Chapter 66

Welcome Home, Big Brother

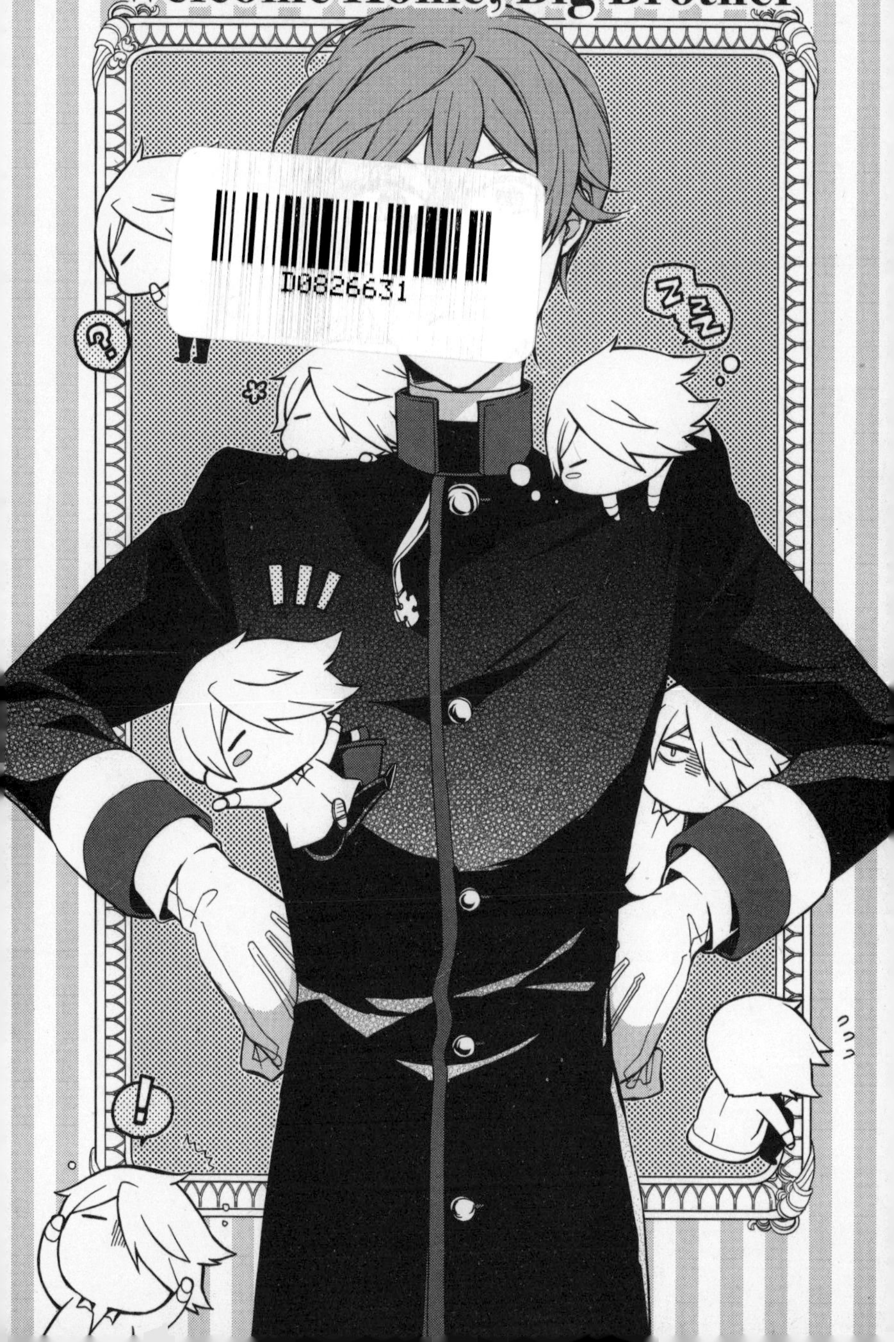

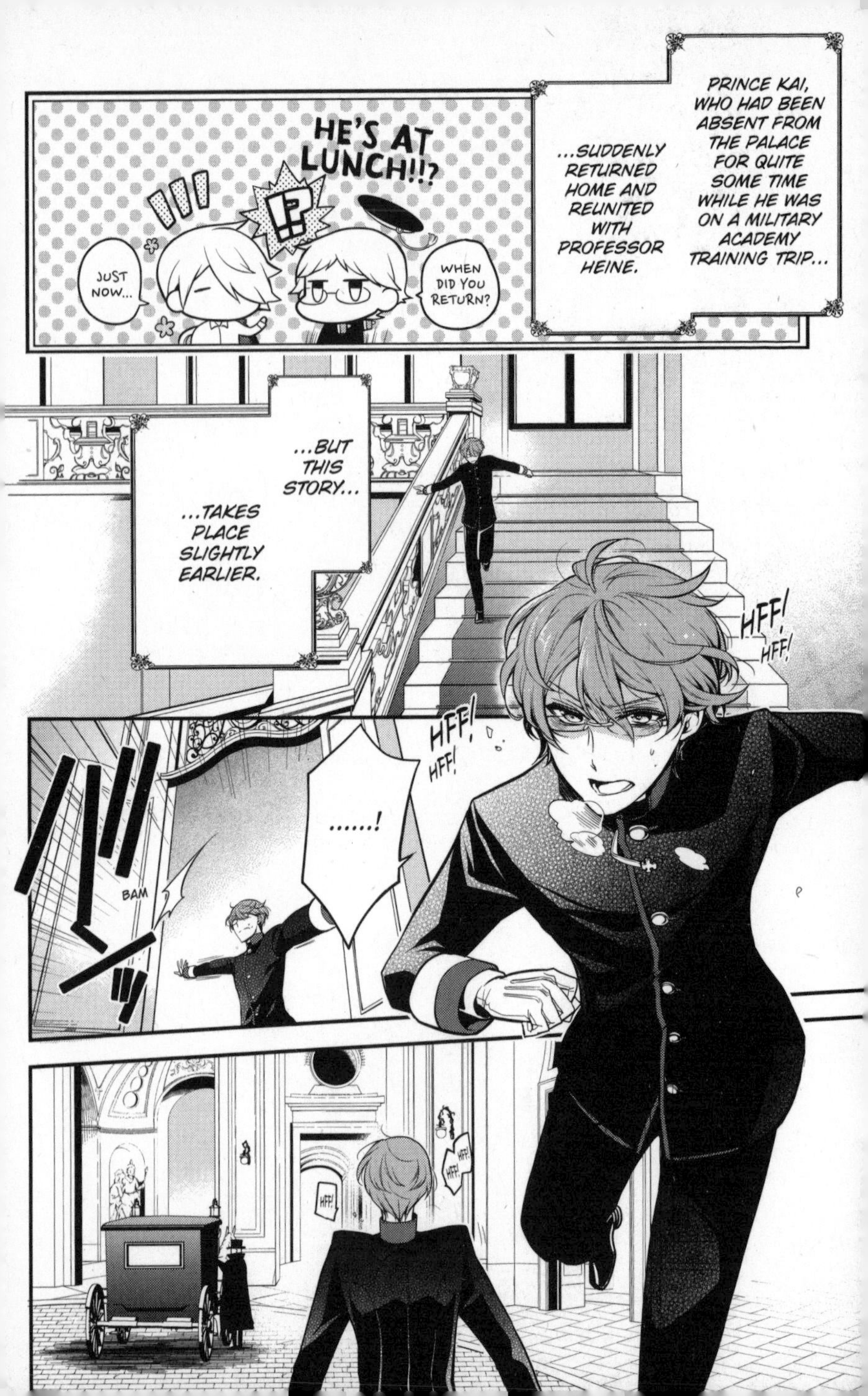
PRINCE KAI, WHO HAD BEEN ABSENT FROM THE PALACE FOR QUITE SOME TIME WHILE HE WAS ON A MILITARY ACADEMY TRAINING TRIP...
...SUDDENLY RETURNED HOME AND REUNITED WITH PROFESSOR HEINE.
WHEN DID YOU RETURN?
JUST NOW...
HE'S AT LUNCH!!?
...BUT THIS STORY...
...TAKES PLACE SLIGHTLY EARLIER.
HFF! HFF!
HFF! HFF!
......!
BAM
HFF! HFF!
HFF!

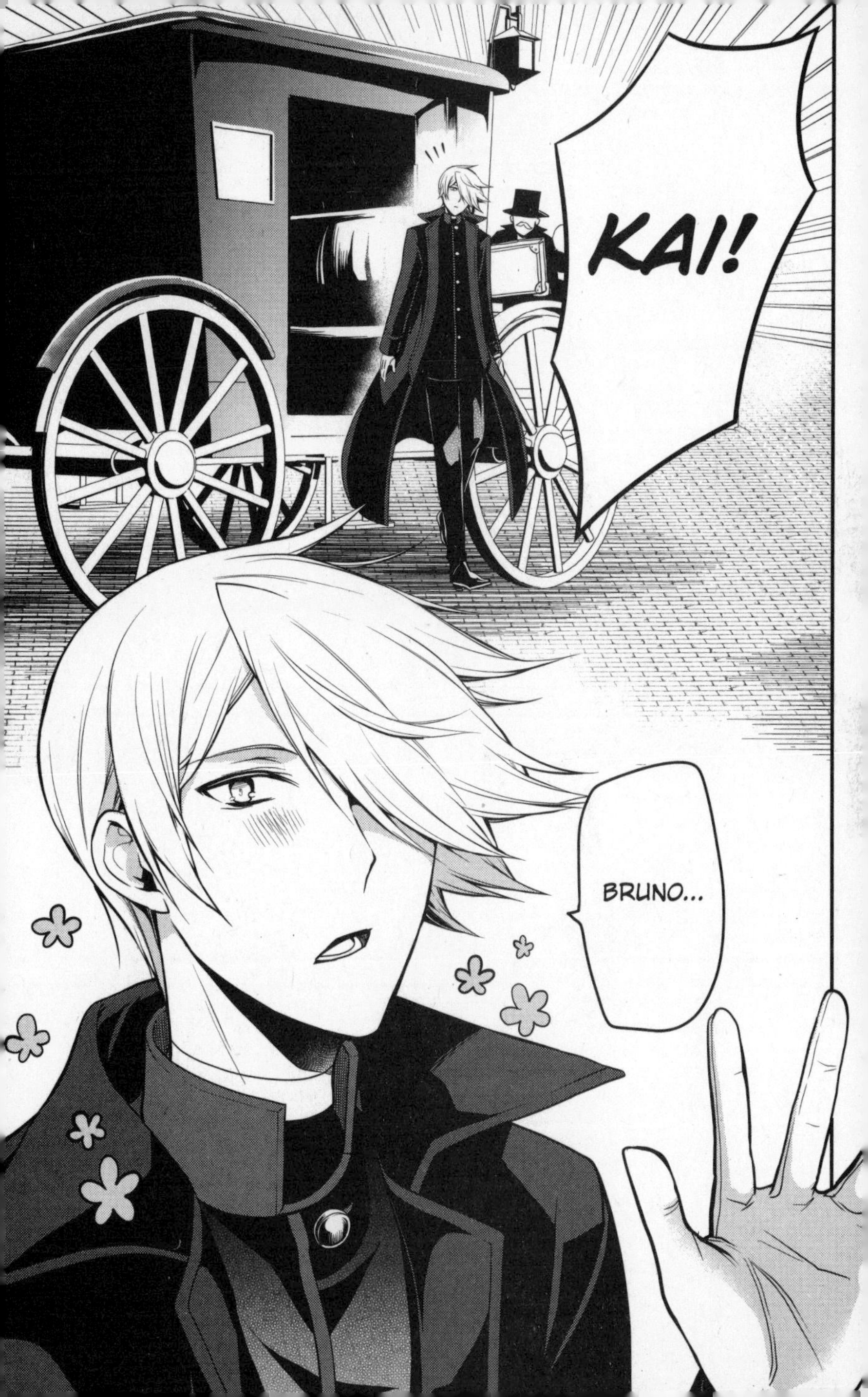
KAI!
BRUNO...

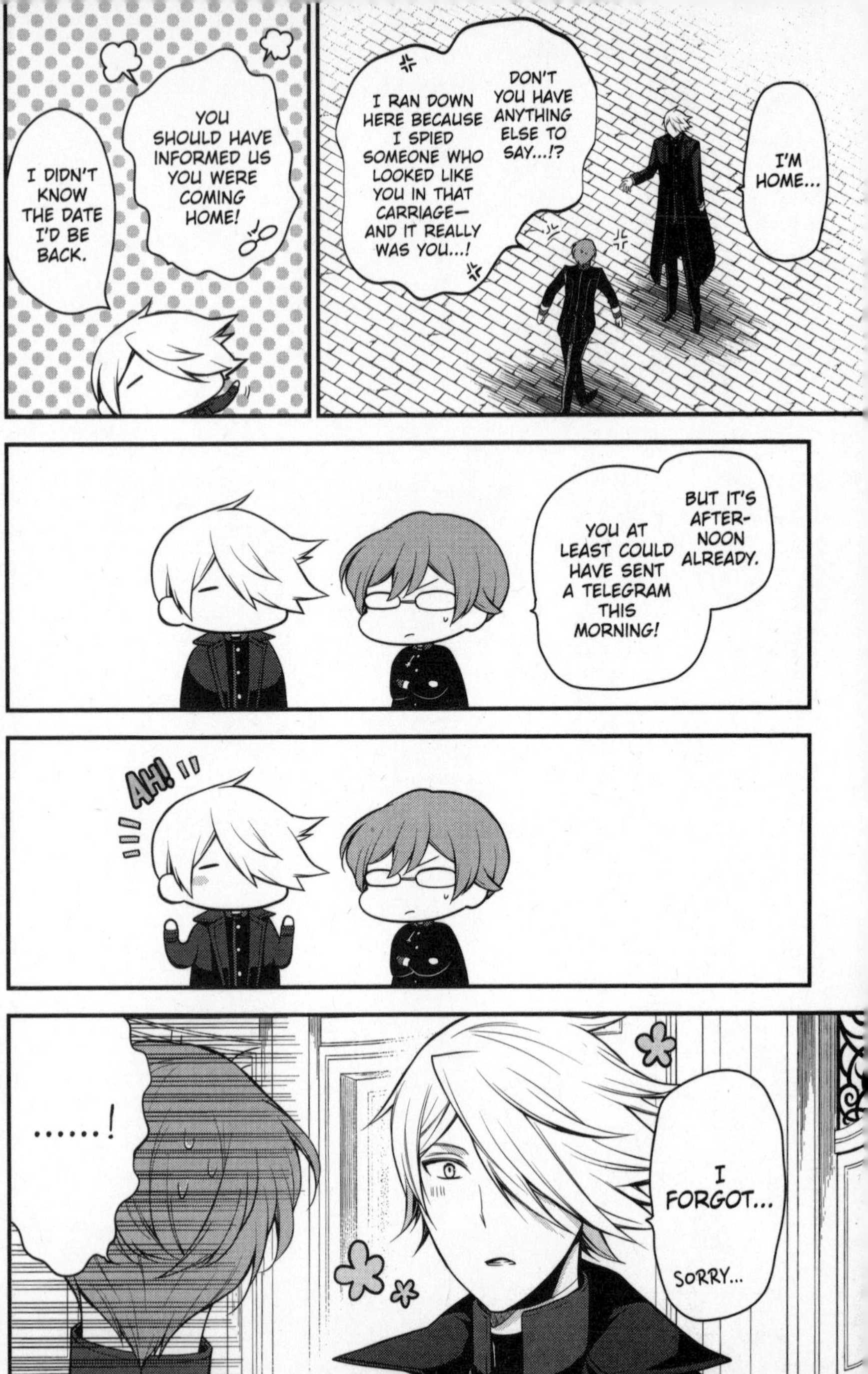
I'M HOME...
DON'T YOU HAVE ANYTHING ELSE TO SAY...!?
I RAN DOWN HERE BECAUSE I SPIED SOMEONE WHO LOOKED LIKE YOU IN THAT CARRIAGE—AND IT REALLY WAS YOU...!
YOU SHOULD HAVE INFORMED US YOU WERE COMING HOME!
I DIDN'T KNOW THE DATE I'D BE BACK.
BUT IT'S AFTER-NOON ALREADY.
YOU AT LEAST COULD HAVE SENT A TELEGRAM THIS MORNING!
AH!
I FORGOT...
SORRY...
......!

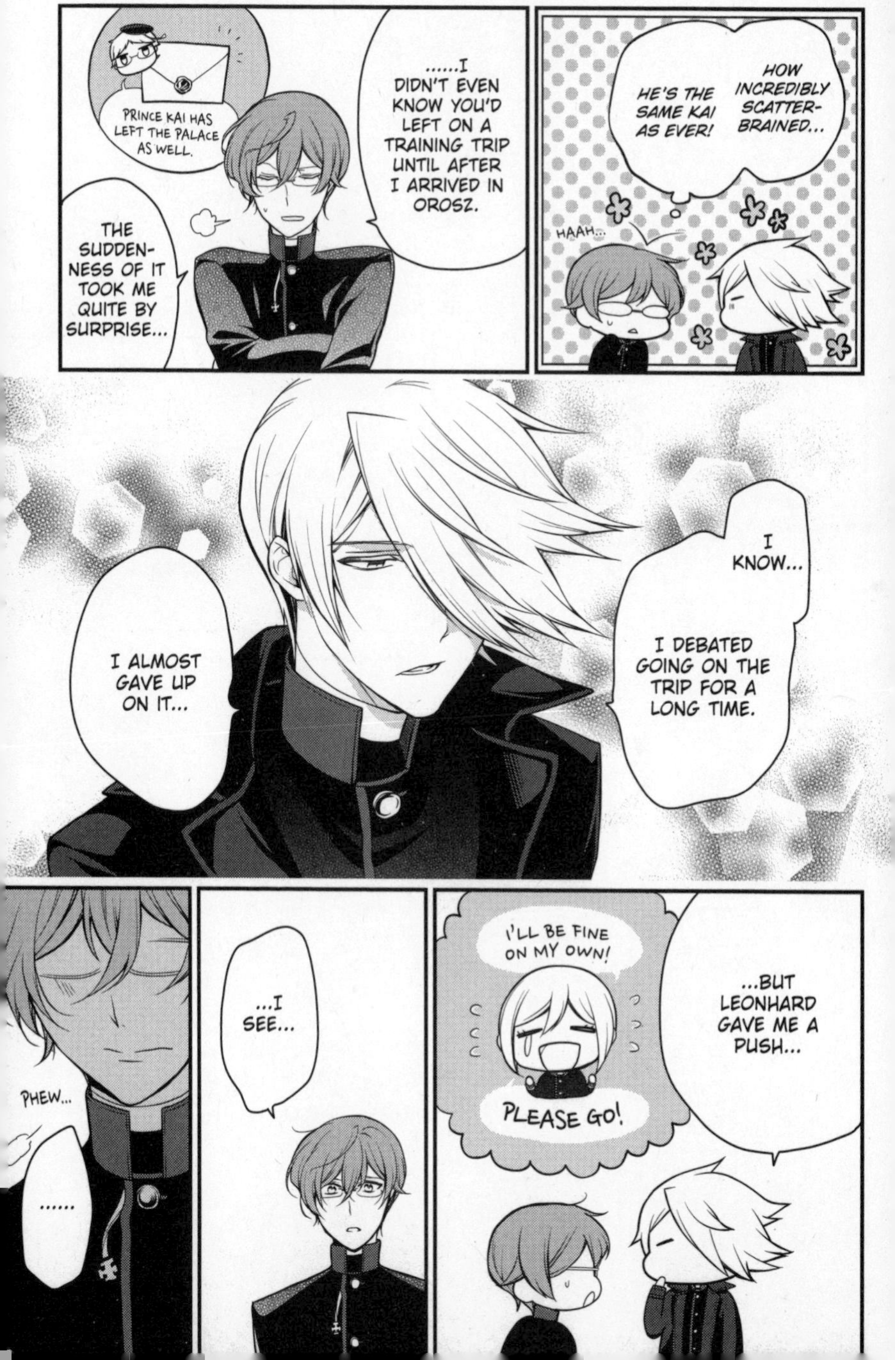
HOW INCREDIBLY SCATTER-BRAINED...
HE'S THE SAME KAI AS EVER!
HAAAH...
......I DIDN'T EVEN KNOW YOU'D LEFT ON A TRAINING TRIP UNTIL AFTER I ARRIVED IN OROSZ.
PRINCE KAI HAS LEFT THE PALACE AS WELL.
THE SUDDENNESS OF IT TOOK ME QUITE BY SURPRISE...
I KNOW...
I DEBATED GOING ON THE TRIP FOR A LONG TIME.
I ALMOST GAVE UP ON IT...
...BUT LEONHARD GAVE ME A PUSH...
I'LL BE FINE ON MY OWN!
PLEASE GO!
...I SEE...
PHEW...
......

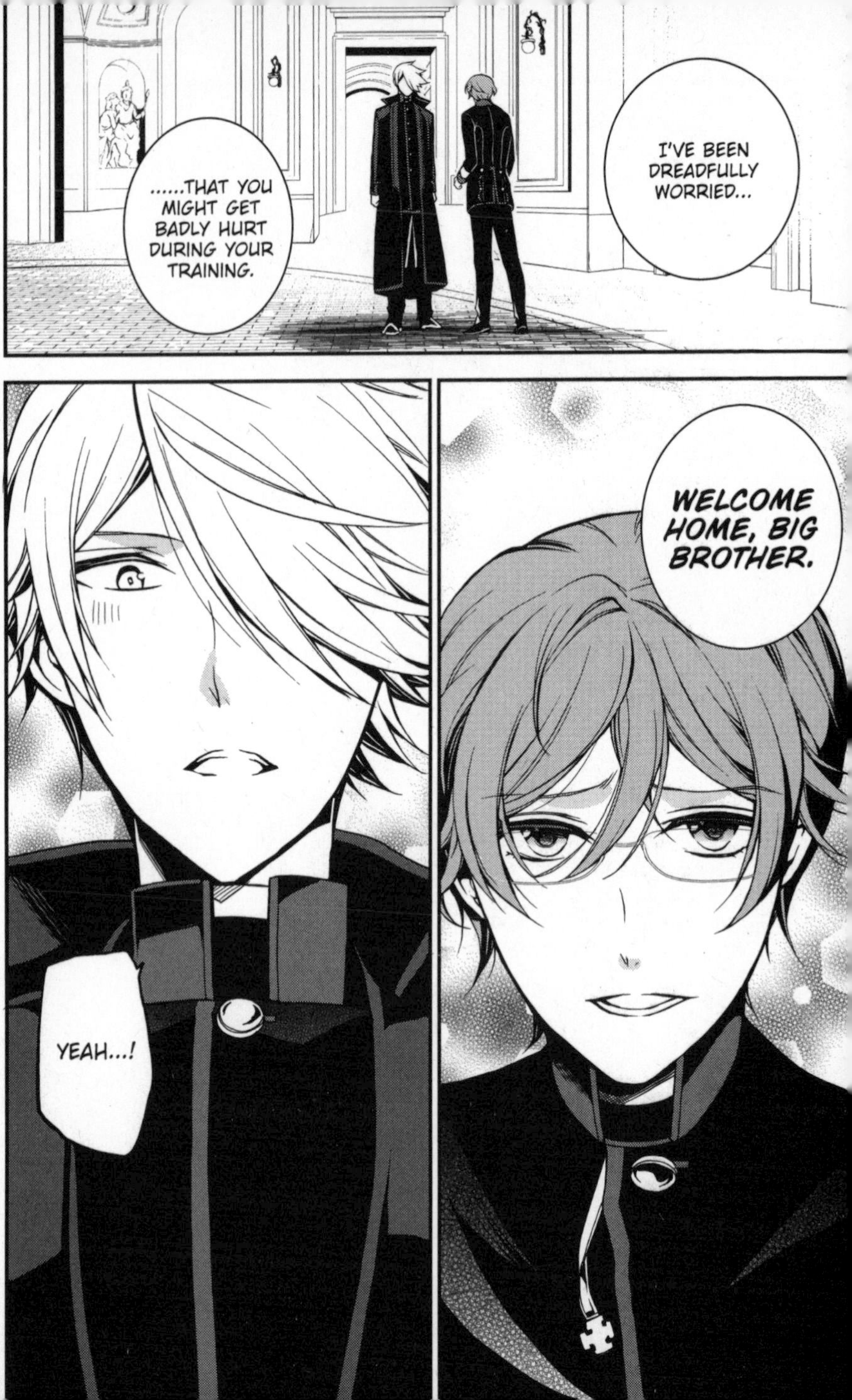
I'VE BEEN DREADFULLY WORRIED...
......THAT YOU MIGHT GET BADLY HURT DURING YOUR TRAINING.
WELCOME HOME, BIG BROTHER.
YEAH...!

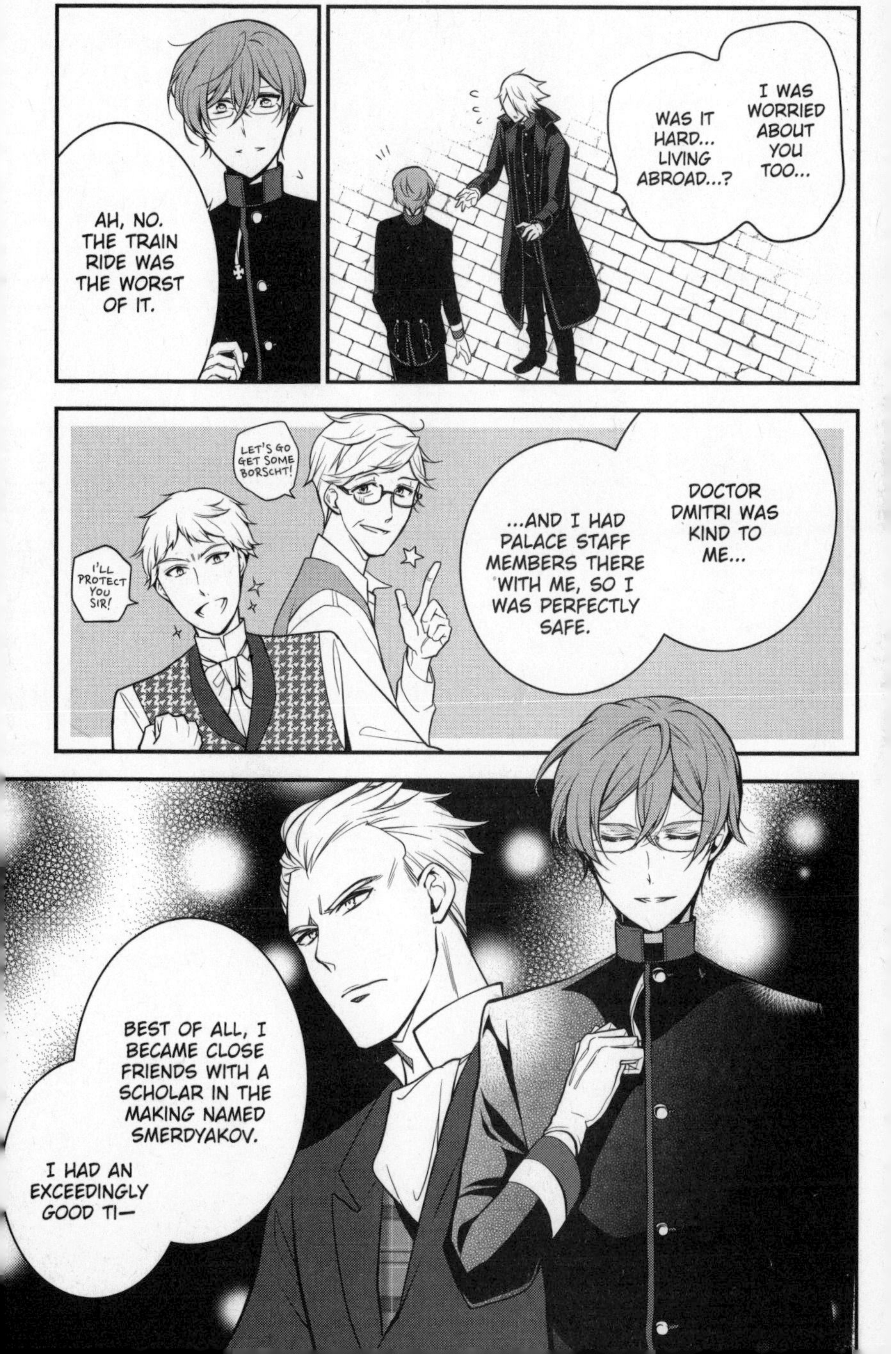
I WAS WORRIED ABOUT YOU TOO...
WAS IT HARD... LIVING ABROAD...?
AH, NO. THE TRAIN RIDE WAS THE WORST OF IT.
DOCTOR DMITRI WAS KIND TO ME...
...AND I HAD PALACE STAFF MEMBERS THERE WITH ME, SO I WAS PERFECTLY SAFE.
LET'S GO GET SOME BORSCHT!
I'LL PROTECT YOU SIR!
BEST OF ALL, I BECAME CLOSE FRIENDS WITH A SCHOLAR IN THE MAKING NAMED SMERDYAKOV.
I HAD AN EXCEEDINGLY GOOD TI—

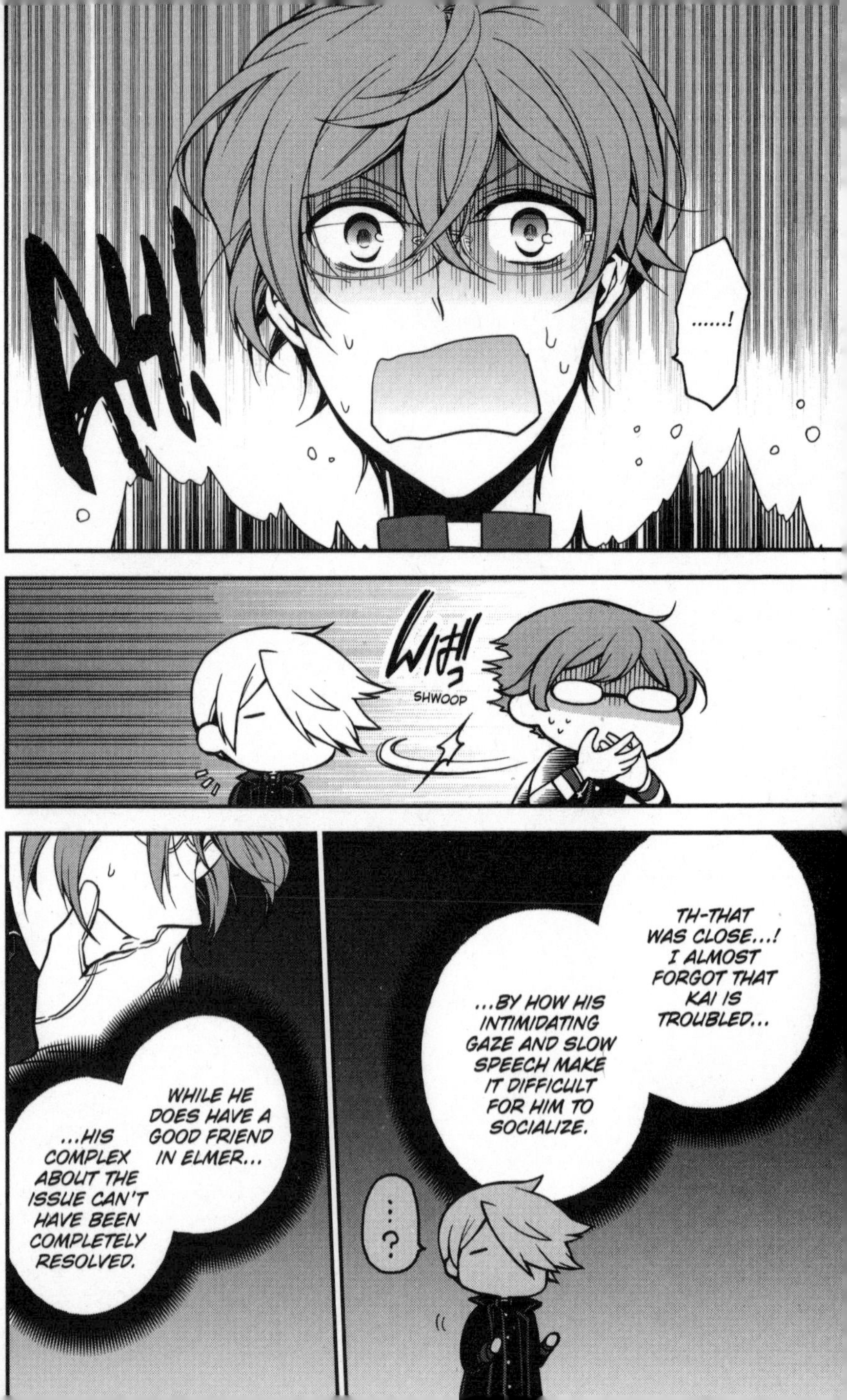
......!
AH!
SHWOOP
TH-THAT WAS CLOSE...! I ALMOST FORGOT THAT KAI IS TROUBLED...
...BY HOW HIS INTIMIDATING GAZE AND SLOW SPEECH MAKE IT DIFFICULT FOR HIM TO SOCIALIZE.
...?
WHILE HE DOES HAVE A GOOD FRIEND IN ELMER...
...HIS COMPLEX ABOUT THE ISSUE CAN'T HAVE BEEN COMPLETELY RESOLVED.

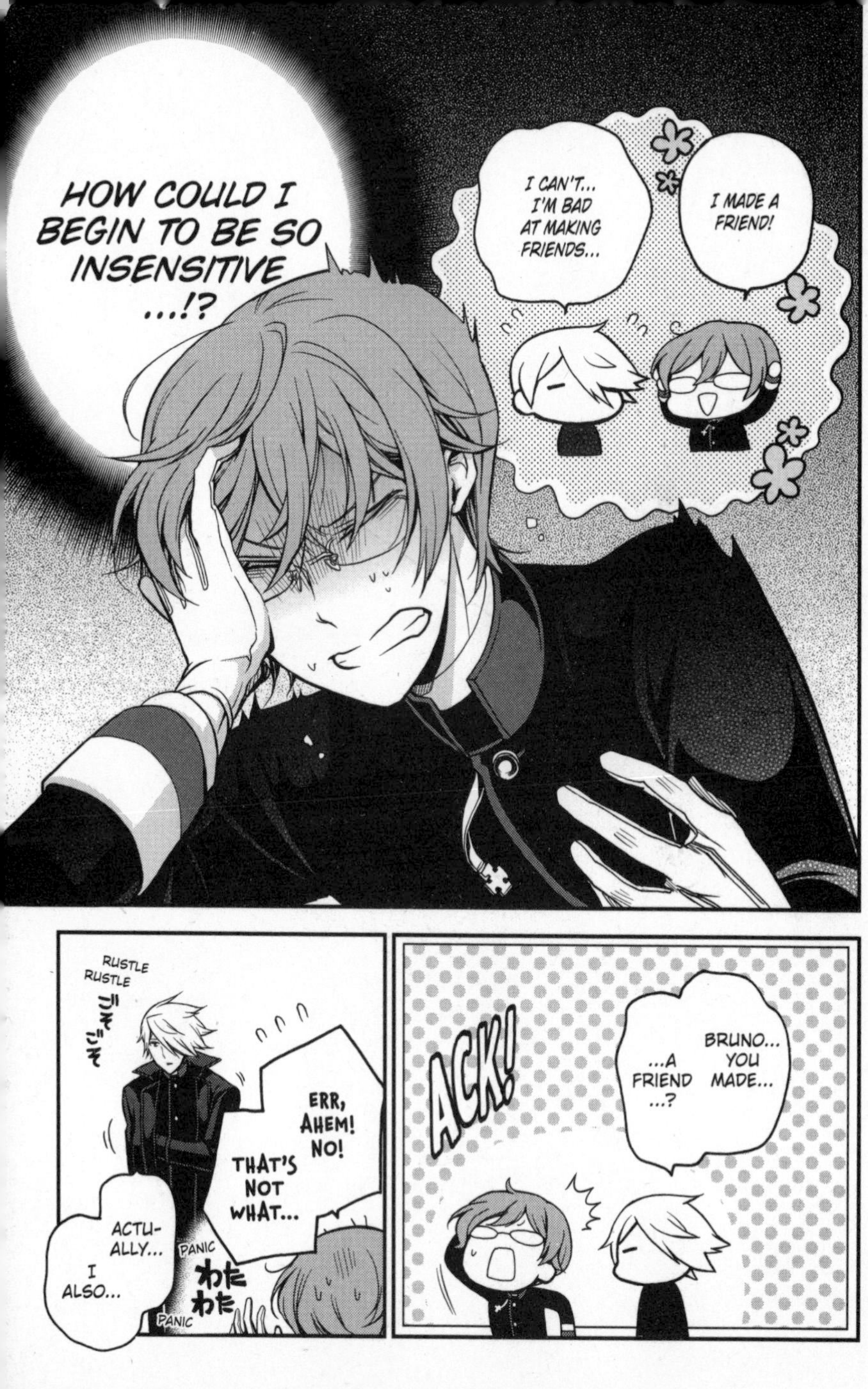
I MADE A FRIEND!
I CAN'T... I'M BAD AT MAKING FRIENDS...
HOW COULD I BEGIN TO BE SO INSENSITIVE ...!?
BRUNO... YOU MADE...
...A FRIEND ...?
ACK!
ERR, AHEM! NO!
THAT'S NOT WHAT...
PANIC
わたわた
PANIC
ACTU-ALLY... I ALSO...
RUSTLE RUSTLE
ごそごそ

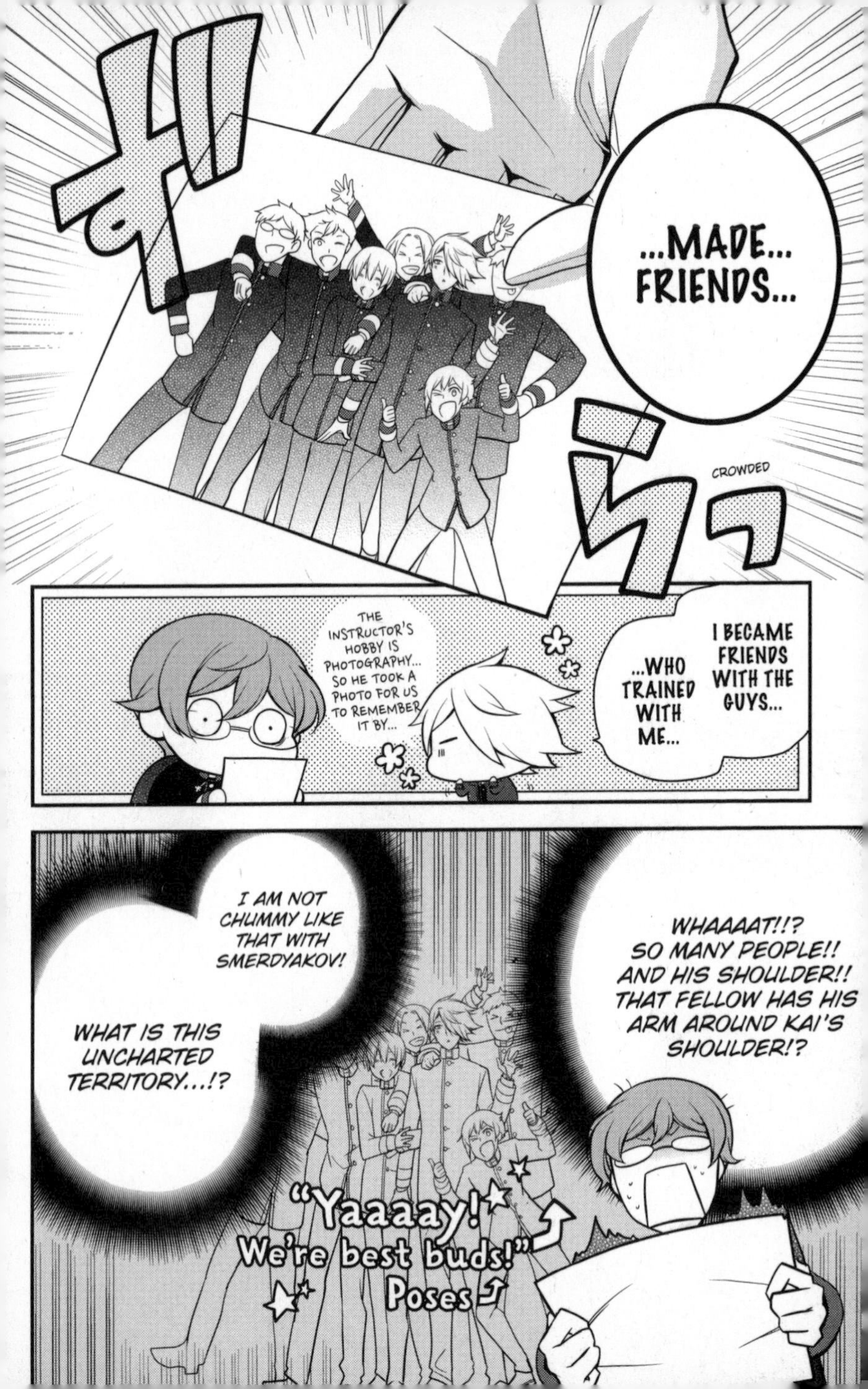
...MADE... FRIENDS...
CROWDED
I BECAME FRIENDS WITH THE GUYS...
...WHO TRAINED WITH ME...
THE INSTRUCTOR'S HOBBY IS PHOTOGRAPHY... SO HE TOOK A PHOTO FOR US TO REMEMBER IT BY...
WHAAAAT!!? SO MANY PEOPLE!! AND HIS SHOULDER!! THAT FELLOW HAS HIS ARM AROUND KAI'S SHOULDER!?
I AM NOT CHUMMY LIKE THAT WITH SMERDYAKOV!
WHAT IS THIS UNCHARTED TERRITORY...!?
"Yaaaaay! We're best buds!"
Poses

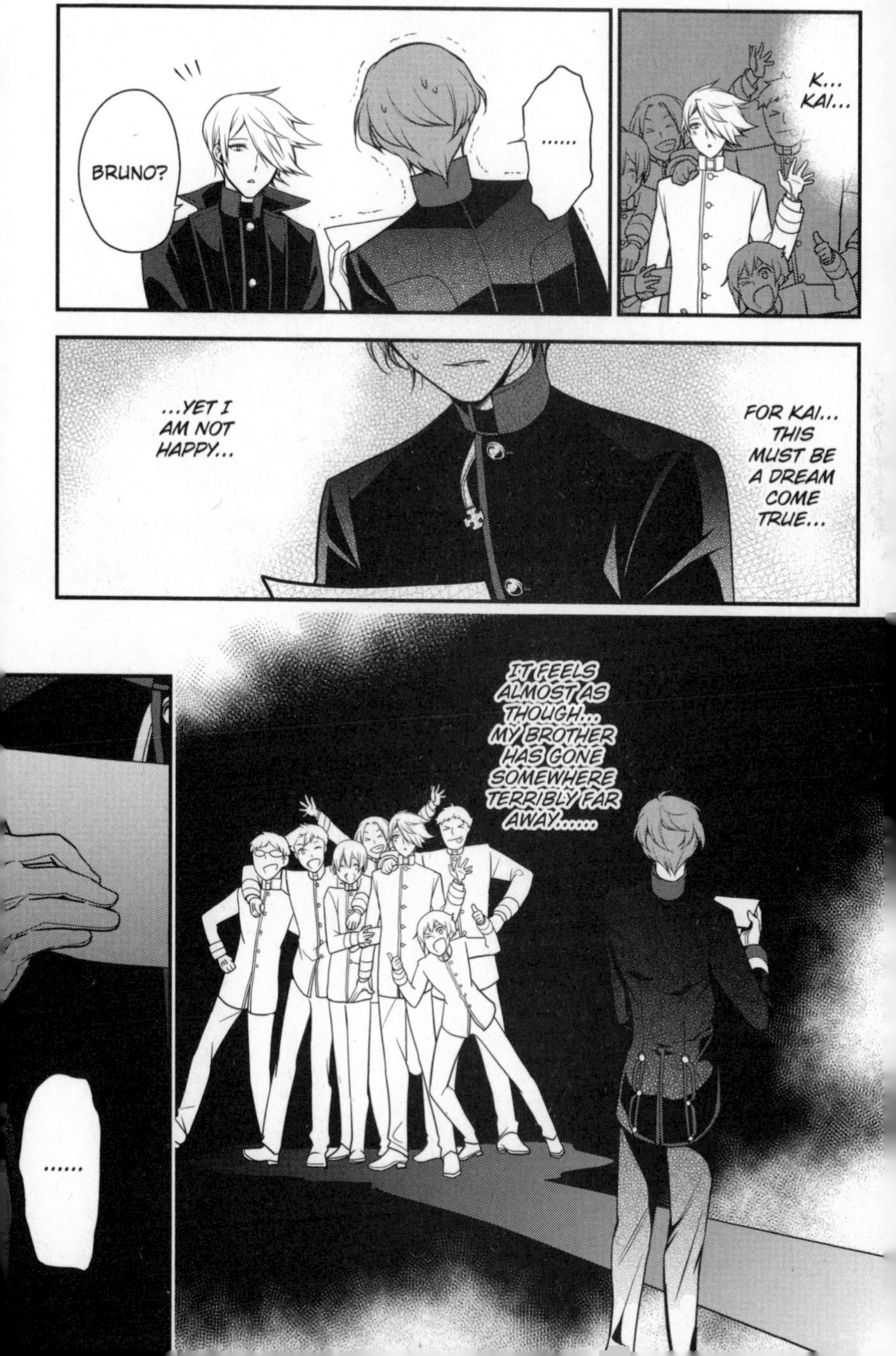
K... KAI...
......
BRUNO?
FOR KAI... THIS MUST BE A DREAM COME TRUE...
...YET I AM NOT HAPPY...
IT FEELS ALMOST AS THOUGH... MY BROTHER HAS GONE SOMEWHERE TERRIBLY FAR AWAY......
......

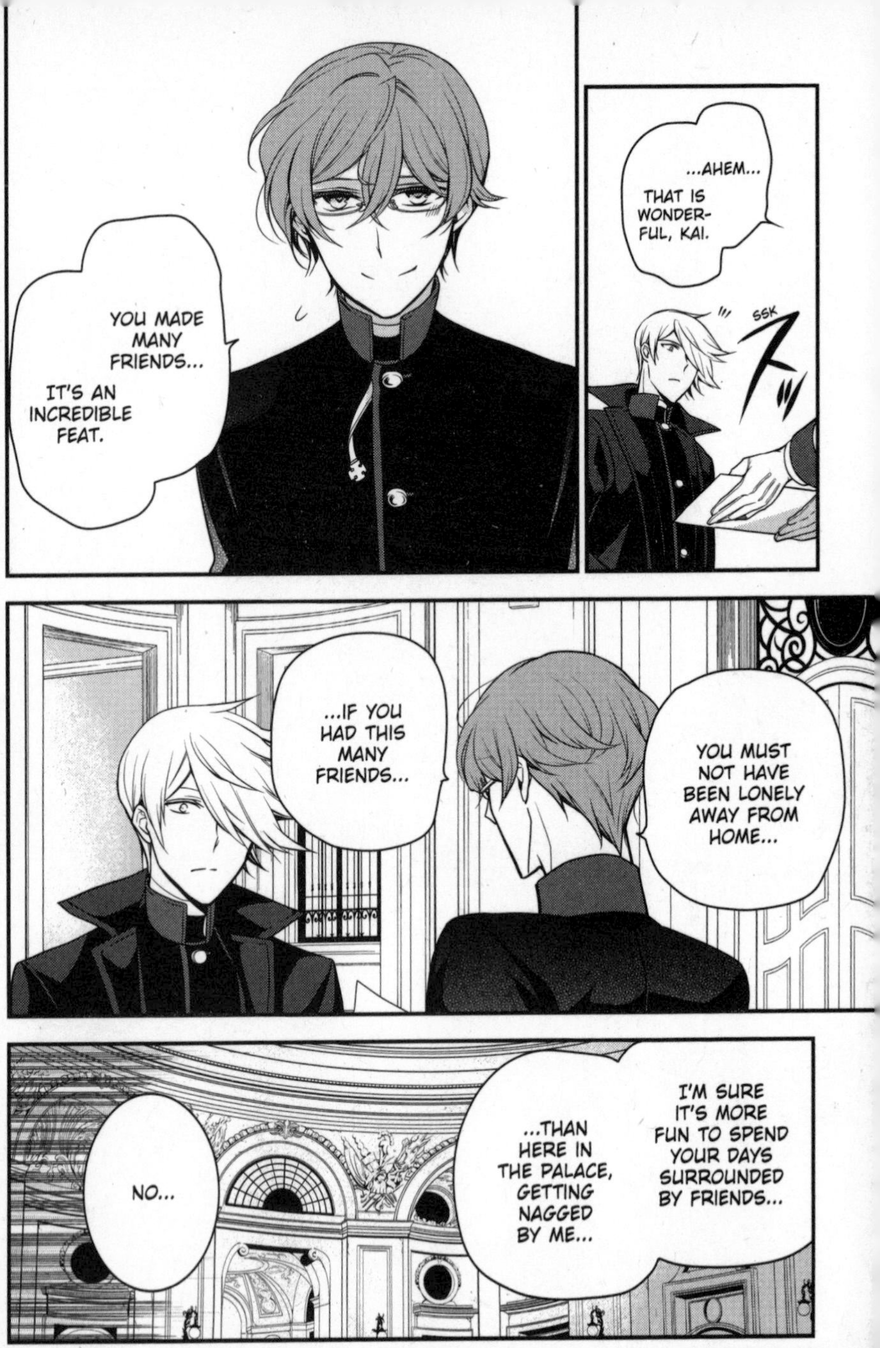
...AHEM... THAT IS WONDER-FUL, KAI.
SSK
YOU MADE MANY FRIENDS...
IT'S AN INCREDIBLE FEAT.
YOU MUST NOT HAVE BEEN LONELY AWAY FROM HOME...
...IF YOU HAD THIS MANY FRIENDS...
I'M SURE IT'S MORE FUN TO SPEND YOUR DAYS SURROUNDED BY FRIENDS...
...THAN HERE IN THE PALACE, GETTING NAGGED BY ME...
NO...

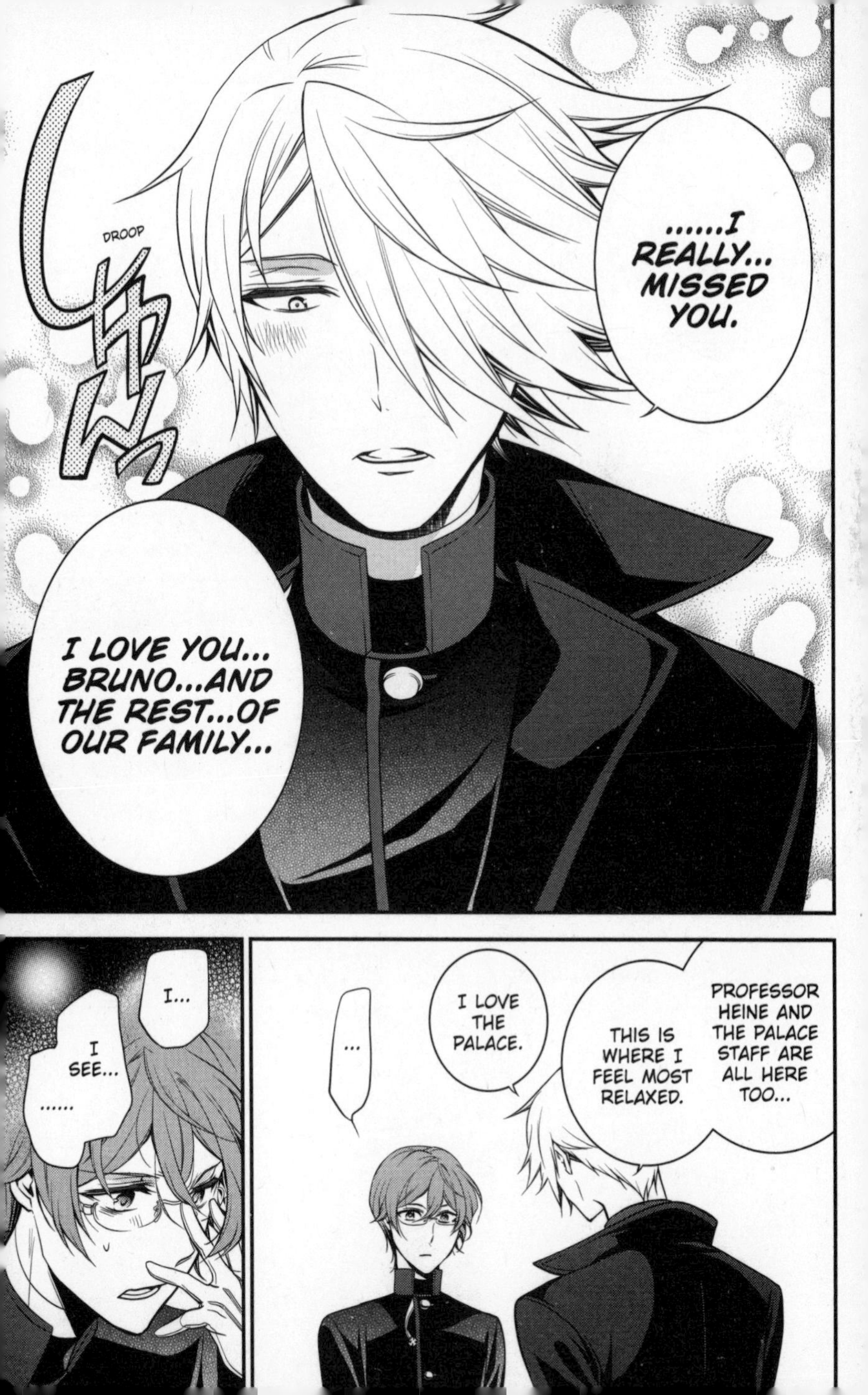
......I REALLY... MISSED YOU.
しゅん
DROOP
I LOVE YOU... BRUNO...AND THE REST...OF OUR FAMILY...
PROFESSOR HEINE AND THE PALACE STAFF ARE ALL HERE TOO...
THIS IS WHERE I FEEL MOST RELAXED.
I LOVE THE PALACE.
...
I...
I SEE...
......

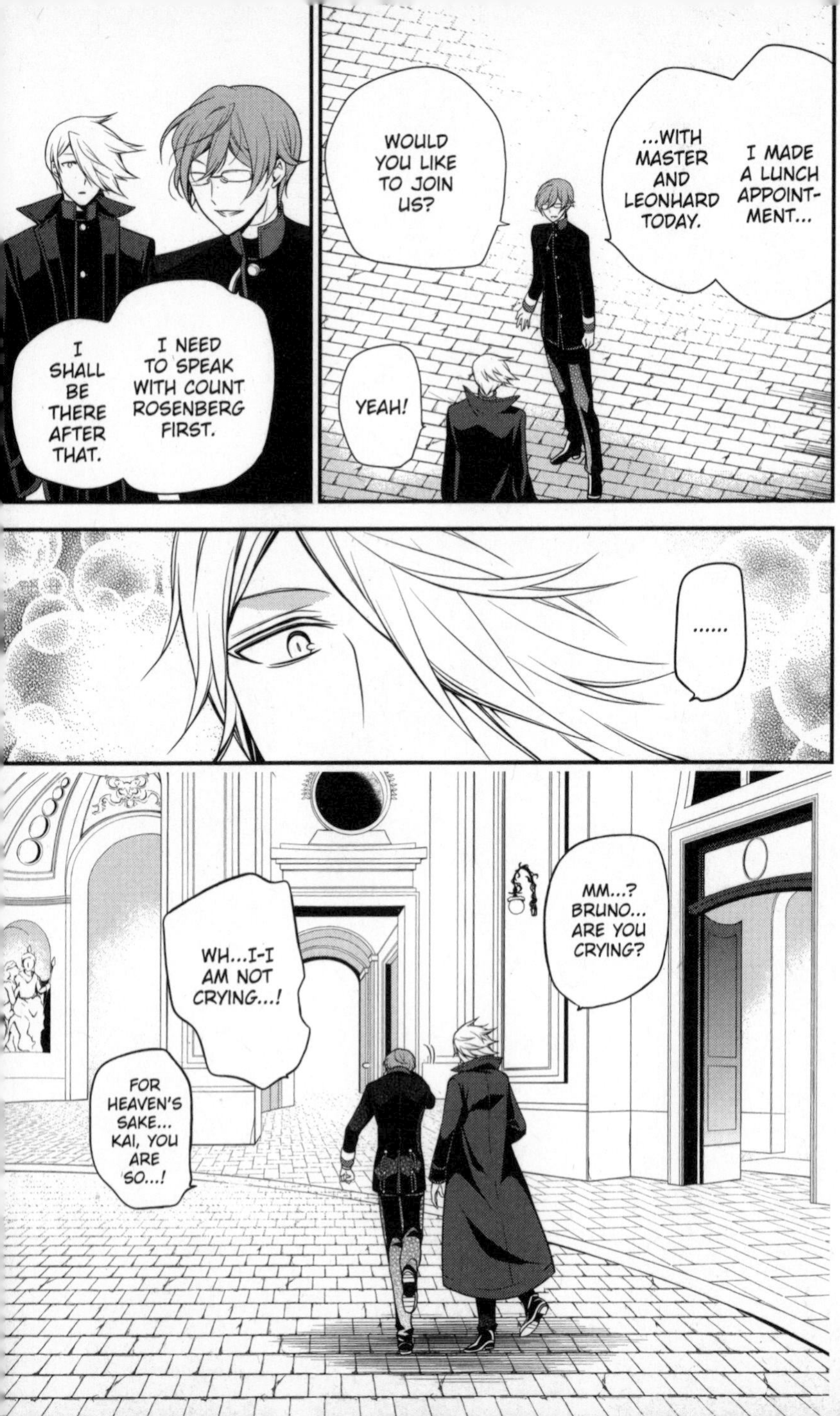
I MADE A LUNCH APPOINTMENT...
...WITH MASTER AND LEONHARD TODAY.
WOULD YOU LIKE TO JOIN US?
YEAH!
I NEED TO SPEAK WITH COUNT ROSENBERG FIRST.
I SHALL BE THERE AFTER THAT.
......
MM...? BRUNO... ARE YOU CRYING?
WH...I-I AM NOT CRYING...!
FOR HEAVEN'S SAKE... KAI, YOU ARE SO...!

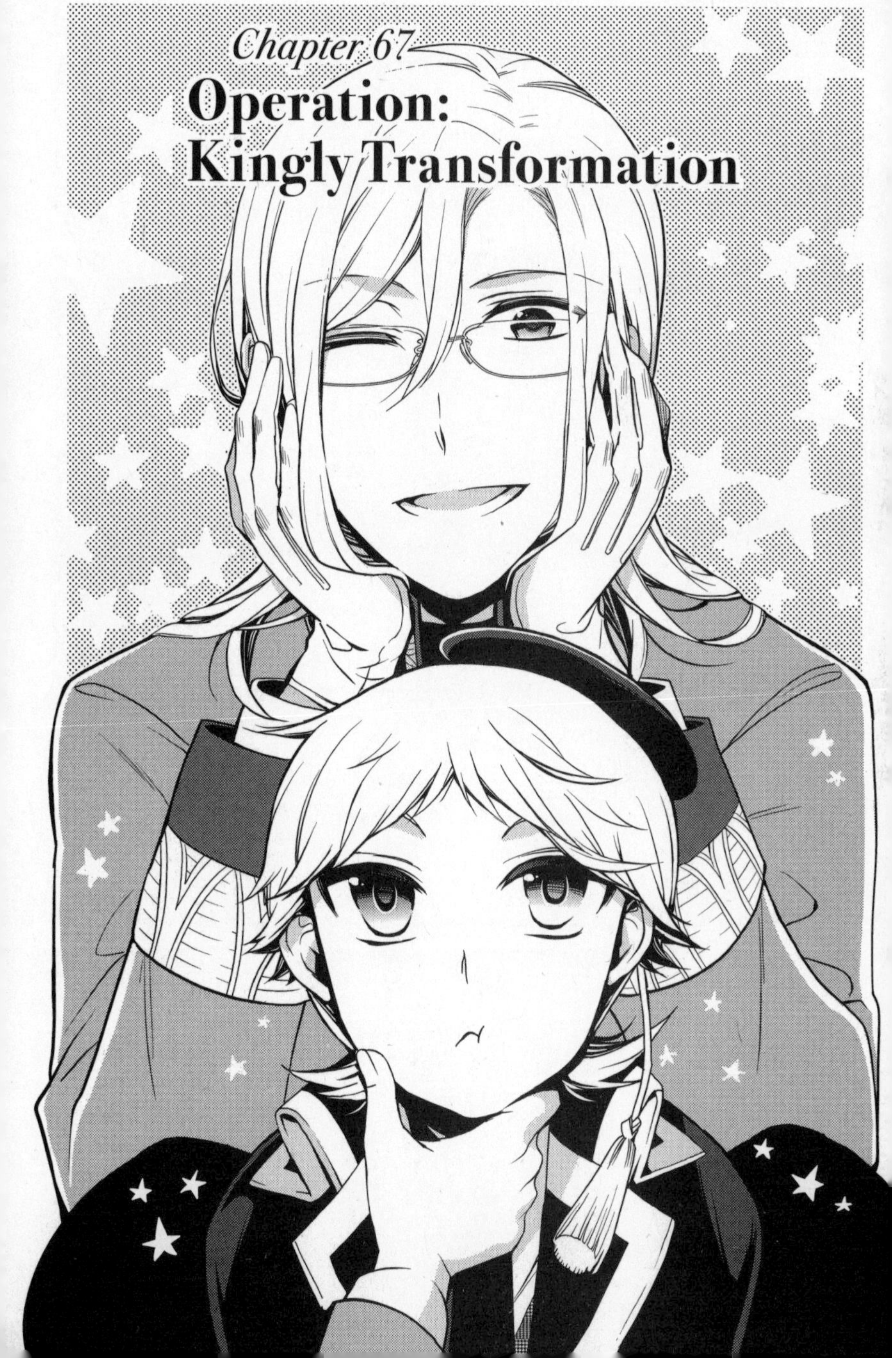
Chapter 67
Operation: Kingly Transformation

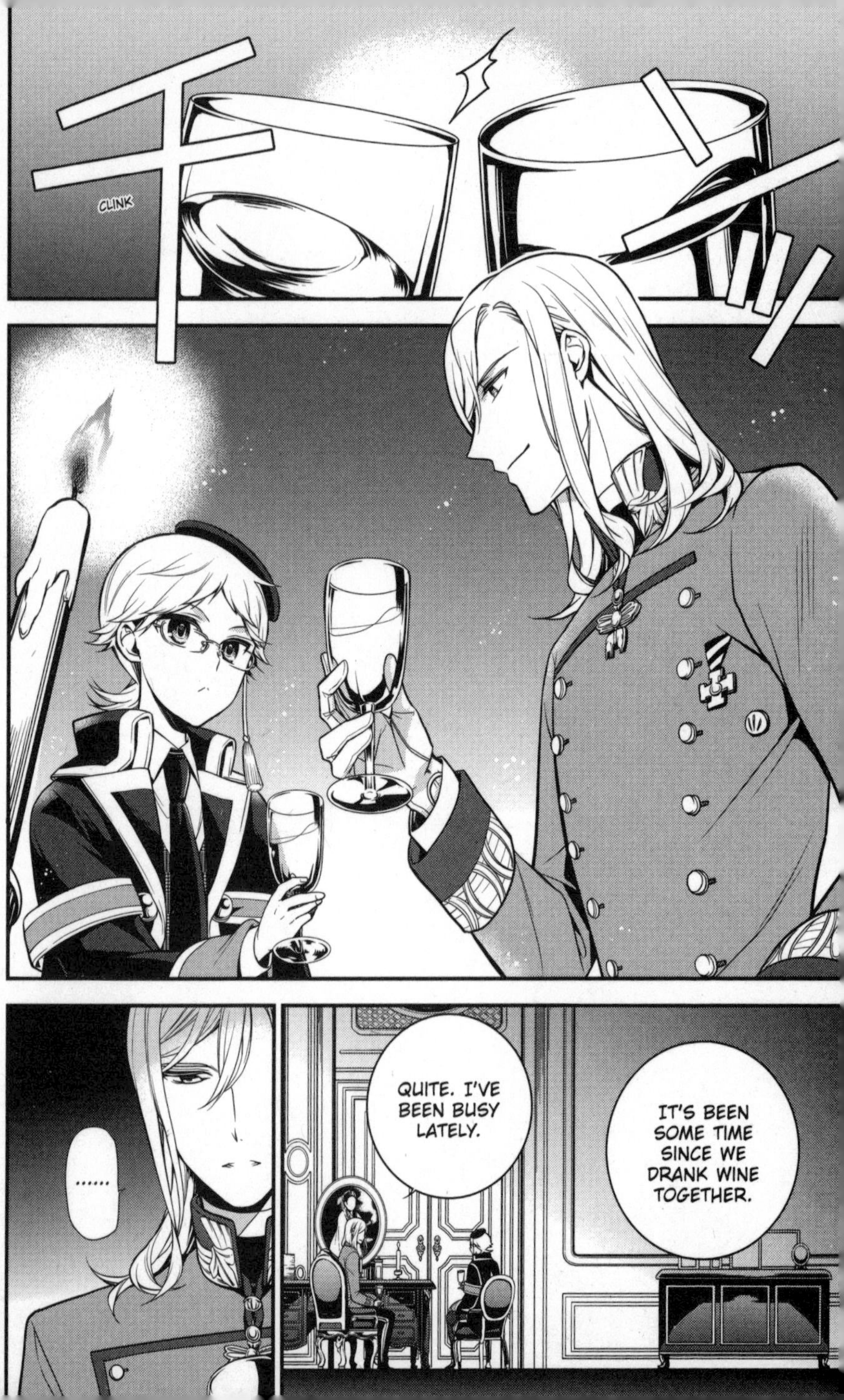
CLINK
IT'S BEEN SOME TIME SINCE WE DRANK WINE TOGETHER.
QUITE. I'VE BEEN BUSY LATELY.
......

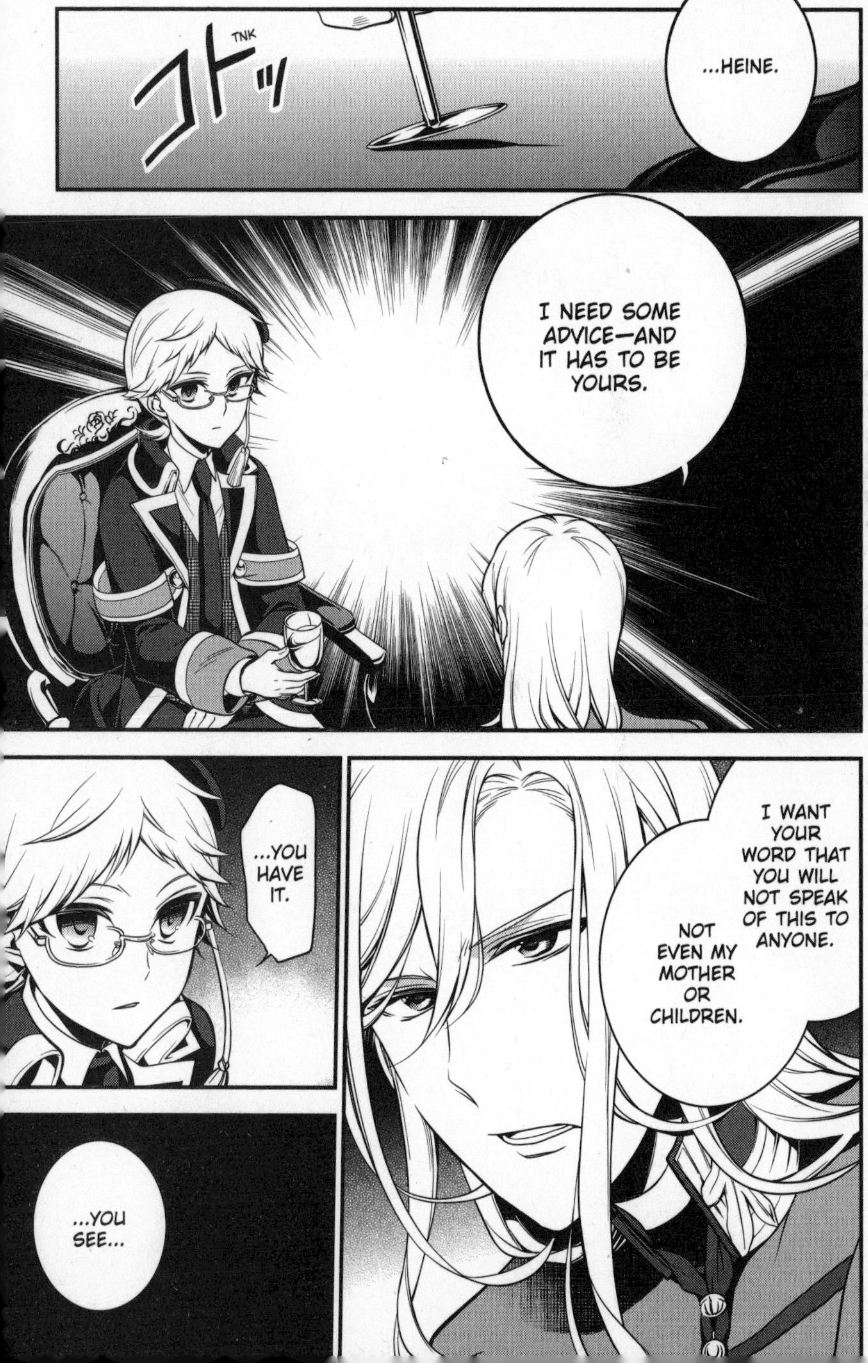
...HEINE.
コトッ
TNK
I NEED SOME ADVICE—AND IT HAS TO BE YOURS.
I WANT YOUR WORD THAT YOU WILL NOT SPEAK OF THIS TO ANYONE.
NOT EVEN MY MOTHER OR CHILDREN.
...YOU HAVE IT.
...YOU SEE...

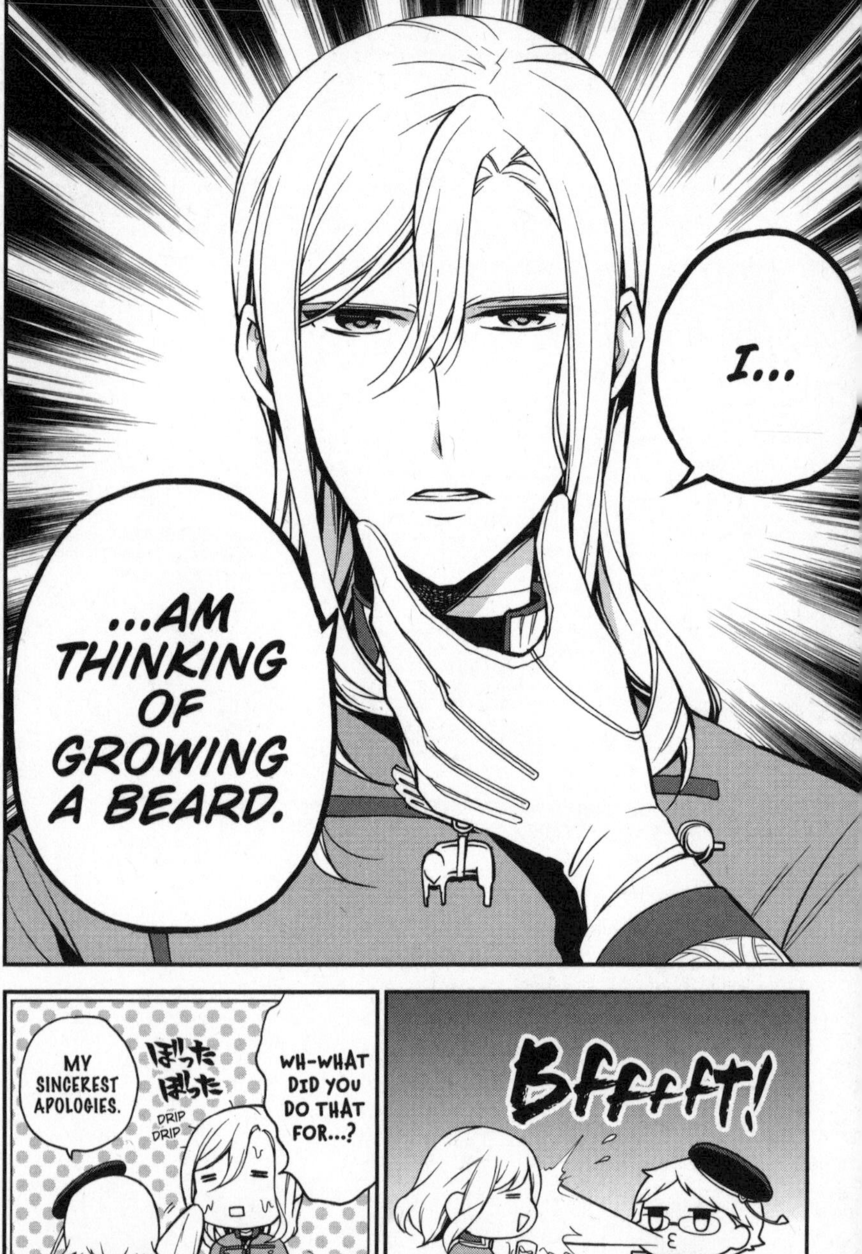
I...
...AM THINKING OF GROWING A BEARD.
BFFFFT!
WH-WHAT DID YOU DO THAT FOR...?
ぽったぽった
DRIP DRIP
MY SINCEREST APOLOGIES.

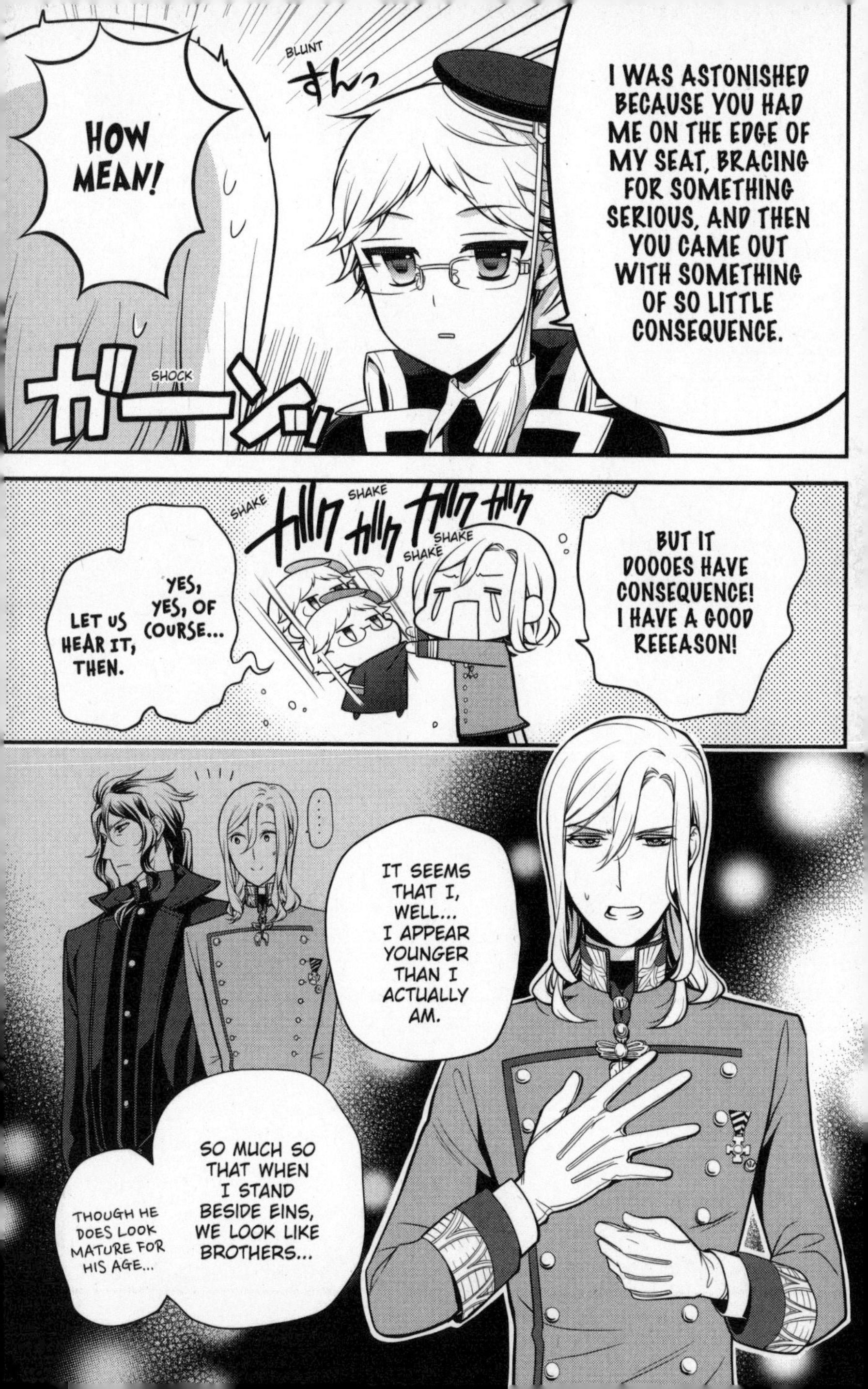
I WAS ASTONISHED BECAUSE YOU HAD ME ON THE EDGE OF MY SEAT, BRACING FOR SOMETHING SERIOUS, AND THEN YOU CAME OUT WITH SOMETHING OF SO LITTLE CONSEQUENCE.
BLUNT
すんっ
HOW MEAN!
SHOCK
ガーンッ
BUT IT DOOOES HAVE CONSEQUENCE! I HAVE A GOOD REEEASON!
SHAKE
SHAKE
SHAKE
SHAKE
ガルク ガルク ガルク ガルク
YES, YES, OF COURSE...
LET US HEAR IT, THEN.
IT SEEMS THAT I, WELL... I APPEAR YOUNGER THAN I ACTUALLY AM.
...
SO MUCH SO THAT WHEN I STAND BESIDE EINS, WE LOOK LIKE BROTHERS...
THOUGH HE DOES LOOK MATURE FOR HIS AGE...

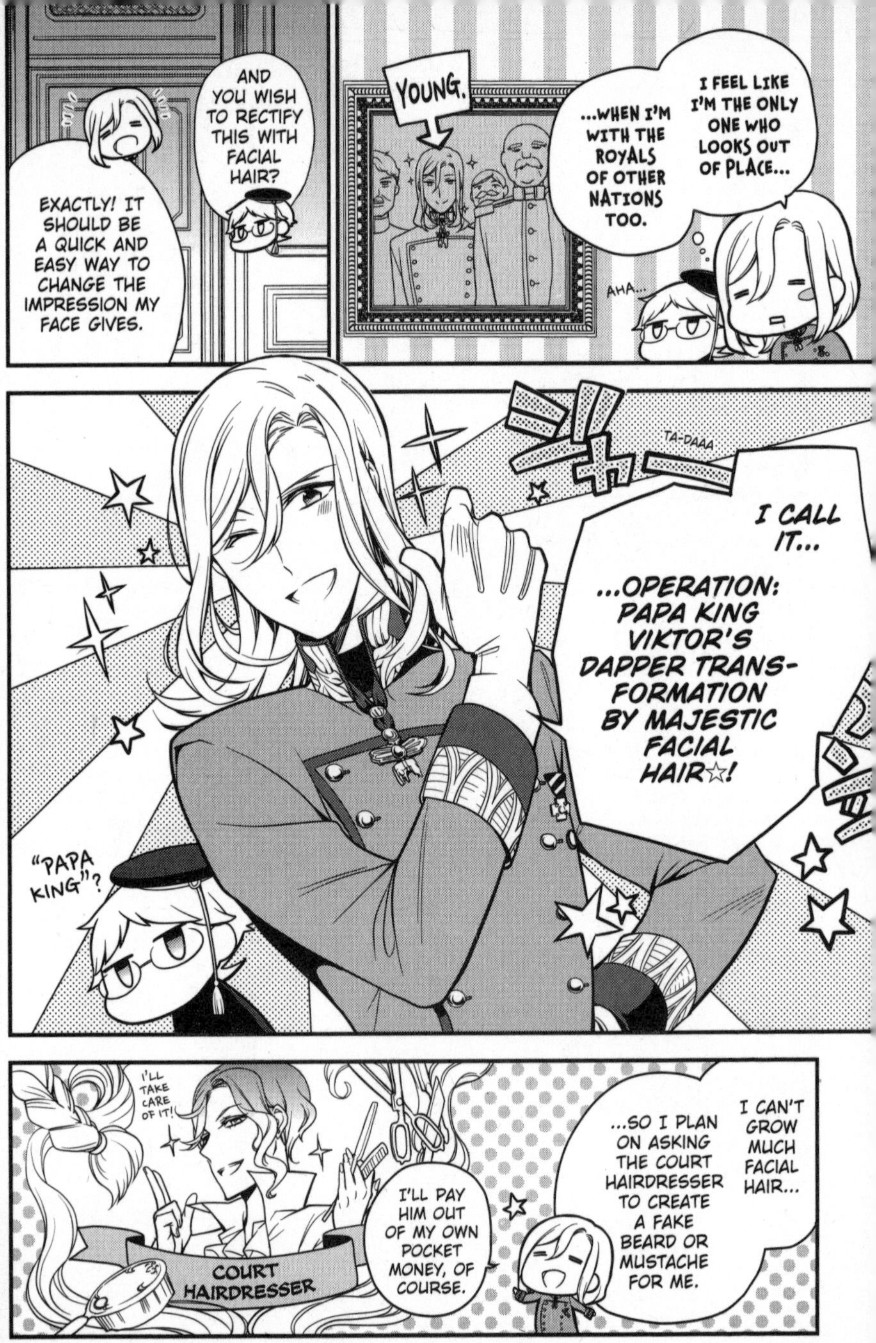
I FEEL LIKE I'M THE ONLY ONE WHO LOOKS OUT OF PLACE...
...WHEN I'M WITH THE ROYALS OF OTHER NATIONS TOO.
YOUNG.
AHA...
AND YOU WISH TO RECTIFY THIS WITH FACIAL HAIR?
EXACTLY! IT SHOULD BE A QUICK AND EASY WAY TO CHANGE THE IMPRESSION MY FACE GIVES.
TA-DAAA
I CALL IT...
...OPERATION: PAPA KING VIKTOR'S DAPPER TRANS-FORMATION BY MAJESTIC FACIAL HAIR☆!
"PAPA KING"?
I CAN'T GROW MUCH FACIAL HAIR...
...SO I PLAN ON ASKING THE COURT HAIRDRESSER TO CREATE A FAKE BEARD OR MUSTACHE FOR ME.
I'LL PAY HIM OUT OF MY OWN POCKET MONEY, OF COURSE.
I'LL TAKE CARE OF IT!
COURT HAIRDRESSER

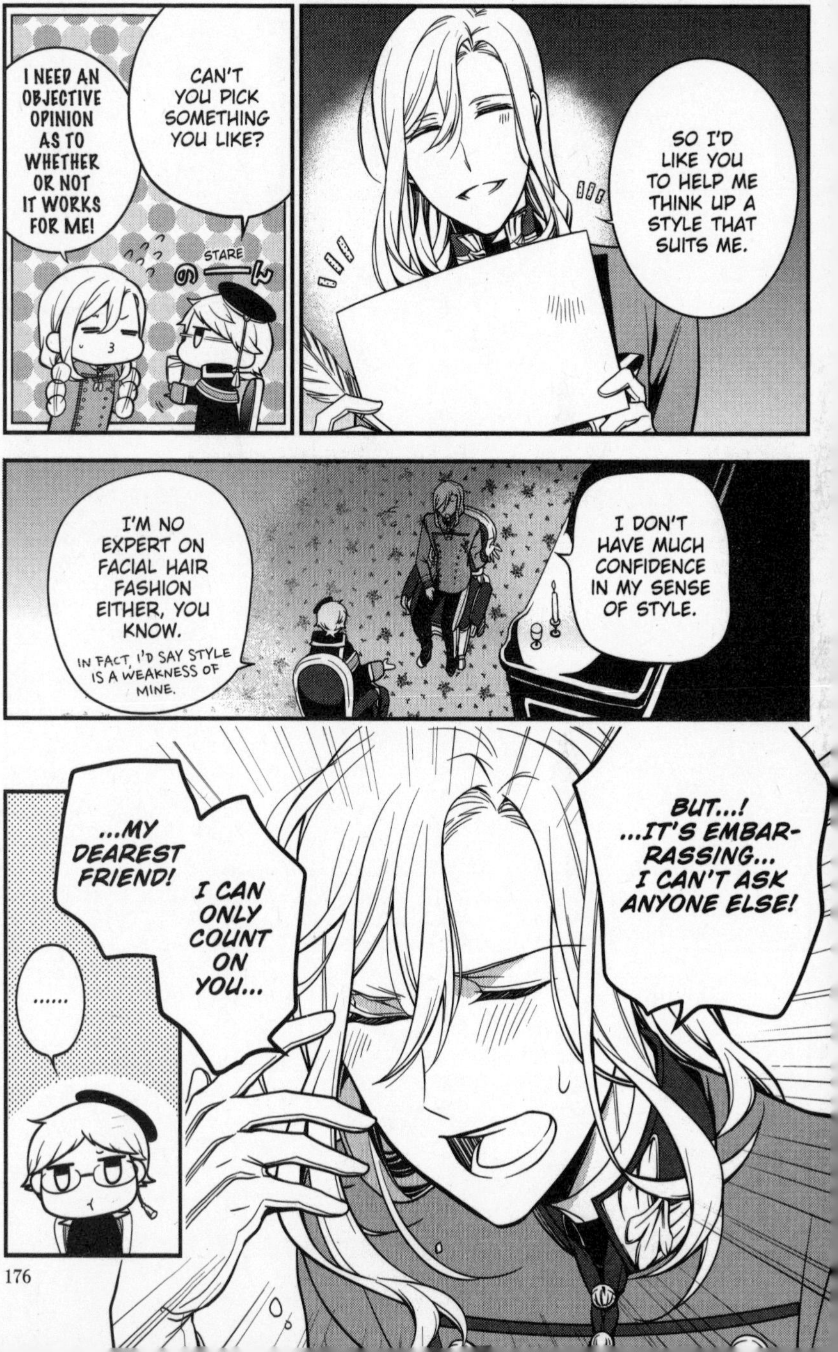

SO I'D LIKE YOU TO HELP ME THINK UP A STYLE THAT SUITS ME.
CAN'T YOU PICK SOMETHING YOU LIKE?
I NEED AN OBJECTIVE OPINION AS TO WHETHER OR NOT IT WORKS FOR ME!
STARE
I DON'T HAVE MUCH CONFIDENCE IN MY SENSE OF STYLE.
I'M NO EXPERT ON FACIAL HAIR FASHION EITHER, YOU KNOW.
IN FACT, I'D SAY STYLE IS A WEAKNESS OF MINE.
BUT...! ...IT'S EMBARRASSING... I CAN'T ASK ANYONE ELSE!
...MY DEAREST FRIEND!
I CAN ONLY COUNT ON YOU...
......

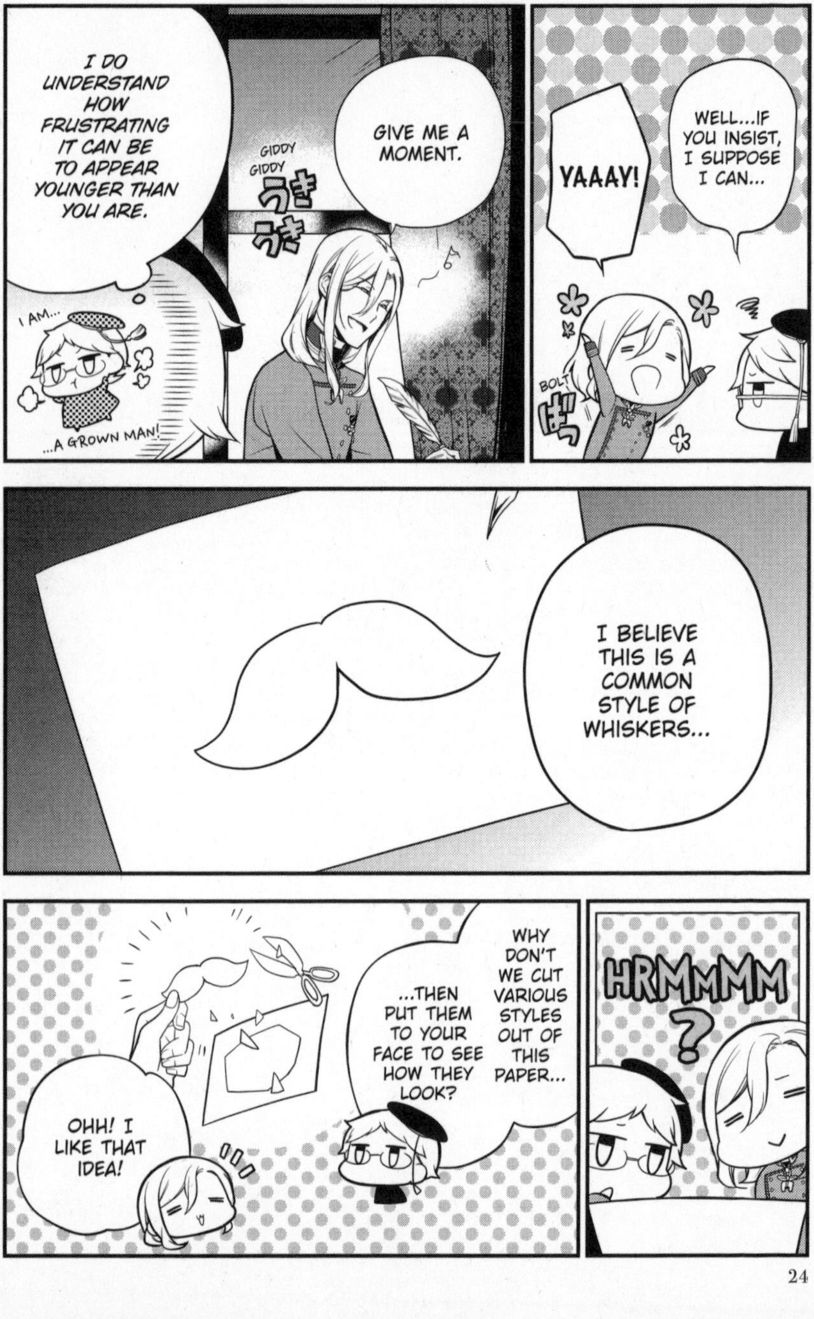
WELL...IF YOU INSIST, I SUPPOSE I CAN...
YAAAY!
BOLT
ぼっ
GIVE ME A MOMENT.
GIDDY GIDDY
うきうき
I DO UNDERSTAND HOW FRUSTRATING IT CAN BE TO APPEAR YOUNGER THAN YOU ARE.
I AM...
...A GROWN MAN!
I BELIEVE THIS IS A COMMON STYLE OF WHISKERS...
HRMMMM
?
WHY DON'T WE CUT VARIOUS STYLES OUT OF THIS PAPER...
...THEN PUT THEM TO YOUR FACE TO SEE HOW THEY LOOK?
OHH! I LIKE THAT IDEA!

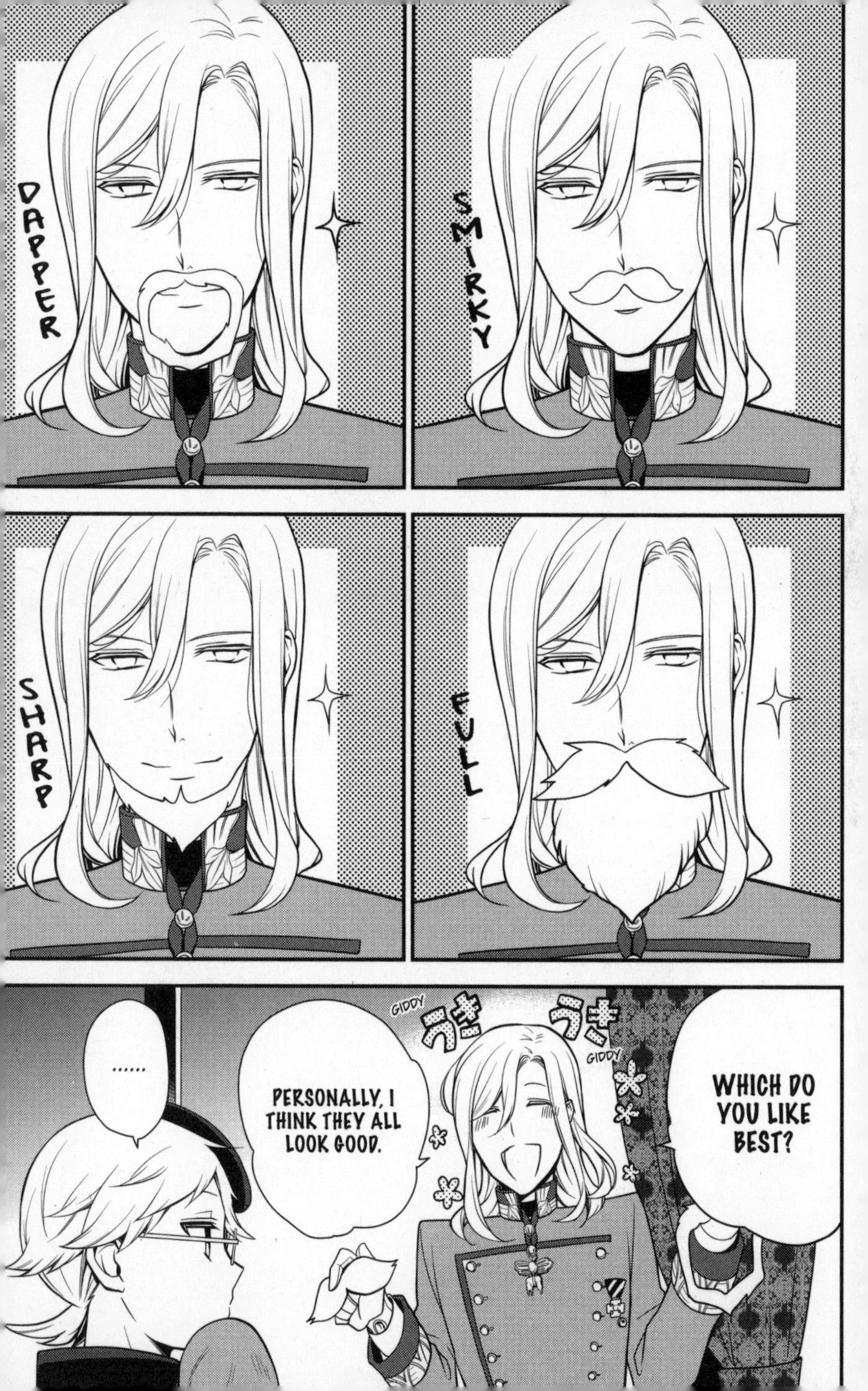
SMIRKY
DAPPER
FULL
SHARP
WHICH DO YOU LIKE BEST?
うき
GIDDY
うき
GIDDY
PERSONALLY, I THINK THEY ALL LOOK GOOD.
......

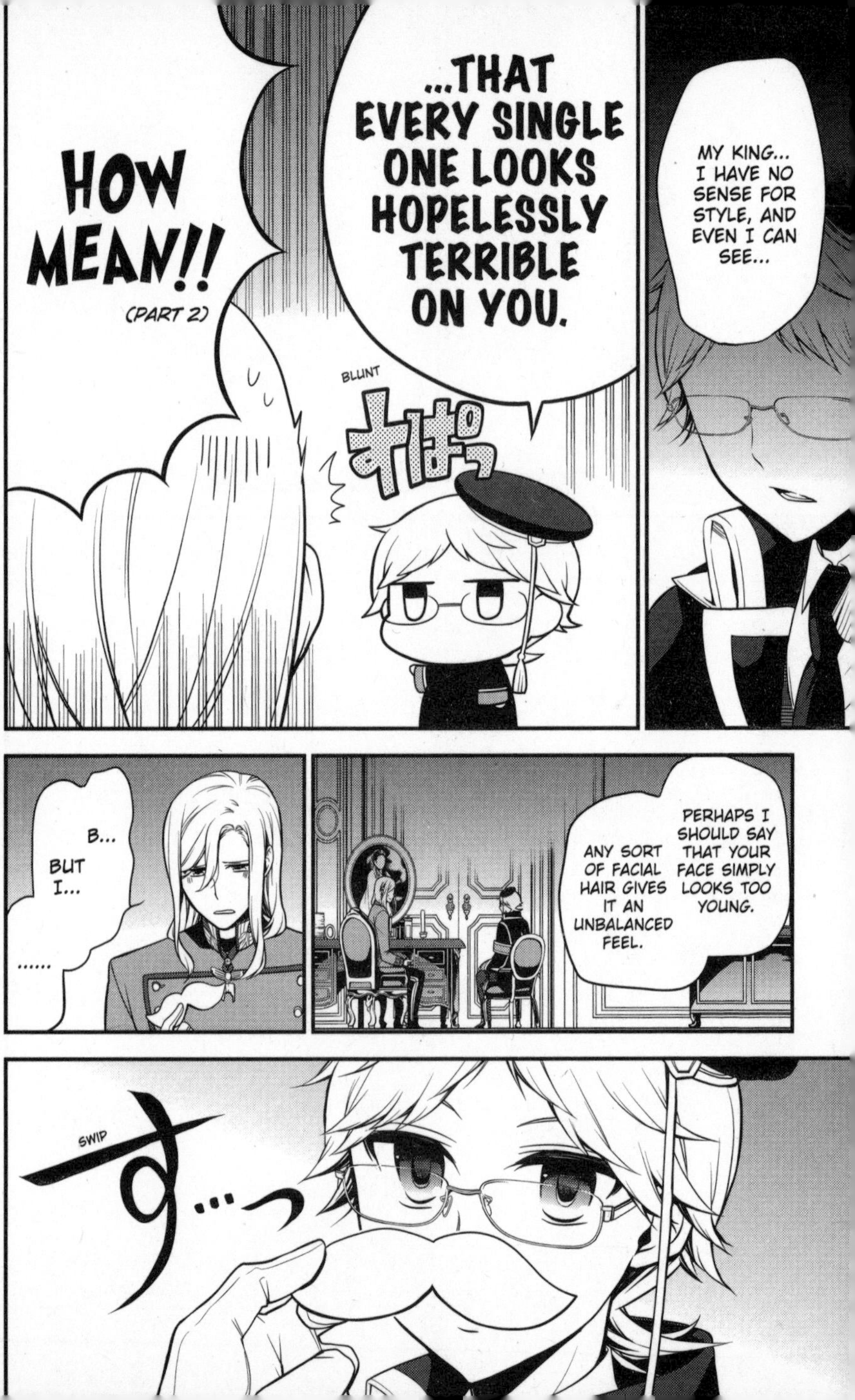
MY KING... I HAVE NO SENSE FOR STYLE, AND EVEN I CAN SEE...
...THAT EVERY SINGLE ONE LOOKS HOPELESSLY TERRIBLE ON YOU.
BLUNT
HOW MEAN!!
(PART 2)
PERHAPS I SHOULD SAY THAT YOUR FACE SIMPLY LOOKS TOO YOUNG.
ANY SORT OF FACIAL HAIR GIVES IT AN UNBALANCED FEEL.
B... BUT I...
......
SWIP

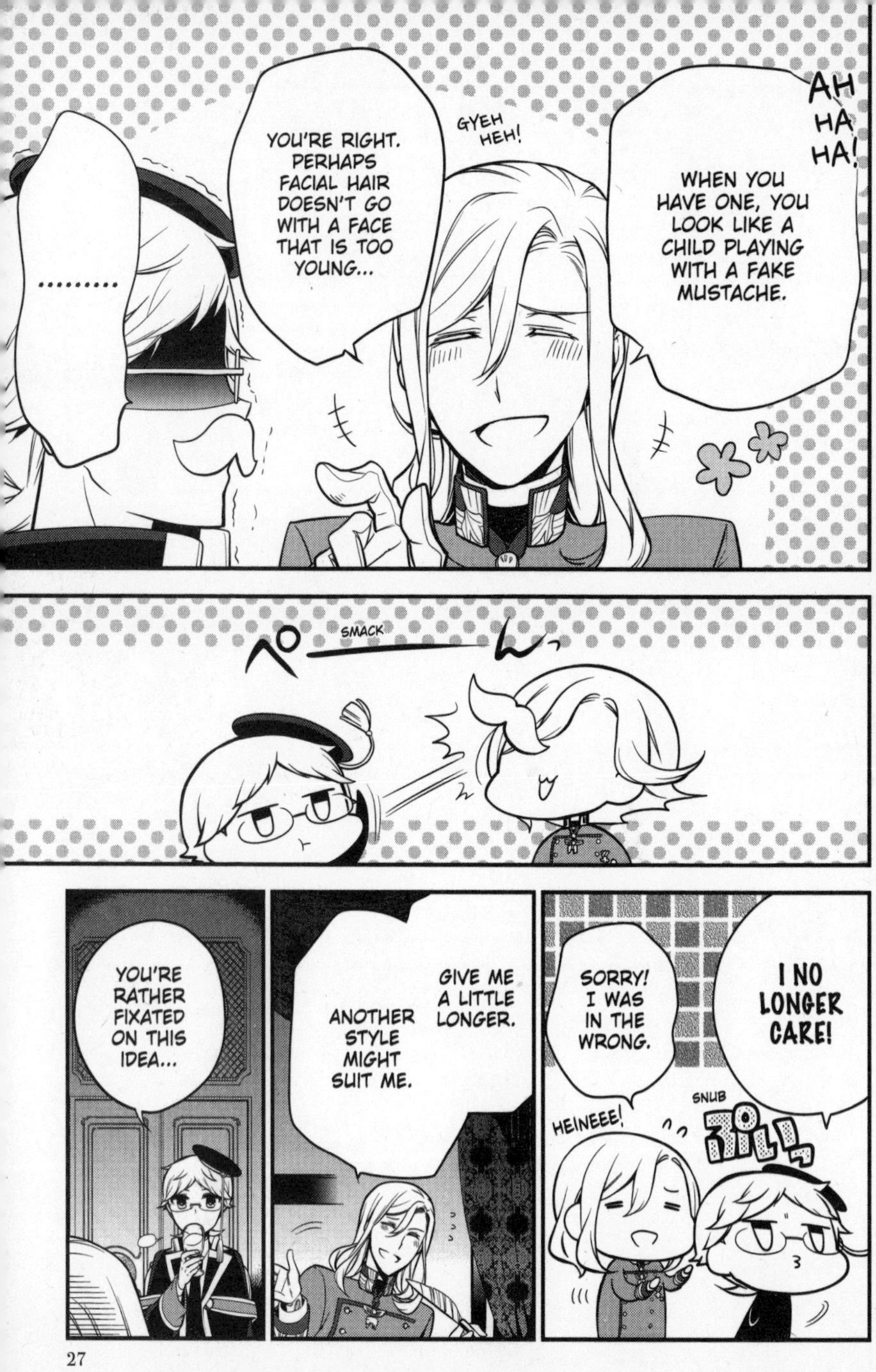
AH HA HA!
WHEN YOU HAVE ONE, YOU LOOK LIKE A CHILD PLAYING WITH A FAKE MUSTACHE.
GYEH HEH!
YOU'RE RIGHT. PERHAPS FACIAL HAIR DOESN'T GO WITH A FACE THAT IS TOO YOUNG...
....
SMACK
I NO LONGER CARE!
SORRY! I WAS IN THE WRONG.
SNUB
HEINEEE!
GIVE ME A LITTLE LONGER.
ANOTHER STYLE MIGHT SUIT ME.
YOU'RE RATHER FIXATED ON THIS IDEA...

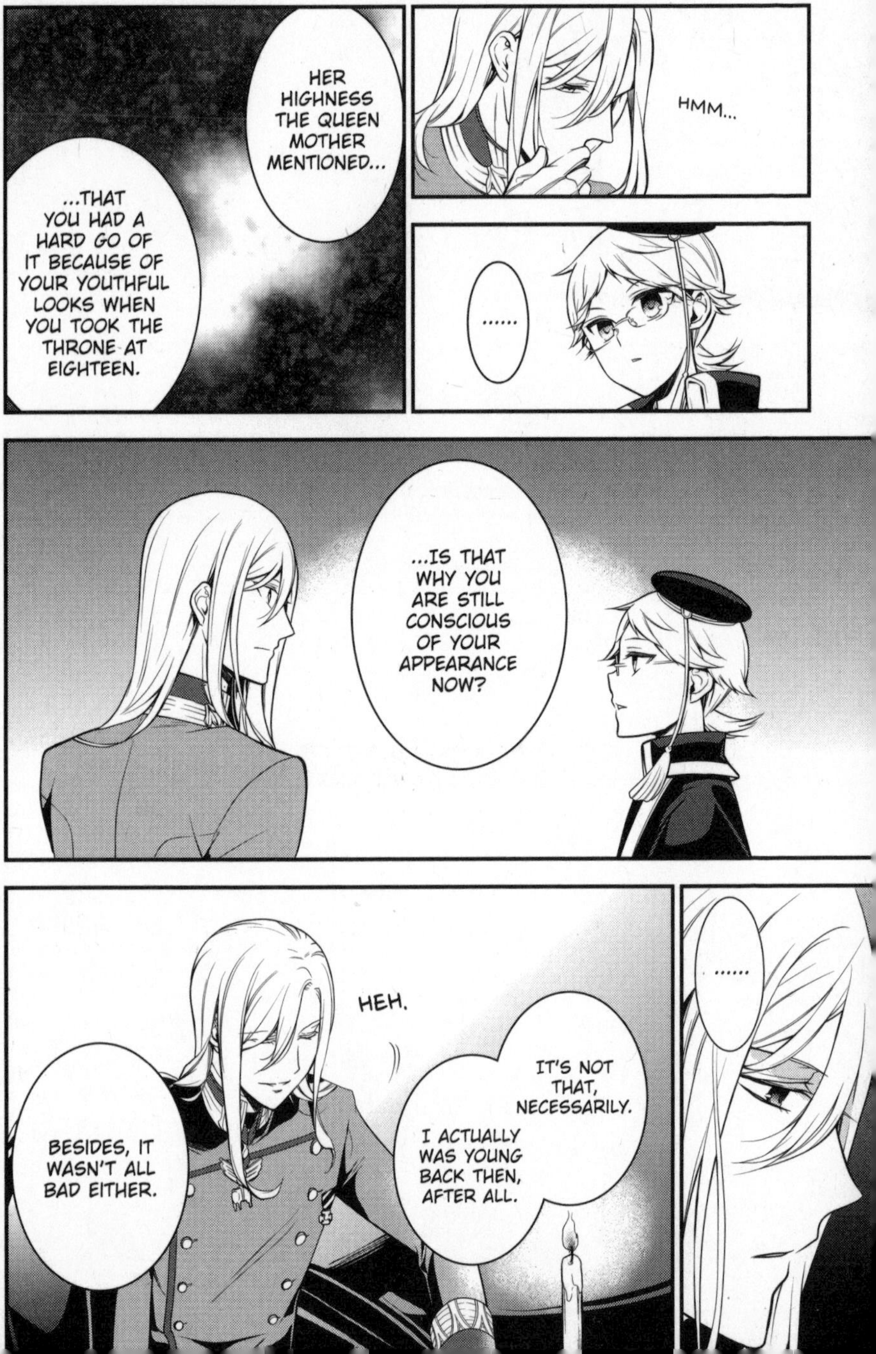
HMM...
......
HER HIGHNESS THE QUEEN MOTHER MENTIONED...
...THAT YOU HAD A HARD GO OF IT BECAUSE OF YOUR YOUTHFUL LOOKS WHEN YOU TOOK THE THRONE AT EIGHTEEN.
...IS THAT WHY YOU ARE STILL CONSCIOUS OF YOUR APPEARANCE NOW?
......
HEH.
IT'S NOT THAT, NECESSARILY.
I ACTUALLY WAS YOUNG BACK THEN, AFTER ALL.
BESIDES, IT WASN'T ALL BAD EITHER.

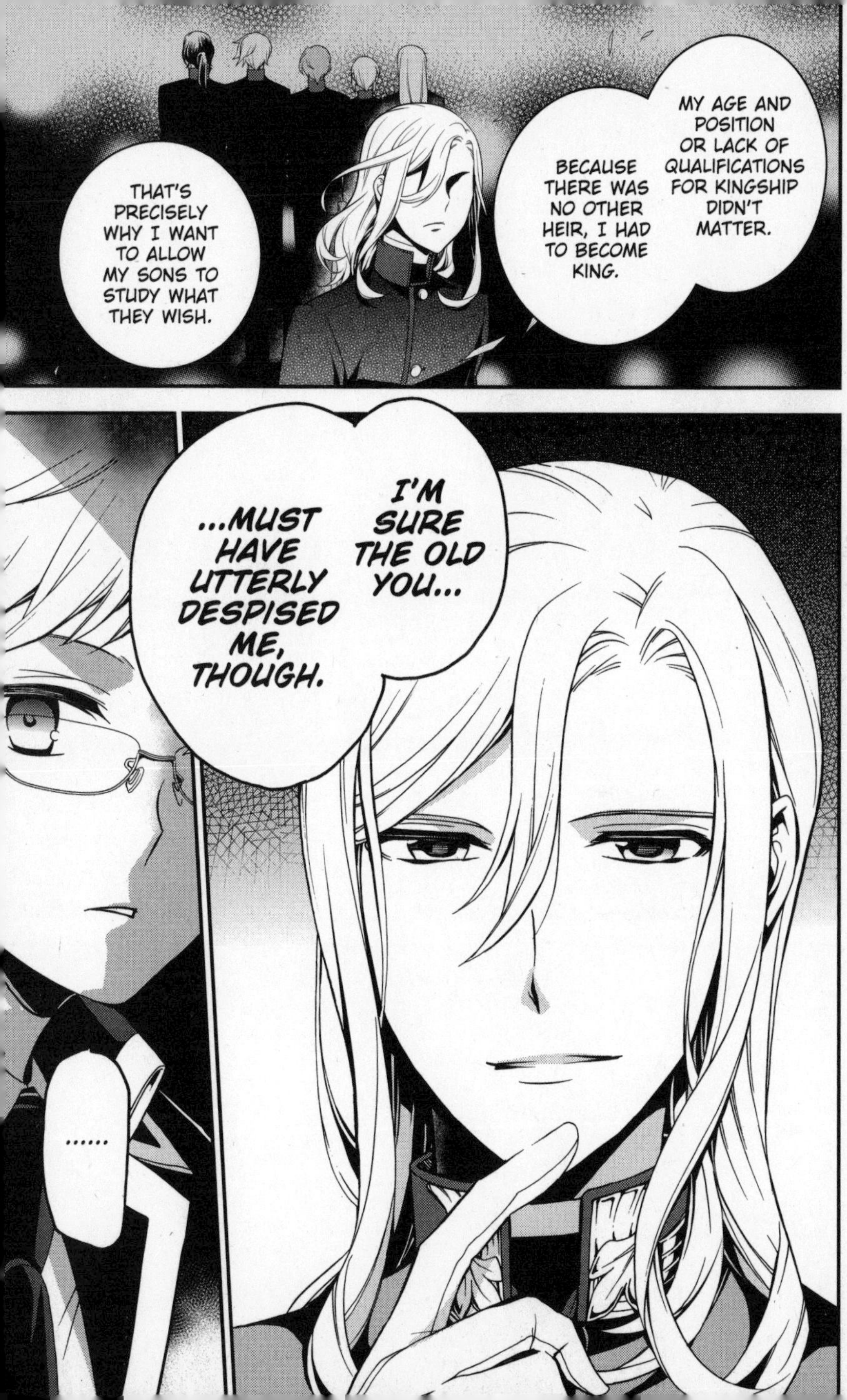
MY AGE AND POSITION OR LACK OF QUALIFICATIONS FOR KINGSHIP DIDN'T MATTER.
BECAUSE THERE WAS NO OTHER HEIR, I HAD TO BECOME KING.
THAT'S PRECISELY WHY I WANT TO ALLOW MY SONS TO STUDY WHAT THEY WISH.
I'M SURE THE OLD YOU...
...MUST HAVE UTTERLY DESPISED ME, THOUGH.
......

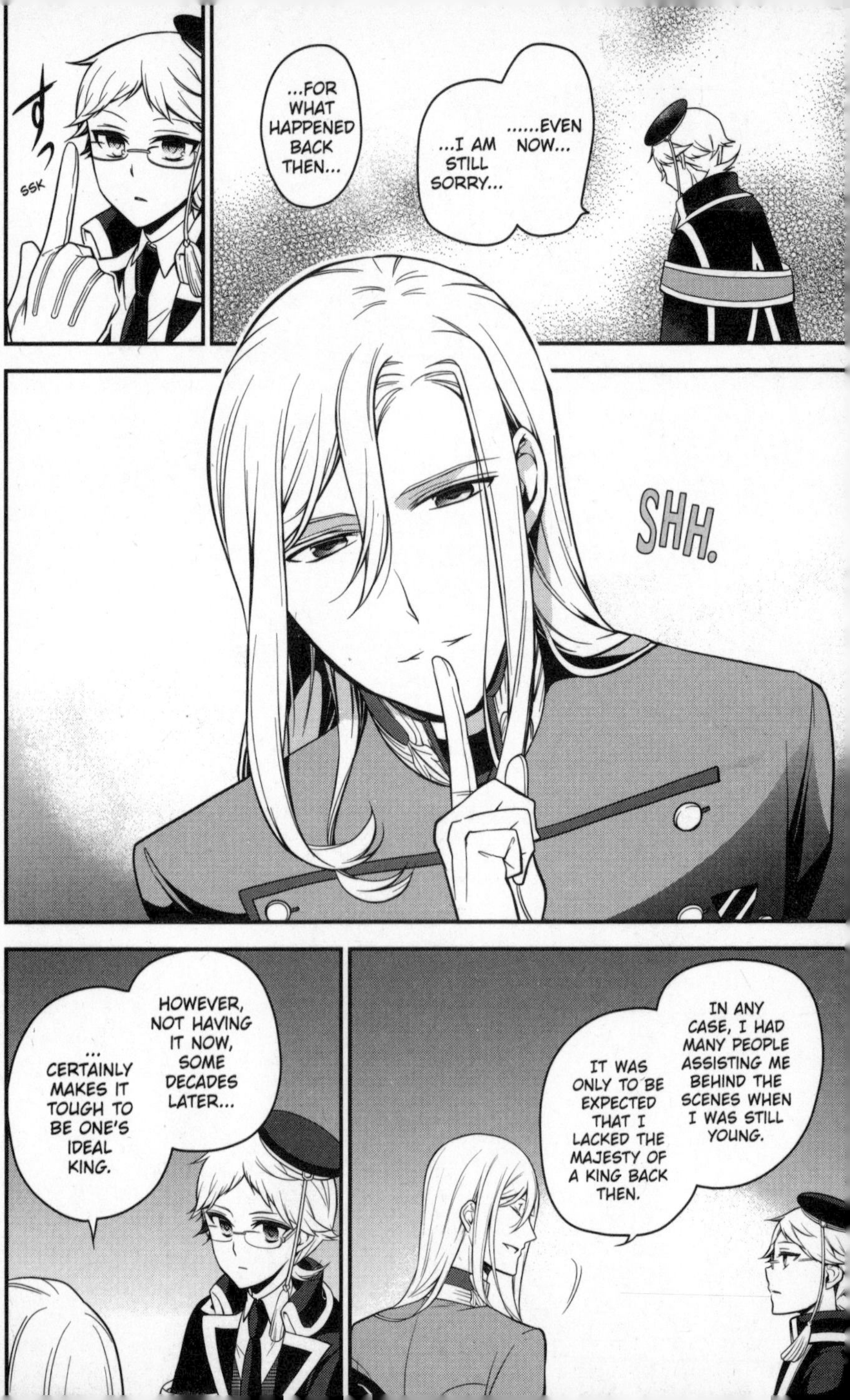
......EVEN NOW... ...I AM STILL SORRY...
...FOR WHAT HAPPENED BACK THEN...
す
SSK
SHH.
IN ANY CASE, I HAD MANY PEOPLE ASSISTING ME BEHIND THE SCENES WHEN I WAS STILL YOUNG.
IT WAS ONLY TO BE EXPECTED THAT I LACKED THE MAJESTY OF A KING BACK THEN.
HOWEVER, NOT HAVING IT NOW, SOME DECADES LATER...
...CERTAINLY MAKES IT TOUGH TO BE ONE'S IDEAL KING.

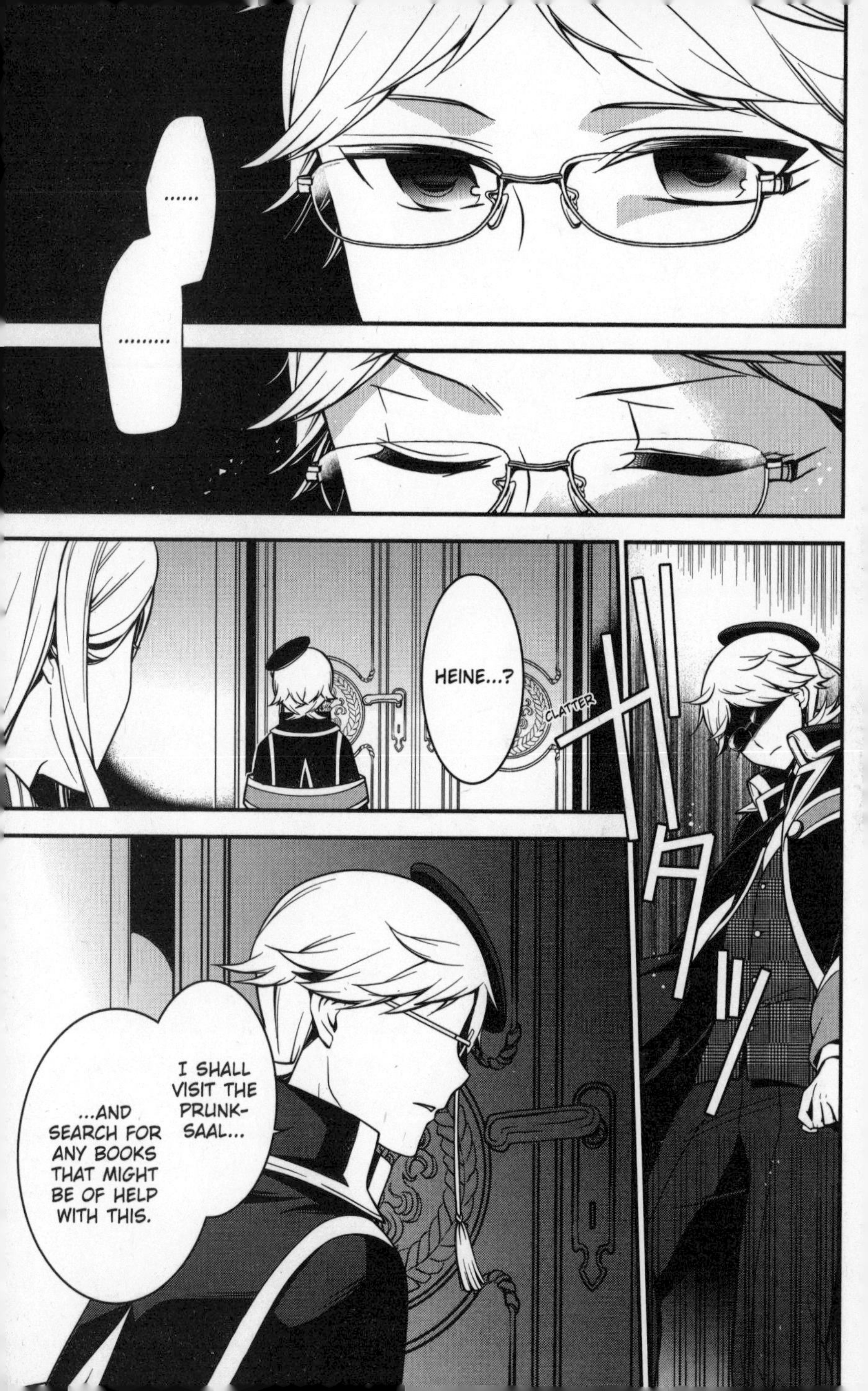
......
....
CLATTER
HEINE...?
I SHALL VISIT THE PRUNK-SAAL...
...AND SEARCH FOR ANY BOOKS THAT MIGHT BE OF HELP WITH THIS.

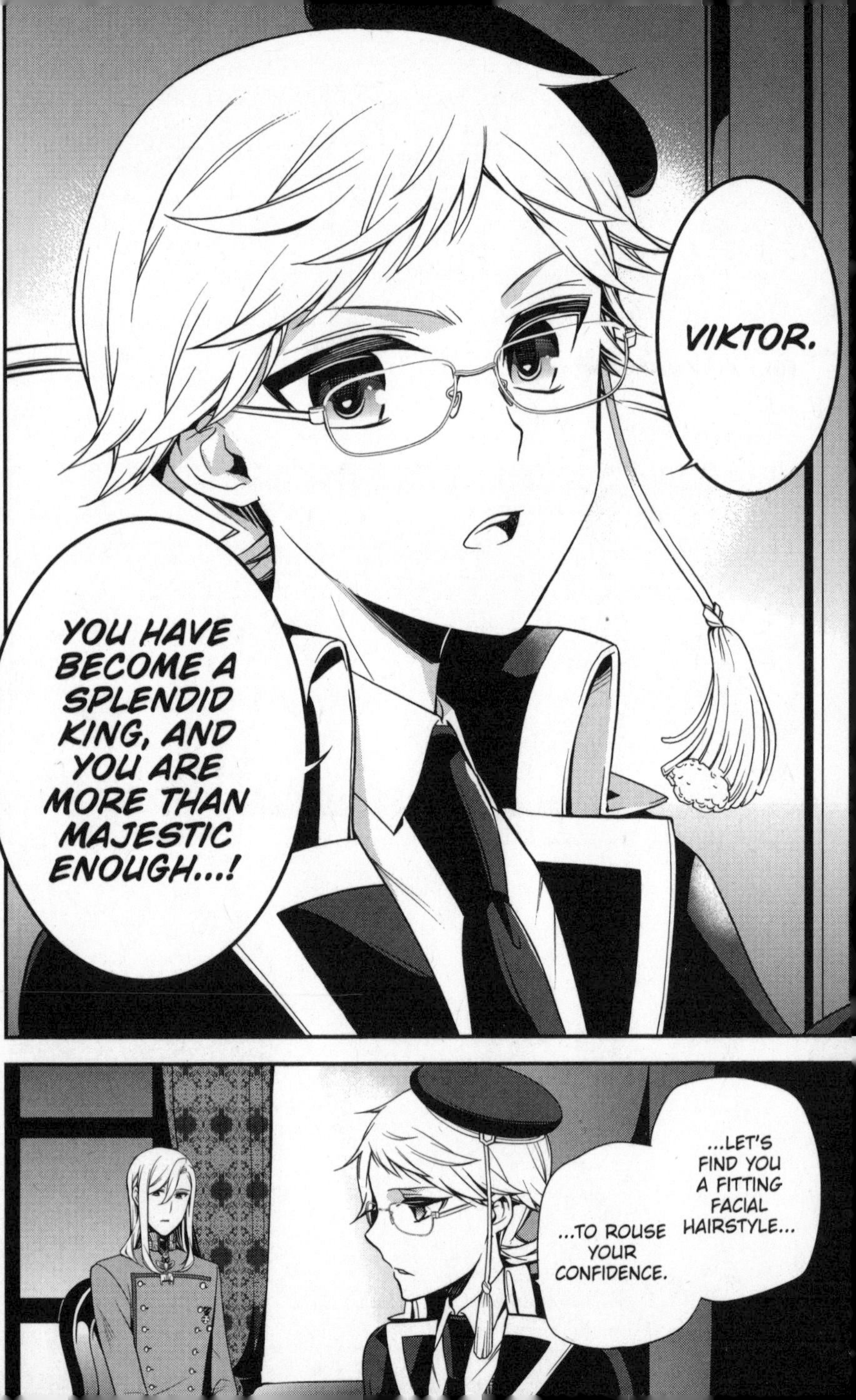
VIKTOR.
YOU HAVE BECOME A SPLENDID KING, AND YOU ARE MORE THAN MAJESTIC ENOUGH...!
...LET'S FIND YOU A FITTING FACIAL HAIRSTYLE...
...TO ROUSE YOUR CONFIDENCE.

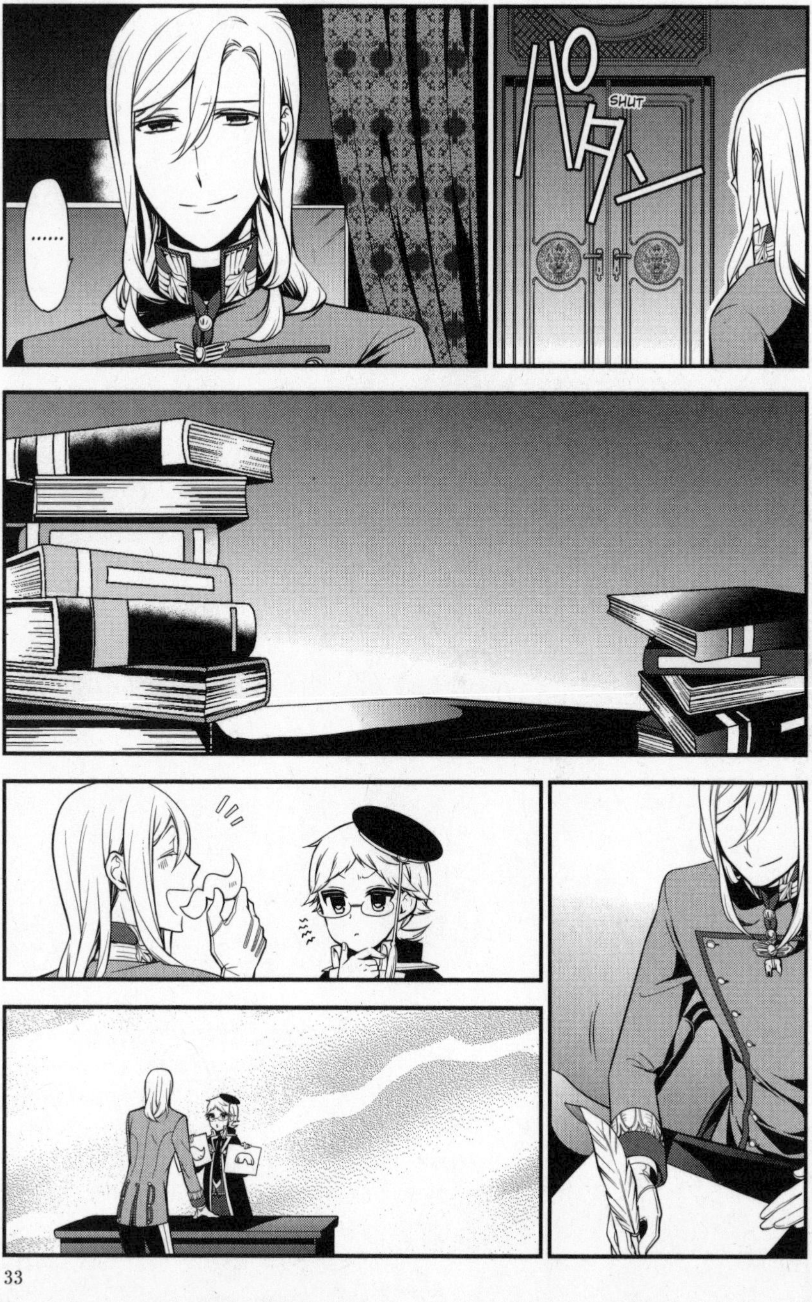
パタン
SHUT
......

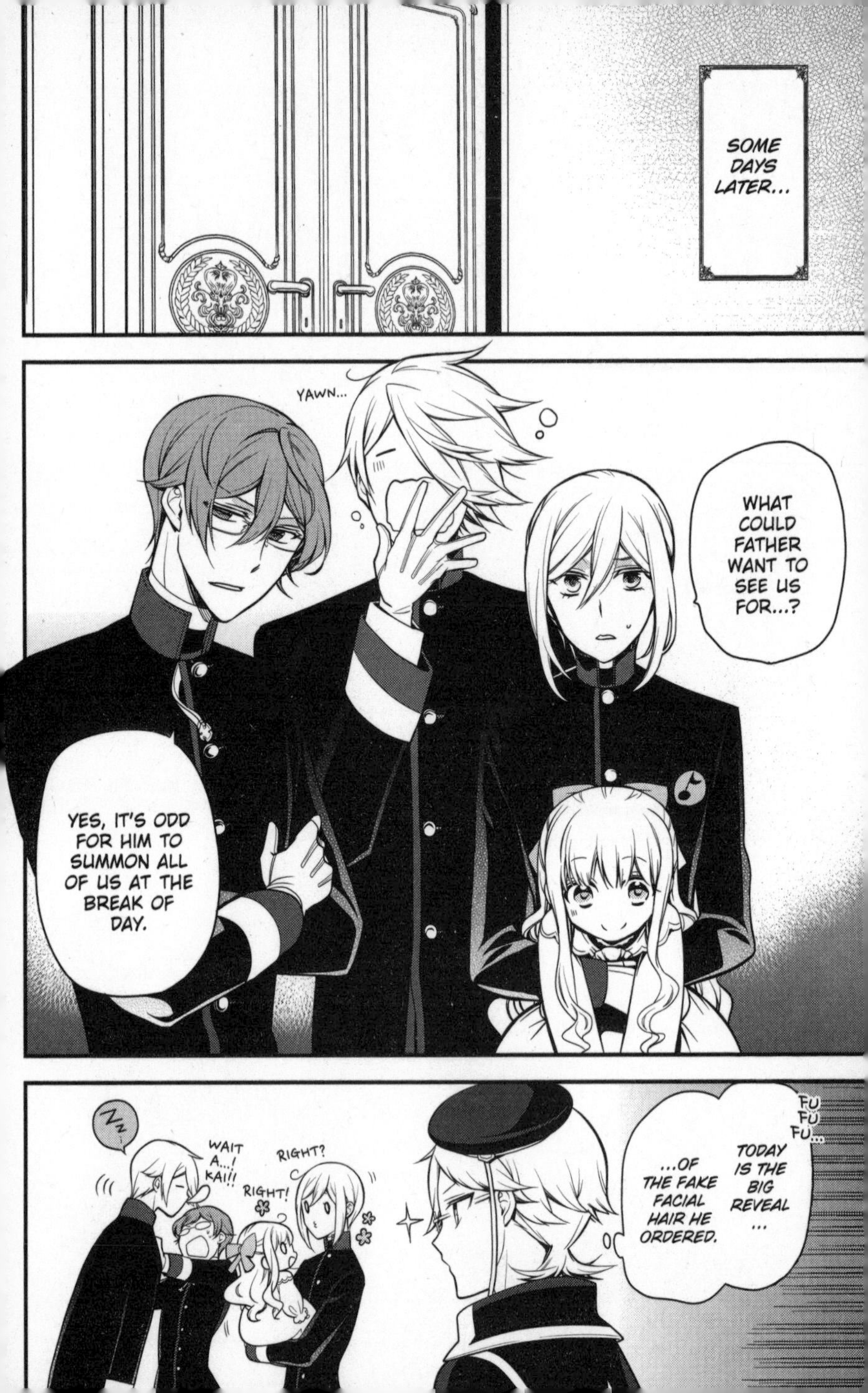
SOME DAYS LATER...
WHAT COULD FATHER WANT TO SEE US FOR...?
YAWN...
YES, IT'S ODD FOR HIM TO SUMMON ALL OF US AT THE BREAK OF DAY.
FU FU FU...
TODAY IS THE BIG REVEAL...
...OF THE FAKE FACIAL HAIR HE ORDERED.
RIGHT?
RIGHT!
WAIT A...! KAI!!
Zz

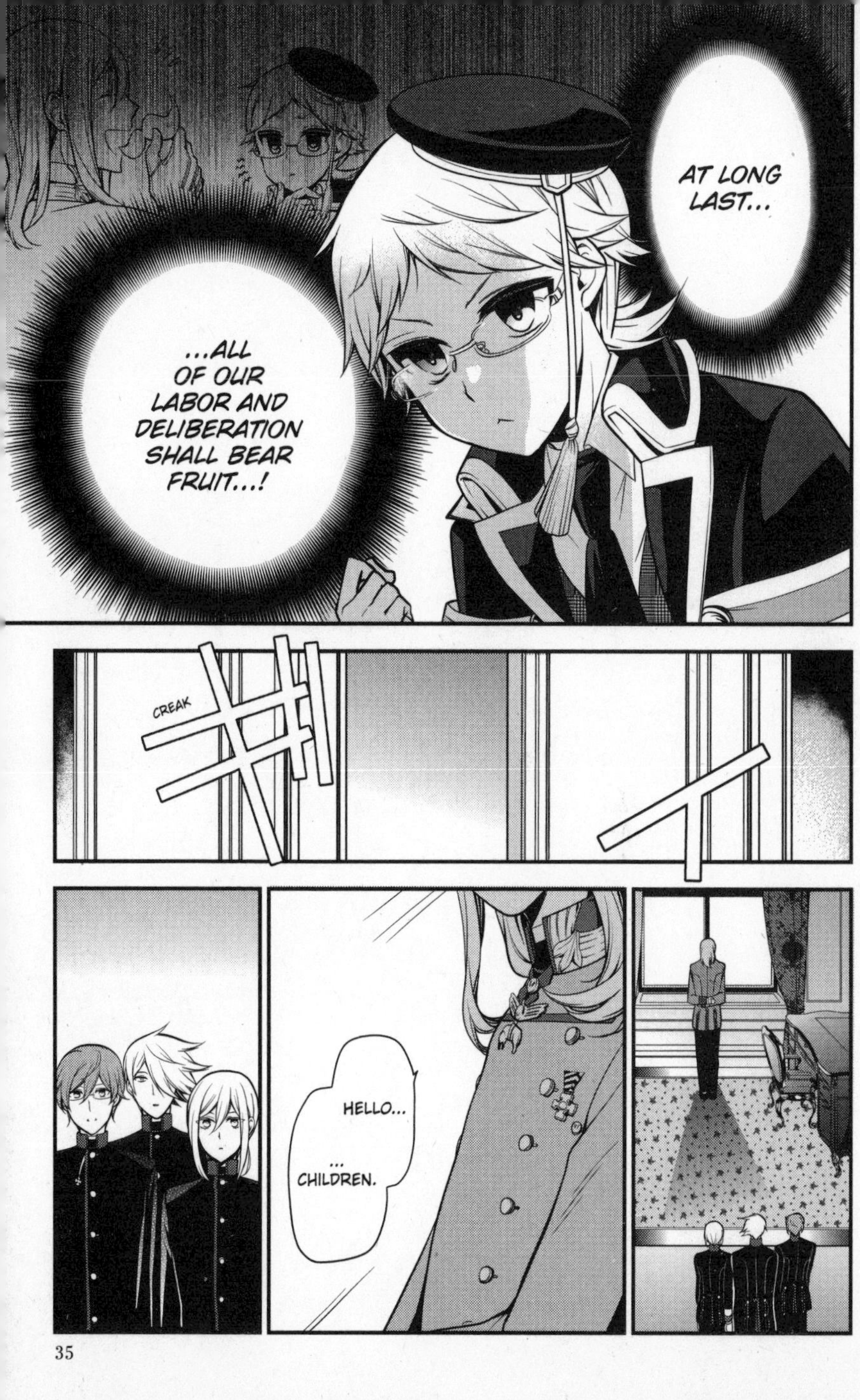
AT LONG LAST...
...ALL OF OUR LABOR AND DELIBERATION SHALL BEAR FRUIT...!
CREAK
HELLO...
... CHILDREN.

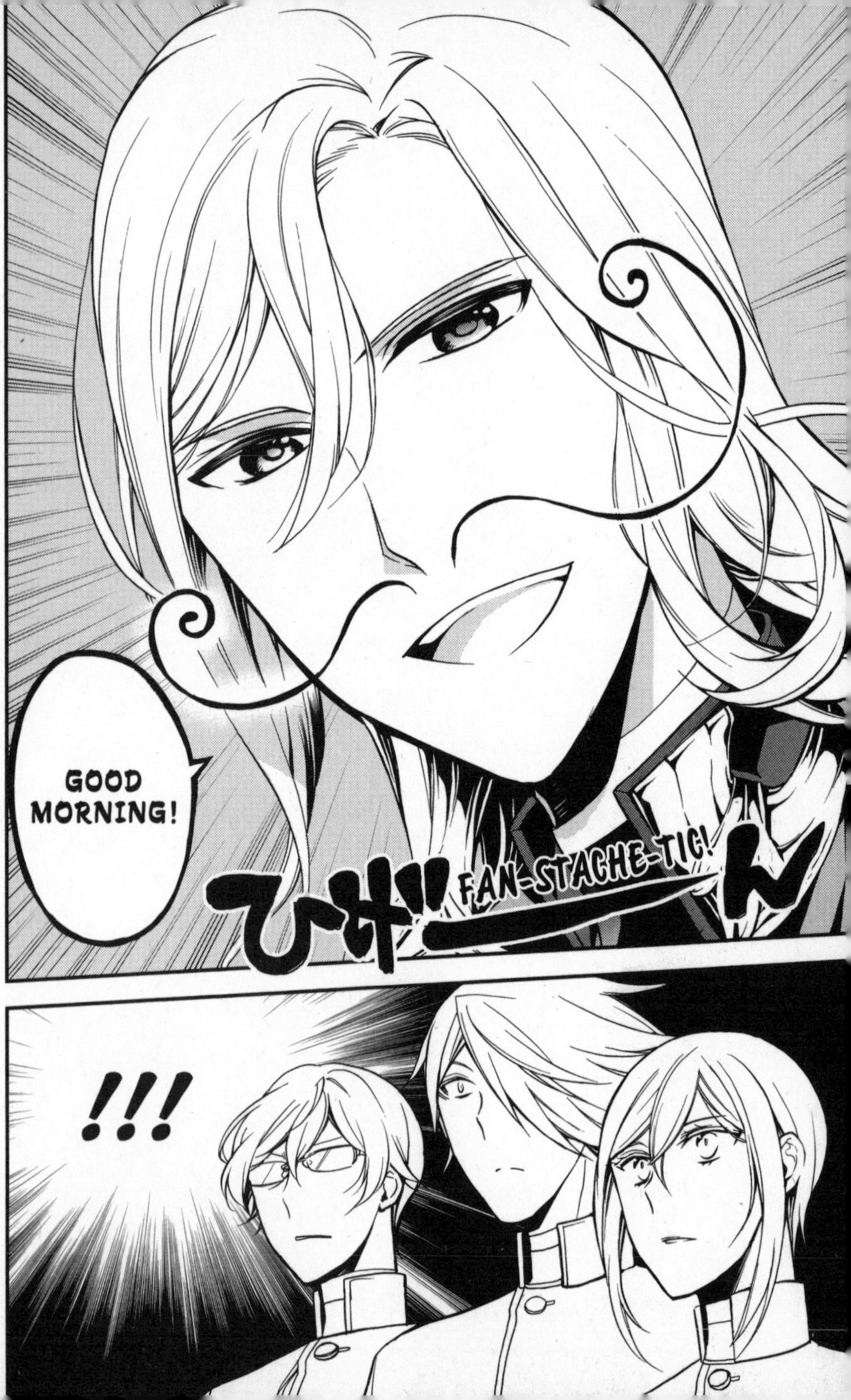
GOOD MORNING!
ひげーん
FAN-STACHE-TIC!
!!!

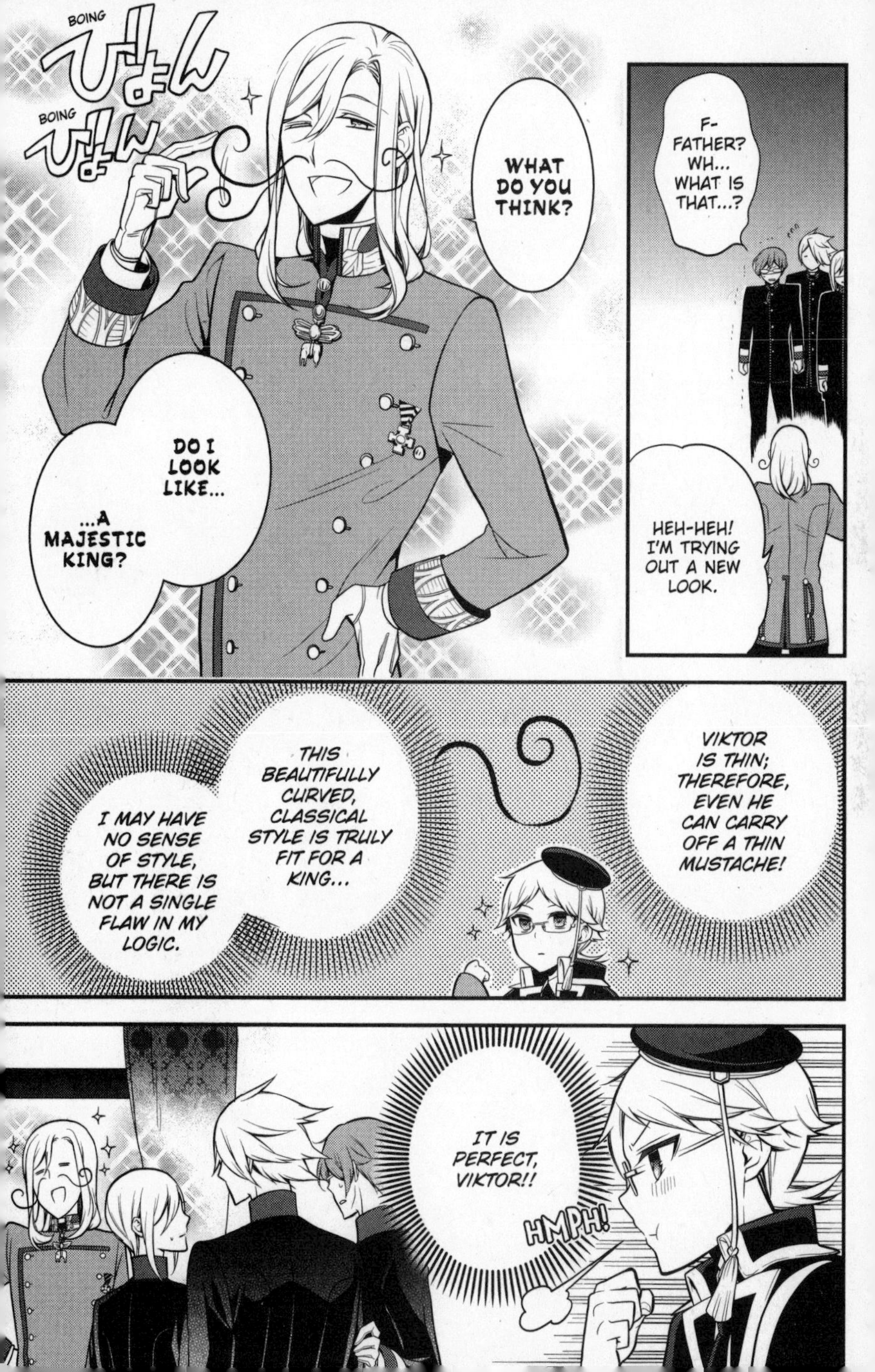
F-FATHER? WH... WHAT IS THAT...?
HEH-HEH! I'M TRYING OUT A NEW LOOK.
BOING
ひよん
BOING
びよん
WHAT DO YOU THINK?
DO I LOOK LIKE...
...A MAJESTIC KING?
VIKTOR IS THIN; THEREFORE, EVEN HE CAN CARRY OFF A THIN MUSTACHE!
THIS BEAUTIFULLY CURVED, CLASSICAL STYLE IS TRULY FIT FOR A KING...
I MAY HAVE NO SENSE OF STYLE, BUT THERE IS NOT A SINGLE FLAW IN MY LOGIC.
IT IS PERFECT, VIKTOR!!
HMPH!

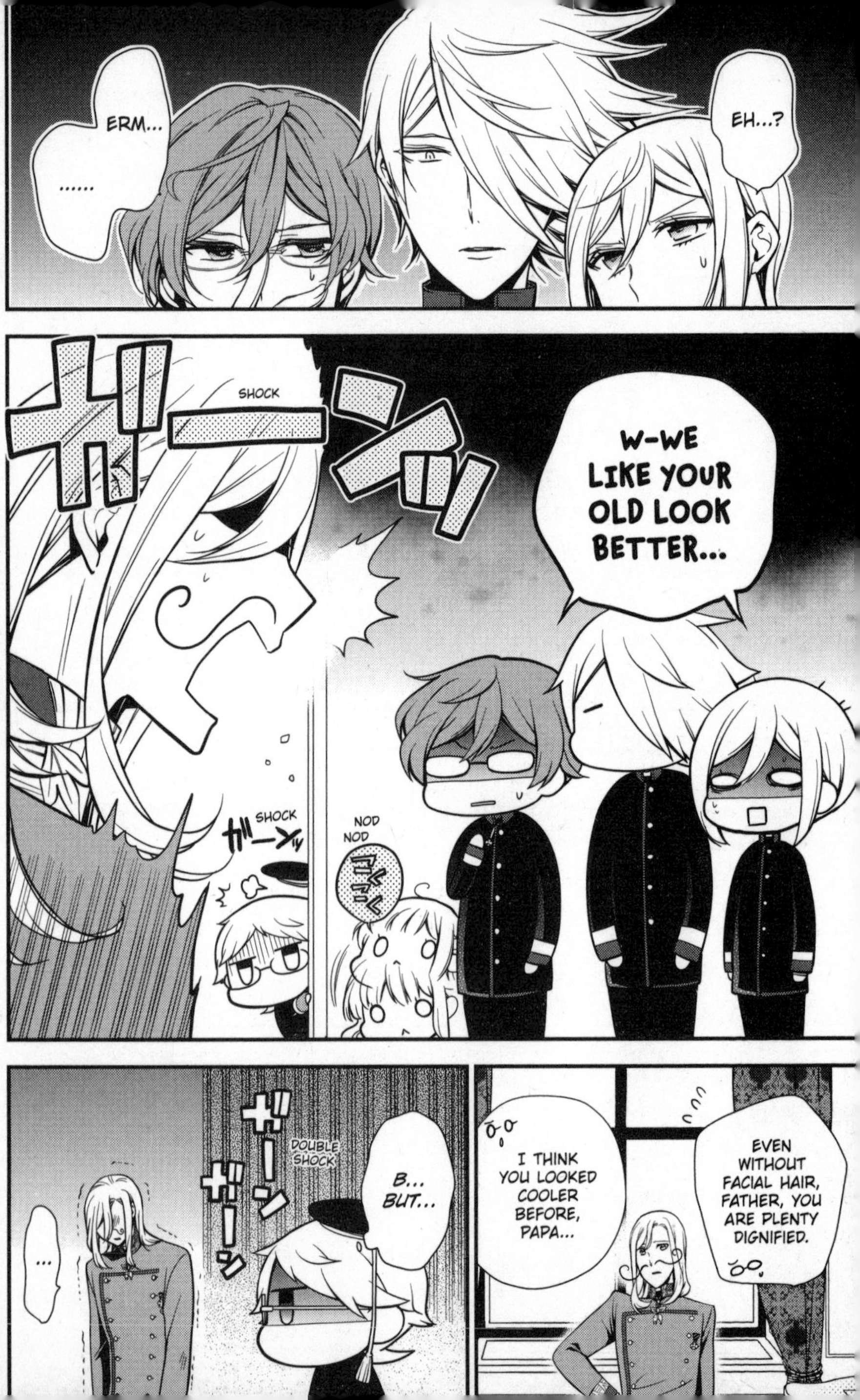
EH...?
ERM...
......
W-WE LIKE YOUR OLD LOOK BETTER...
NOD NOD
SHOCK
SHOCK
EVEN WITHOUT FACIAL HAIR, FATHER, YOU ARE PLENTY DIGNIFIED.
I THINK YOU LOOKED COOLER BEFORE, PAPA...
DOUBLE SHOCK
B... BUT...
...

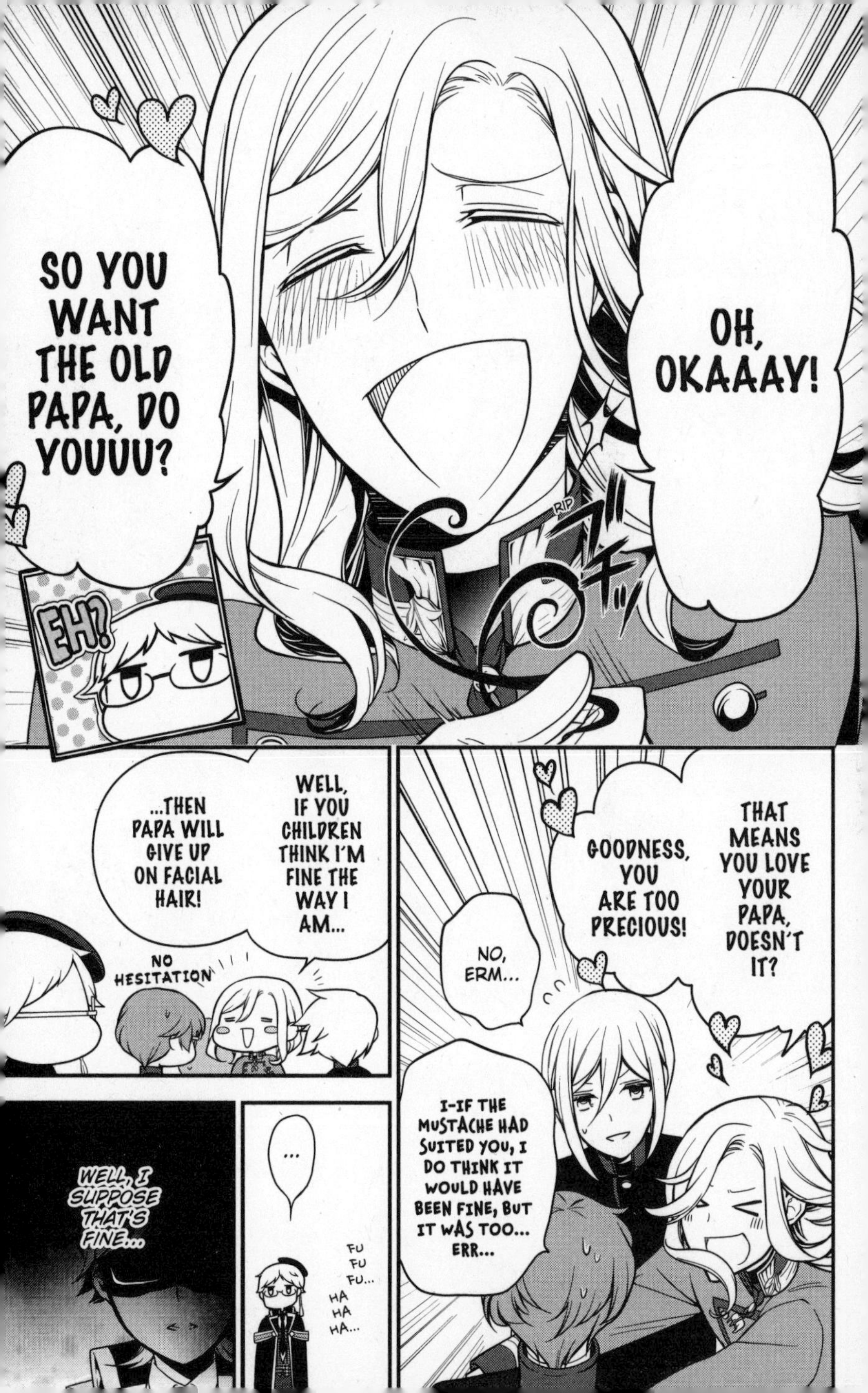
OH, OKAAAY!
SO YOU WANT THE OLD PAPA, DO YOUUU?
RIP
EH?
THAT MEANS YOU LOVE YOUR PAPA, DOESN'T IT?
GOODNESS, YOU ARE TOO PRECIOUS!
NO, ERM...
I-IF THE MUSTACHE HAD SUITED YOU, I DO THINK IT WOULD HAVE BEEN FINE, BUT IT WAS TOO... ERR...
WELL, IF YOU CHILDREN THINK I'M FINE THE WAY I AM...
...THEN PAPA WILL GIVE UP ON FACIAL HAIR!
NO HESITATION
...
FU FU FU...
HA HA HA...
WELL, I SUPPOSE THAT'S FINE...

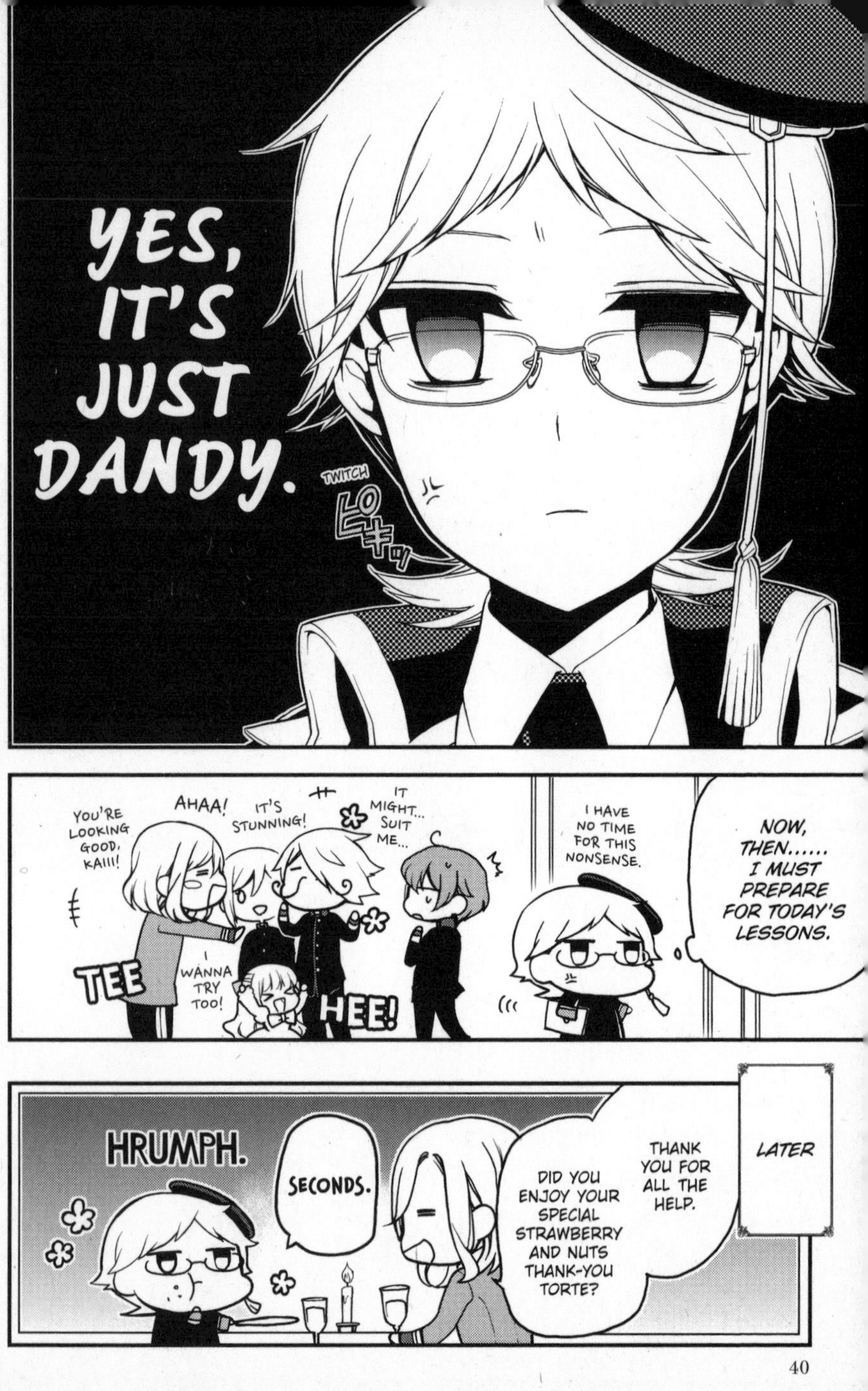
YES, IT'S JUST DANDY.
TWITCH
NOW, THEN...... I MUST PREPARE FOR TODAY'S LESSONS.
I HAVE NO TIME FOR THIS NONSENSE.
IT MIGHT... SUIT ME...
IT'S STUNNING!
AHAA!
YOU'RE LOOKING GOOD, KAIII!
I WANNA TRY TOO!
HEE!
TEE
LATER
THANK YOU FOR ALL THE HELP.
DID YOU ENJOY YOUR SPECIAL STRAWBERRY AND NUTS THANK-YOU TORTE?
SECONDS.
HRUMPH.

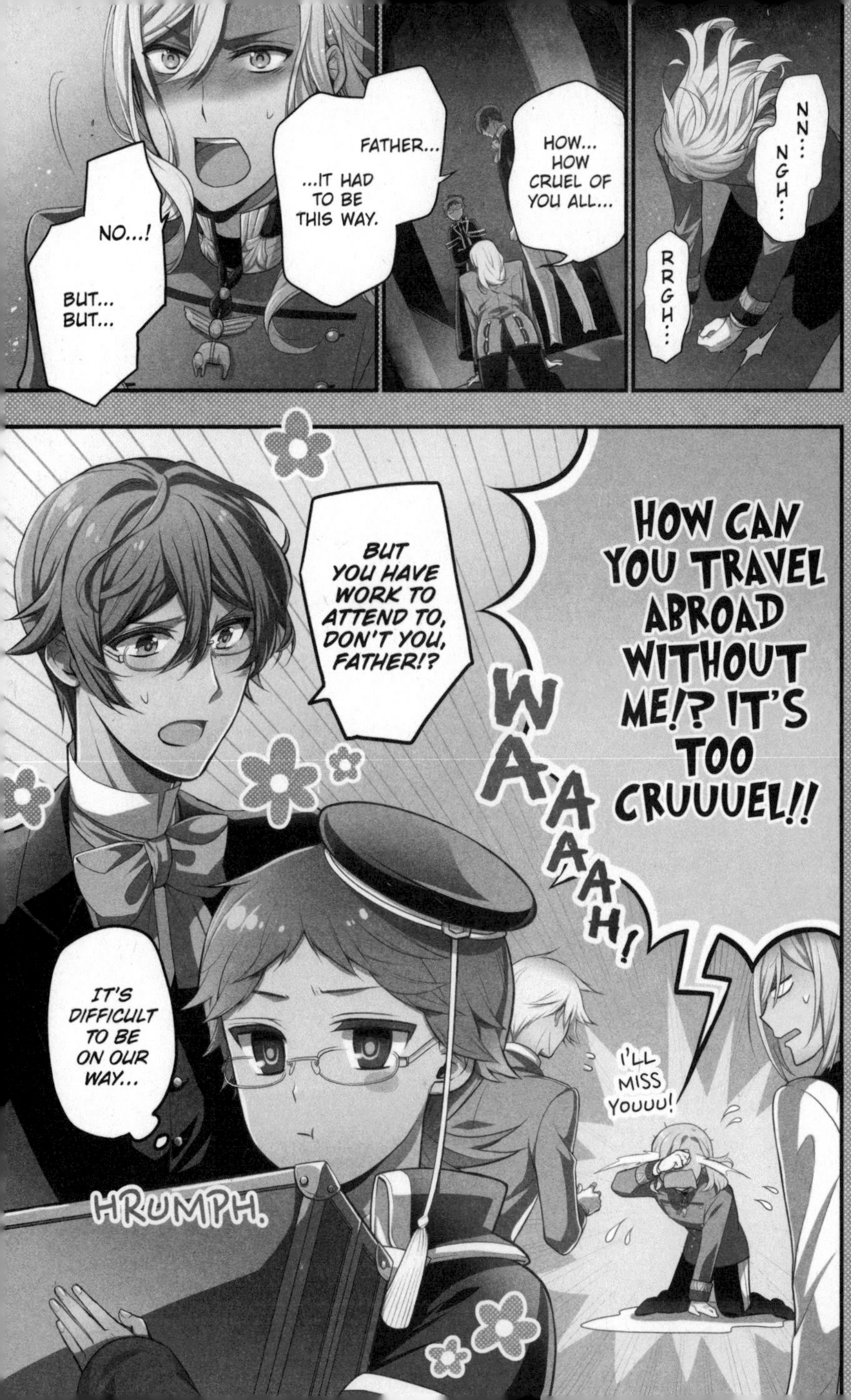
NN... NGH...
RRGH...
HOW... HOW CRUEL OF YOU ALL...
FATHER...
...IT HAD TO BE THIS WAY.
NO...!
BUT... BUT...
HOW CAN YOU TRAVEL ABROAD WITHOUT ME!? IT'S TOO CRUUUEL!!
WAAAAAH!
BUT YOU HAVE WORK TO ATTEND TO, DON'T YOU, FATHER!?
I'LL MISS YOUUU!
IT'S DIFFICULT TO BE ON OUR WAY...
HRUMPH.

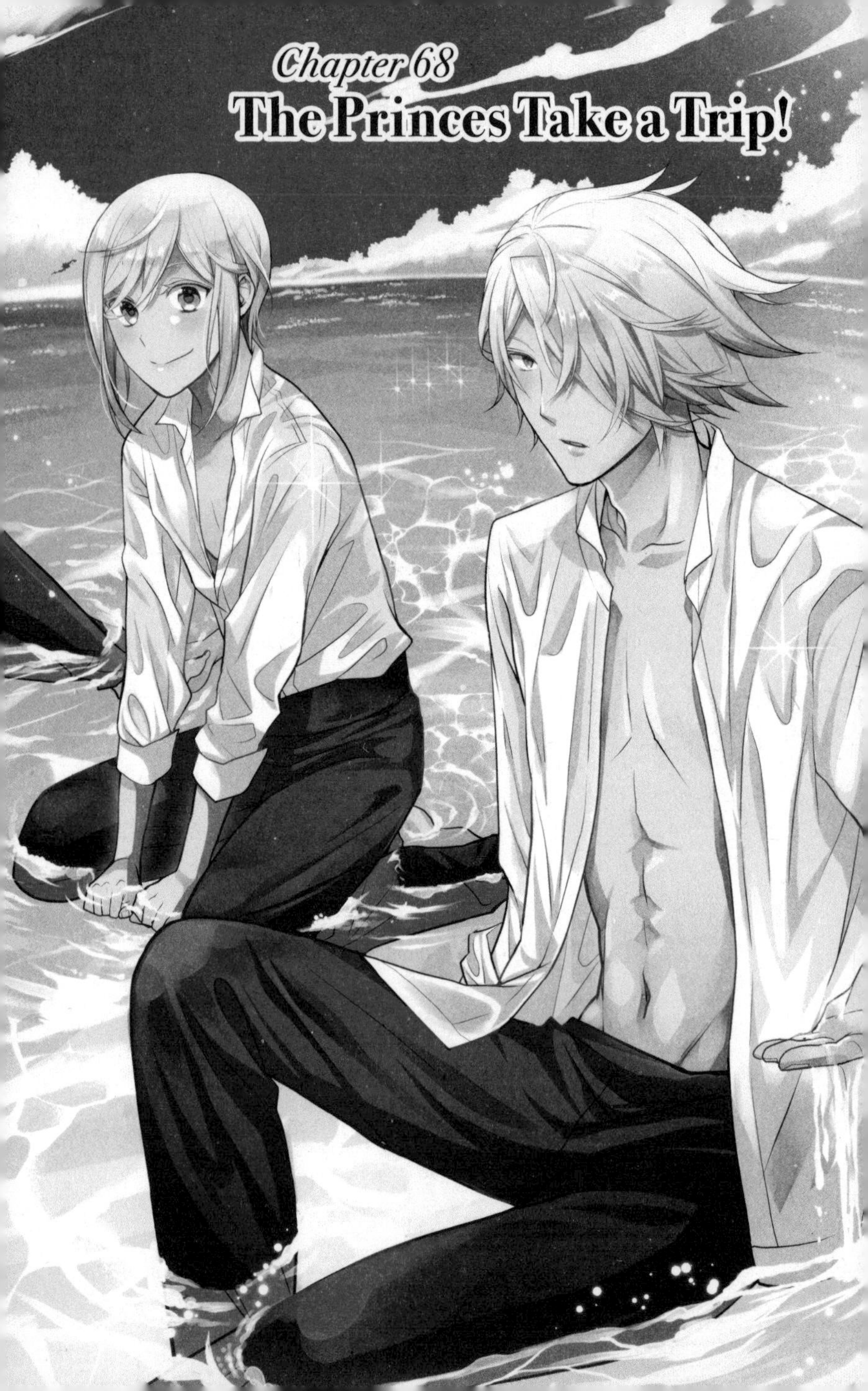
Chapter 68
The Princes Take a Trip!

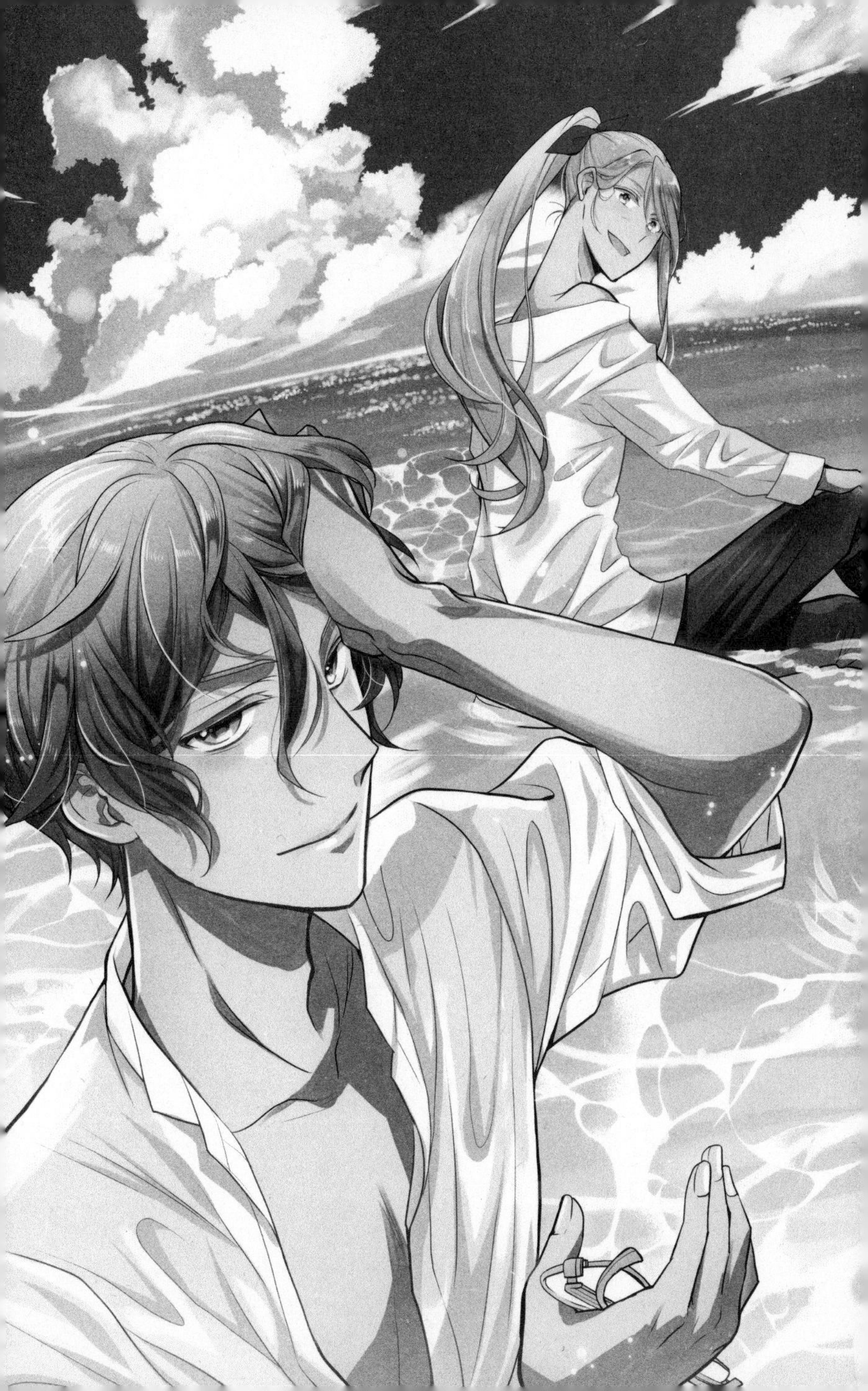

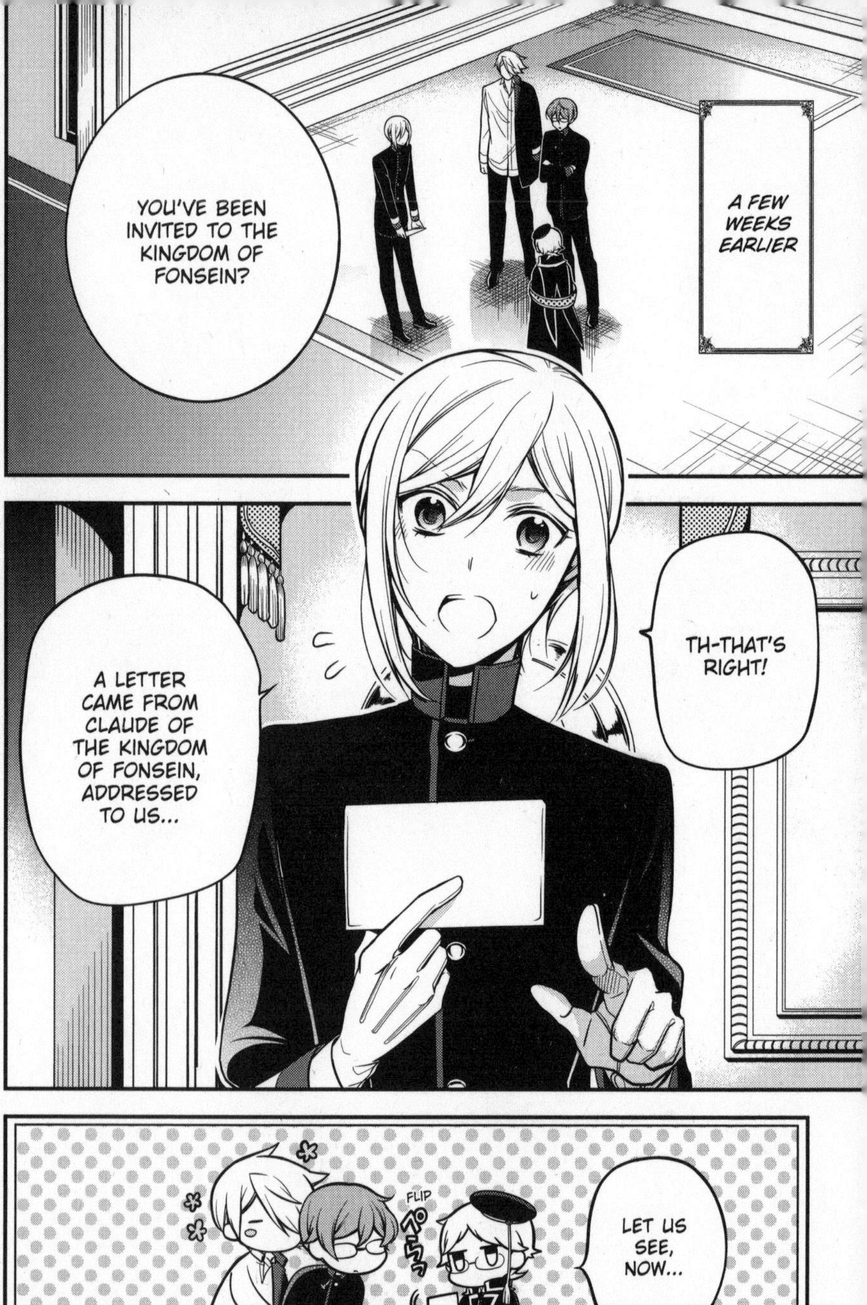
A FEW WEEKS EARLIER
YOU'VE BEEN INVITED TO THE KINGDOM OF FONSEIN?
TH-THAT'S RIGHT!
A LETTER CAME FROM CLAUDE OF THE KINGDOM OF FONSEIN, ADDRESSED TO US...
LET US SEE, NOW...
FLIP

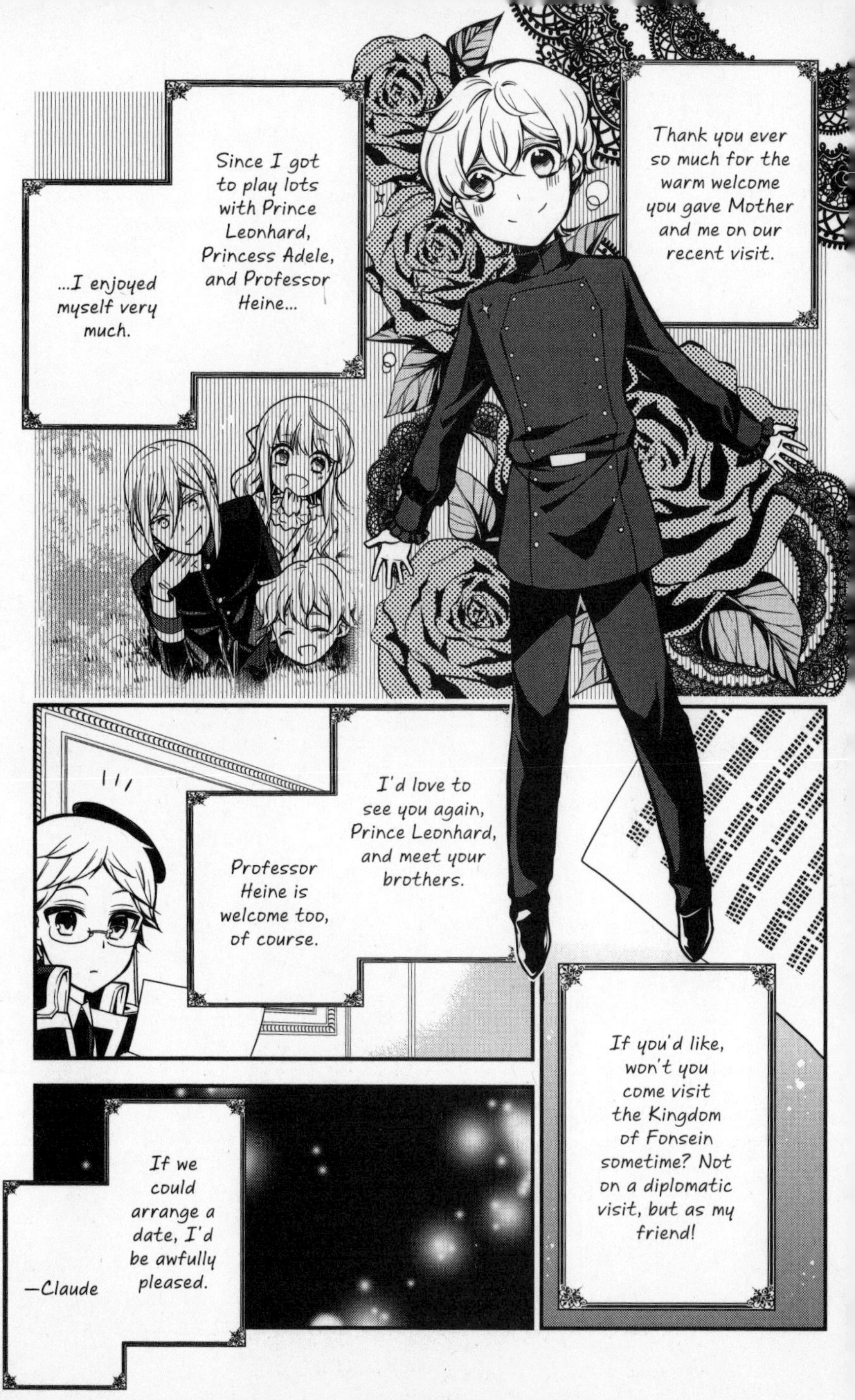
Thank you ever so much for the warm welcome you gave Mother and me on our recent visit.
Since I got to play lots with Prince Leonhard, Princess Adele, and Professor Heine...
...I enjoyed myself very much.
I'd love to see you again, Prince Leonhard, and meet your brothers.
Professor Heine is welcome too, of course.
If you'd like, won't you come visit the Kingdom of Fonsein sometime? Not on a diplomatic visit, but as my friend!
If we could arrange a date, I'd be awfully pleased.
—Claude

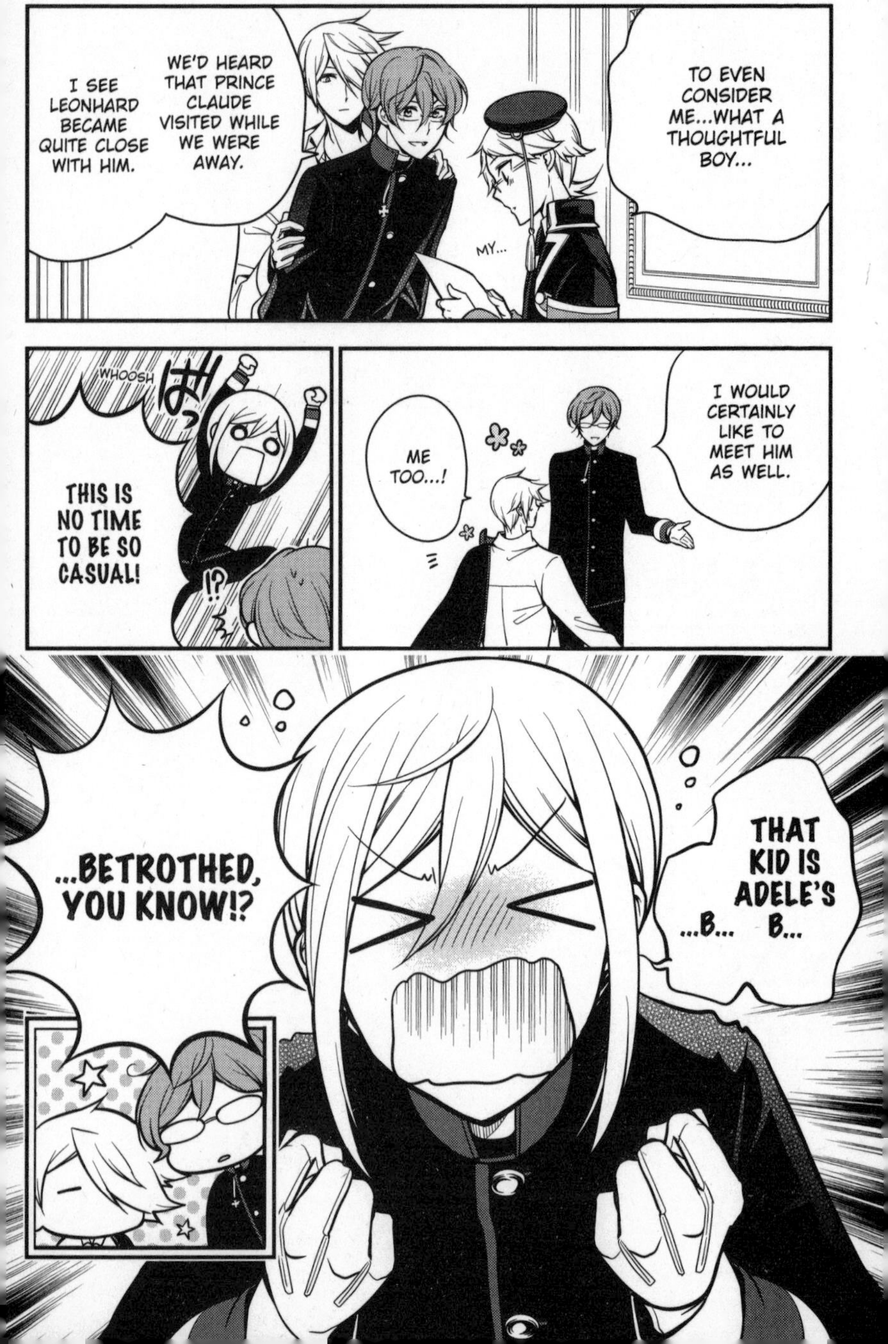

TO EVEN CONSIDER ME...WHAT A THOUGHTFUL BOY...
MY...
WE'D HEARD THAT PRINCE CLAUDE VISITED WHILE WE WERE AWAY.
I SEE LEONHARD BECAME QUITE CLOSE WITH HIM.
I WOULD CERTAINLY LIKE TO MEET HIM AS WELL.
ME TOO...!
WHOOSH
ぱっ
THIS IS NO TIME TO BE SO CASUAL!
!?
THAT KID IS ADELE'S ...B... B...
...BETROTHED, YOU KNOW!?

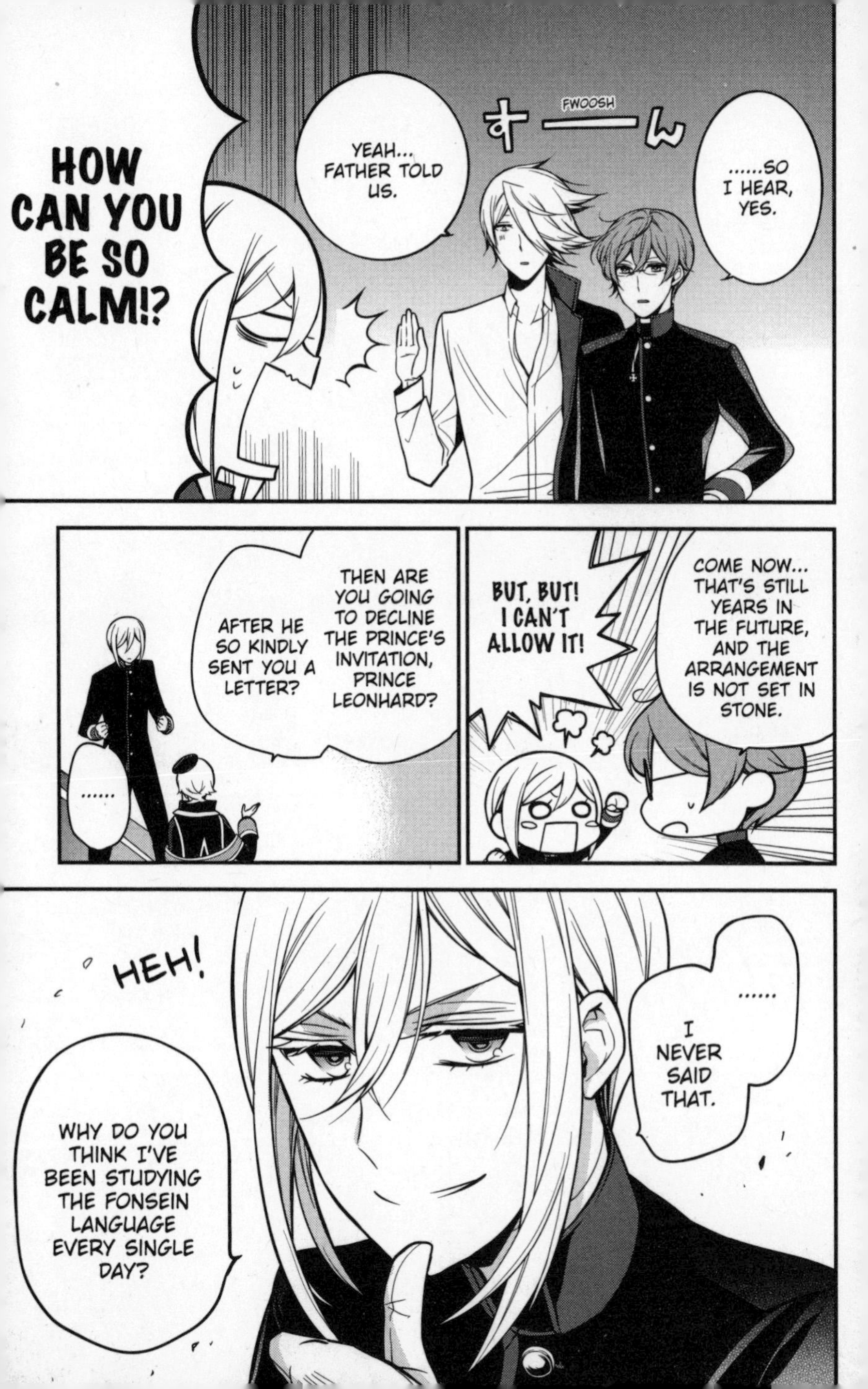
......SO I HEAR, YES.
FWOOSH
すーん
YEAH... FATHER TOLD US.
HOW CAN YOU BE SO CALM!?
COME NOW... THAT'S STILL YEARS IN THE FUTURE, AND THE ARRANGEMENT IS NOT SET IN STONE.
BUT, BUT! I CAN'T ALLOW IT!
THEN ARE YOU GOING TO DECLINE THE PRINCE'S INVITATION, PRINCE LEONHARD?
AFTER HE SO KINDLY SENT YOU A LETTER?
......
......
I NEVER SAID THAT.
HEH!
WHY DO YOU THINK I'VE BEEN STUDYING THE FONSEIN LANGUAGE EVERY SINGLE DAY?

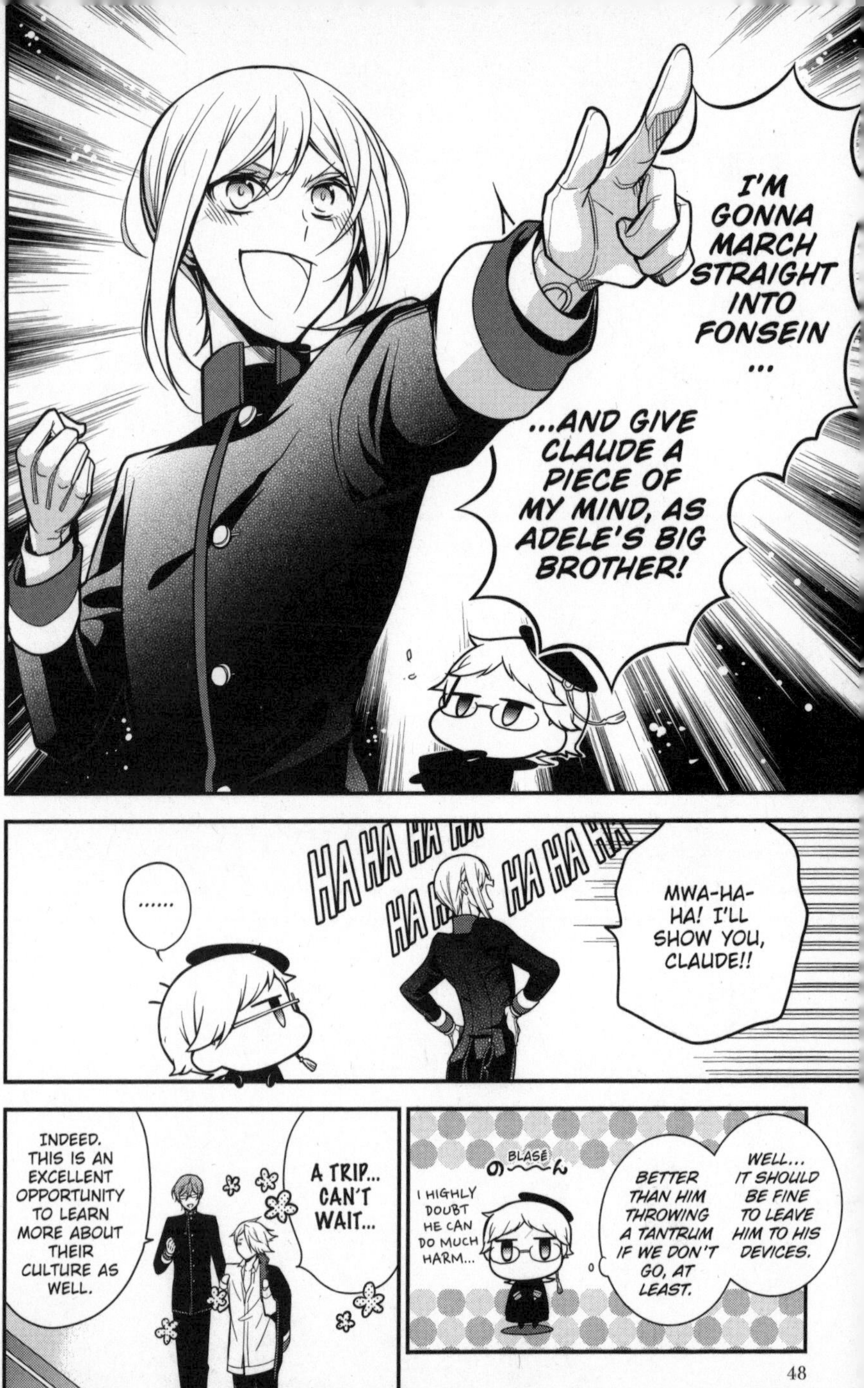
I'M GONNA MARCH STRAIGHT INTO FONSEIN ...
...AND GIVE CLAUDE A PIECE OF MY MIND, AS ADELE'S BIG BROTHER!
MWA-HA-HA! I'LL SHOW YOU, CLAUDE!!
HA HA HA
HA HA HA
......
WELL... IT SHOULD BE FINE TO LEAVE HIM TO HIS DEVICES.
BETTER THAN HIM THROWING A TANTRUM IF WE DON'T GO, AT LEAST.
BLASÉ
I HIGHLY DOUBT HE CAN DO MUCH HARM...
A TRIP... CAN'T WAIT...
INDEED. THIS IS AN EXCELLENT OPPORTUNITY TO LEARN MORE ABOUT THEIR CULTURE AS WELL.

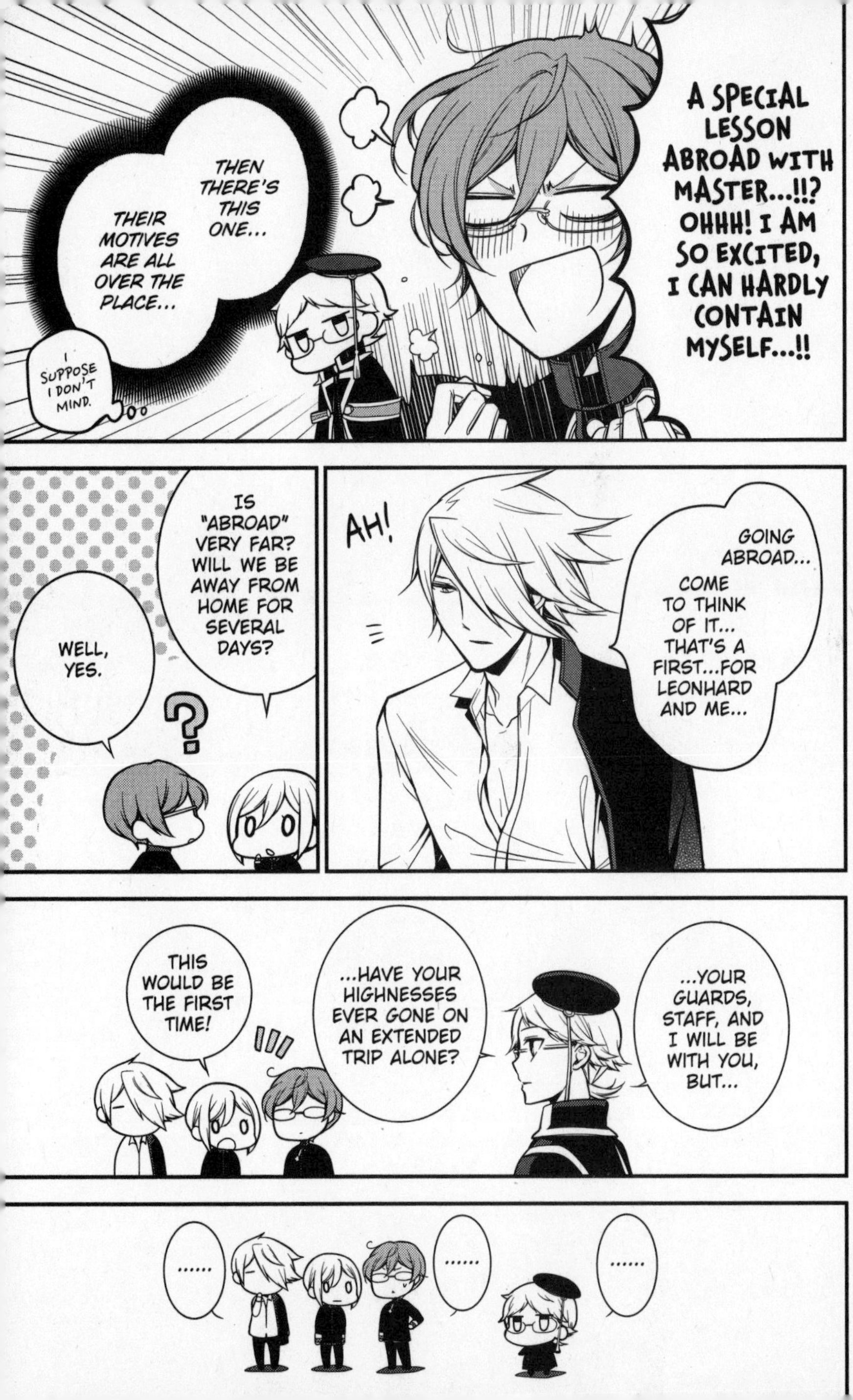
A SPECIAL LESSON ABROAD WITH MASTER...!!? OHHH! I AM SO EXCITED, I CAN HARDLY CONTAIN MYSELF...!!
THEN THERE'S THIS ONE...
THEIR MOTIVES ARE ALL OVER THE PLACE...
I SUPPOSE I DON'T MIND.
GOING ABROAD... COME TO THINK OF IT... THAT'S A FIRST...FOR LEONHARD AND ME...
AH!
IS "ABROAD" VERY FAR? WILL WE BE AWAY FROM HOME FOR SEVERAL DAYS?
WELL, YES.
?
...YOUR GUARDS, STAFF, AND I WILL BE WITH YOU, BUT...
...HAVE YOUR HIGHNESSES EVER GONE ON AN EXTENDED TRIP ALONE?
THIS WOULD BE THE FIRST TIME!
......
......
......

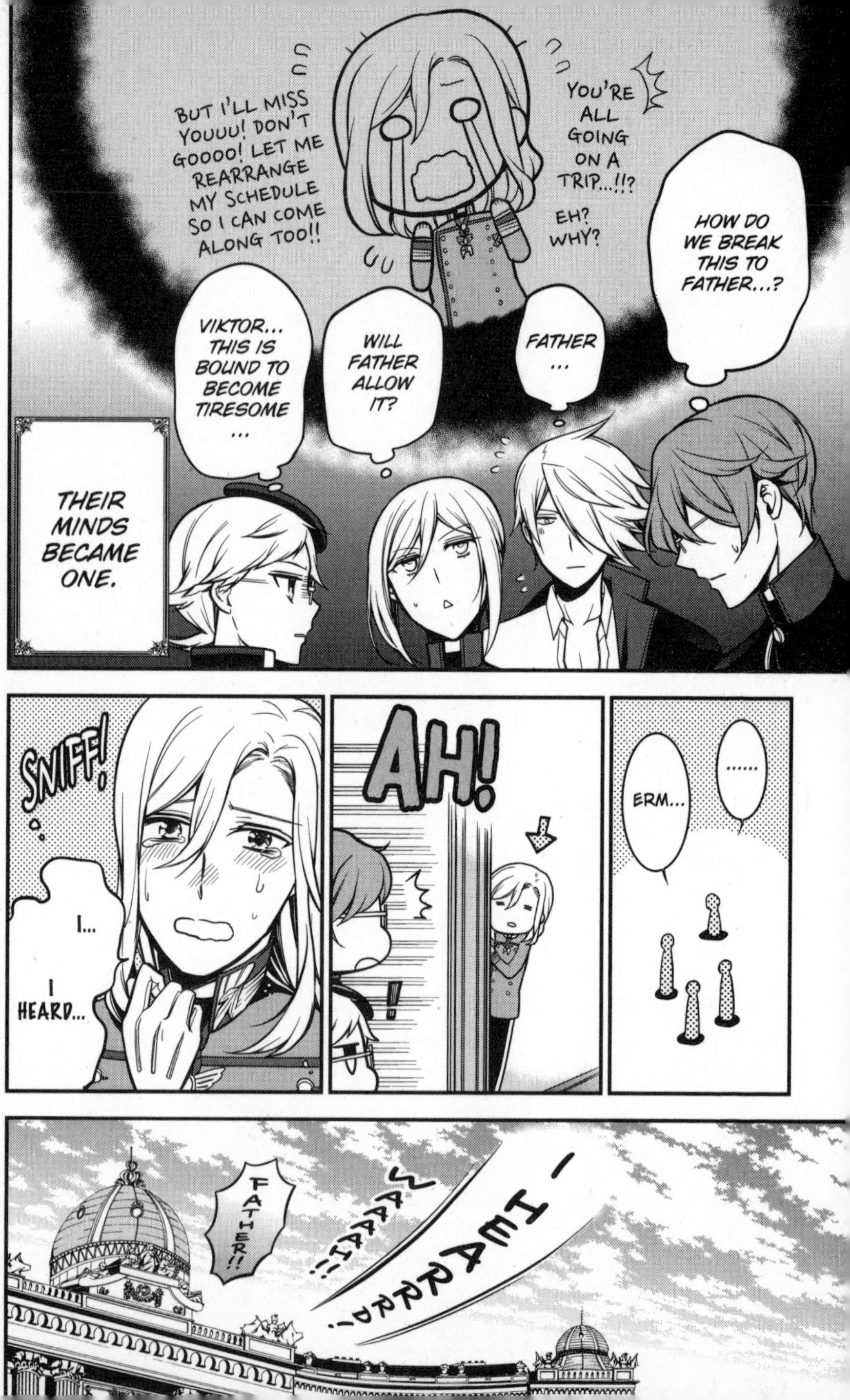
HOW DO WE BREAK THIS TO FATHER...?
FATHER ...
WILL FATHER ALLOW IT?
VIKTOR... THIS IS BOUND TO BECOME TIRESOME ...
YOU'RE ALL GOING ON A TRIP...!!?
EH? WHY?
BUT I'LL MISS YOUUU! DON'T GOOOO! LET ME REARRANGE MY SCHEDULE SO I CAN COME ALONG TOO!!
THEIR MINDS BECAME ONE.
......
ERM...
AH!
SNIFF!
I...
I HEARD...
I HEARRRD-!
WAAAAH!!
FATHER!!

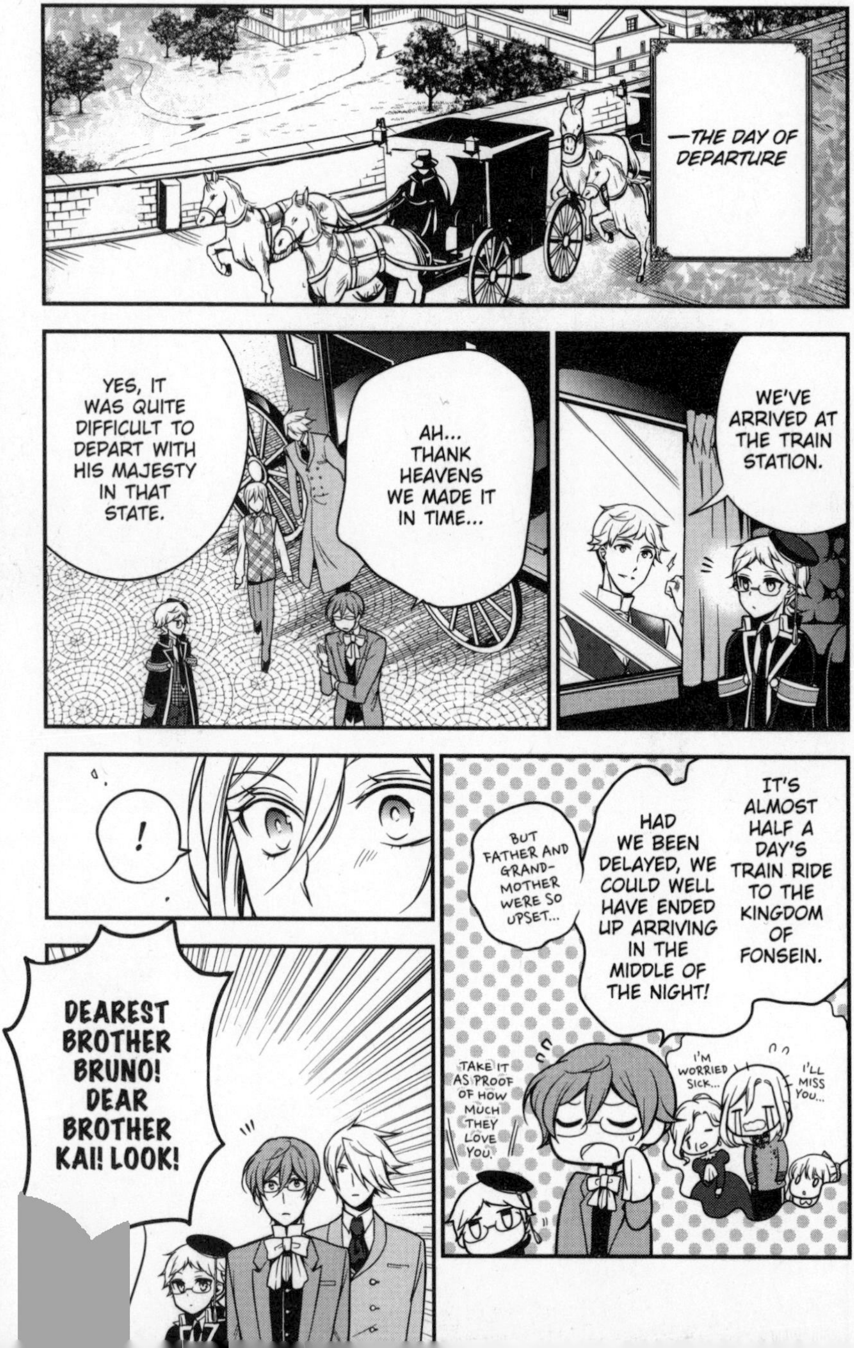
—THE DAY OF DEPARTURE
WE'VE ARRIVED AT THE TRAIN STATION.
AH... THANK HEAVENS WE MADE IT IN TIME...
YES, IT WAS QUITE DIFFICULT TO DEPART WITH HIS MAJESTY IN THAT STATE.
IT'S ALMOST HALF A DAY'S TRAIN RIDE TO THE KINGDOM OF FONSEIN.
HAD WE BEEN DELAYED, WE COULD WELL HAVE ENDED UP ARRIVING IN THE MIDDLE OF THE NIGHT!
BUT FATHER AND GRAND-MOTHER WERE SO UPSET...
I'LL MISS YOU...
I'M WORRIED SICK...
TAKE IT AS PROOF OF HOW MUCH THEY LOVE YOU.
!
DEAREST BROTHER BRUNO! DEAR BROTHER KAI! LOOK!

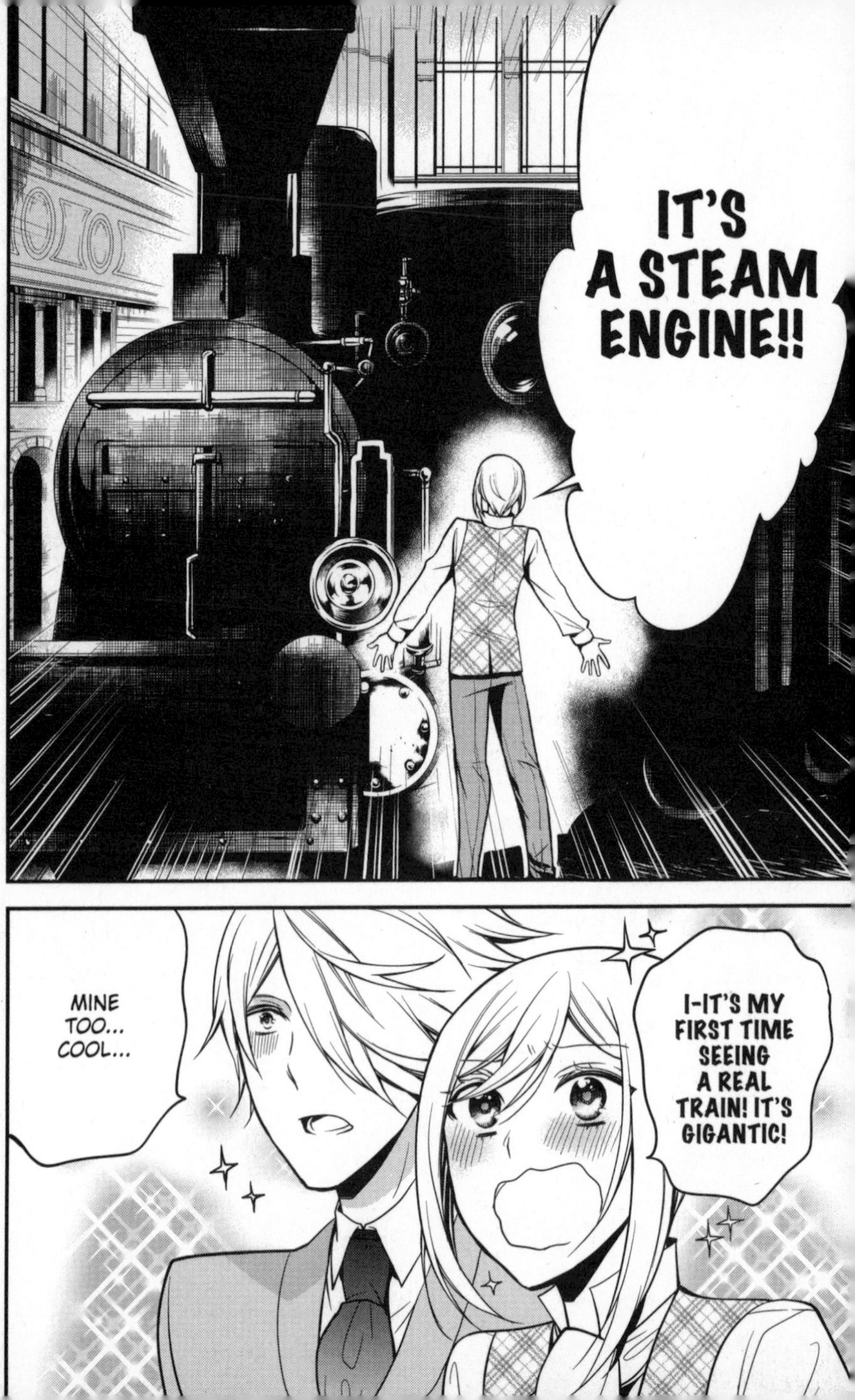
IT'S A STEAM ENGINE!!
I-IT'S MY FIRST TIME SEEING A REAL TRAIN! IT'S GIGANTIC!
MINE TOO... COOL...

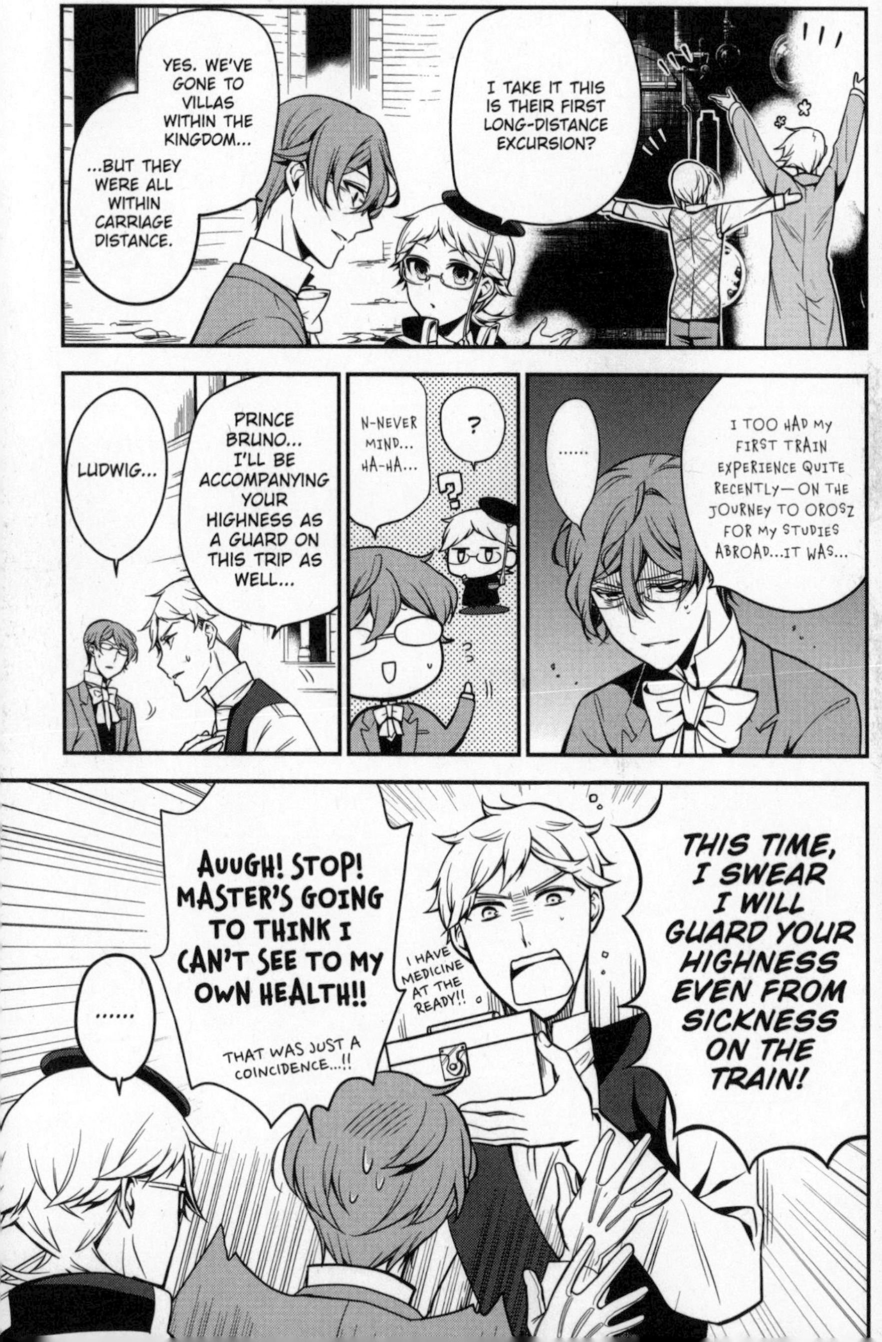
I TAKE IT THIS IS THEIR FIRST LONG-DISTANCE EXCURSION?
YES. WE'VE GONE TO VILLAS WITHIN THE KINGDOM...
...BUT THEY WERE ALL WITHIN CARRIAGE DISTANCE.
I TOO HAD MY FIRST TRAIN EXPERIENCE QUITE RECENTLY—ON THE JOURNEY TO OROSZ FOR MY STUDIES ABROAD...IT WAS...
......
?
N-NEVER MIND... HA-HA...
PRINCE BRUNO... I'LL BE ACCOMPANYING YOUR HIGHNESS AS A GUARD ON THIS TRIP AS WELL...
LUDWIG...
THIS TIME, I SWEAR I WILL GUARD YOUR HIGHNESS EVEN FROM SICKNESS ON THE TRAIN!
I HAVE MEDICINE AT THE READY!!
AUUGH! STOP! MASTER'S GOING TO THINK I CAN'T SEE TO MY OWN HEALTH!!
THAT WAS JUST A COINCIDENCE...!!
......

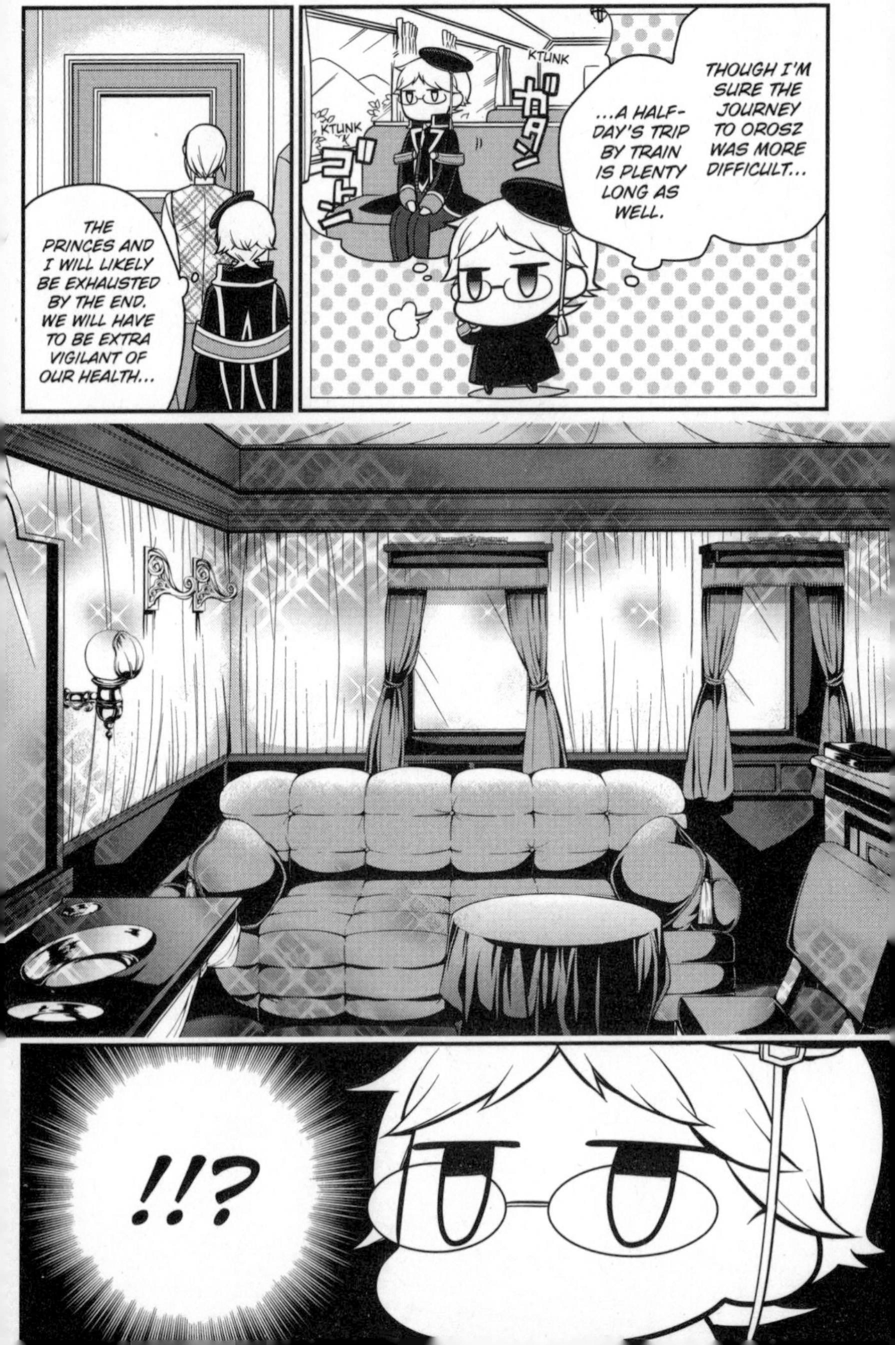
THOUGH I'M SURE THE JOURNEY TO OROSZ WAS MORE DIFFICULT...
...A HALF-DAY'S TRIP BY TRAIN IS PLENTY LONG AS WELL.
KTUNK
KTUNK
THE PRINCES AND I WILL LIKELY BE EXHAUSTED BY THE END. WE WILL HAVE TO BE EXTRA VIGILANT OF OUR HEALTH...
!!?

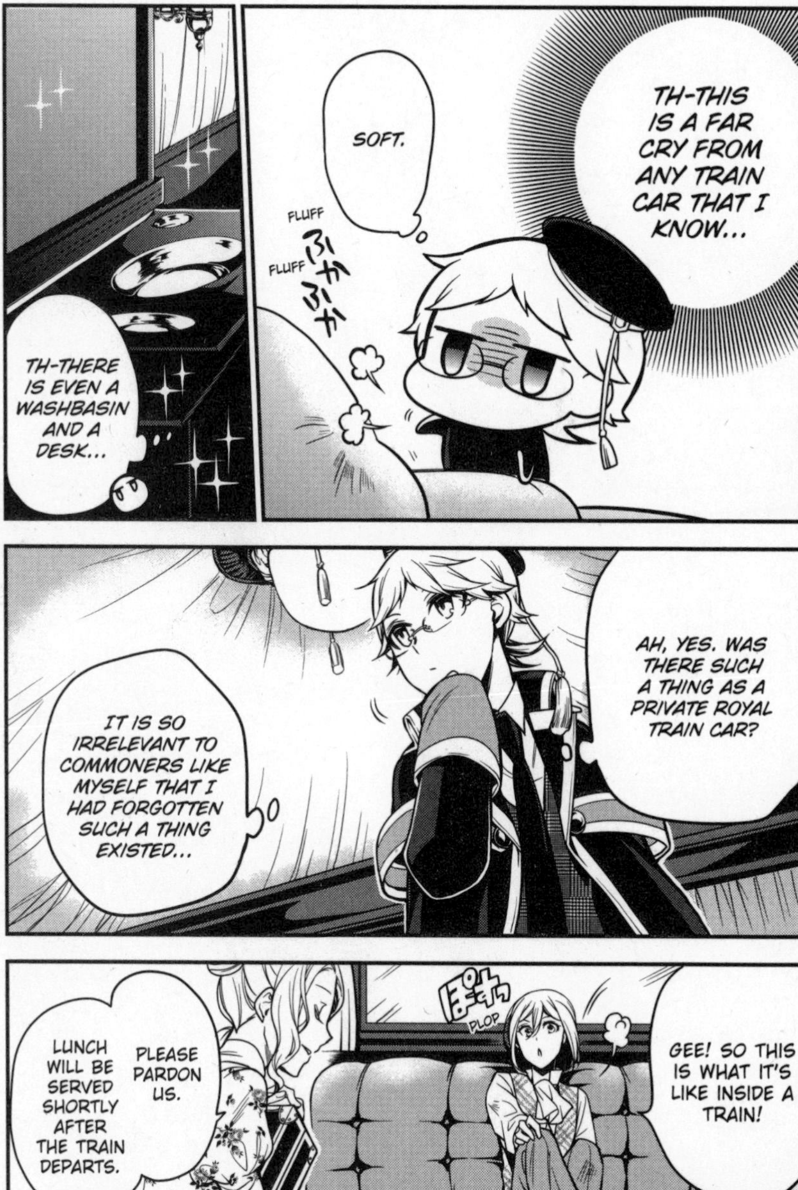
TH-THIS IS A FAR CRY FROM ANY TRAIN CAR THAT I KNOW...
SOFT.
ふかふか
FLUFF FLUFF
TH-THERE IS EVEN A WASHBASIN AND A DESK...
AH, YES. WAS THERE SUCH A THING AS A PRIVATE ROYAL TRAIN CAR?
IT IS SO IRRELEVANT TO COMMONERS LIKE MYSELF THAT I HAD FORGOTTEN SUCH A THING EXISTED...
GEE! SO THIS IS WHAT IT'S LIKE INSIDE A TRAIN!
ぽすっ
PLOP
PLEASE PARDON US.
LUNCH WILL BE SERVED SHORTLY AFTER THE TRAIN DEPARTS.

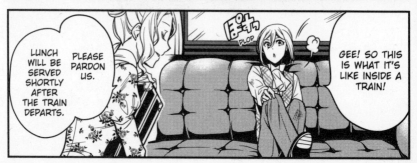

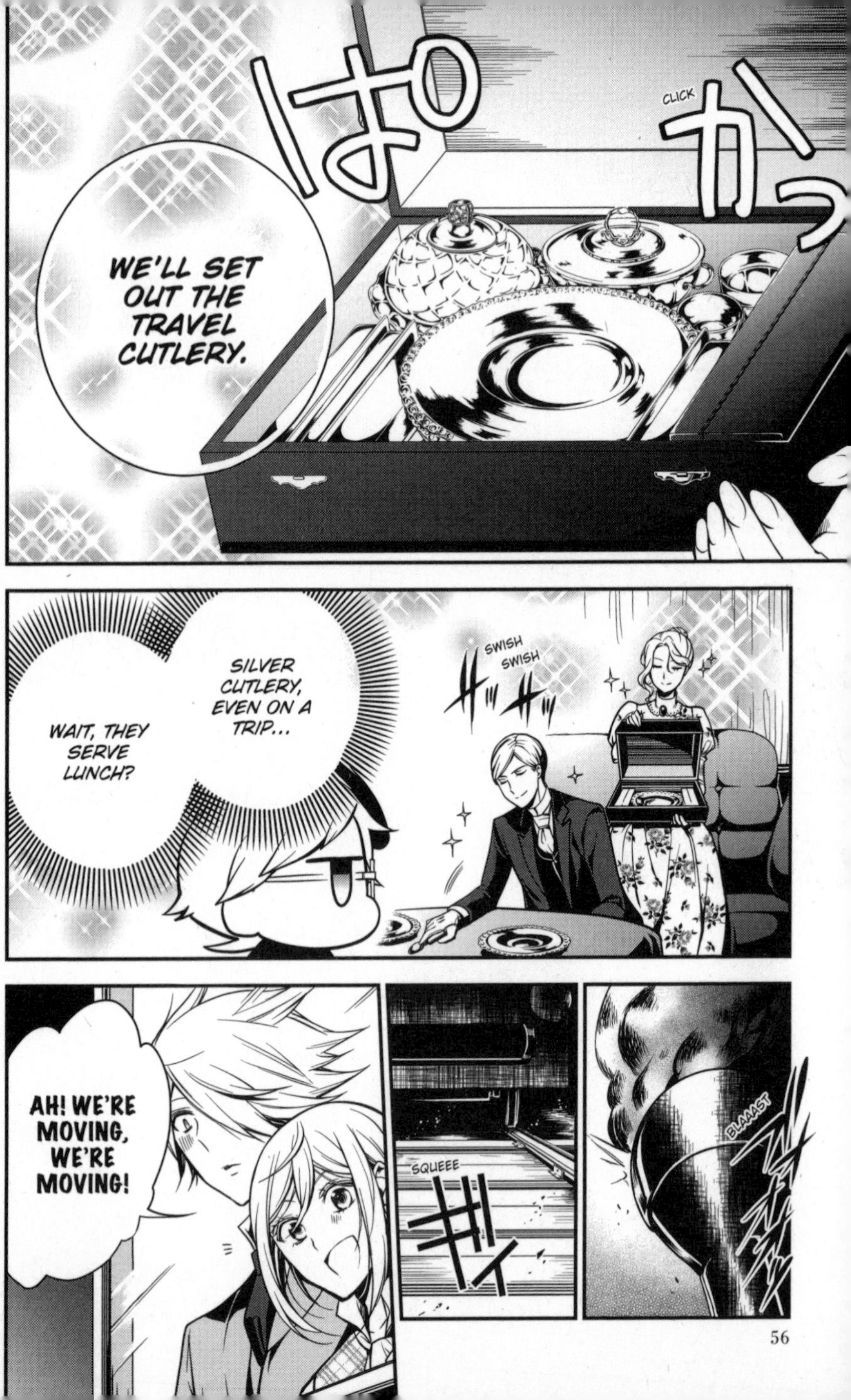
CLICK
WE'LL SET OUT THE TRAVEL CUTLERY.
SWISH SWISH
SILVER CUTLERY, EVEN ON A TRIP...
WAIT, THEY SERVE LUNCH?
BLAAAST
SQUEEE
AH! WE'RE MOVING, WE'RE MOVING!

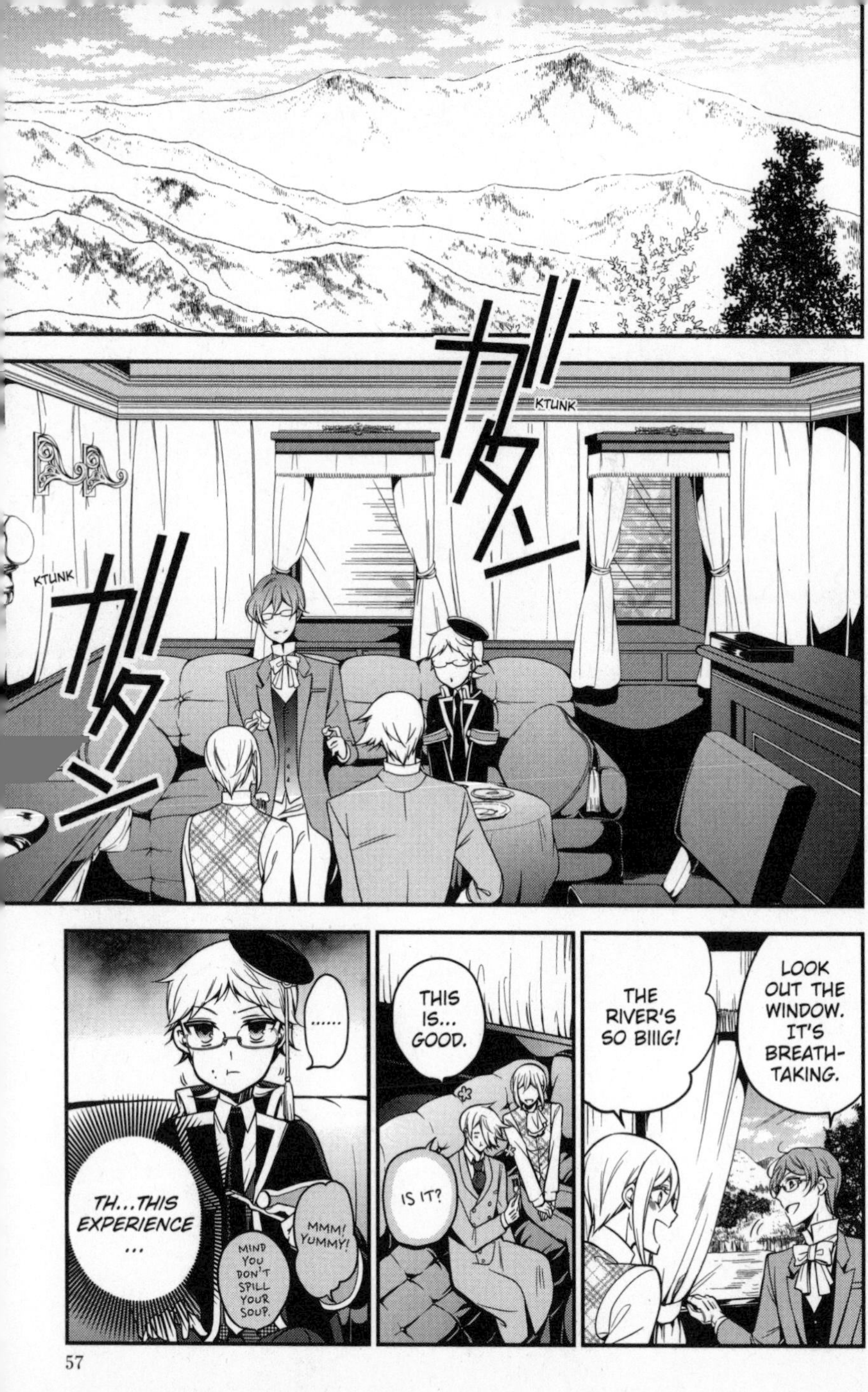
KTUNK
KTUNK
LOOK OUT THE WINDOW. IT'S BREATH-TAKING.
THE RIVER'S SO BIIIG!
THIS IS... GOOD.
IS IT?
......
MMM! YUMMY!
MIND YOU DON'T SPILL YOUR SOUP.
TH...THIS EXPERIENCE ...

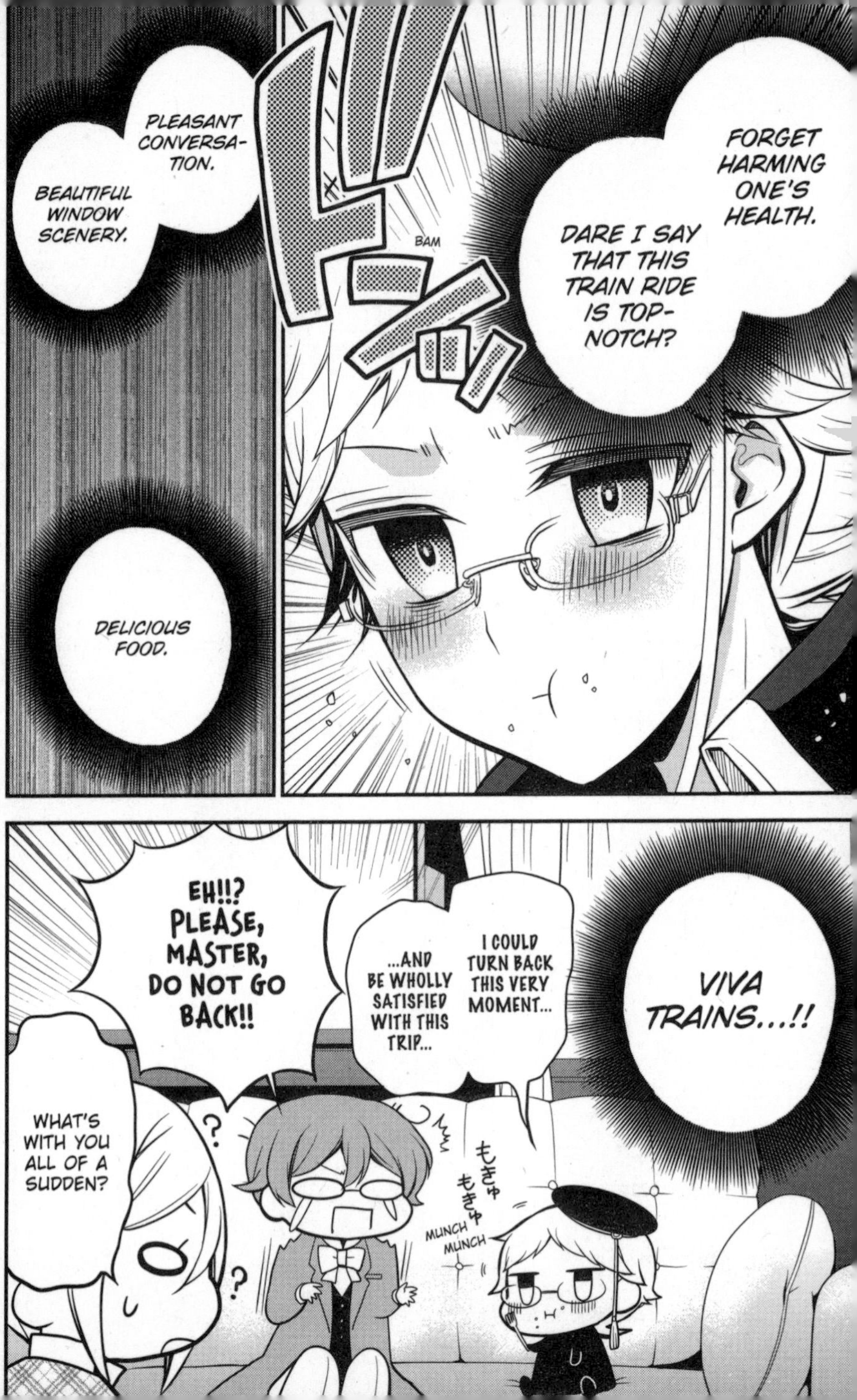
FORGET HARMING ONE'S HEALTH.
DARE I SAY THAT THIS TRAIN RIDE IS TOP-NOTCH?
BAM
PLEASANT CONVERSA-TION.
BEAUTIFUL WINDOW SCENERY.
DELICIOUS FOOD.
VIVA TRAINS...!!
I COULD TURN BACK THIS VERY MOMENT...
...AND BE WHOLLY SATISFIED WITH THIS TRIP...
EH!!? PLEASE, MASTER, DO NOT GO BACK!!
もきゅもきゅ
MUNCH MUNCH
WHAT'S WITH YOU ALL OF A SUDDEN?

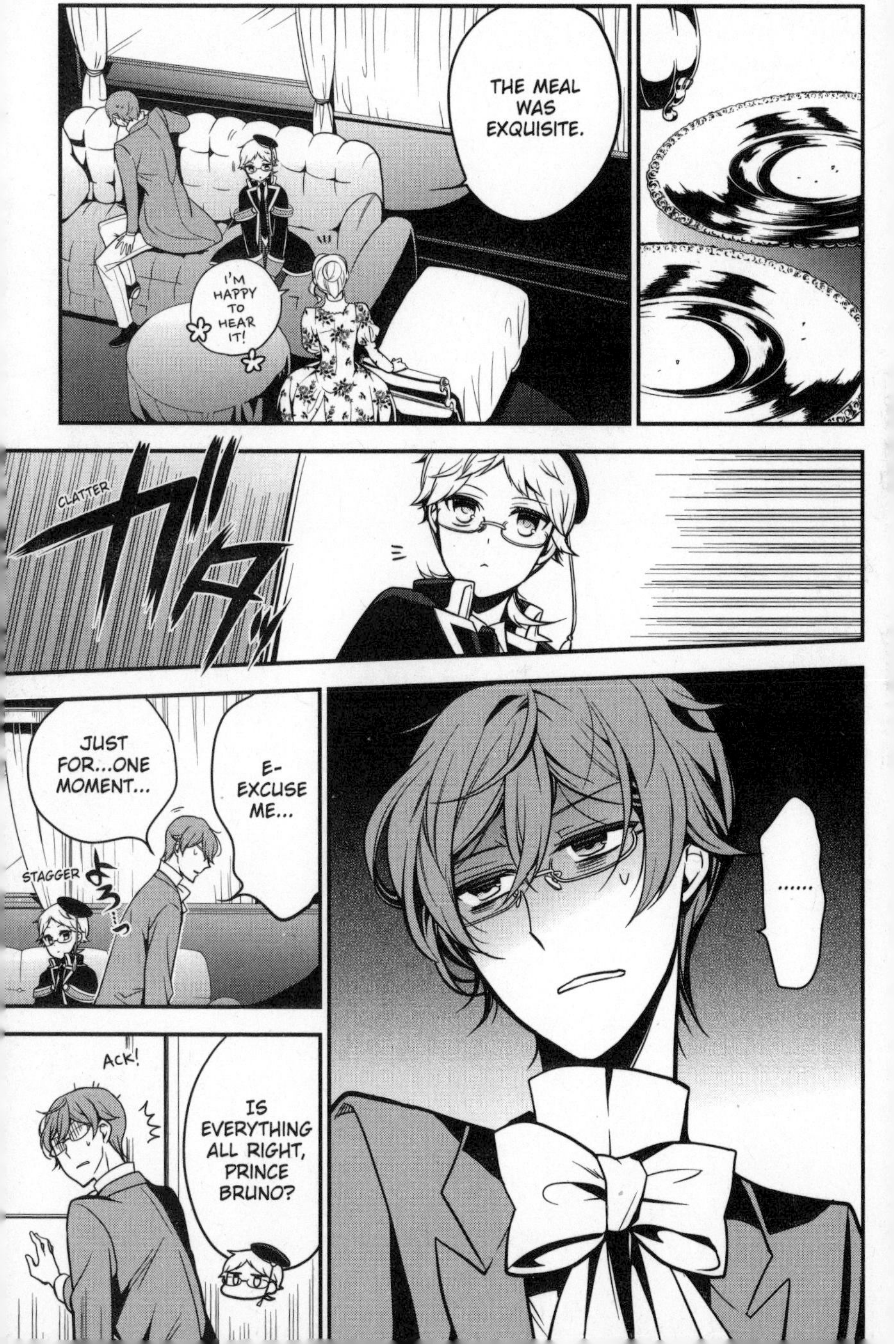
THE MEAL WAS EXQUISITE.
I'M HAPPY TO HEAR IT!
CLATTER
......
E-EXCUSE ME...
JUST FOR...ONE MOMENT...
STAGGER
IS EVERYTHING ALL RIGHT, PRINCE BRUNO?
ACK!

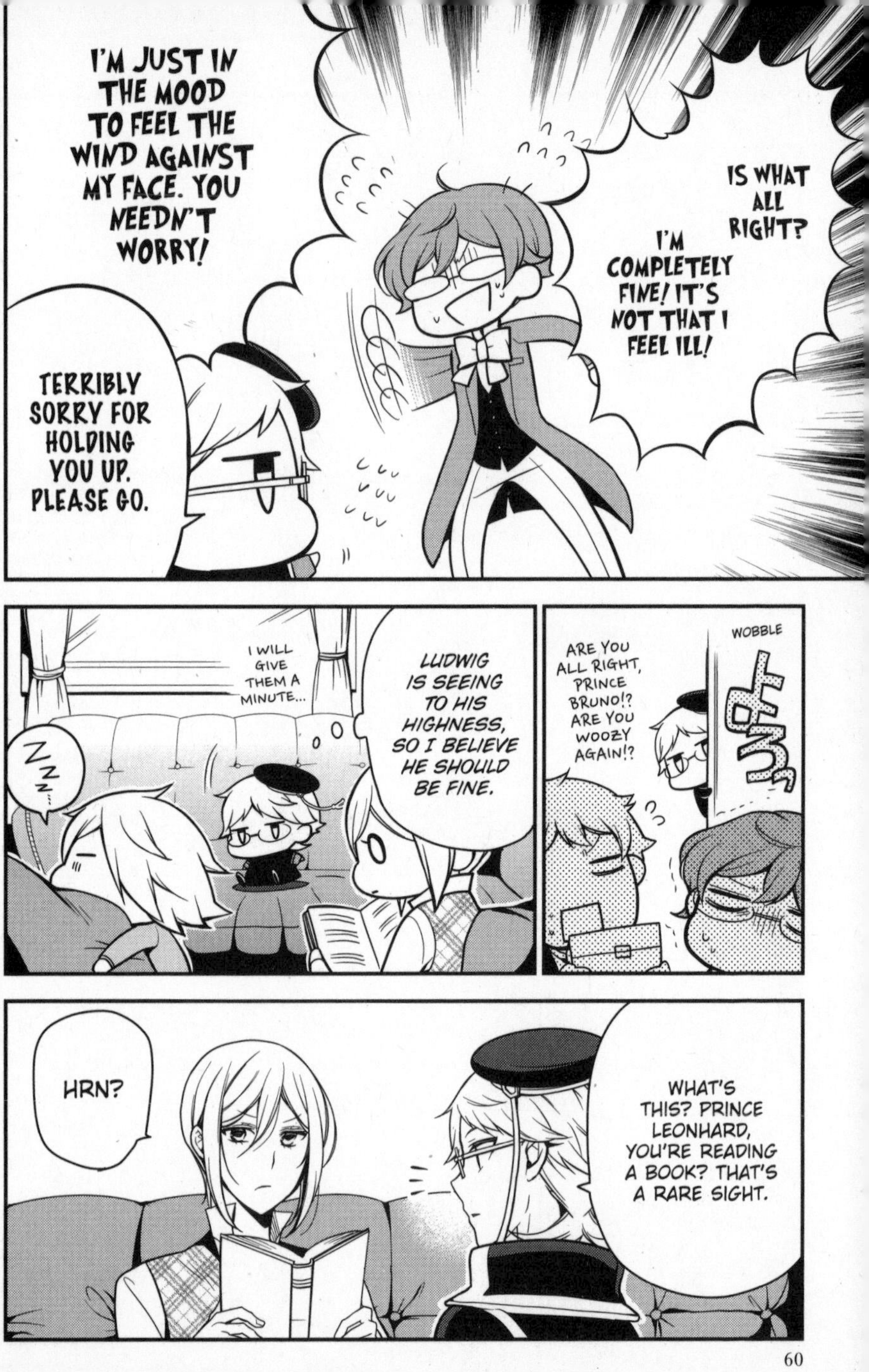

IS WHAT ALL RIGHT?
I'M COMPLETELY FINE! IT'S NOT THAT I FEEL ILL!
I'M JUST IN THE MOOD TO FEEL THE WIND AGAINST MY FACE. YOU NEEDN'T WORRY!
TERRIBLY SORRY FOR HOLDING YOU UP. PLEASE GO.
WOBBLE
よろっ
ARE YOU ALL RIGHT, PRINCE BRUNO!? ARE YOU WOOZY AGAIN!?
LUDWIG IS SEEING TO HIS HIGHNESS, SO I BELIEVE HE SHOULD BE FINE.
I WILL GIVE THEM A MINUTE...
ZZZ...
WHAT'S THIS? PRINCE LEONHARD, YOU'RE READING A BOOK? THAT'S A RARE SIGHT.
HRN?

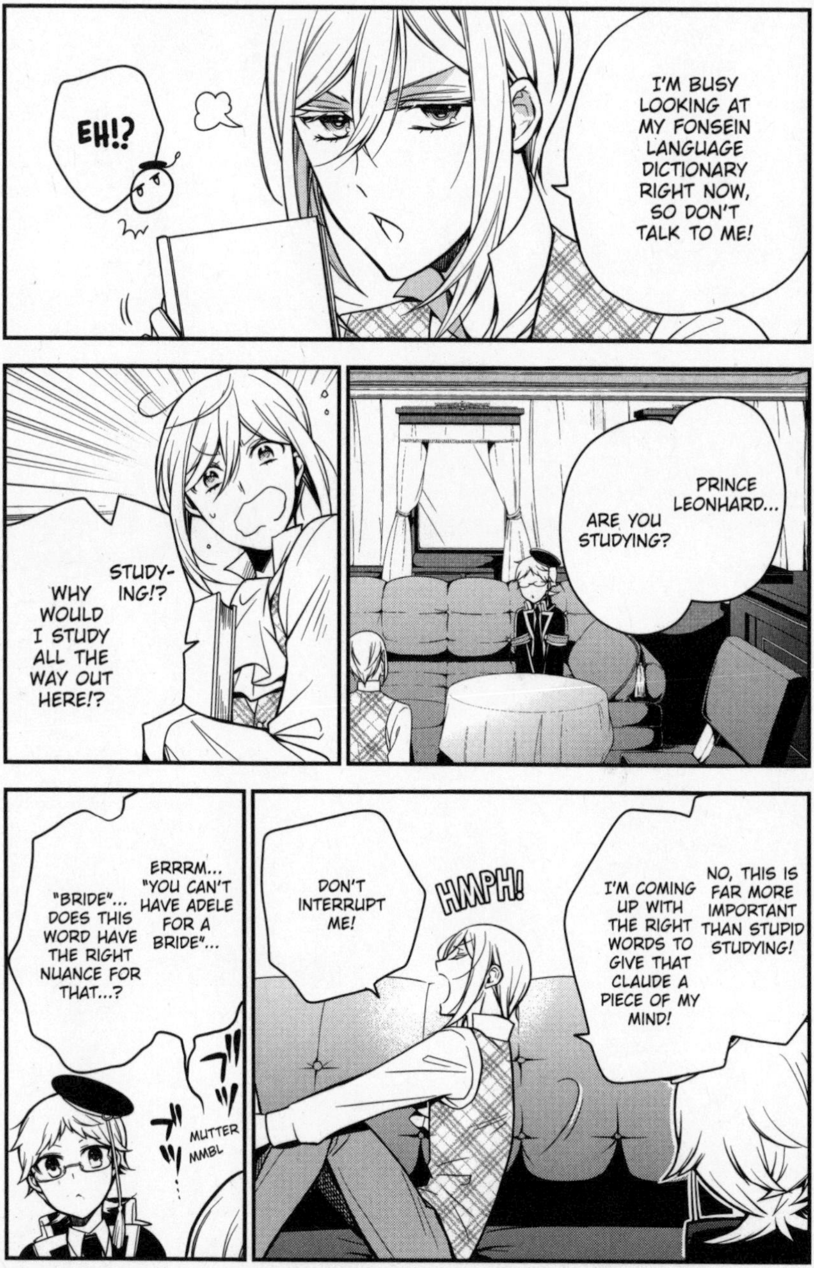
I'M BUSY LOOKING AT MY FONSEIN LANGUAGE DICTIONARY RIGHT NOW, SO DON'T TALK TO ME!
EH!?
PRINCE LEONHARD...
ARE YOU STUDYING?
STUDYING!?
WHY WOULD I STUDY ALL THE WAY OUT HERE!?
NO, THIS IS FAR MORE IMPORTANT THAN STUPID STUDYING!
I'M COMING UP WITH THE RIGHT WORDS TO GIVE THAT CLAUDE A PIECE OF MY MIND!
HMPH!
DON'T INTERRUPT ME!
ERRRM... "YOU CAN'T HAVE ADELE FOR A BRIDE"...
"BRIDE"... DOES THIS WORD HAVE THE RIGHT NUANCE FOR THAT...?
MUTTER MMBL

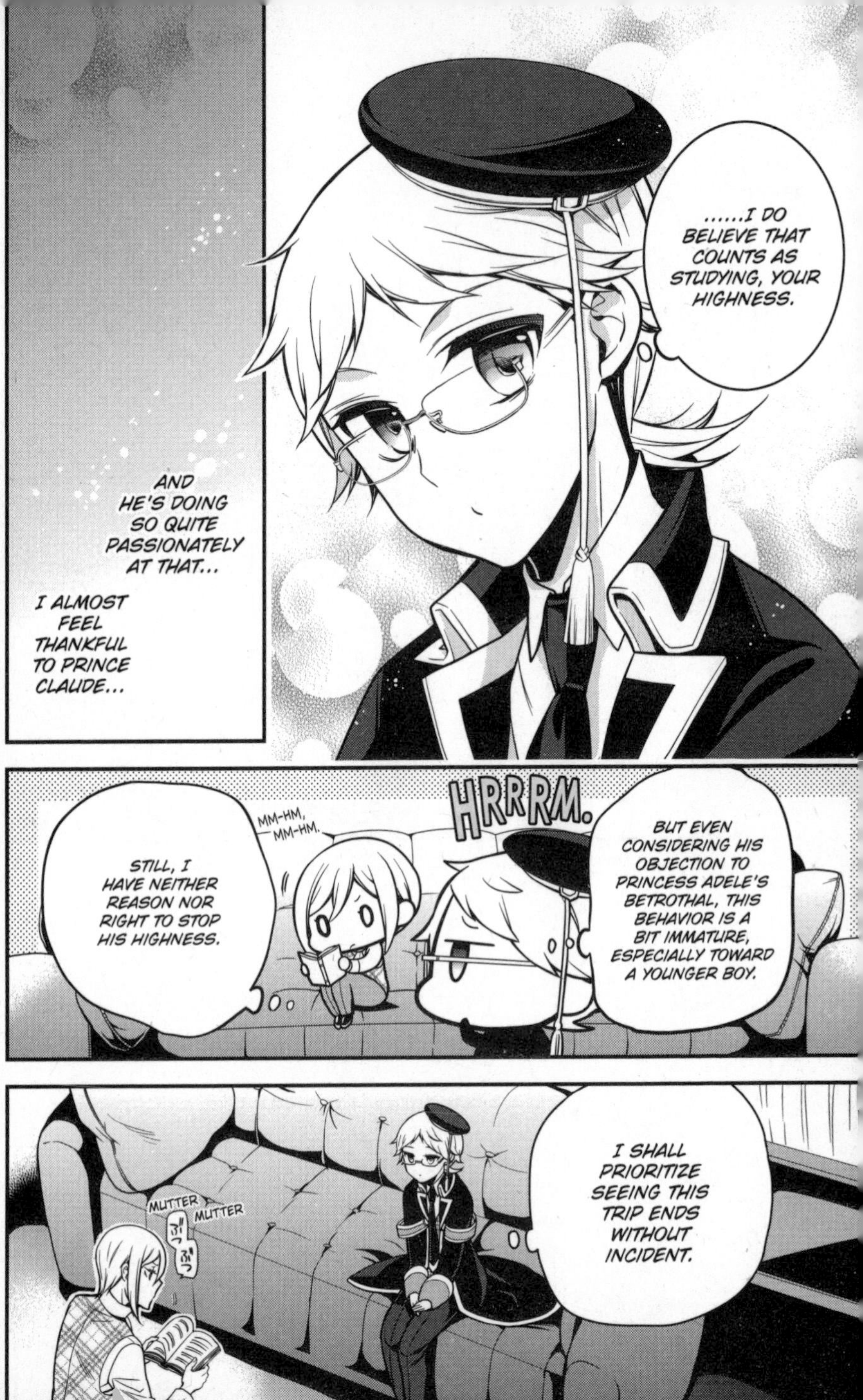
......I DO BELIEVE THAT COUNTS AS STUDYING, YOUR HIGHNESS.
AND HE'S DOING SO QUITE PASSIONATELY AT THAT...
I ALMOST FEEL THANKFUL TO PRINCE CLAUDE...
HRRRM.
BUT EVEN CONSIDERING HIS OBJECTION TO PRINCESS ADELE'S BETROTHAL, THIS BEHAVIOR IS A BIT IMMATURE, ESPECIALLY TOWARD A YOUNGER BOY.
MM-HM, MM-HM.
STILL, I HAVE NEITHER REASON NOR RIGHT TO STOP HIS HIGHNESS.
I SHALL PRIORITIZE SEEING THIS TRIP ENDS WITHOUT INCIDENT.
MUTTER MUTTER
ぶつぶつ

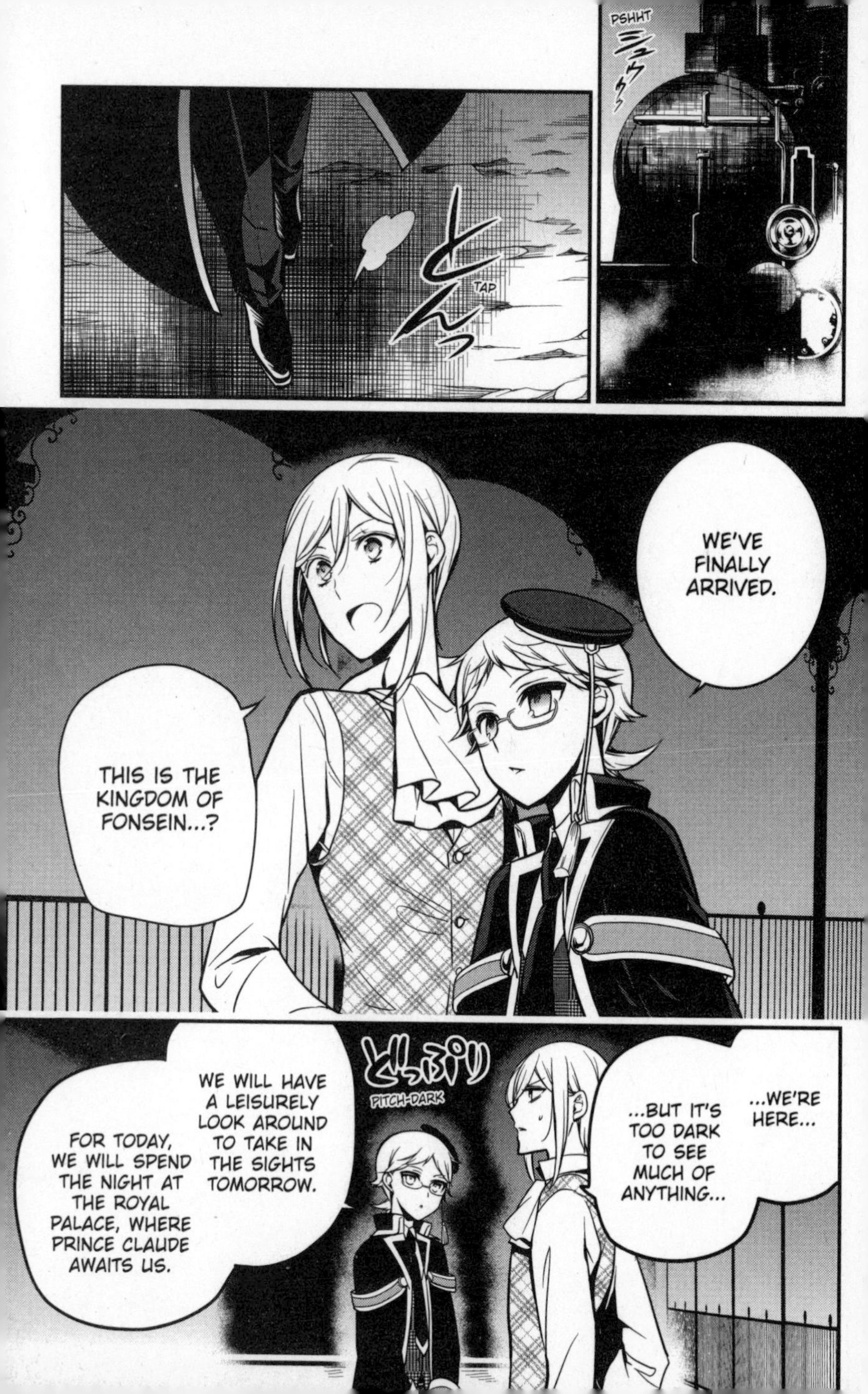
PSHHT
TAP
WE'VE FINALLY ARRIVED.
THIS IS THE KINGDOM OF FONSEIN...?
...WE'RE HERE...
...BUT IT'S TOO DARK TO SEE MUCH OF ANYTHING...
PITCH-DARK
FOR TODAY, WE WILL SPEND THE NIGHT AT THE ROYAL PALACE, WHERE PRINCE CLAUDE AWAITS US.
WE WILL HAVE A LEISURELY LOOK AROUND TO TAKE IN THE SIGHTS TOMORROW.

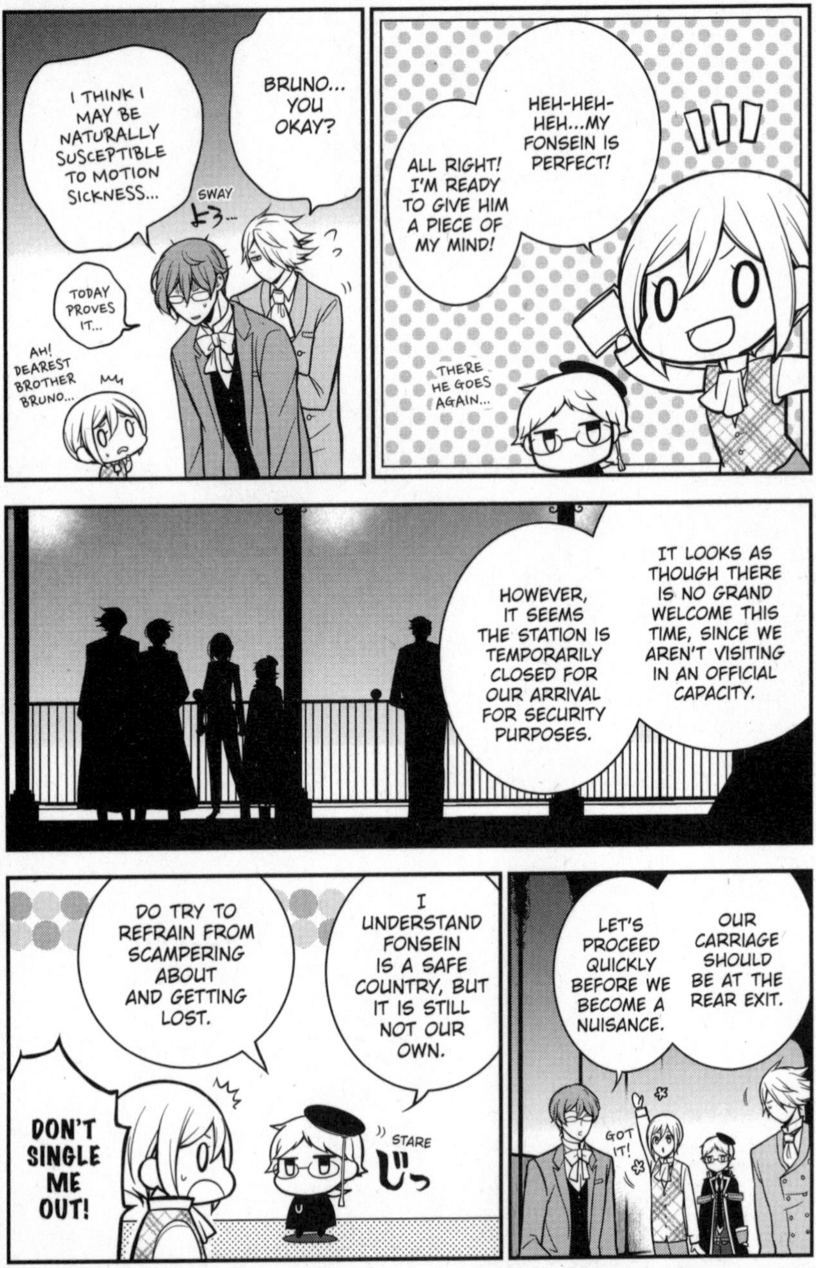
HEH-HEH-HEH...MY FONSEIN IS PERFECT!
ALL RIGHT! I'M READY TO GIVE HIM A PIECE OF MY MIND!
THERE HE GOES AGAIN...
BRUNO... YOU OKAY?
I THINK I MAY BE NATURALLY SUSCEPTIBLE TO MOTION SICKNESS...
SWAY
よろ...
TODAY PROVES IT...
AH! DEAREST BROTHER BRUNO...
IT LOOKS AS THOUGH THERE IS NO GRAND WELCOME THIS TIME, SINCE WE AREN'T VISITING IN AN OFFICIAL CAPACITY.
HOWEVER, IT SEEMS THE STATION IS TEMPORARILY CLOSED FOR OUR ARRIVAL FOR SECURITY PURPOSES.
OUR CARRIAGE SHOULD BE AT THE REAR EXIT.
LET'S PROCEED QUICKLY BEFORE WE BECOME A NUISANCE.
GOT IT!
I UNDERSTAND FONSEIN IS A SAFE COUNTRY, BUT IT IS STILL NOT OUR OWN.
DO TRY TO REFRAIN FROM SCAMPERING ABOUT AND GETTING LOST.
STARE
じっ
DON'T SINGLE ME OUT!

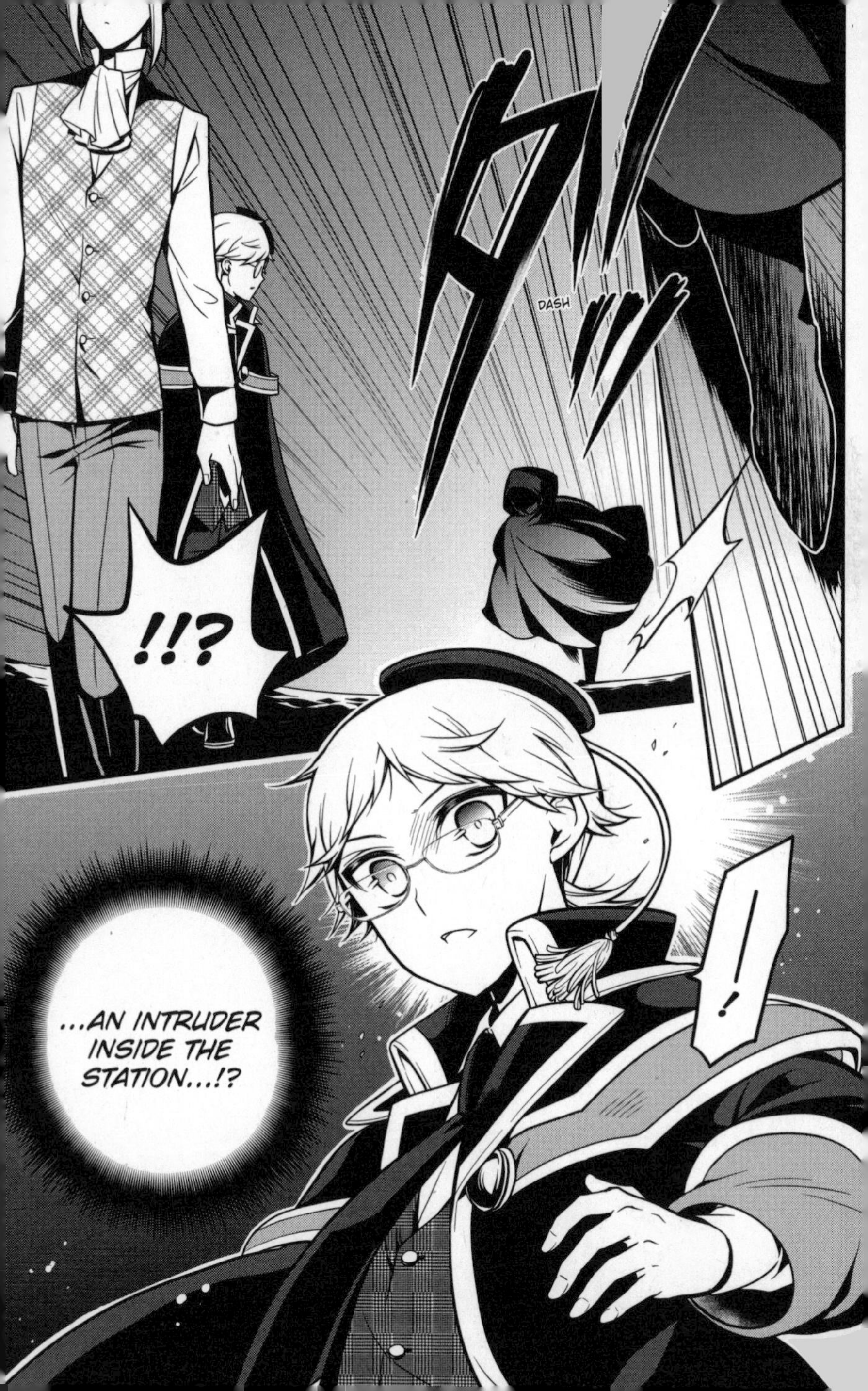
DASH
!!?
!
...AN INTRUDER INSIDE THE STATION...!?

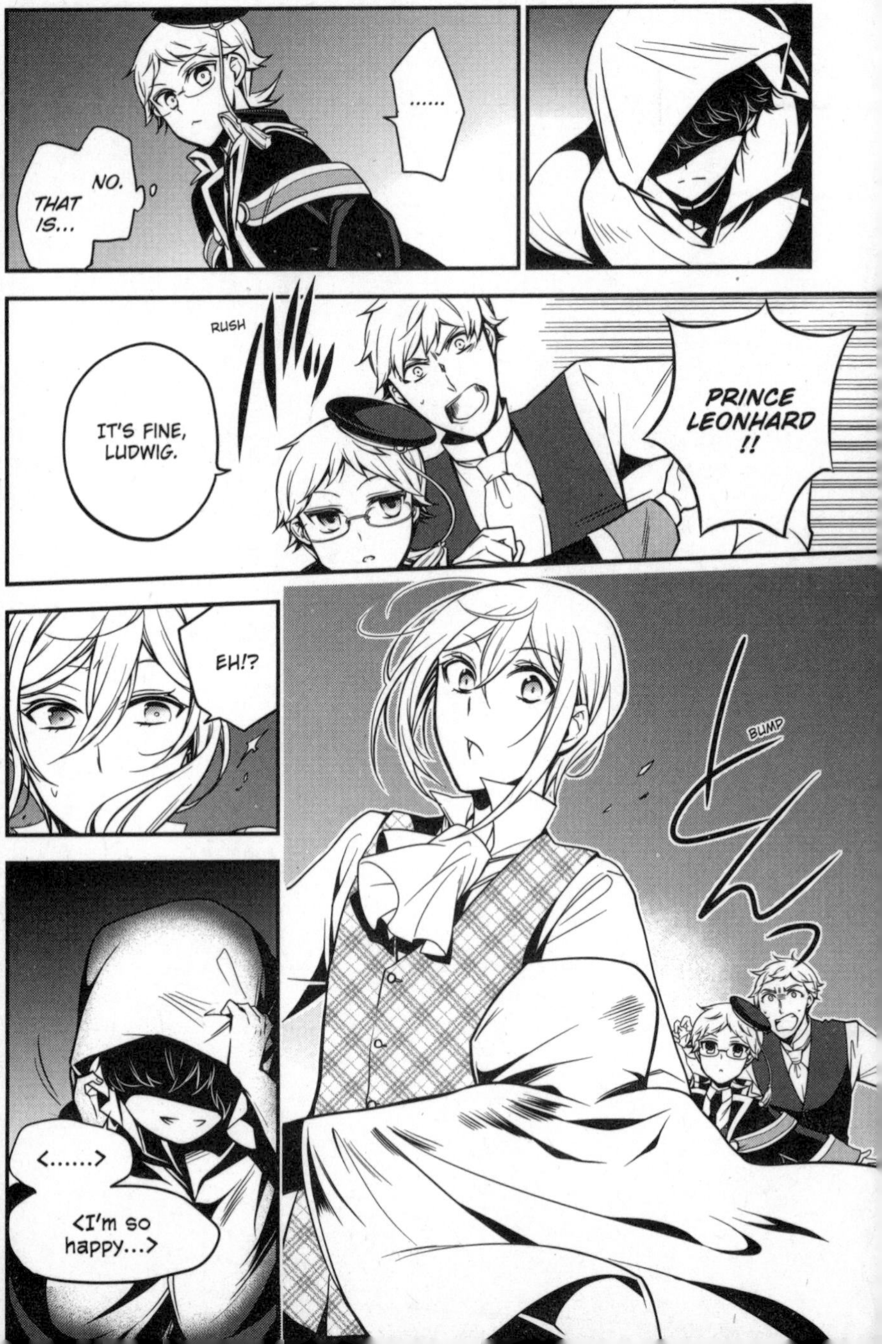
......
NO. THAT IS...
PRINCE LEONHARD !!
RUSH
IT'S FINE, LUDWIG.
BUMP
EH!?
<......>
<I'm so happy...>

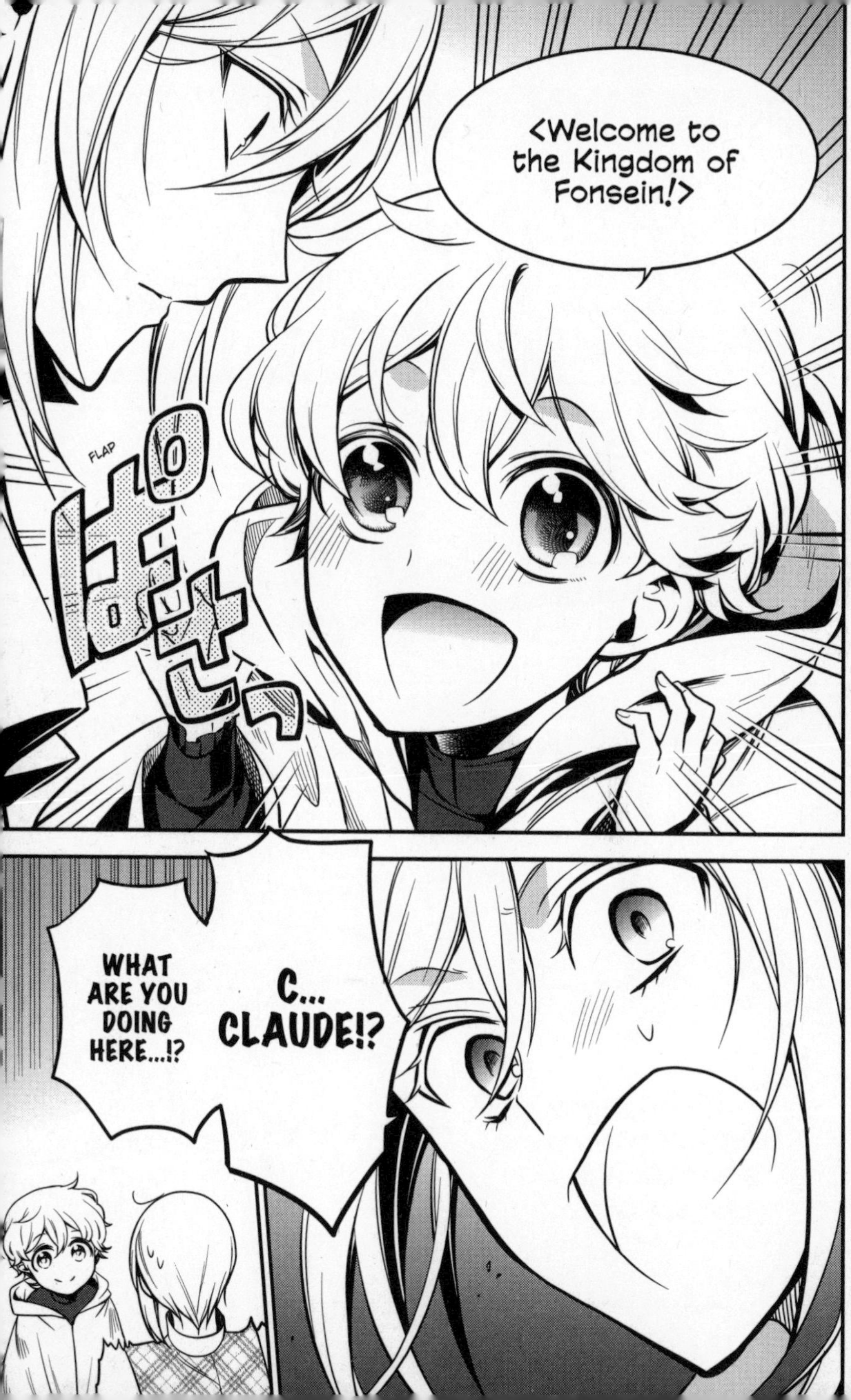
<Welcome to the Kingdom of Fonsein!>
FLAP
C... CLAUDE!?
WHAT ARE YOU DOING HERE...!?

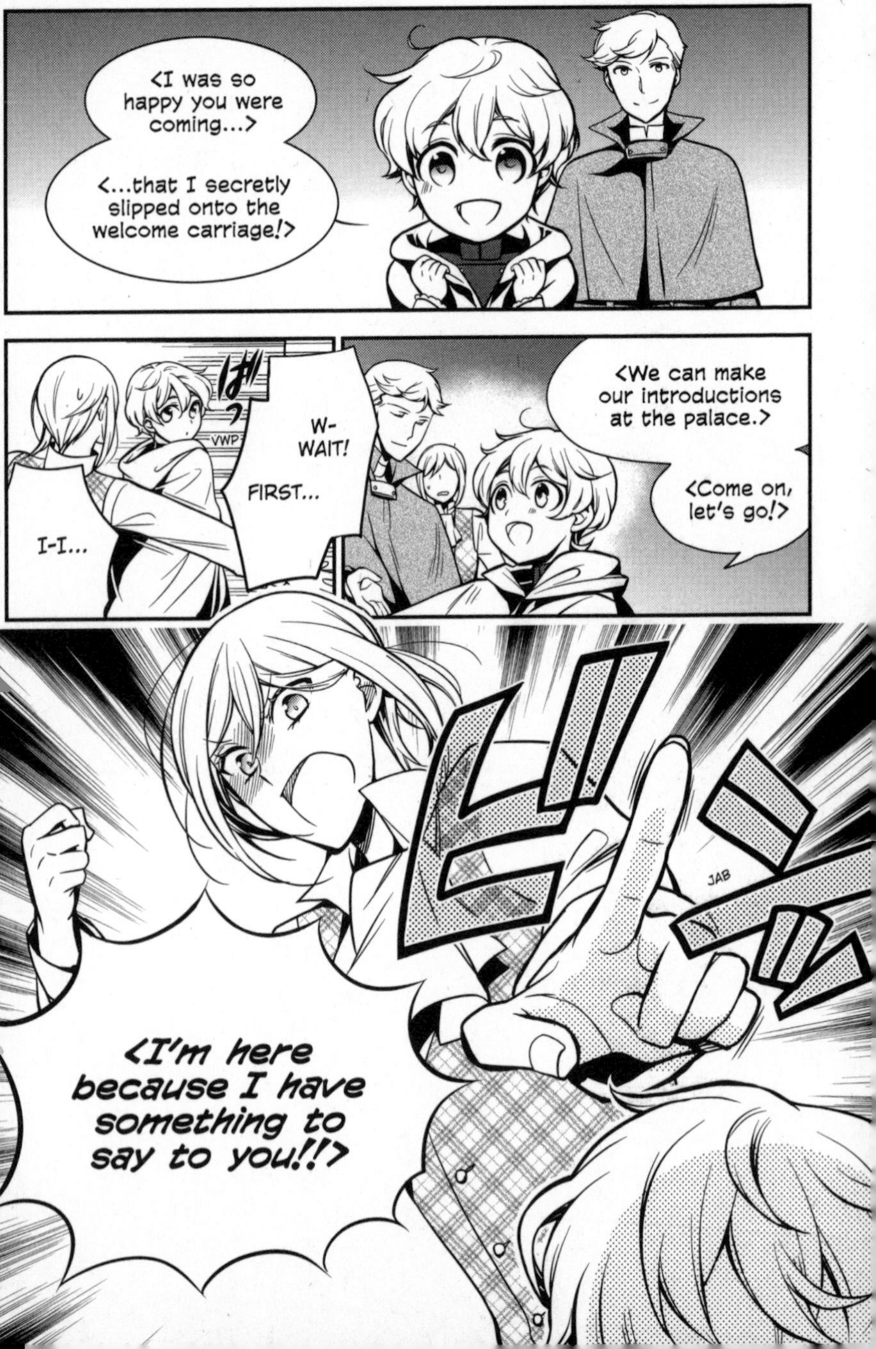
<I was so happy you were coming...>
<...that I secretly slipped onto the welcome carriage!>
<We can make our introductions at the palace.>
<Come on, let's go!>
W- WAIT!
FIRST...
ぱっ
VWP
I-I...
JAB
<I'm here because I have something to say to you!!>

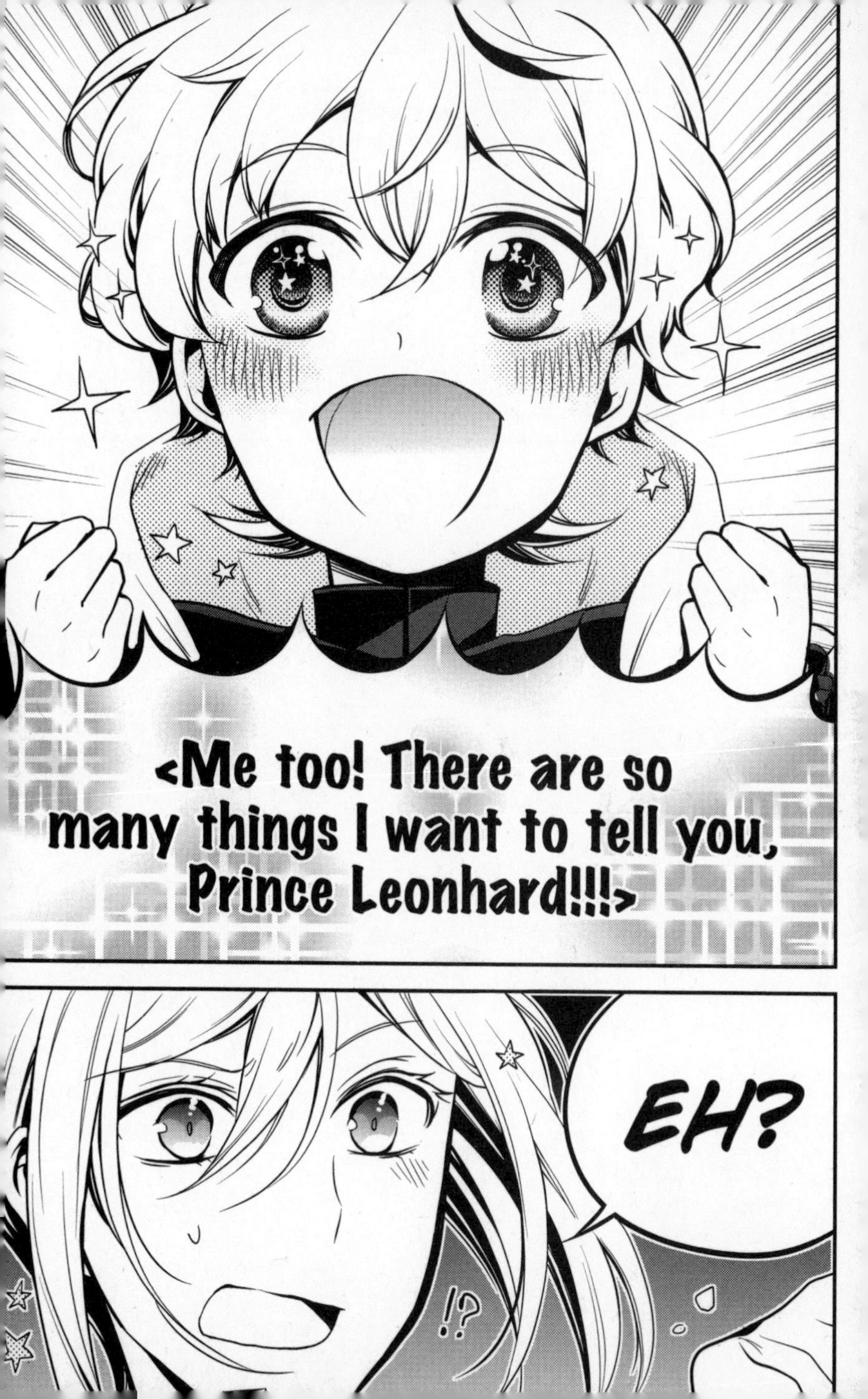

<Me too! There are so many things I want to tell you, Prince Leonhard!!!>
EH?
!?

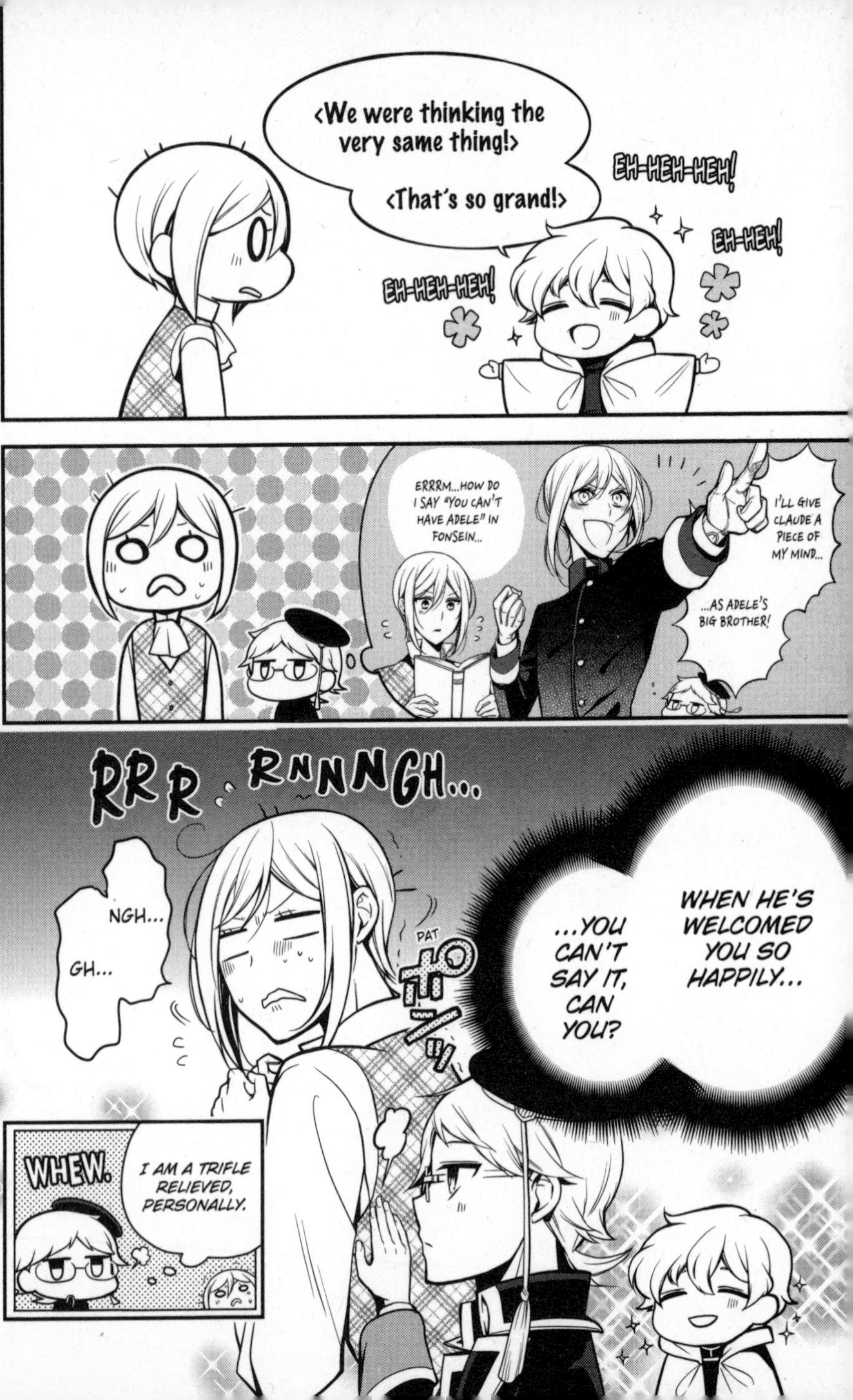
‹We were thinking the very same thing!›
‹That's so grand!›
EH-HEH-HEH!
EH-HEH!
EH-HEH-HEH!
I'LL GIVE CLAUDE A PIECE OF MY MIND...
...AS ADELE'S BIG BROTHER!
ERRRM...HOW DO I SAY "YOU CAN'T HAVE ADELE" IN FONSEIN...
RRR... RNNNGH...
WHEN HE'S WELCOMED YOU SO HAPPILY...
...YOU CAN'T SAY IT, CAN YOU?
PAT
NGH...
GH...
WHEW.
I AM A TRIFLE RELIEVED, PERSONALLY.

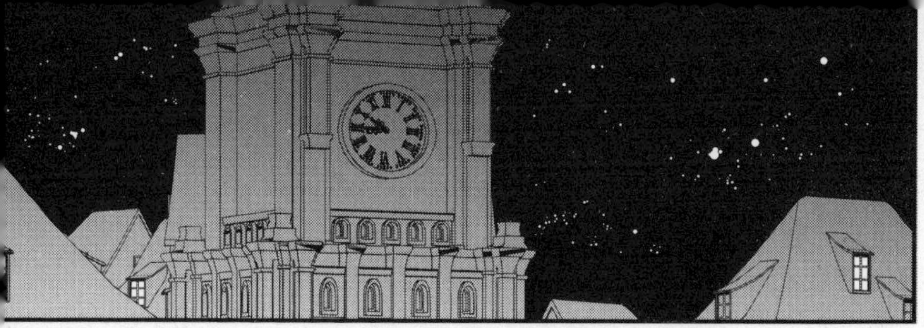

Chapter 69
Princes of Two Kingdoms

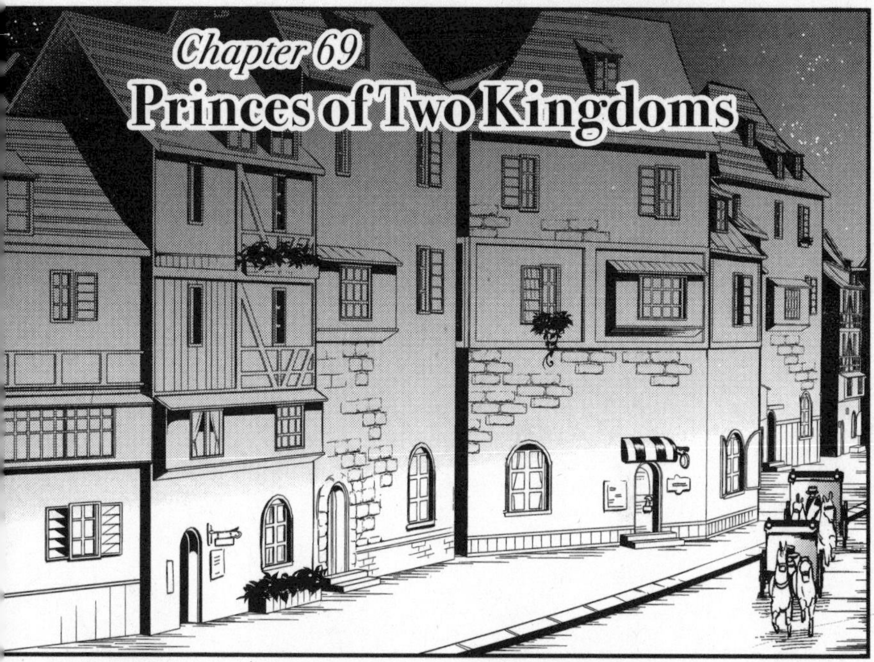

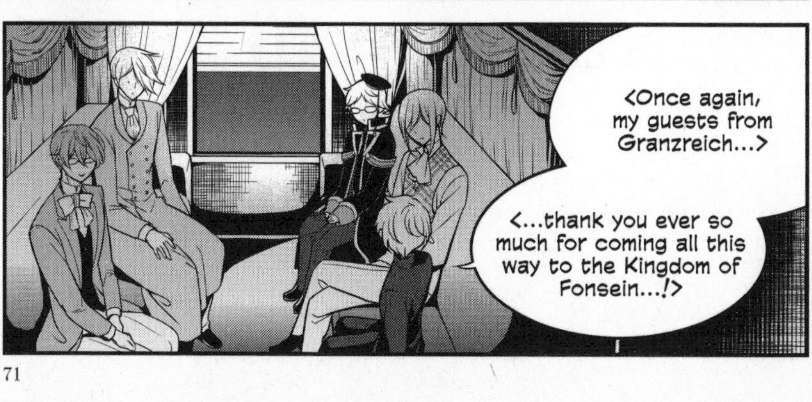
<Once again, my guests from Granzreich...>
<...thank you ever so much for coming all this way to the Kingdom of Fonsein...!>

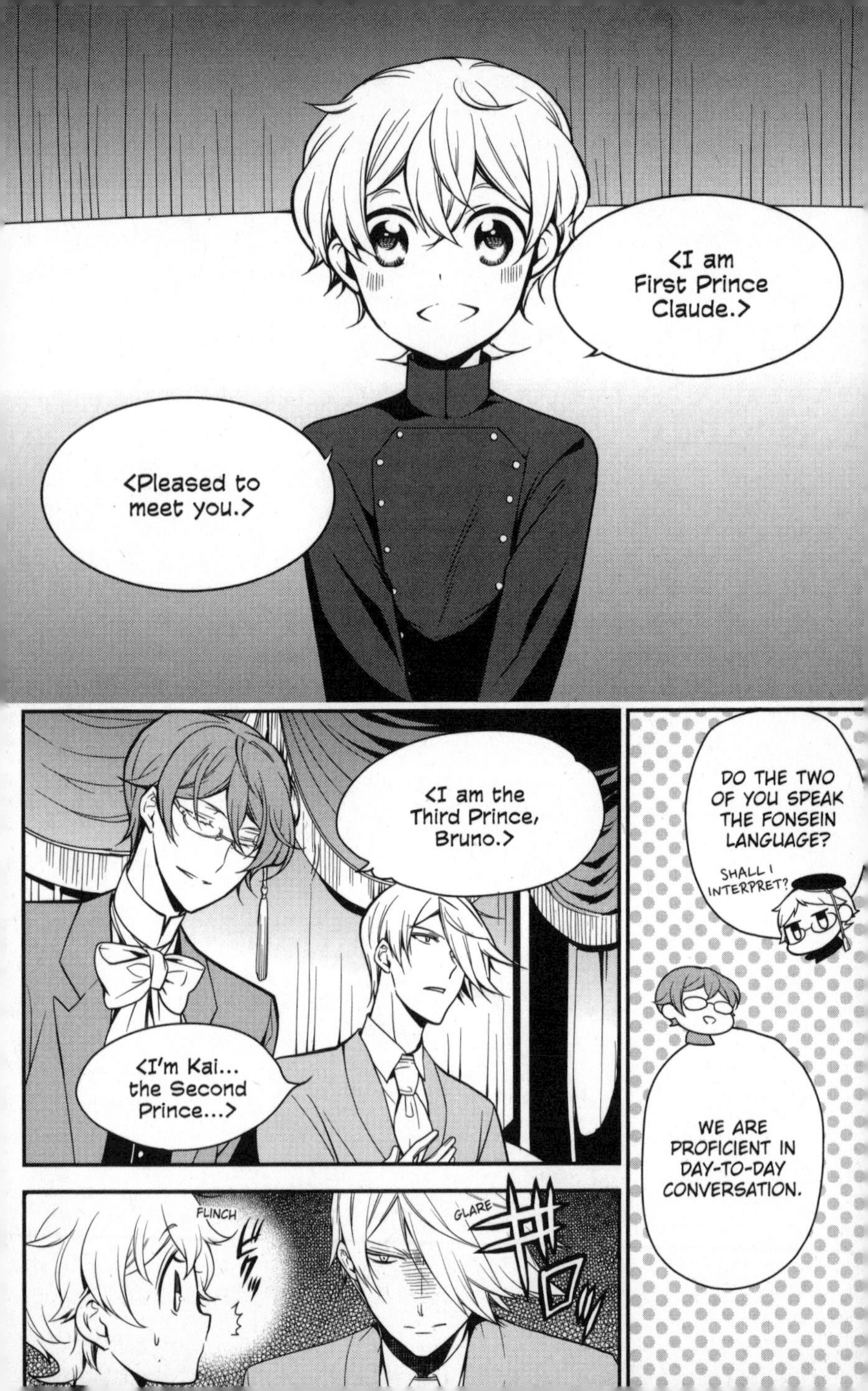
<I am First Prince Claude.>
<Pleased to meet you.>
DO THE TWO OF YOU SPEAK THE FONSEIN LANGUAGE?
SHALL I INTERPRET?
WE ARE PROFICIENT IN DAY-TO-DAY CONVERSATION.
<I am the Third Prince, Bruno.>
<I'm Kai... the Second Prince...>
GLARE
FLINCH

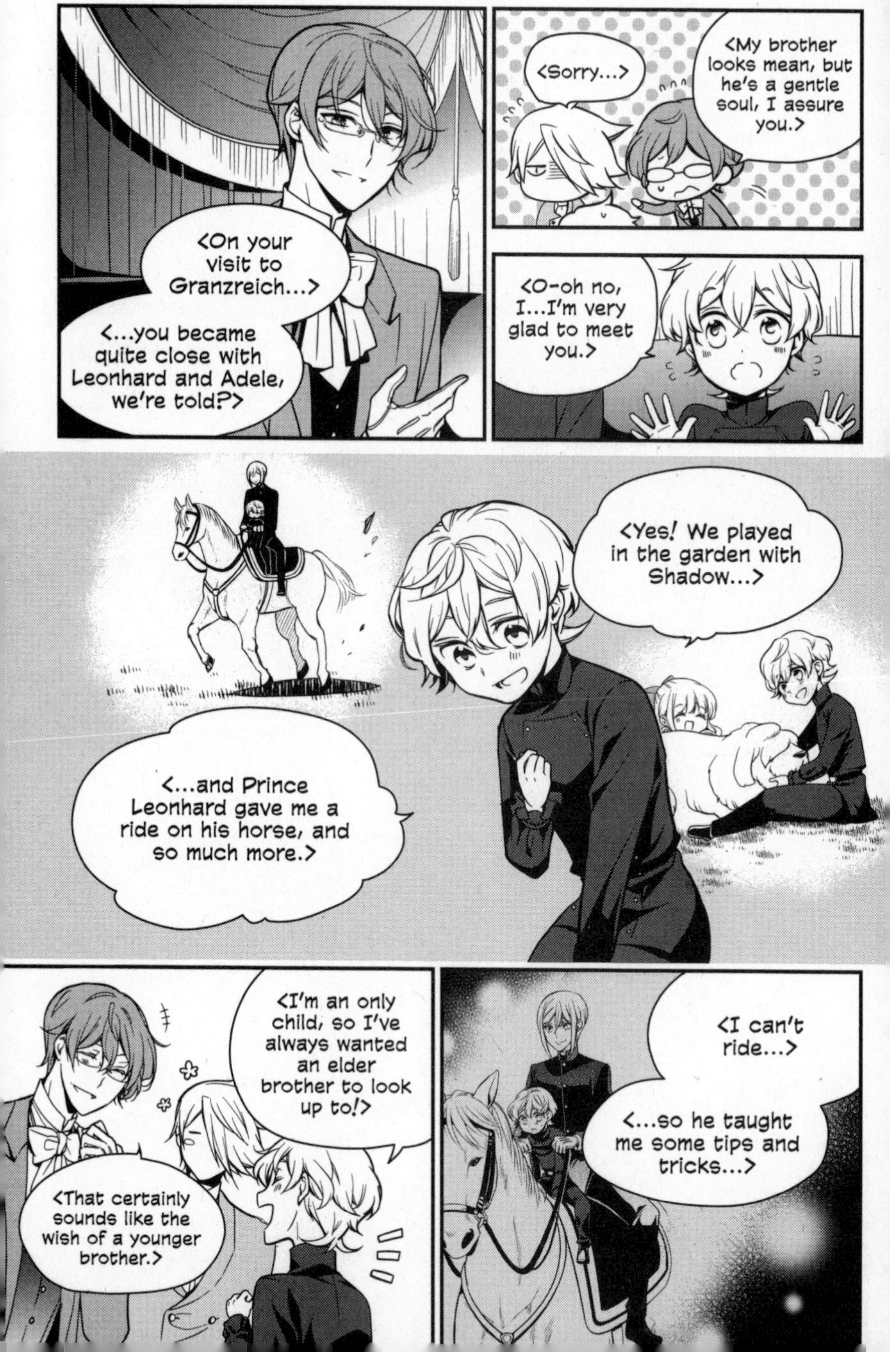
<My brother looks mean, but he's a gentle soul, I assure you.>
<Sorry...>
<O-oh no, I...I'm very glad to meet you.>
<On your visit to Granzreich...>
<...you became quite close with Leonhard and Adele, we're told?>
<Yes! We played in the garden with Shadow...>
<...and Prince Leonhard gave me a ride on his horse, and so much more.>
<I can't ride...>
<...so he taught me some tips and tricks...>
<I'm an only child, so I've always wanted an elder brother to look up to!>
<That certainly sounds like the wish of a younger brother.>

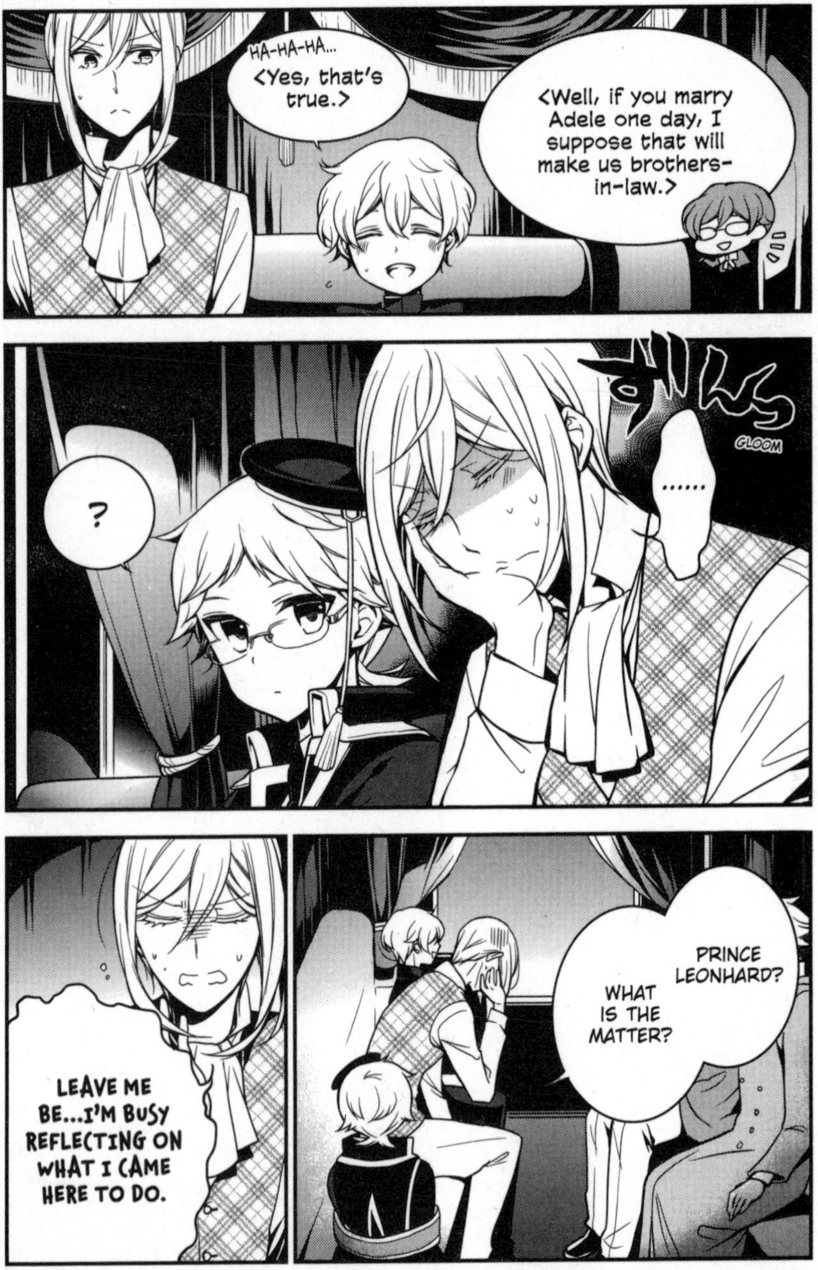
<Well, if you marry Adele one day, I suppose that will make us brothers-in-law.>
HA-HA-HA...
<Yes, that's true.>
GLOOM
......
?
PRINCE LEONHARD?
WHAT IS THE MATTER?
LEAVE ME BE...I'M BUSY REFLECTING ON WHAT I CAME HERE TO DO.

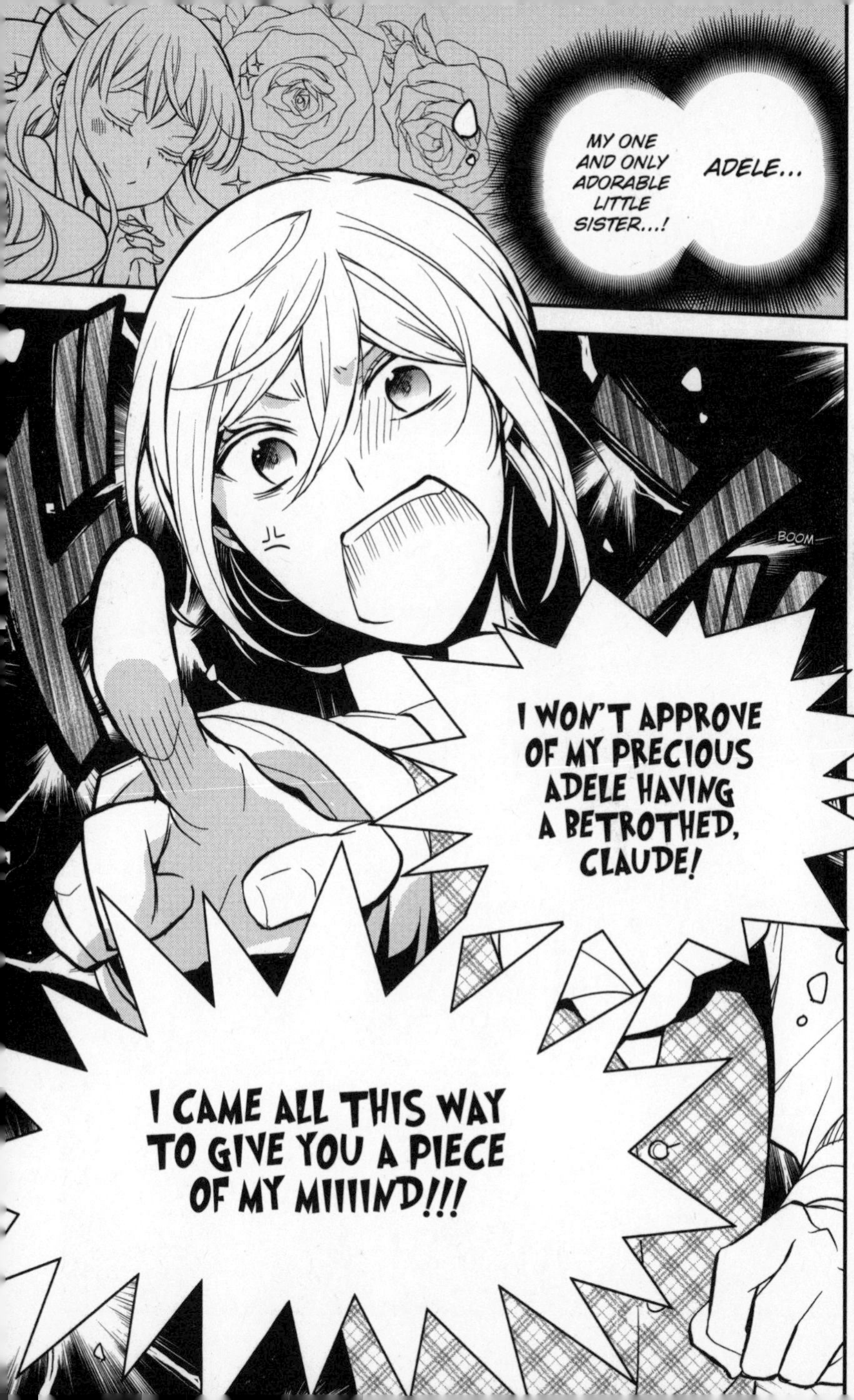
ADELE...
MY ONE AND ONLY ADORABLE LITTLE SISTER...!
BOOM
I WON'T APPROVE OF MY PRECIOUS ADELE HAVING A BETROTHED, CLAUDE!
I CAME ALL THIS WAY TO GIVE YOU A PIECE OF MY MIIIIND!!!

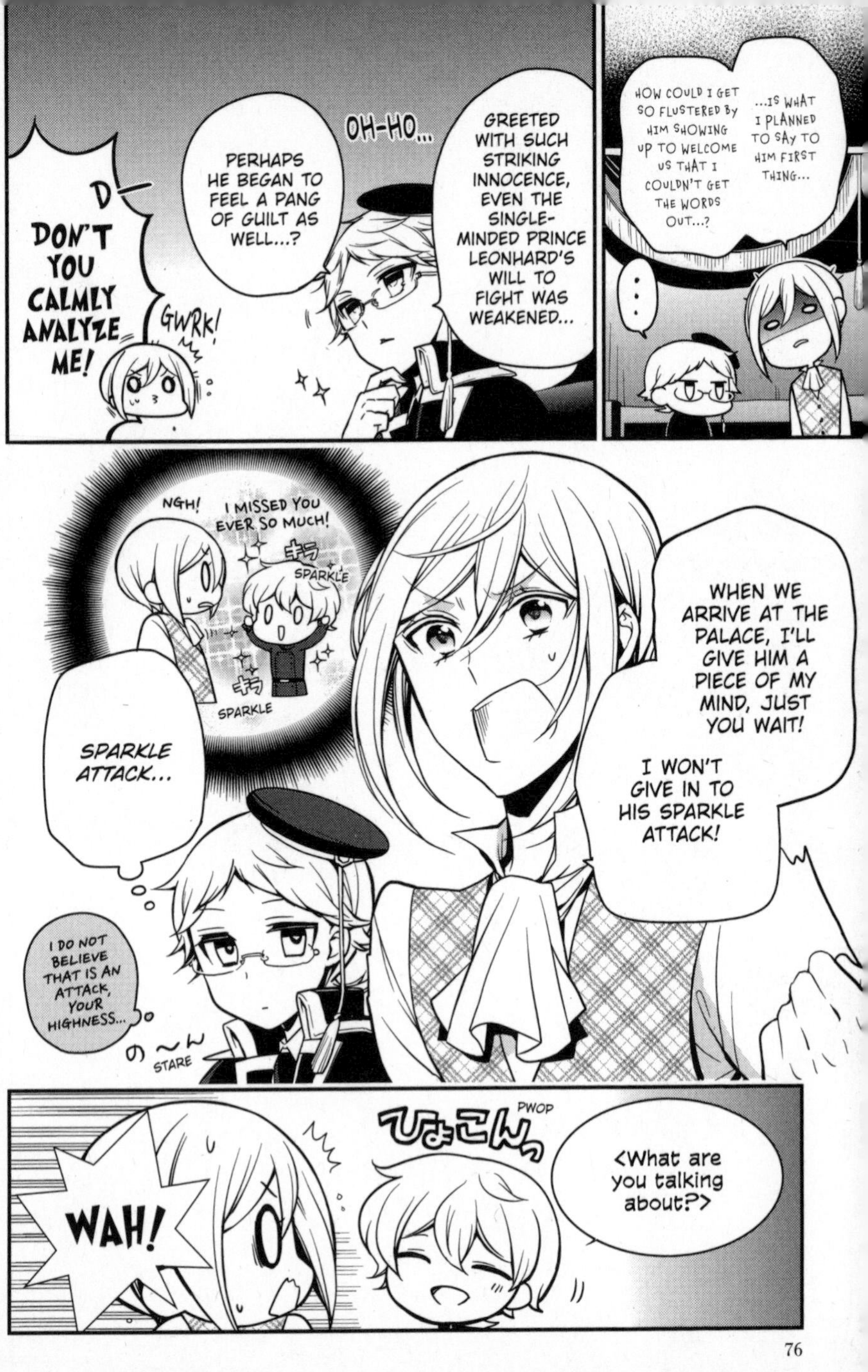
HOW COULD I GET SO FLUSTERED BY HIM SHOWING UP TO WELCOME US THAT I COULDN'T GET THE WORDS OUT...?
...IS WHAT I PLANNED TO SAY TO HIM FIRST THING...
...
GREETED WITH SUCH STRIKING INNOCENCE, EVEN THE SINGLE-MINDED PRINCE LEONHARD'S WILL TO FIGHT WAS WEAKENED...
OH-HO...
PERHAPS HE BEGAN TO FEEL A PANG OF GUILT AS WELL...?
D— DON'T YOU CALMLY ANALYZE ME!
GWRK!
WHEN WE ARRIVE AT THE PALACE, I'LL GIVE HIM A PIECE OF MY MIND, JUST YOU WAIT!
I WON'T GIVE IN TO HIS SPARKLE ATTACK!
I MISSED YOU EVER SO MUCH!
NGH!
キラ SPARKLE
キラ SPARKLE
SPARKLE ATTACK...
I DO NOT BELIEVE THAT IS AN ATTACK, YOUR HIGHNESS...
の～ん STARE
<What are you talking about?>
ひょこん PWOP
WAH!

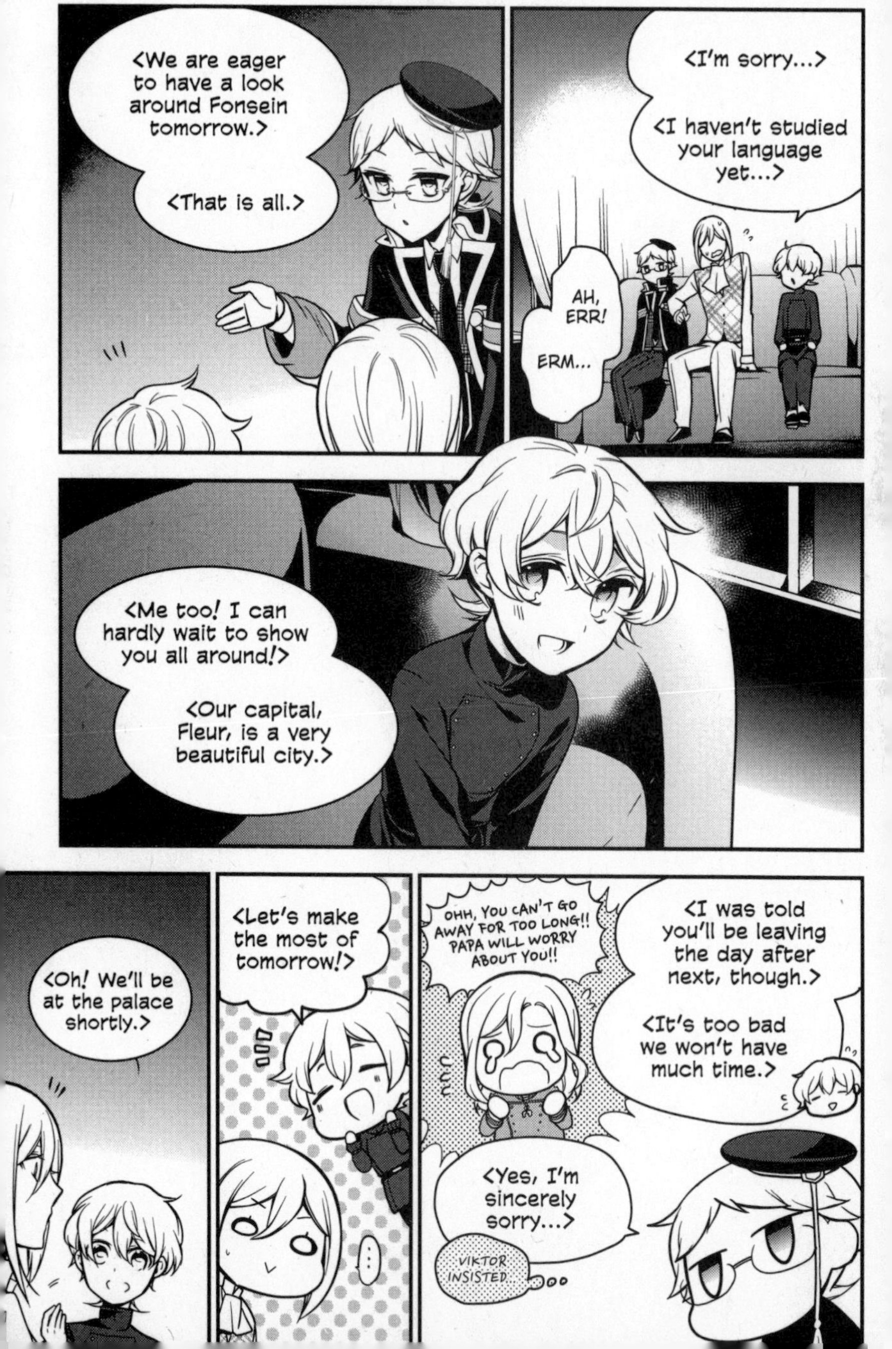
<I'm sorry...>
<I haven't studied your language yet...>
AH, ERR!
ERM...
<We are eager to have a look around Fonsein tomorrow.>
<That is all.>
<Me too! I can hardly wait to show you all around!>
<Our capital, Fleur, is a very beautiful city.>
<I was told you'll be leaving the day after next, though.>
<It's too bad we won't have much time.>
OHH, YOU CAN'T GO AWAY FOR TOO LONG!! PAPA WILL WORRY ABOUT YOU!!
<Yes, I'm sincerely sorry...>
VIKTOR INSISTED.
<Let's make the most of tomorrow!>
...
<Oh! We'll be at the palace shortly.>

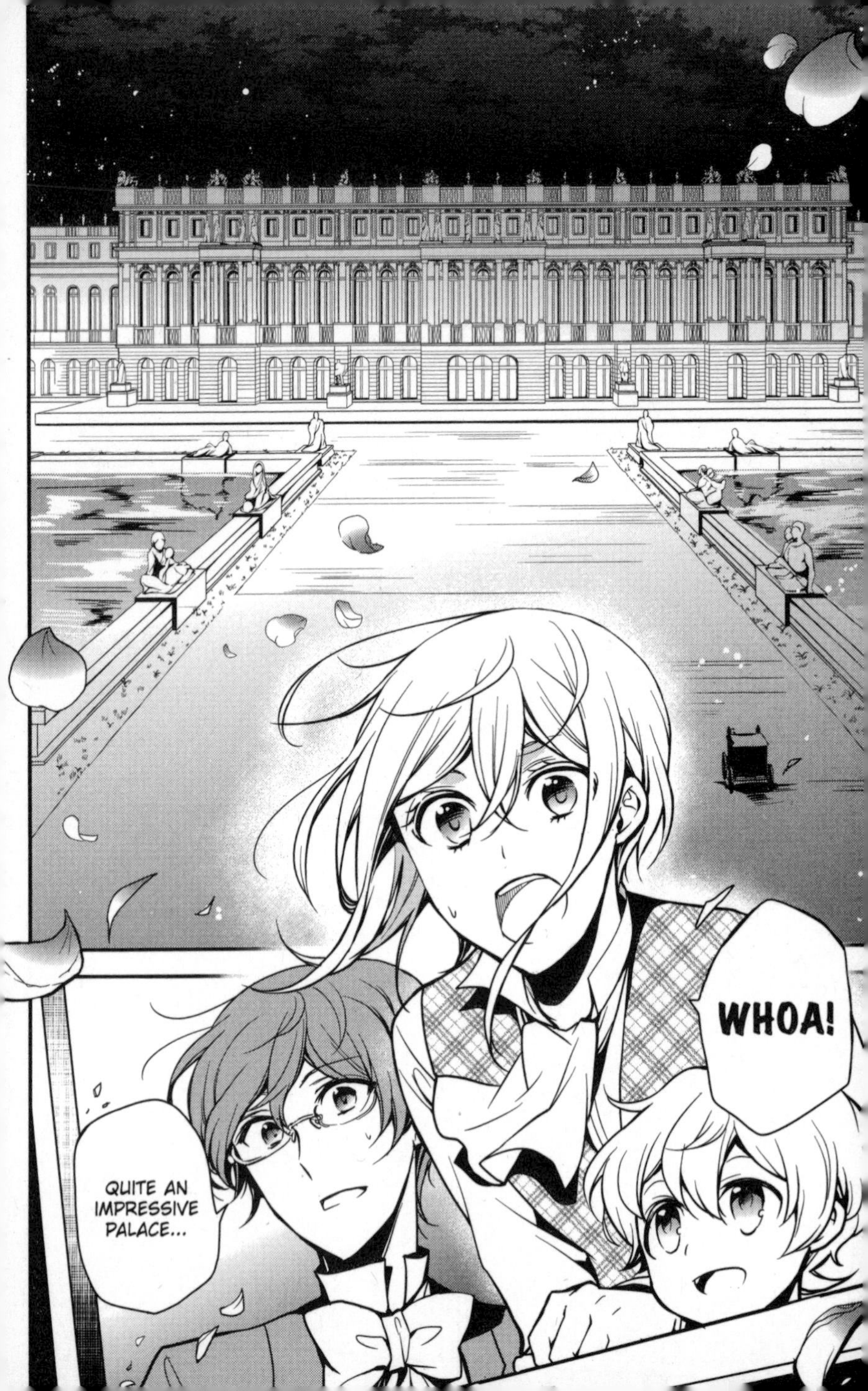
WHOA!
QUITE AN IMPRESSIVE PALACE...

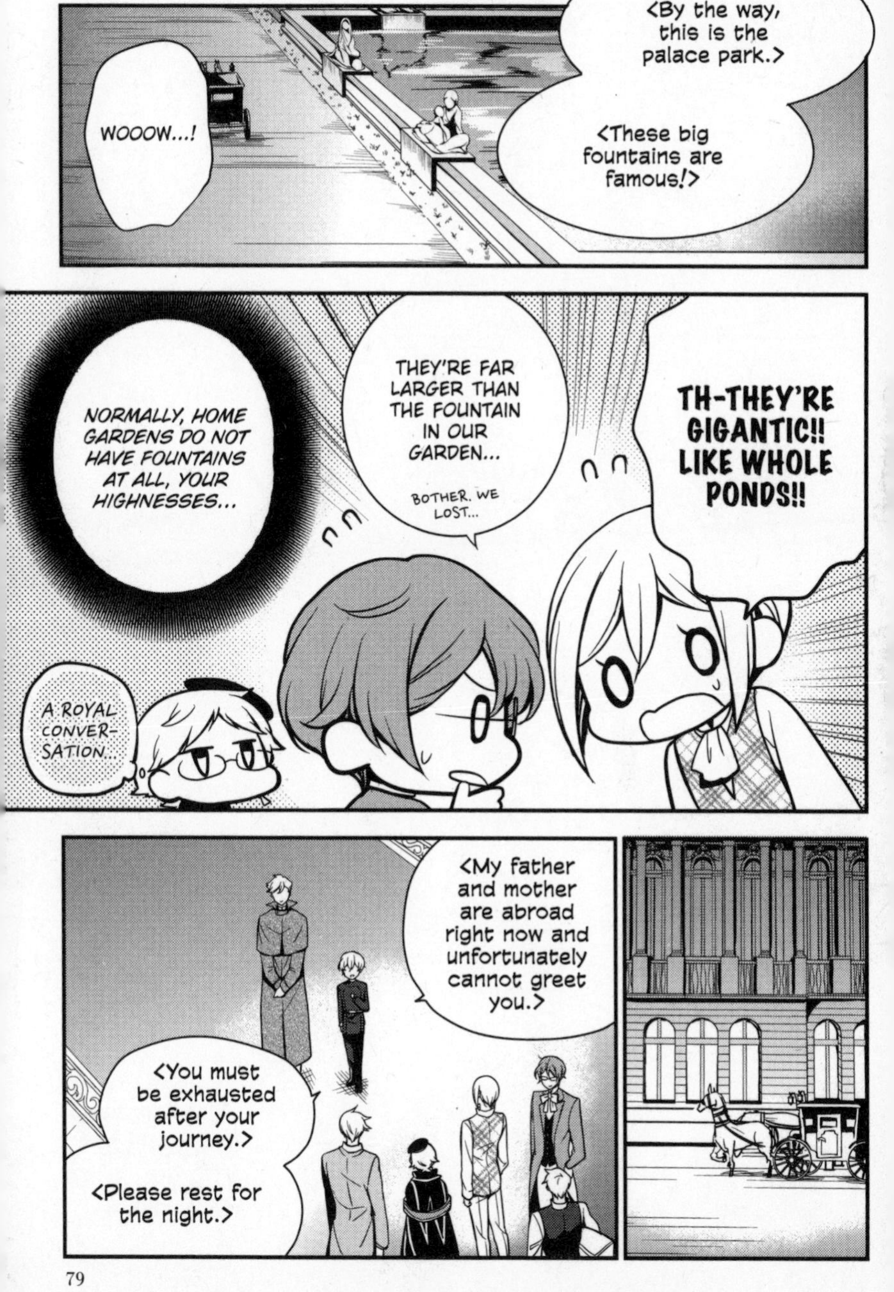
<By the way, this is the palace park.>
<These big fountains are famous!>
WOOOW...!
TH-THEY'RE GIGANTIC!! LIKE WHOLE PONDS!!
THEY'RE FAR LARGER THAN THE FOUNTAIN IN OUR GARDEN...
BOTHER. WE LOST...
NORMALLY, HOME GARDENS DO NOT HAVE FOUNTAINS AT ALL, YOUR HIGHNESSES...
A ROYAL CONVERSATION...
<My father and mother are abroad right now and unfortunately cannot greet you.>
<You must be exhausted after your journey.>
<Please rest for the night.>

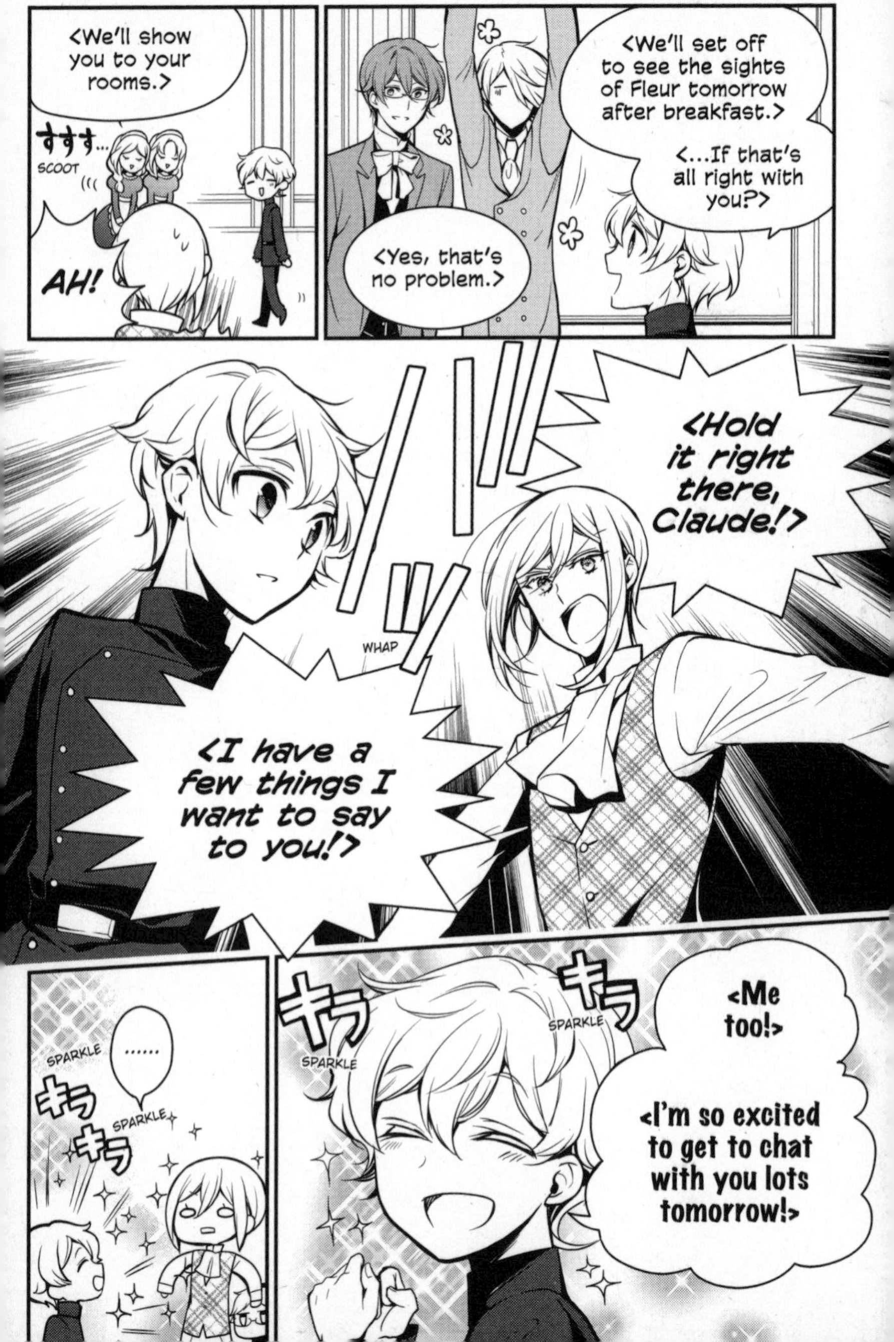
<We'll set off to see the sights of Fleur tomorrow after breakfast.>
<...If that's all right with you?>
<Yes, that's no problem.>
<We'll show you to your rooms.>
すすす...
SCOOT
AH!
<Hold it right there, Claude!>
WHAP
<I have a few things I want to say to you!>
キラ
SPARKLE
キラ
SPARKLE
<Me too!>
<I'm so excited to get to chat with you lots tomorrow!>
......
SPARKLE
キラ
SPARKLE
キラ

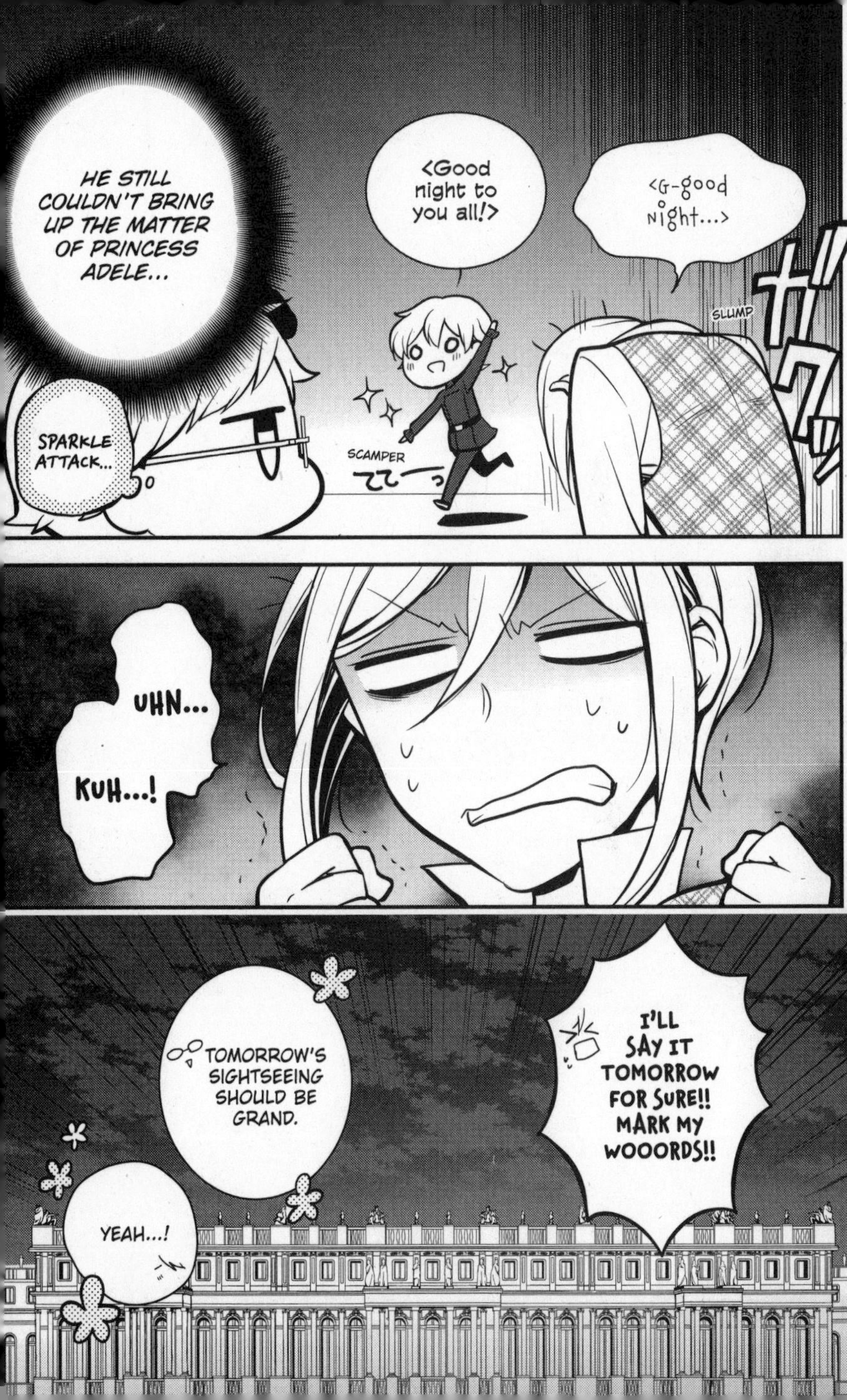
<G-good night...>
SLUMP
<Good night to you all!>
SCAMPER
HE STILL COULDN'T BRING UP THE MATTER OF PRINCESS ADELE...
SPARKLE ATTACK...
UHN...
KUH...!
I'LL SAY IT TOMORROW FOR SURE!! MARK MY WOOORDS!!
TOMORROW'S SIGHTSEEING SHOULD BE GRAND.
YEAH...!

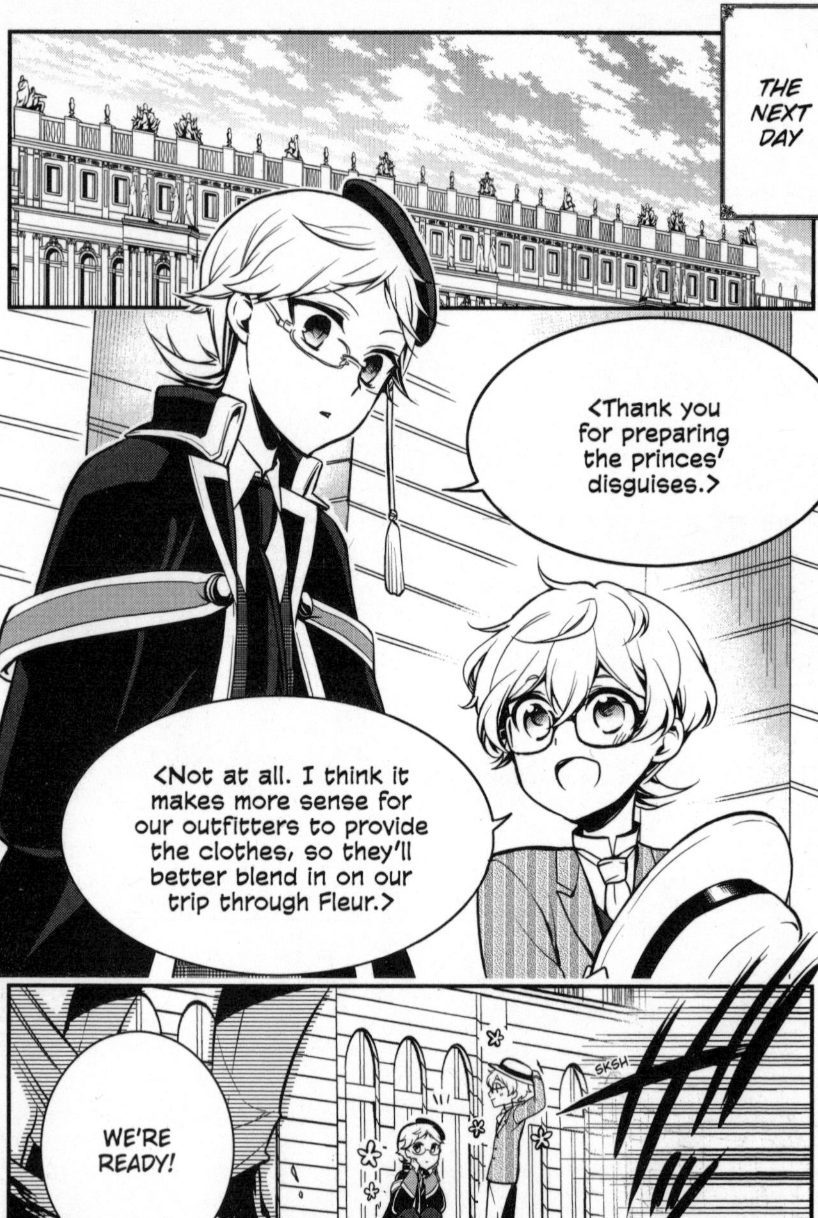
THE NEXT DAY
<Thank you for preparing the princes' disguises.>
<Not at all. I think it makes more sense for our outfitters to provide the clothes, so they'll better blend in on our trip through Fleur.>
SKSH
WE'RE READY!

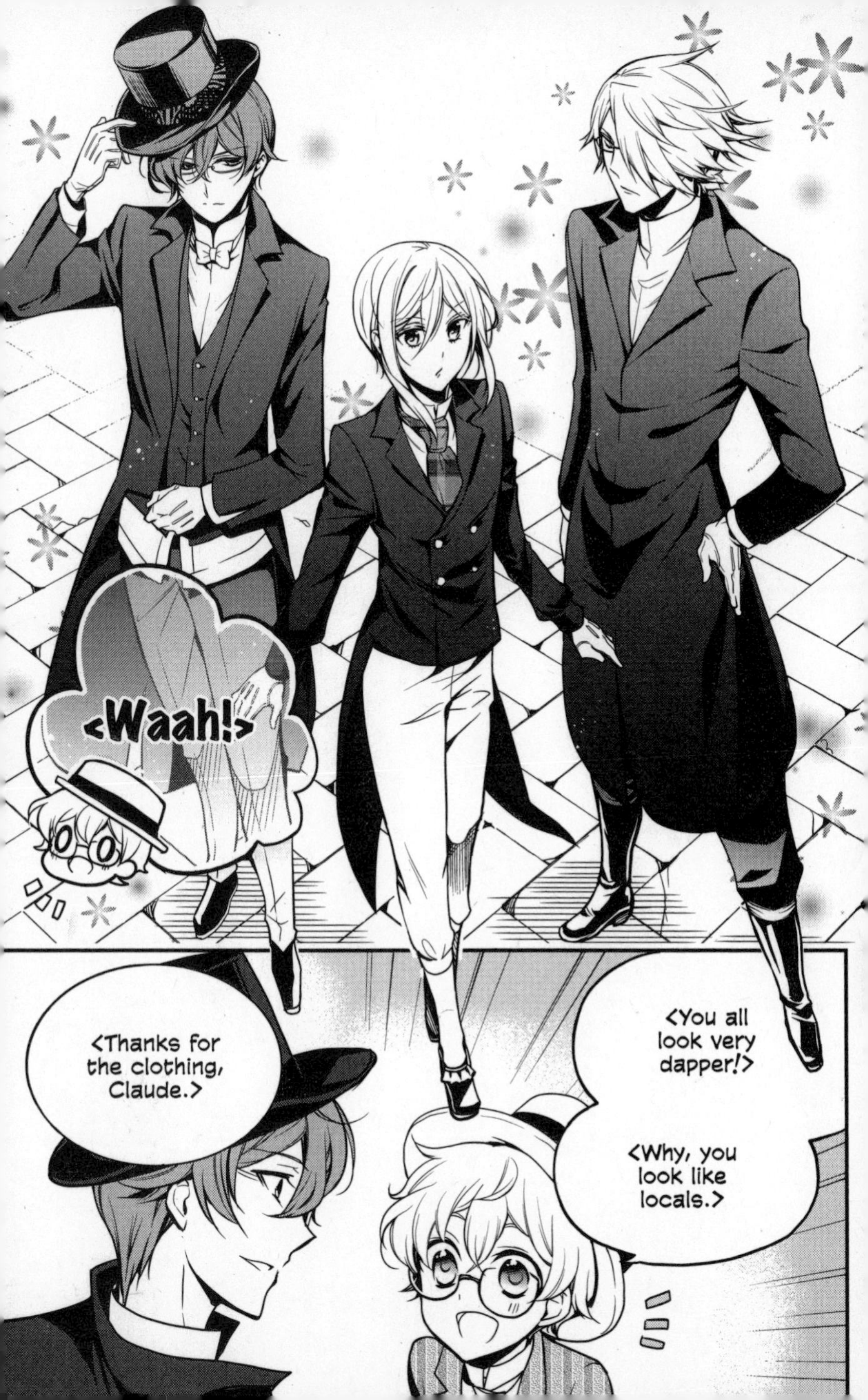
<Waah!>
<You all look very dapper!>
<Why, you look like locals.>
<Thanks for the clothing, Claude.>

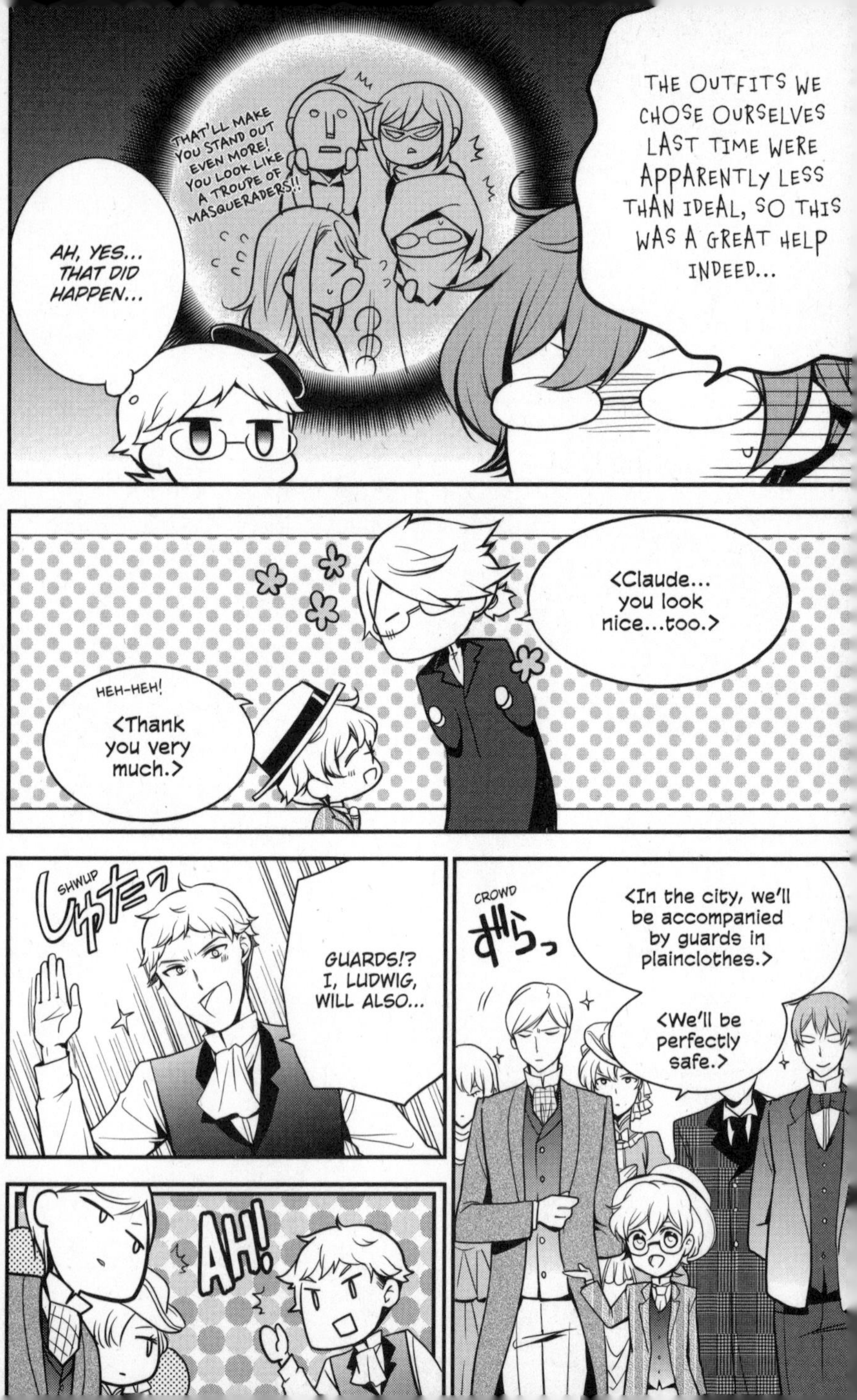
THE OUTFITS WE CHOSE OURSELVES LAST TIME WERE APPARENTLY LESS THAN IDEAL, SO THIS WAS A GREAT HELP INDEED...
THAT'LL MAKE YOU STAND OUT EVEN MORE! YOU LOOK LIKE A TROUPE OF MASQUERADERS!!
AH, YES... THAT DID HAPPEN...
<Claude... you look nice...too.>
HEH-HEH!
<Thank you very much.>
CROWD
ずらっ
<In the city, we'll be accompanied by guards in plainclothes.>
<We'll be perfectly safe.>
SHWUP
しゅたっ
GUARDS!? I, LUDWIG, WILL ALSO...
AH!

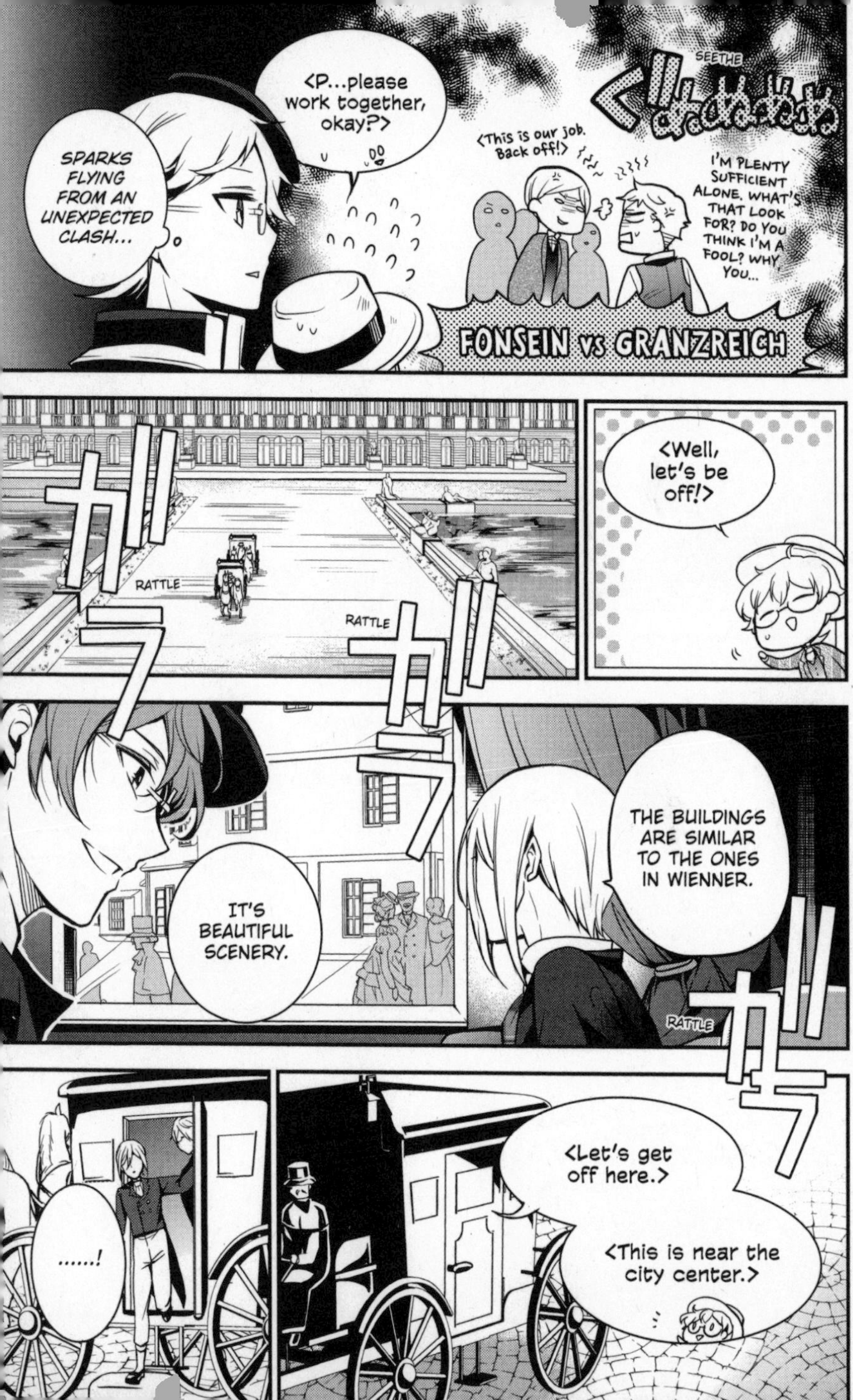
SEETHE
I'M PLENTY SUFFICIENT ALONE. WHAT'S THAT LOOK FOR? DO YOU THINK I'M A FOOL? WHY YOU...
<This is our job. Back off!>
FONSEIN vs GRANZREICH
<P...please work together, okay?>
SPARKS FLYING FROM AN UNEXPECTED CLASH...
<Well, let's be off!>
ガラ
RATTLE
ガラ
RATTLE
THE BUILDINGS ARE SIMILAR TO THE ONES IN WIENNER.
ガラ
RATTLE
IT'S BEAUTIFUL SCENERY.
<Let's get off here.>
<This is near the city center.>
......!

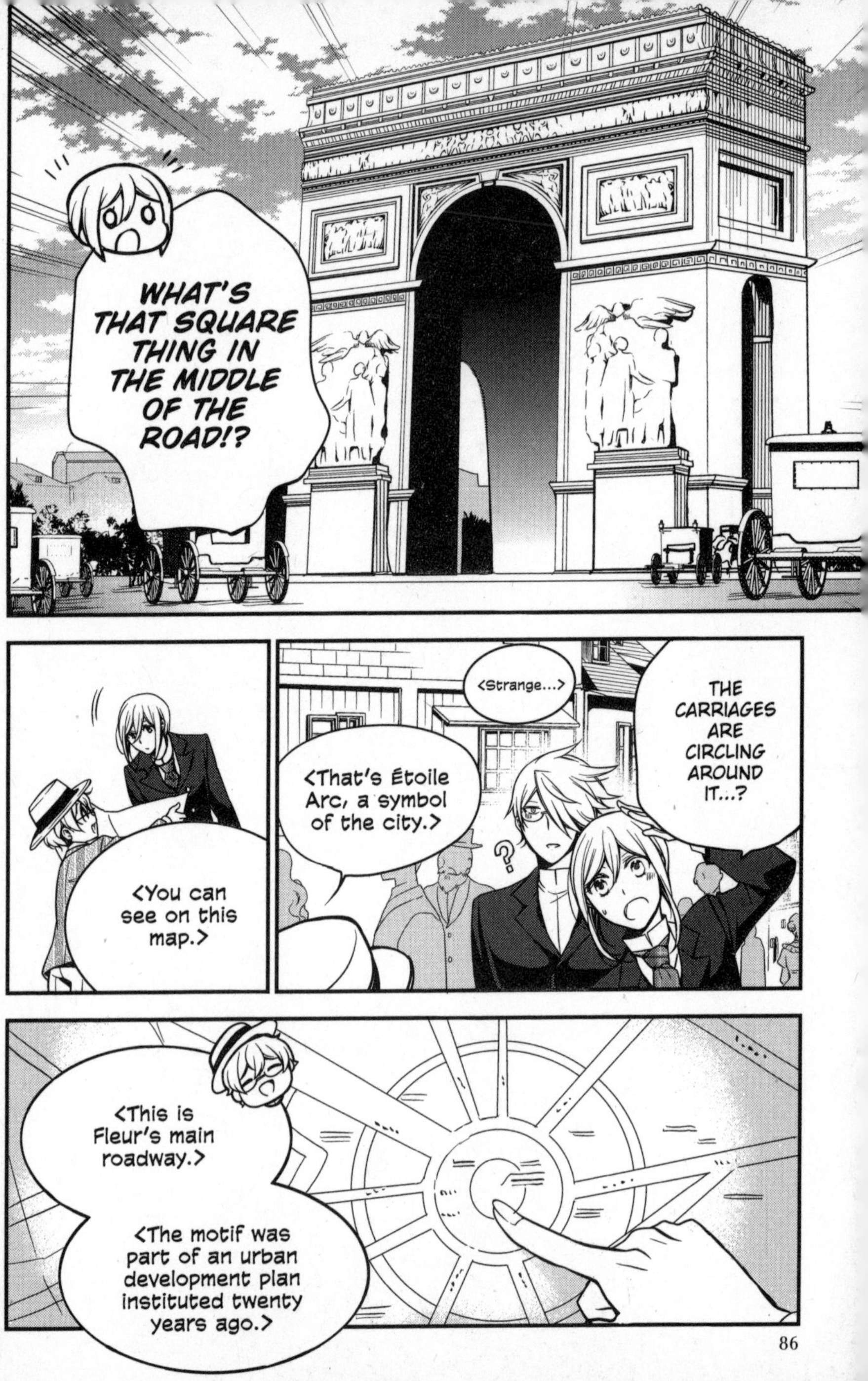
WHAT'S THAT SQUARE THING IN THE MIDDLE OF THE ROAD!?
THE CARRIAGES ARE CIRCLING AROUND IT...?
<Strange...>
<That's Étoile Arc, a symbol of the city.>
<You can see on this map.>
<This is Fleur's main roadway.>
<The motif was part of an urban development plan instituted twenty years ago.>

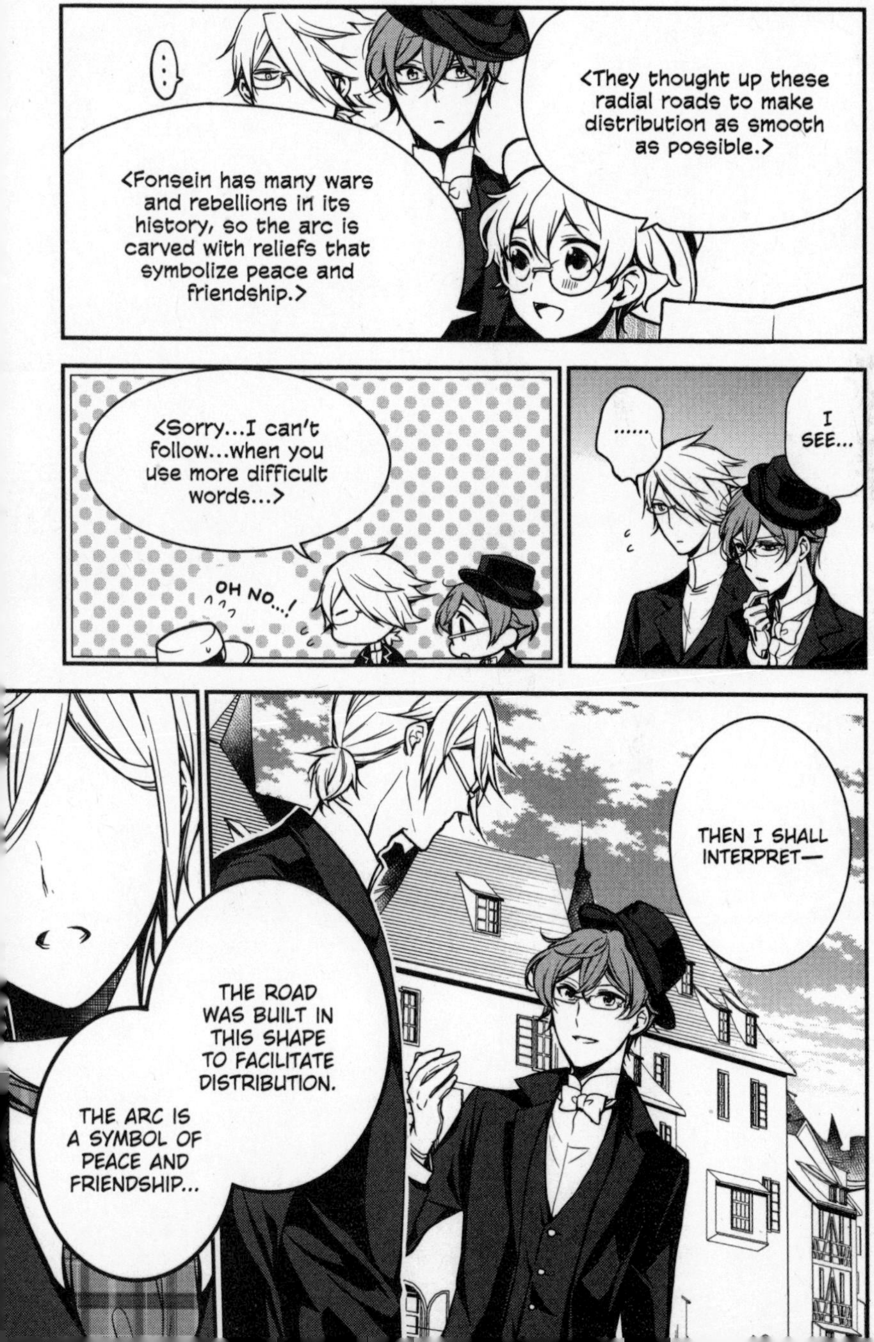
<They thought up these radial roads to make distribution as smooth as possible.>
...
<Fonsein has many wars and rebellions in its history, so the arc is carved with reliefs that symbolize peace and friendship.>
I SEE...
......
<Sorry...I can't follow...when you use more difficult words...>
OH NO...!
THEN I SHALL INTERPRET—
THE ROAD WAS BUILT IN THIS SHAPE TO FACILITATE DISTRIBUTION.
THE ARC IS A SYMBOL OF PEACE AND FRIENDSHIP...

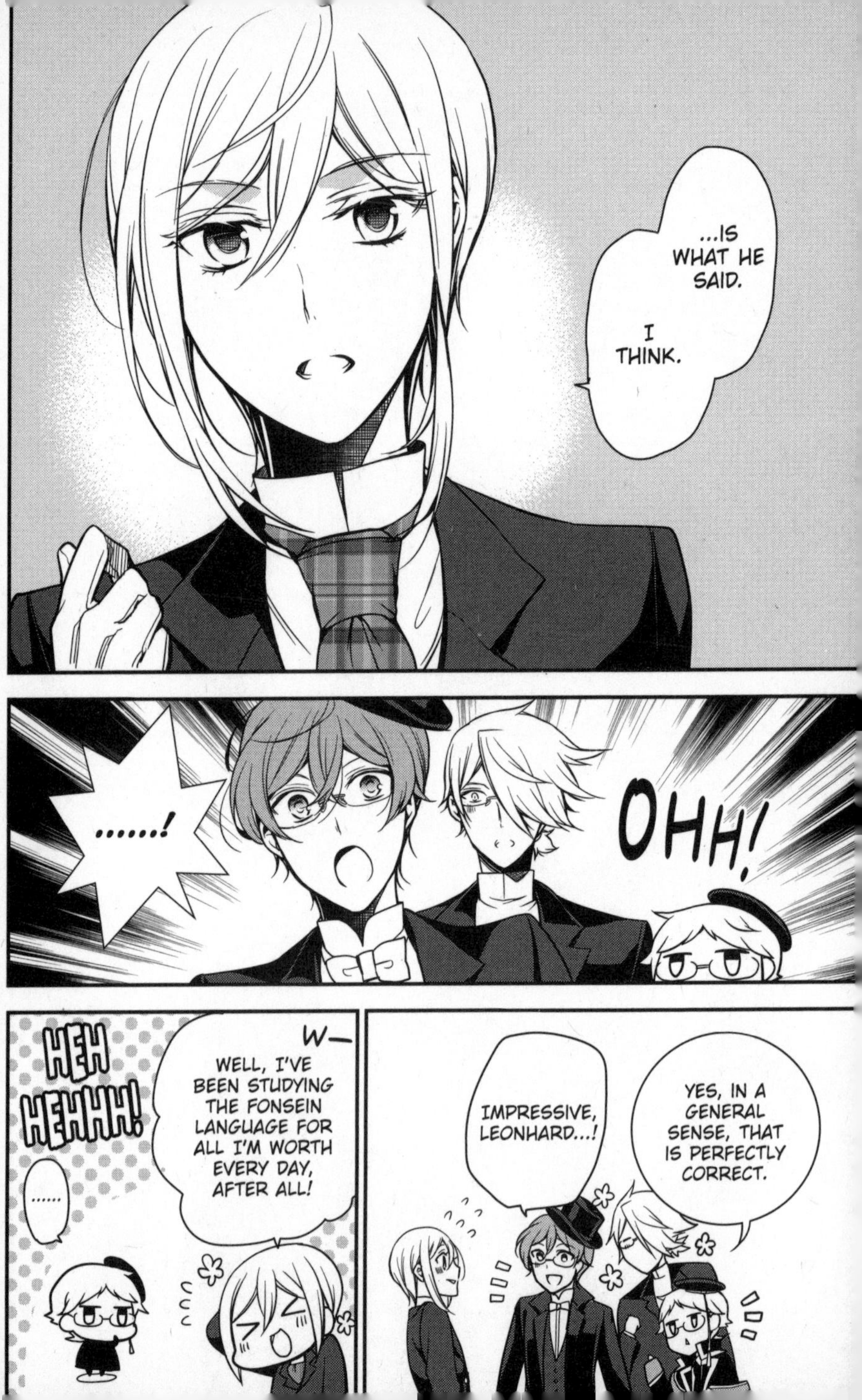

...IS WHAT HE SAID.
I THINK.
OHH!
......!
YES, IN A GENERAL SENSE, THAT IS PERFECTLY CORRECT.
IMPRESSIVE, LEONHARD...!
W—
WELL, I'VE BEEN STUDYING THE FONSEIN LANGUAGE FOR ALL I'M WORTH EVERY DAY, AFTER ALL!
HEH HEHHH!
......

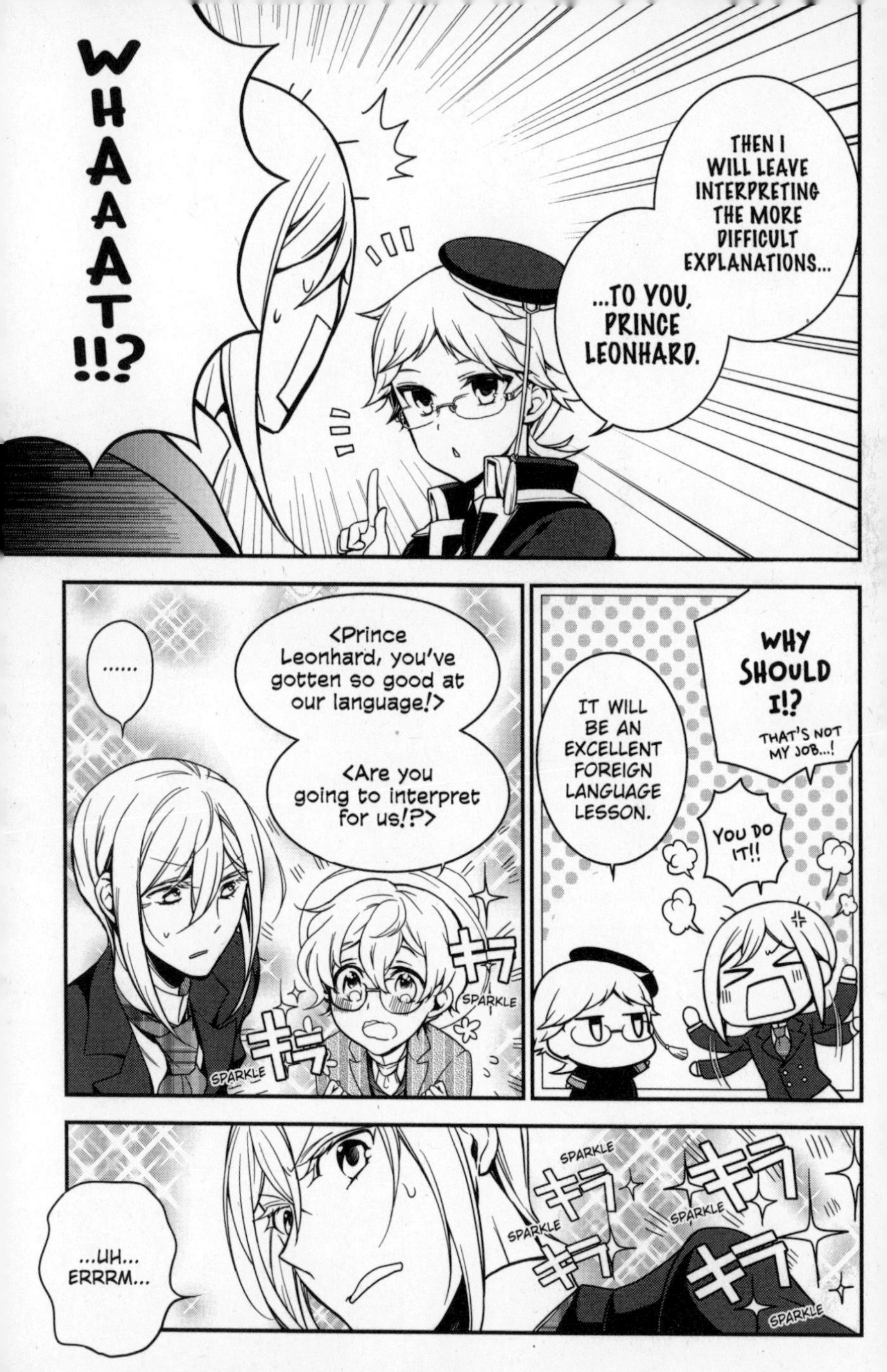
THEN I WILL LEAVE INTERPRETING THE MORE DIFFICULT EXPLANATIONS...
...TO YOU, PRINCE LEONHARD.
WHAAAT!!?
WHY SHOULD I!?
THAT'S NOT MY JOB...!
IT WILL BE AN EXCELLENT FOREIGN LANGUAGE LESSON.
YOU DO IT!!
<Prince Leonhard, you've gotten so good at our language!>
<Are you going to interpret for us!?>
......
キラ SPARKLE
キラ SPARKLE
キラ SPARKLE
キラ SPARKLE
キラ SPARKLE
キラ SPARKLE
...UH... ERRRM...

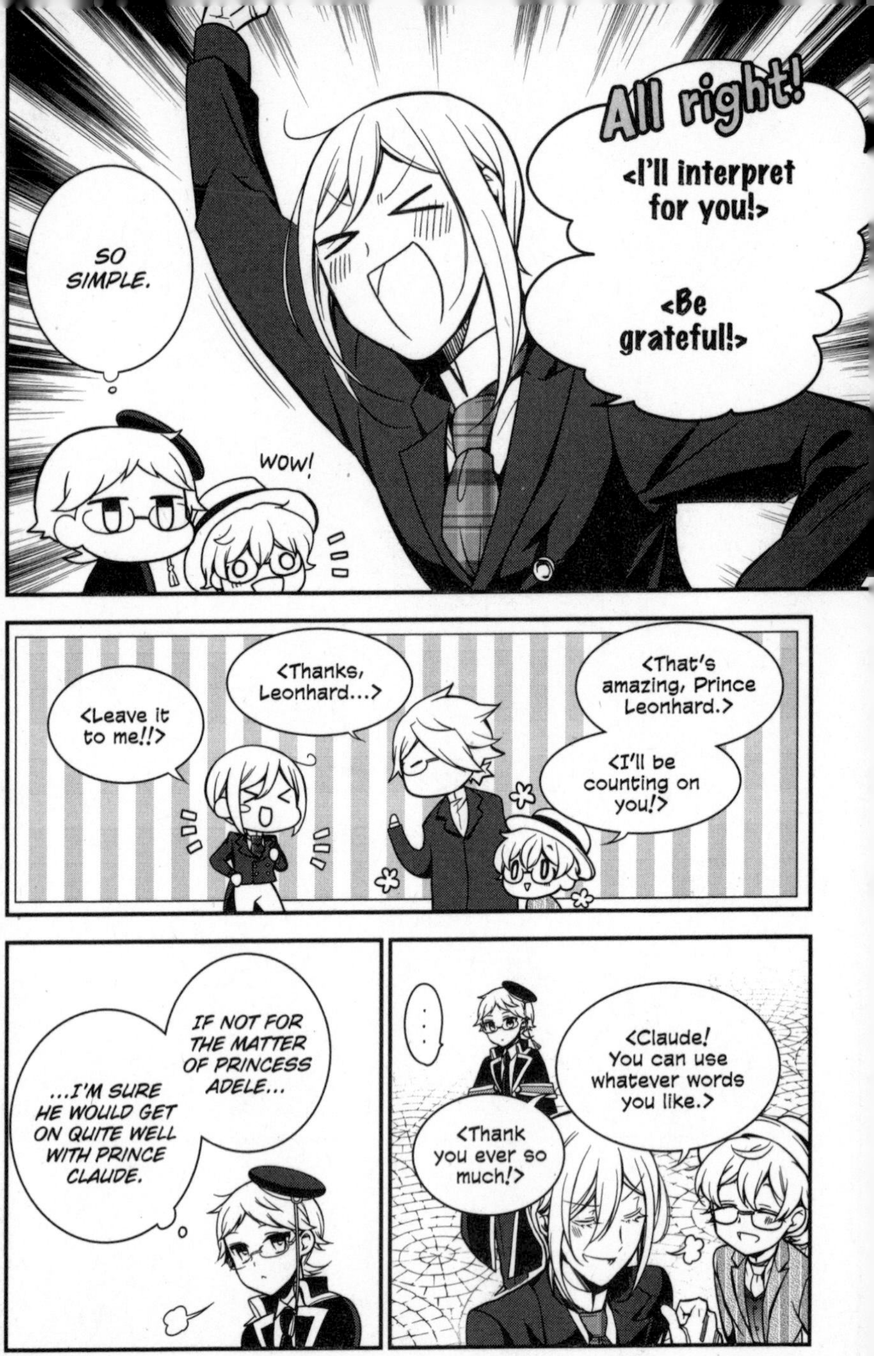
All right!
<I'll interpret for you!>
<Be grateful!>
SO SIMPLE.
WOW!
<That's amazing, Prince Leonhard.>
<I'll be counting on you!>
<Thanks, Leonhard...>
<Leave it to me!!>
<Claude! You can use whatever words you like.>
...
<Thank you ever so much!>
IF NOT FOR THE MATTER OF PRINCESS ADELE...
...I'M SURE HE WOULD GET ON QUITE WELL WITH PRINCE CLAUDE.

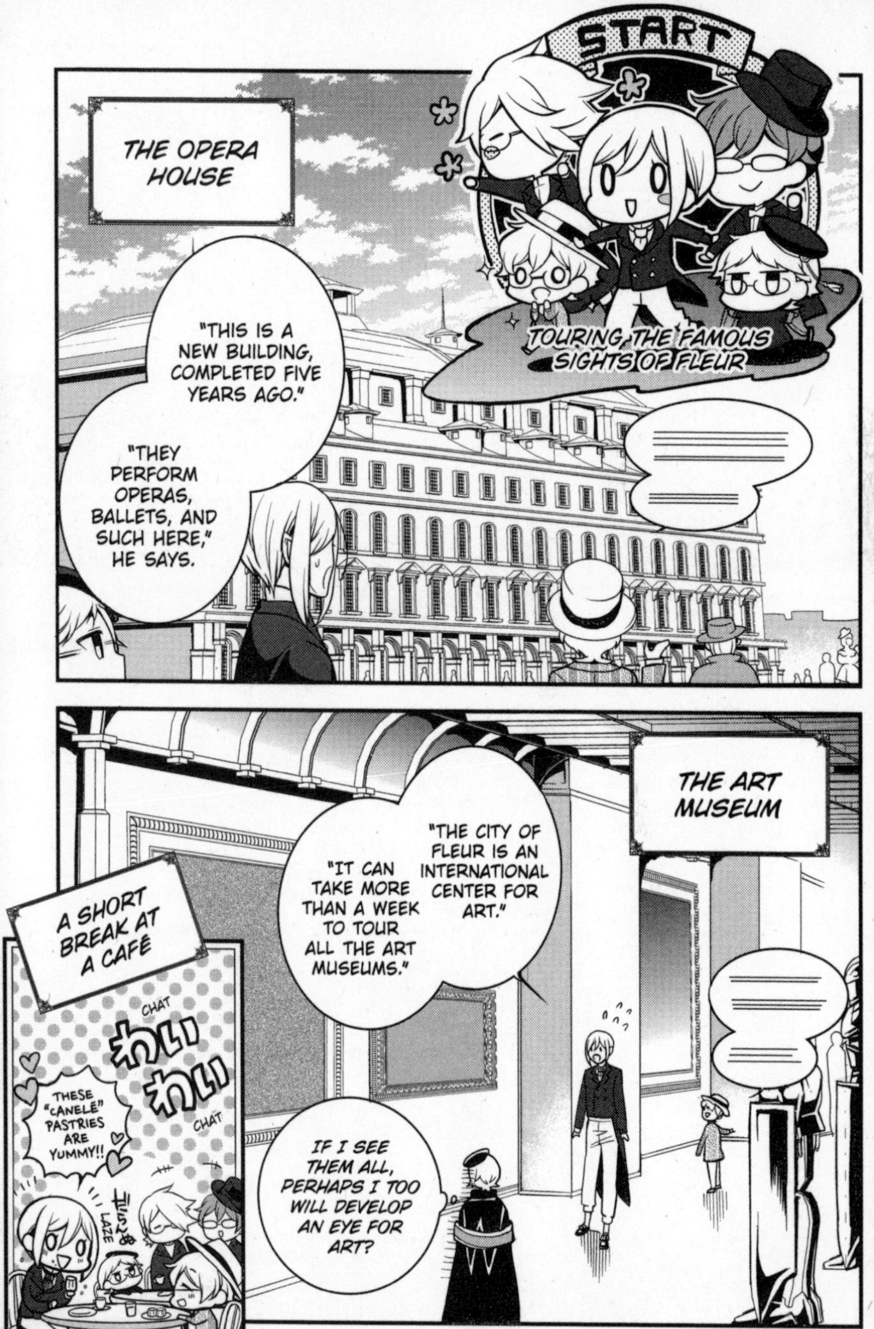
START
TOURING THE FAMOUS SIGHTS OF FLEUR
THE OPERA HOUSE
"THIS IS A NEW BUILDING, COMPLETED FIVE YEARS AGO."
"THEY PERFORM OPERAS, BALLETS, AND SUCH HERE," HE SAYS.
THE ART MUSEUM
"THE CITY OF FLEUR IS AN INTERNATIONAL CENTER FOR ART."
"IT CAN TAKE MORE THAN A WEEK TO TOUR ALL THE ART MUSEUMS."
IF I SEE THEM ALL, PERHAPS I TOO WILL DEVELOP AN EYE FOR ART?
A SHORT BREAK AT A CAFÉ
わい わい
CHAT
CHAT
THESE "CANELÉ" PASTRIES ARE YUMMY!!
LAZE

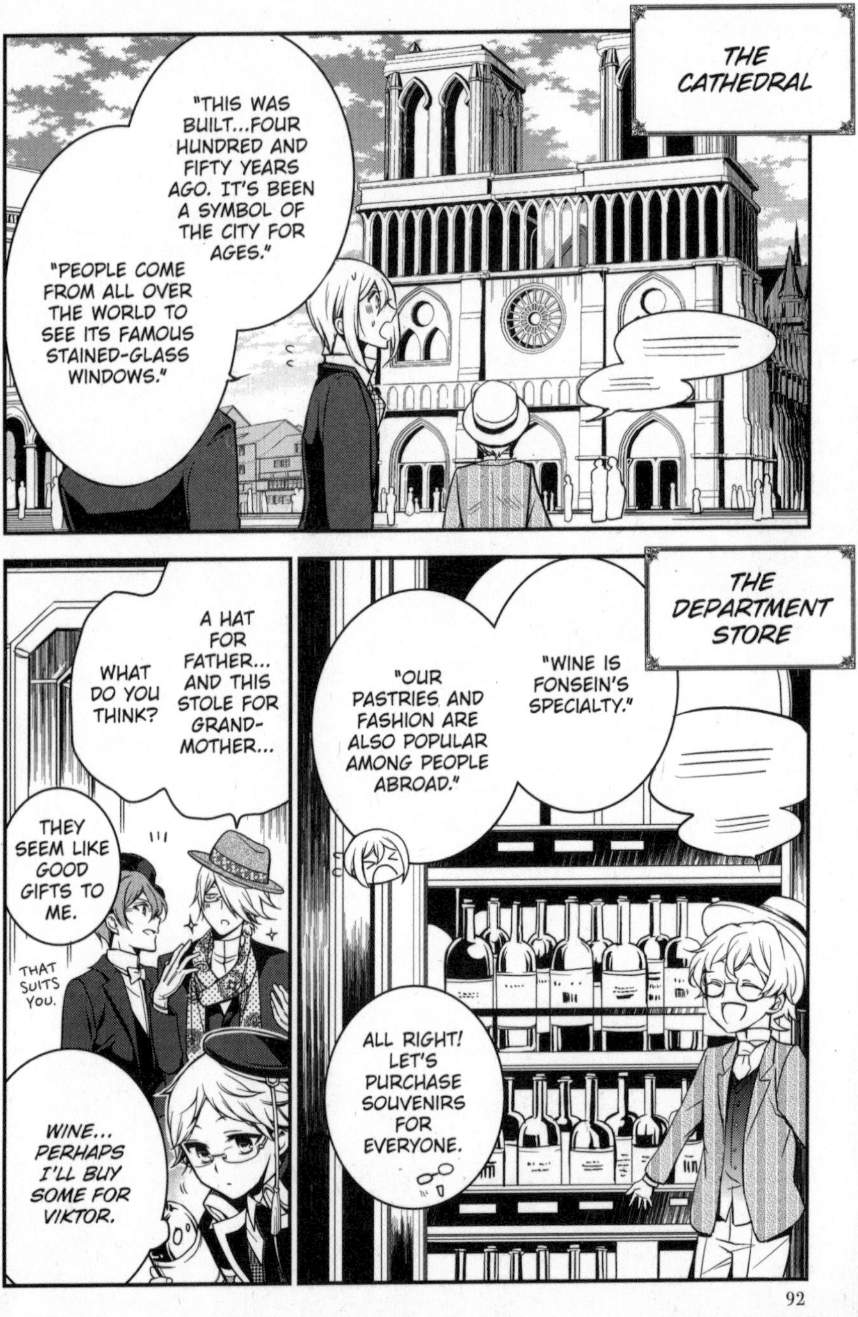
THE CATHEDRAL
"THIS WAS BUILT...FOUR HUNDRED AND FIFTY YEARS AGO. IT'S BEEN A SYMBOL OF THE CITY FOR AGES."
"PEOPLE COME FROM ALL OVER THE WORLD TO SEE ITS FAMOUS STAINED-GLASS WINDOWS."
THE DEPARTMENT STORE
"WINE IS FONSEIN'S SPECIALTY."
"OUR PASTRIES AND FASHION ARE ALSO POPULAR AMONG PEOPLE ABROAD."
ALL RIGHT! LET'S PURCHASE SOUVENIRS FOR EVERYONE.
A HAT FOR FATHER... AND THIS STOLE FOR GRAND-MOTHER...
WHAT DO YOU THINK?
THEY SEEM LIKE GOOD GIFTS TO ME.
THAT SUITS YOU.
WINE... PERHAPS I'LL BUY SOME FOR VIKTOR.

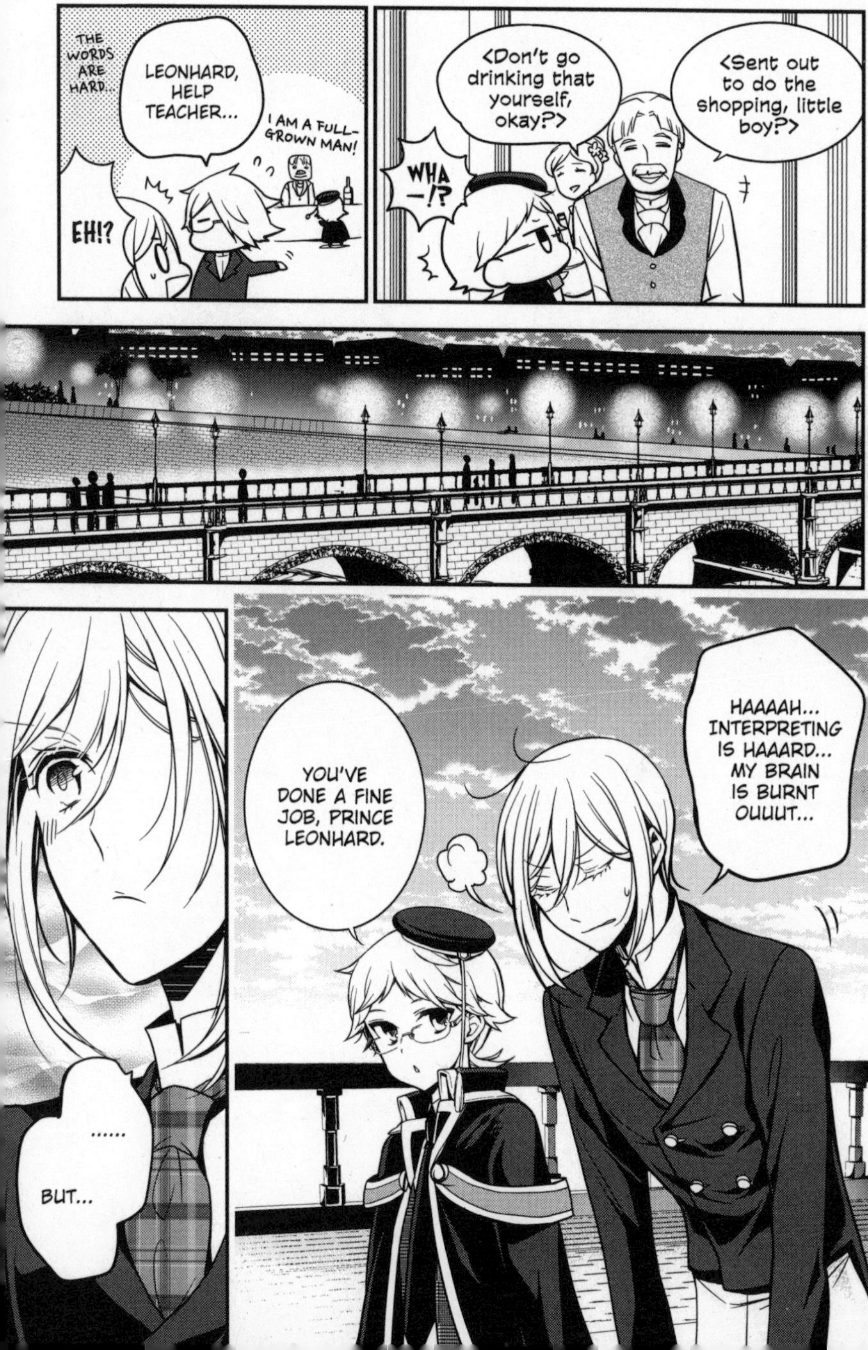
<Sent out to do the shopping, little boy?>
<Don't go drinking that yourself, okay?>
WHA—!?
LEONHARD, HELP TEACHER...
THE WORDS ARE HARD...
I AM A FULL-GROWN MAN!
EH!?
HAAAAH... INTERPRETING IS HAAARD... MY BRAIN IS BURNT OUUUT...
YOU'VE DONE A FINE JOB, PRINCE LEONHARD.
......
BUT...

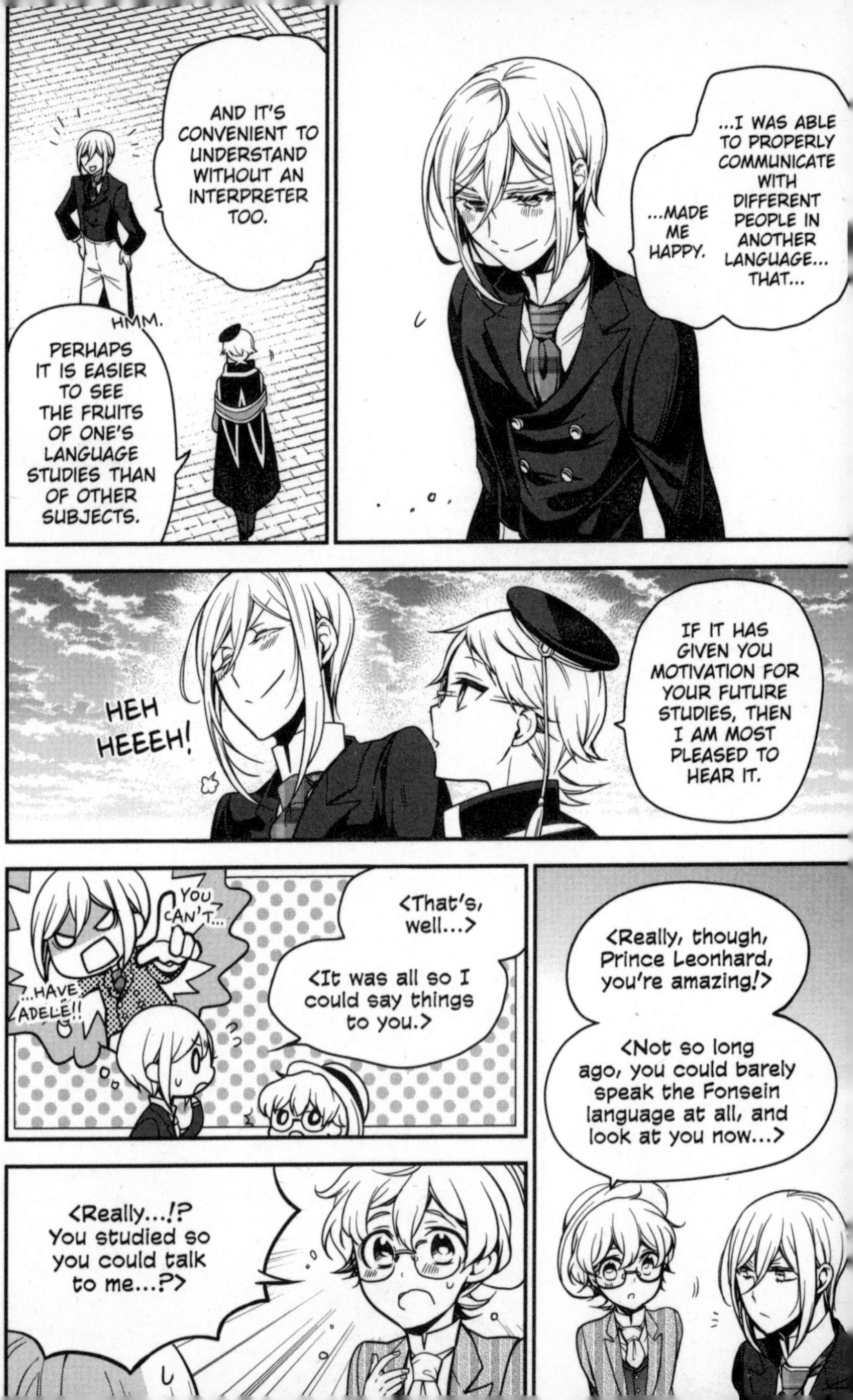
...I WAS ABLE TO PROPERLY COMMUNICATE WITH DIFFERENT PEOPLE IN ANOTHER LANGUAGE... THAT...
...MADE ME HAPPY.
AND IT'S CONVENIENT TO UNDERSTAND WITHOUT AN INTERPRETER TOO.
HMM.
PERHAPS IT IS EASIER TO SEE THE FRUITS OF ONE'S LANGUAGE STUDIES THAN OF OTHER SUBJECTS.
IF IT HAS GIVEN YOU MOTIVATION FOR YOUR FUTURE STUDIES, THEN I AM MOST PLEASED TO HEAR IT.
HEH HEEEH!
<Really, though, Prince Leonhard, you're amazing!>
<Not so long ago, you could barely speak the Fonsein language at all, and look at you now...>
<That's, well...>
<It was all so I could say things to you.>
YOU CAN'T...
...HAVE ADELE!!
<Really...!? You studied so you could talk to me...?>

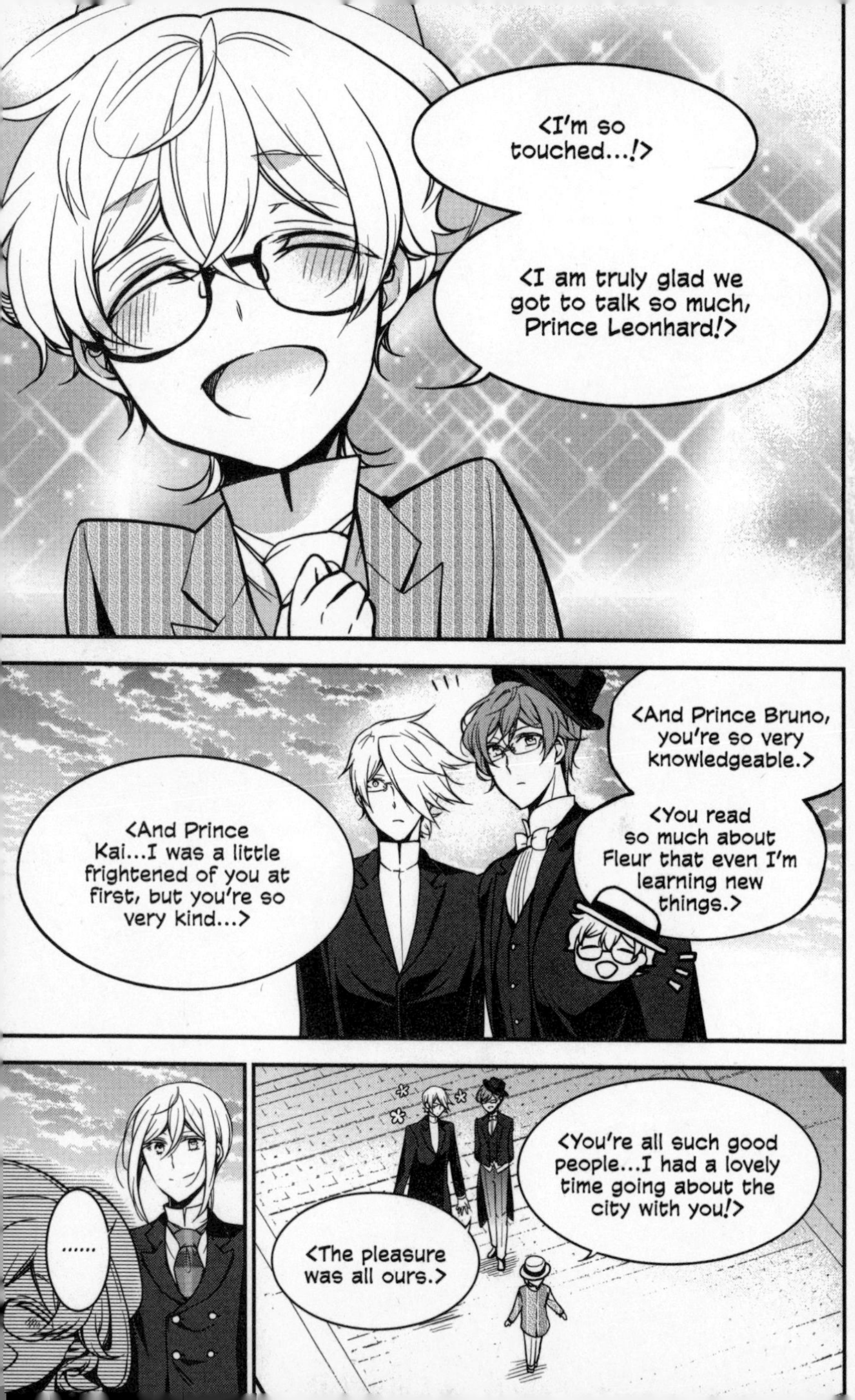
<I'm so touched...!>
<I am truly glad we got to talk so much, Prince Leonhard!>
<And Prince Bruno, you're so very knowledgeable.>
<You read so much about Fleur that even I'm learning new things.>
<And Prince Kai...I was a little frightened of you at first, but you're so very kind...>
<You're all such good people...I had a lovely time going about the city with you!>
<The pleasure was all ours.>
......

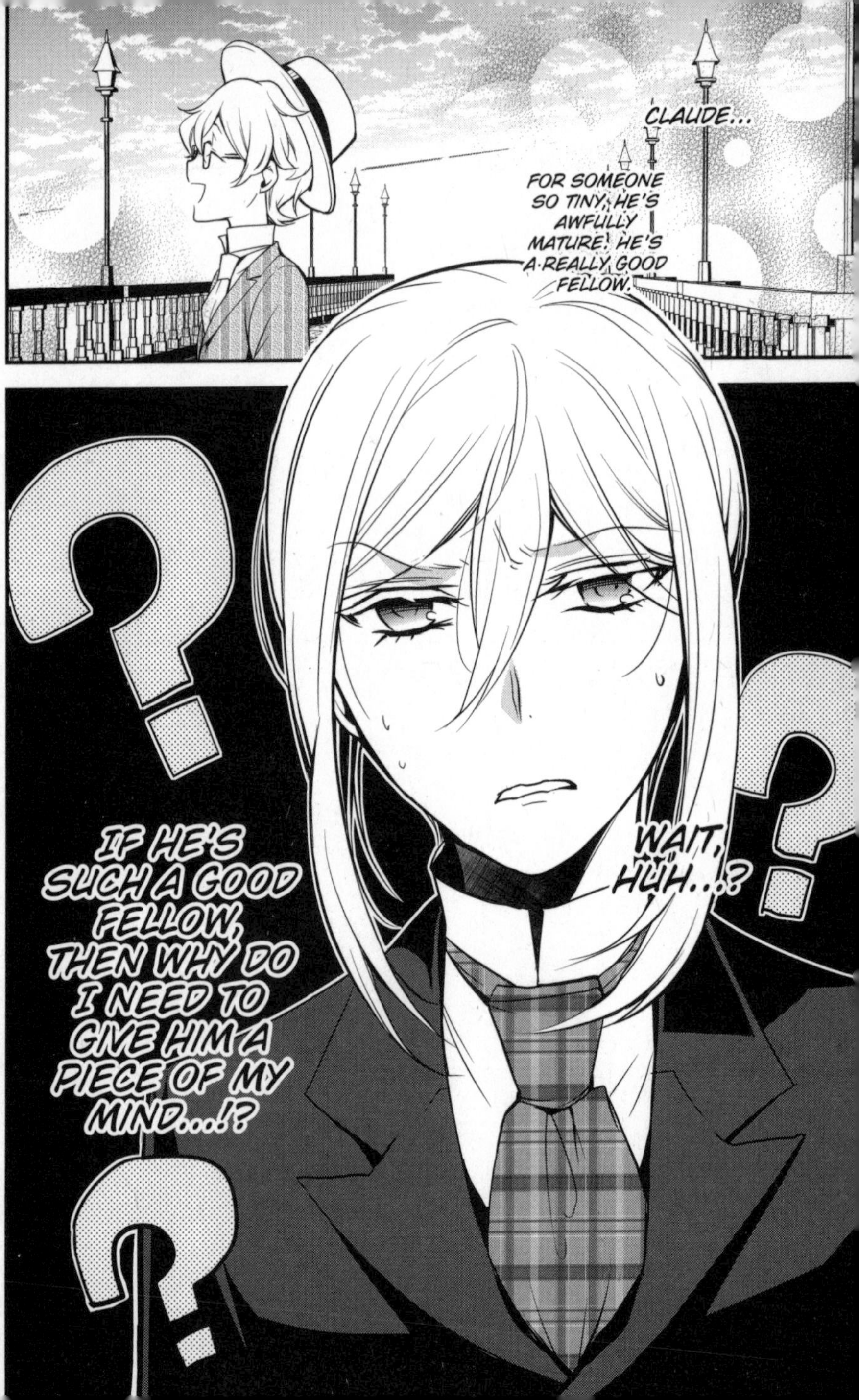
CLAUDE...
FOR SOMEONE SO TINY, HE'S AWFULLY MATURE! HE'S A REALLY GOOD FELLOW.
WAIT, HUH...!?
IF HE'S SUCH A GOOD FELLOW, THEN WHY DO I NEED TO GIVE HIM A PIECE OF MY MIND...!?

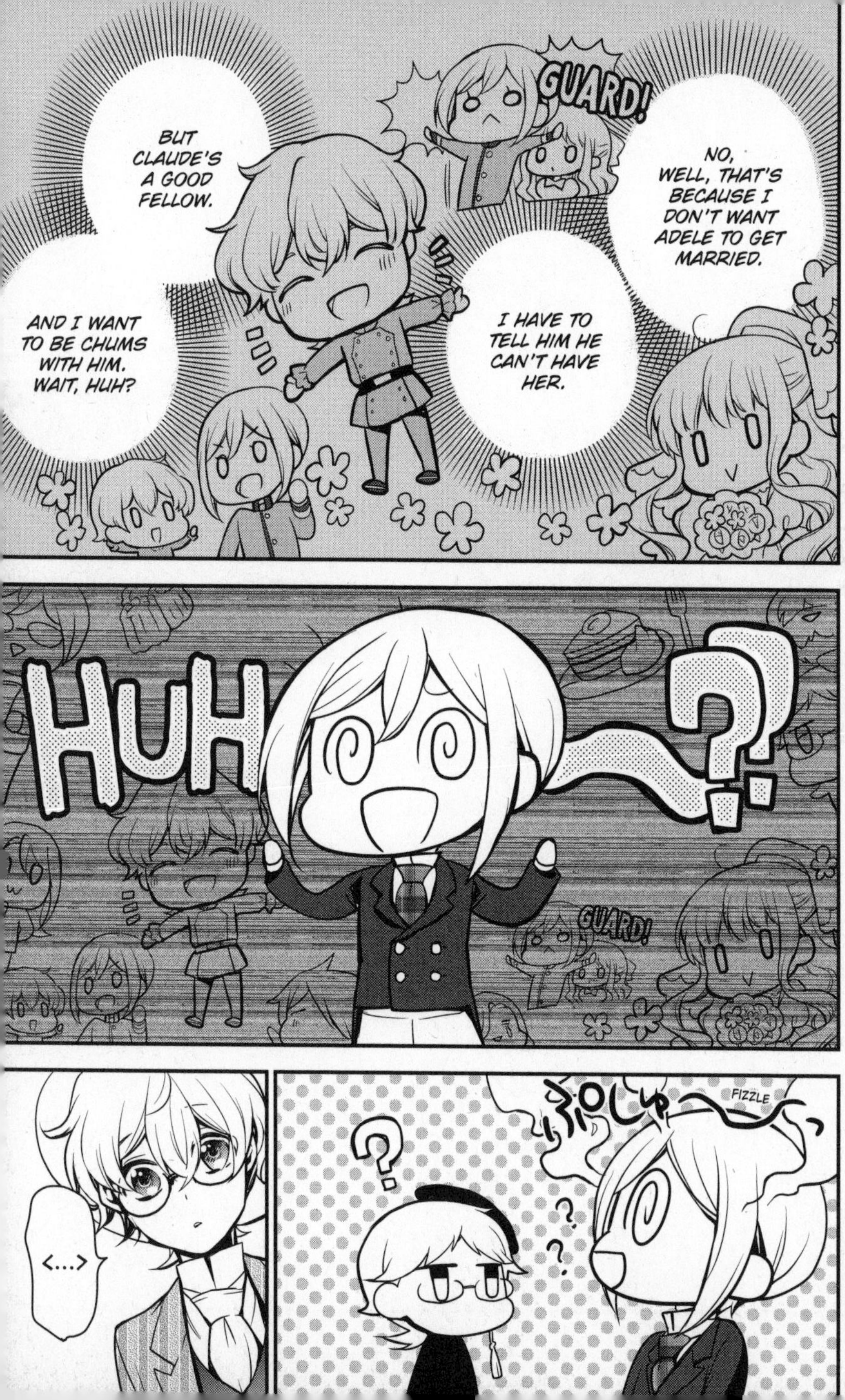

NO, WELL, THAT'S BECAUSE I DON'T WANT ADELE TO GET MARRIED.
GUARD!
I HAVE TO TELL HIM HE CAN'T HAVE HER.
BUT CLAUDE'S A GOOD FELLOW.
AND I WANT TO BE CHUMS WITH HIM. WAIT, HUH?
HUH~??
GUARD!
FIZZLE
?
??
<...>

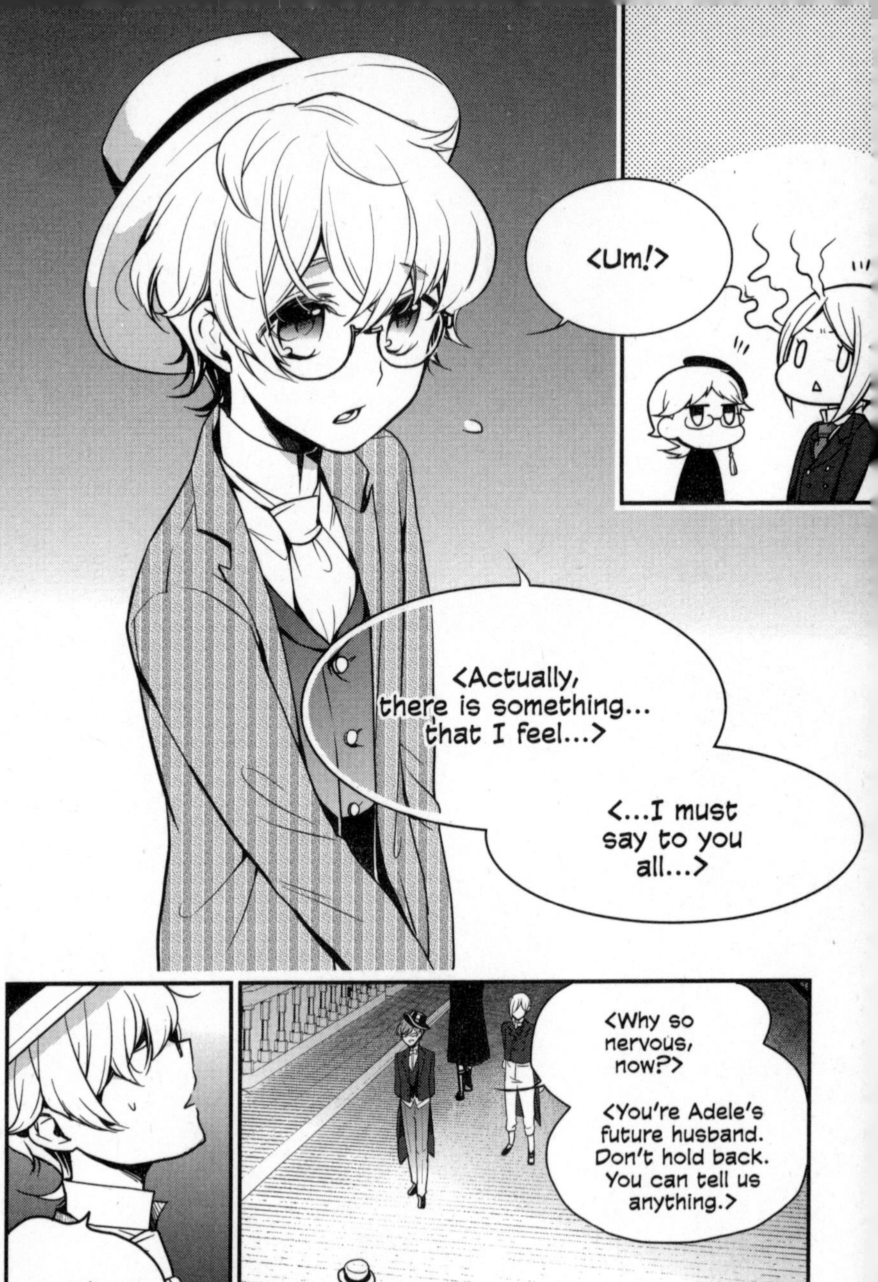
<Um!>
<Actually, there is something... that I feel...>
<...I must say to you all...>
<Why so nervous, now?>
<You're Adele's future husband. Don't hold back. You can tell us anything.>
<...It's...>

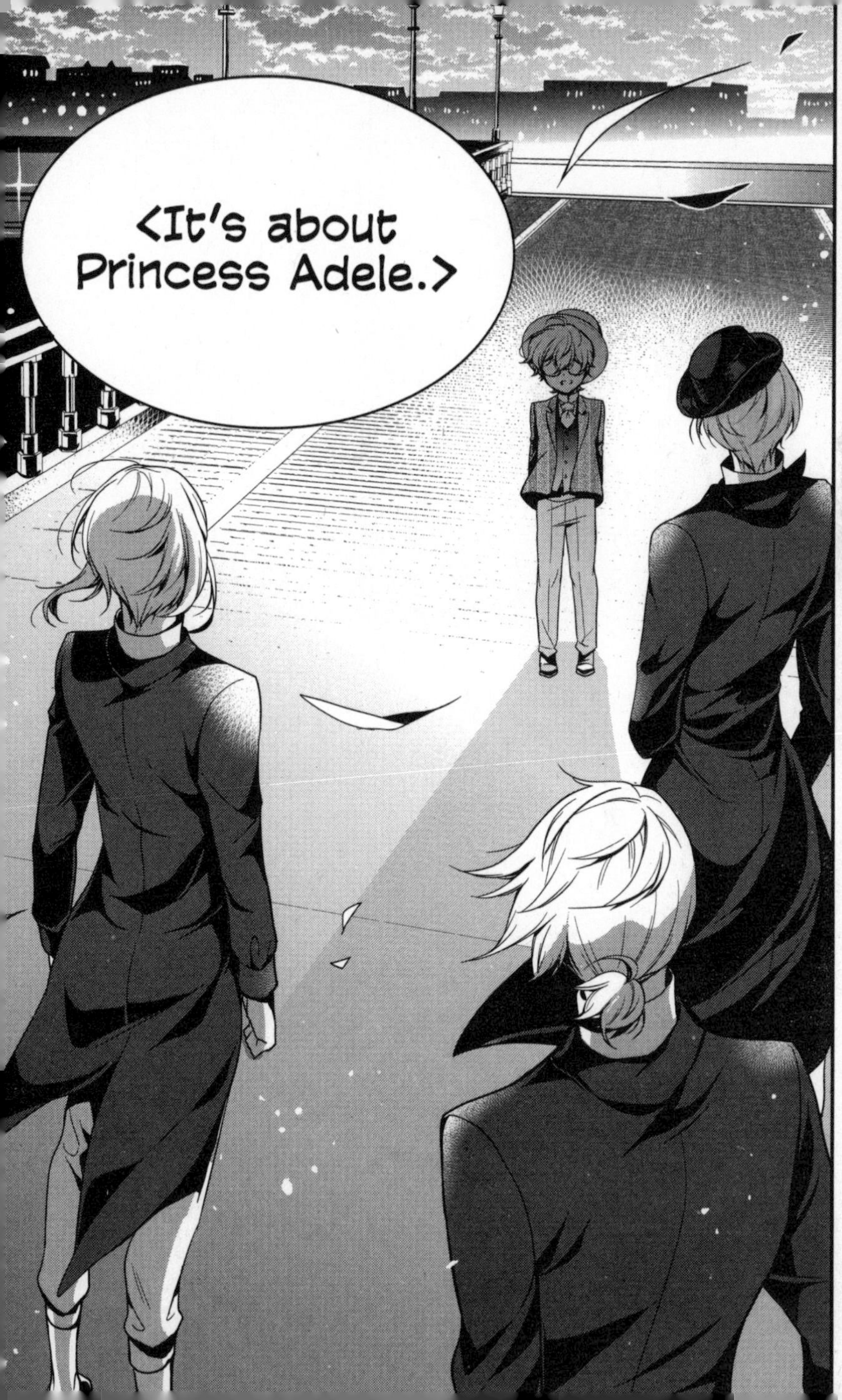
<It's about Princess Adele.>

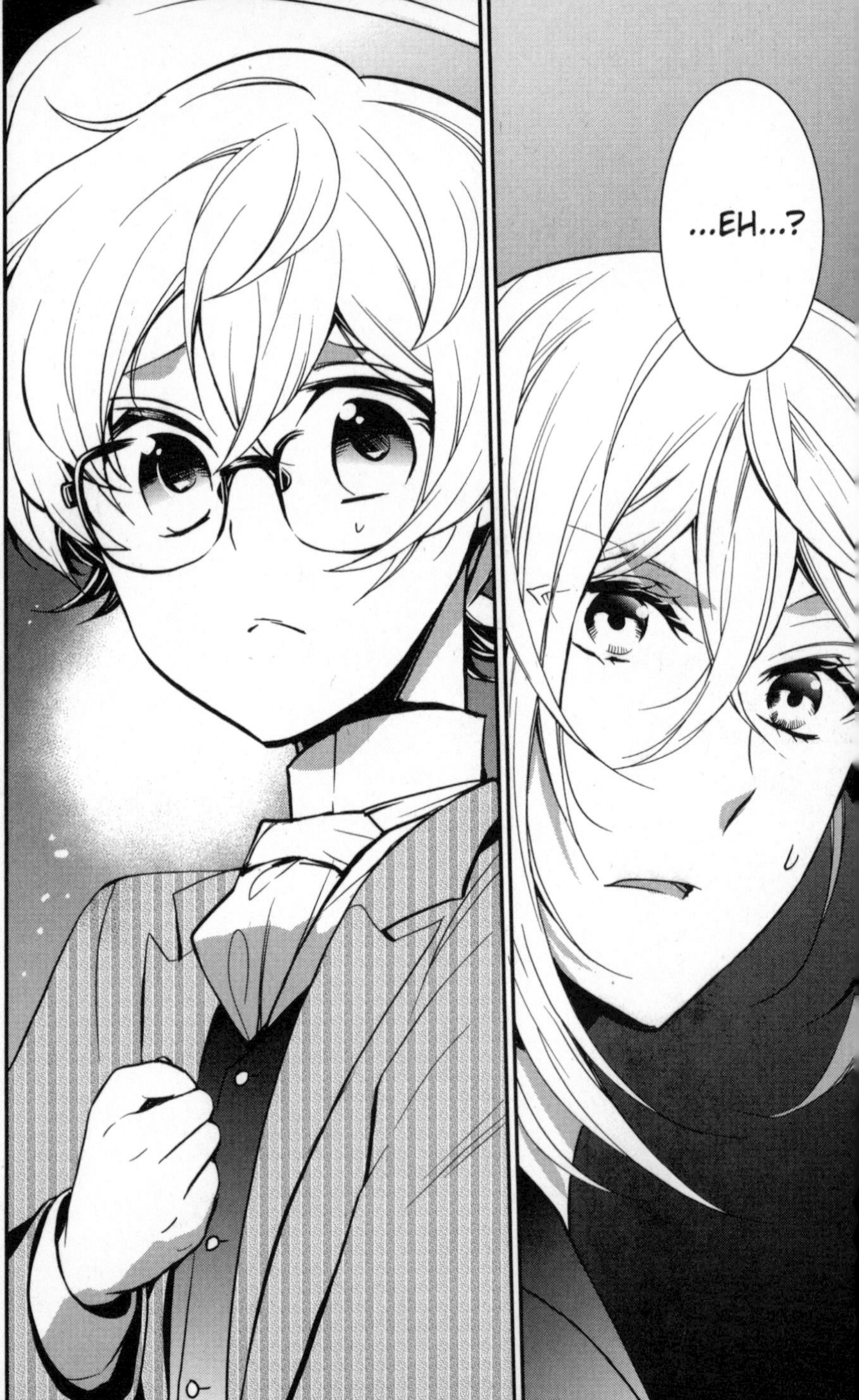
...EH...?

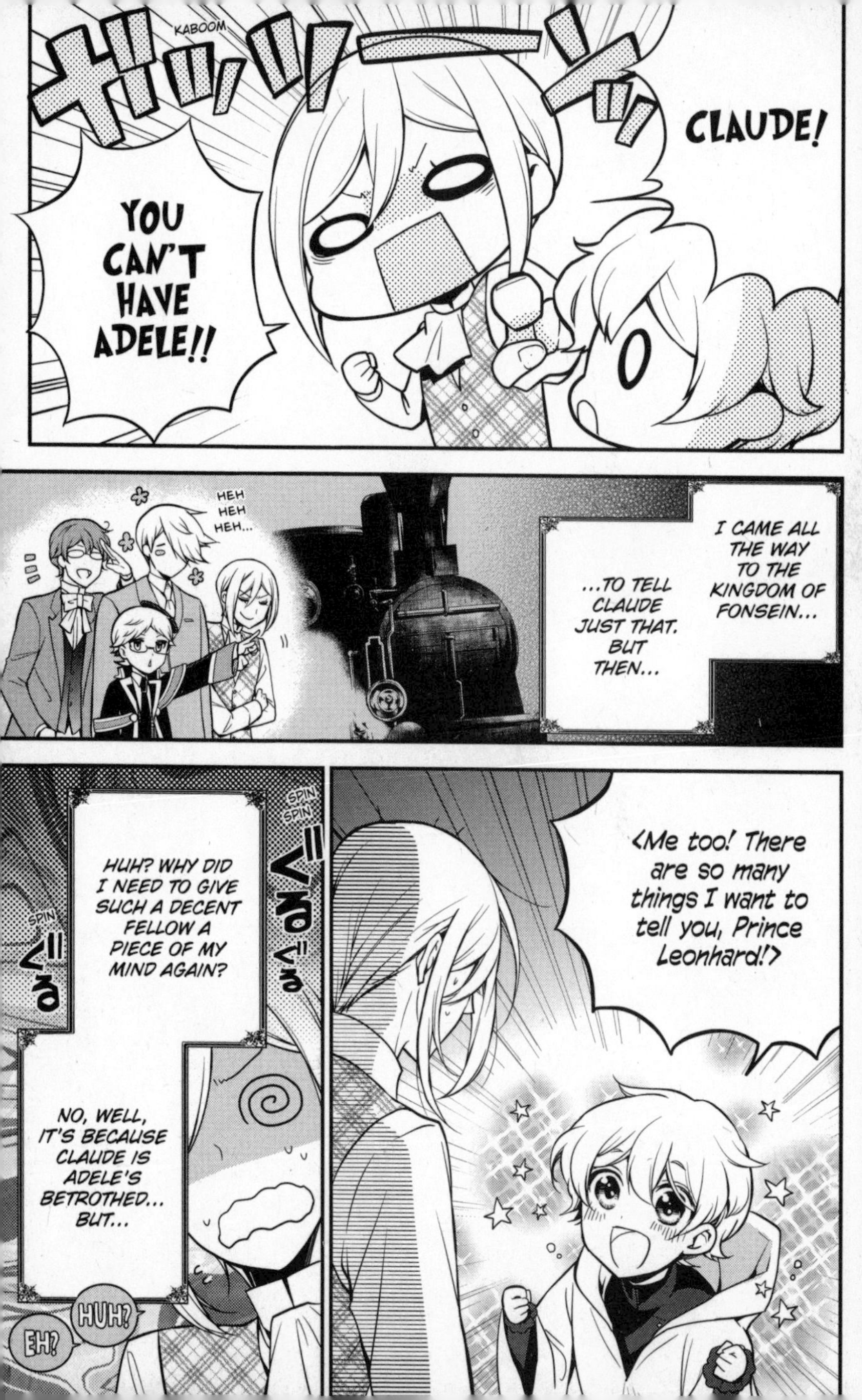
KABOOM
CLAUDE!
YOU CAN'T HAVE ADELE!!
I CAME ALL THE WAY TO THE KINGDOM OF FONSEIN...
...TO TELL CLAUDE JUST THAT. BUT THEN...
HEH HEH HEH...
<Me too! There are so many things I want to tell you, Prince Leonhard!>
SPIN SPIN
HUH? WHY DID I NEED TO GIVE SUCH A DECENT FELLOW A PIECE OF MY MIND AGAIN?
SPIN
NO, WELL, IT'S BECAUSE CLAUDE IS ADELE'S BETROTHED... BUT...
HUH?
EH?

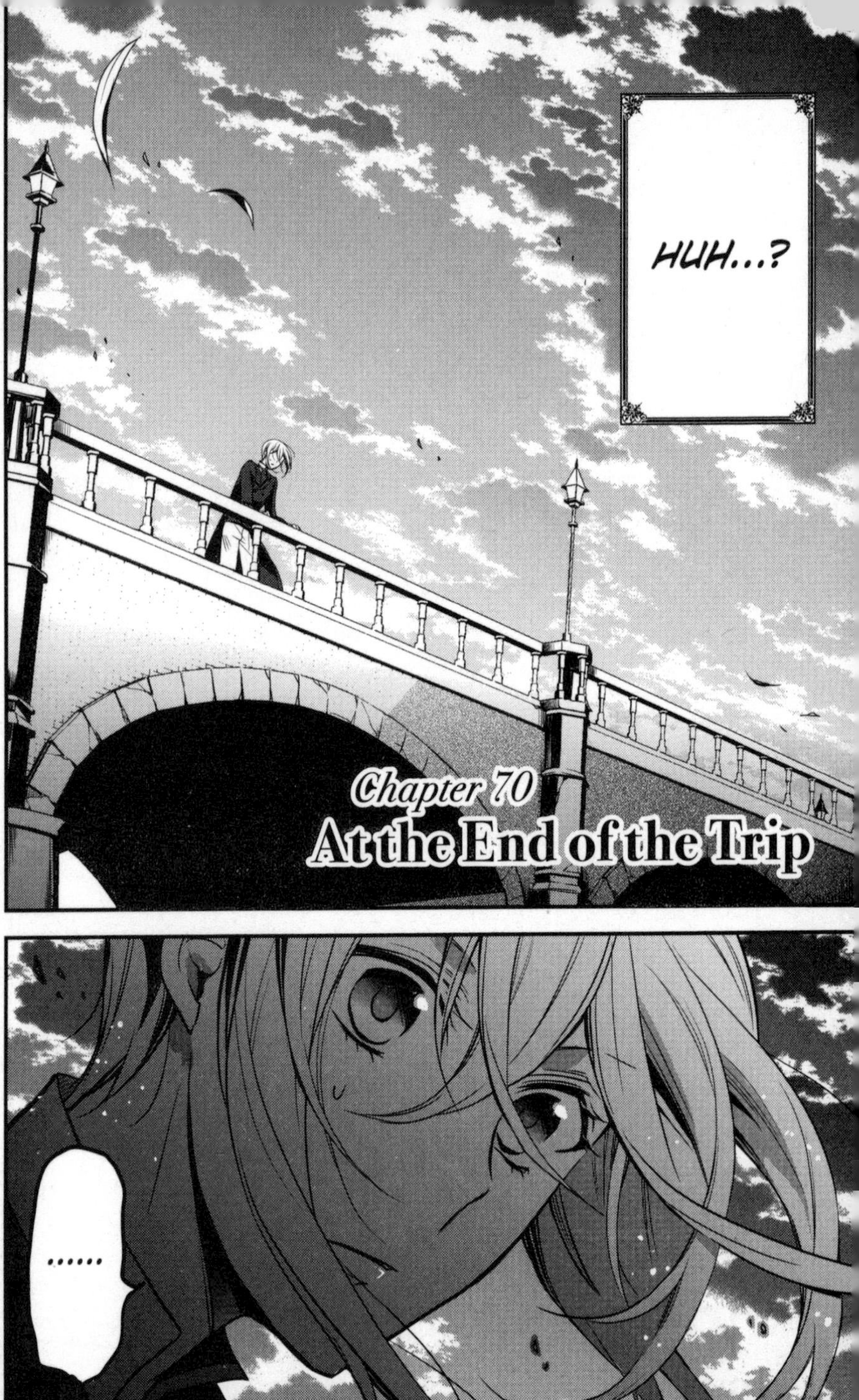
HUH...?
Chapter 70
At the End of the Trip
......

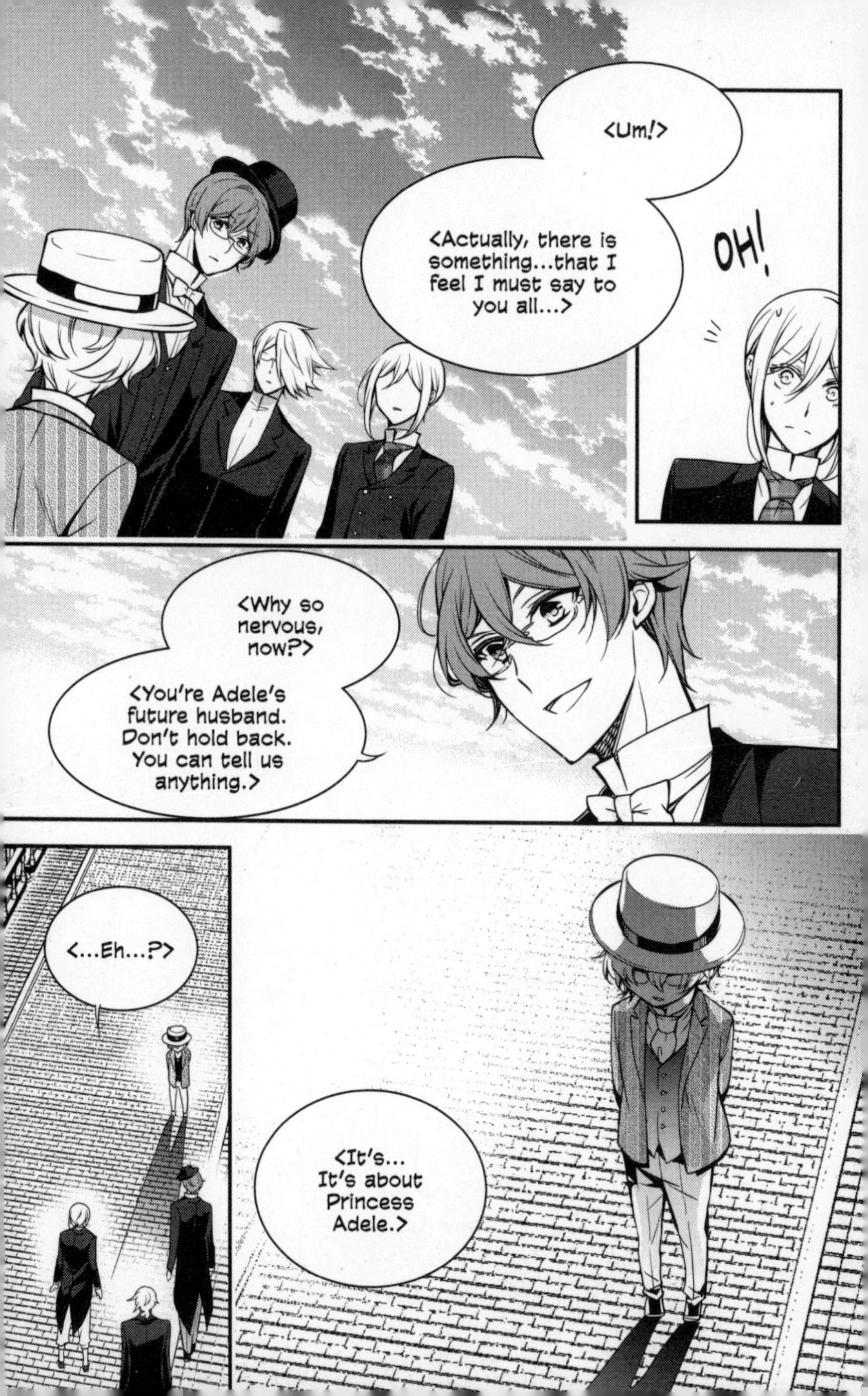
<Um!>
OH!
<Actually, there is something...that I feel I must say to you all...>
<Why so nervous, now?>
<You're Adele's future husband. Don't hold back. You can tell us anything.>
<It's... It's about Princess Adele.>
<...Eh...?>

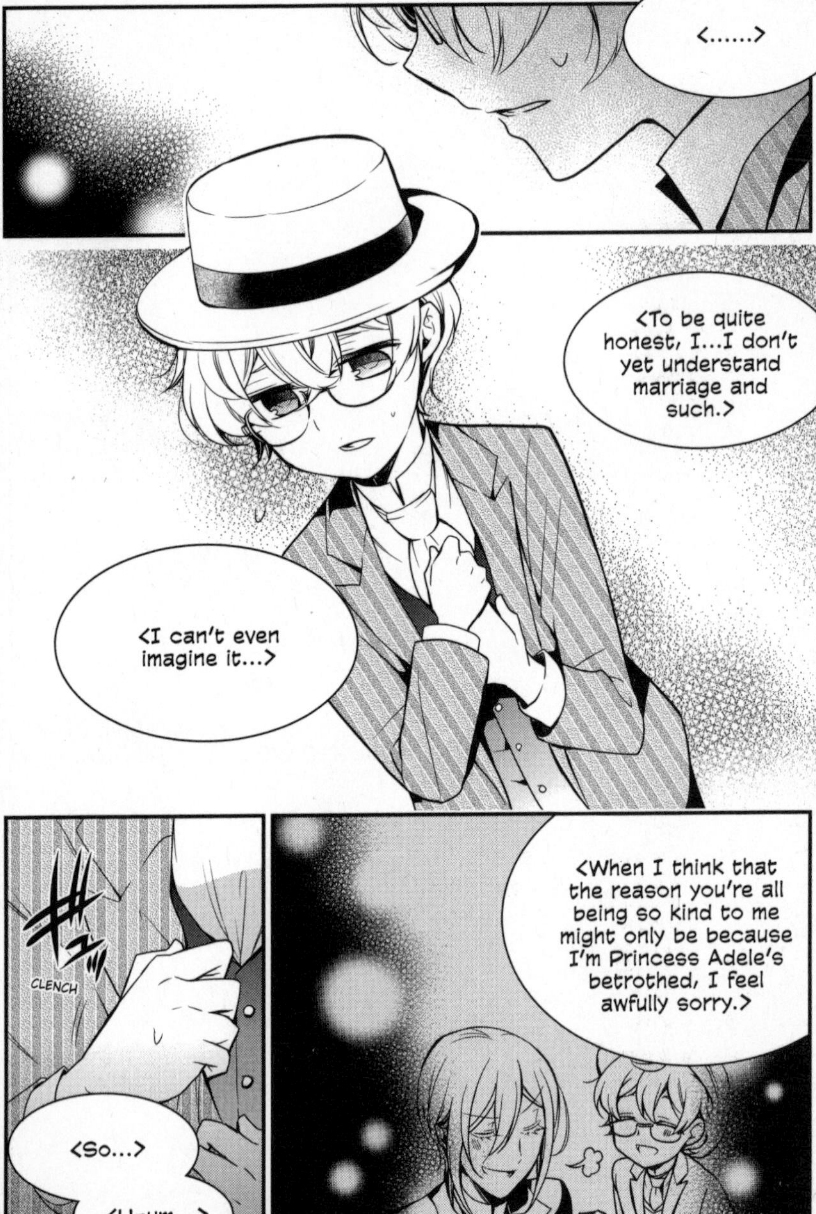
<......>
<To be quite honest, I...I don't yet understand marriage and such.>
<I can't even imagine it...>
<When I think that the reason you're all being so kind to me might only be because I'm Princess Adele's betrothed, I feel awfully sorry.>
CLENCH
<So...>
<U-um...>

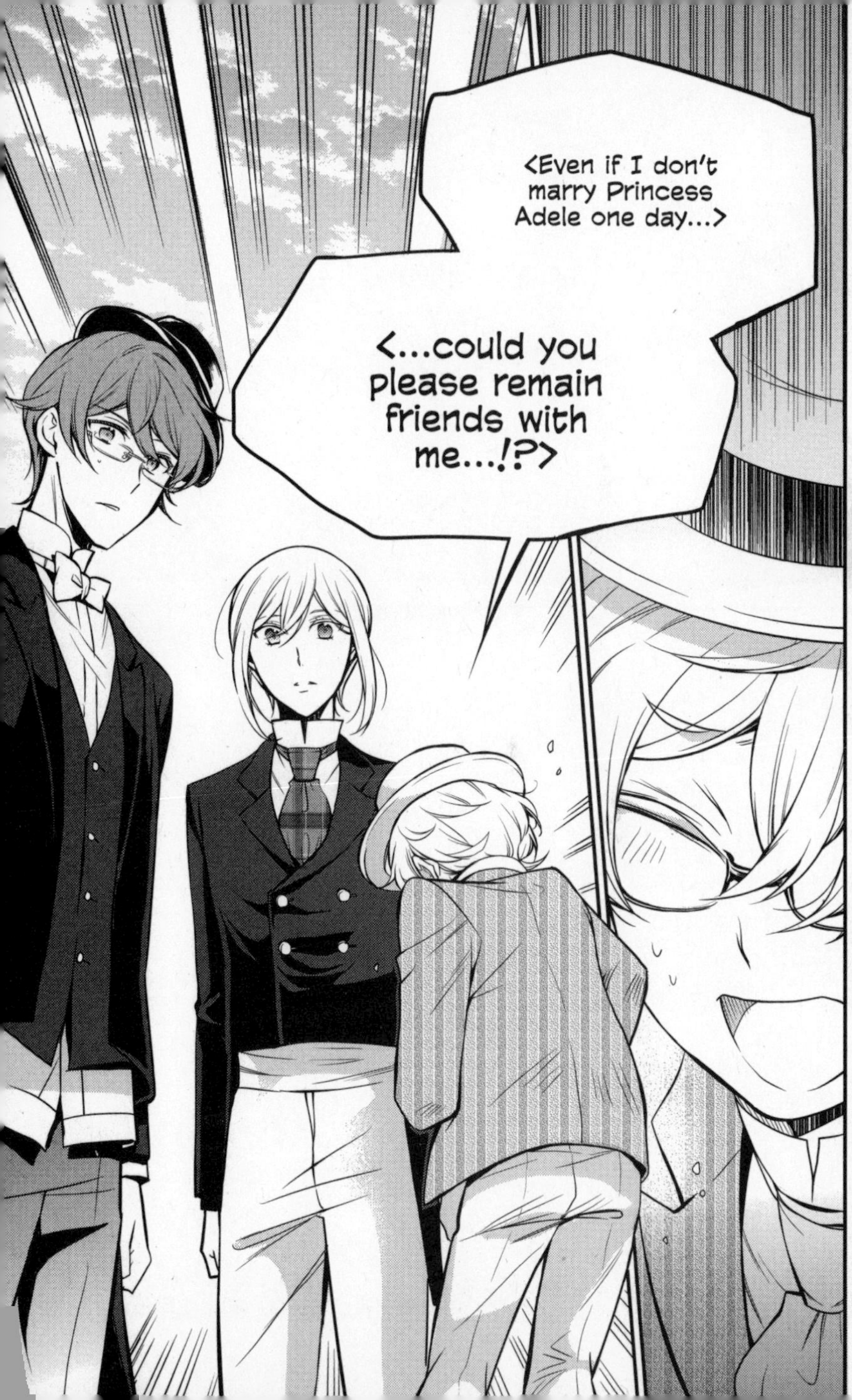
<Even if I don't marry Princess Adele one day...>
<...could you please remain friends with me...!?>

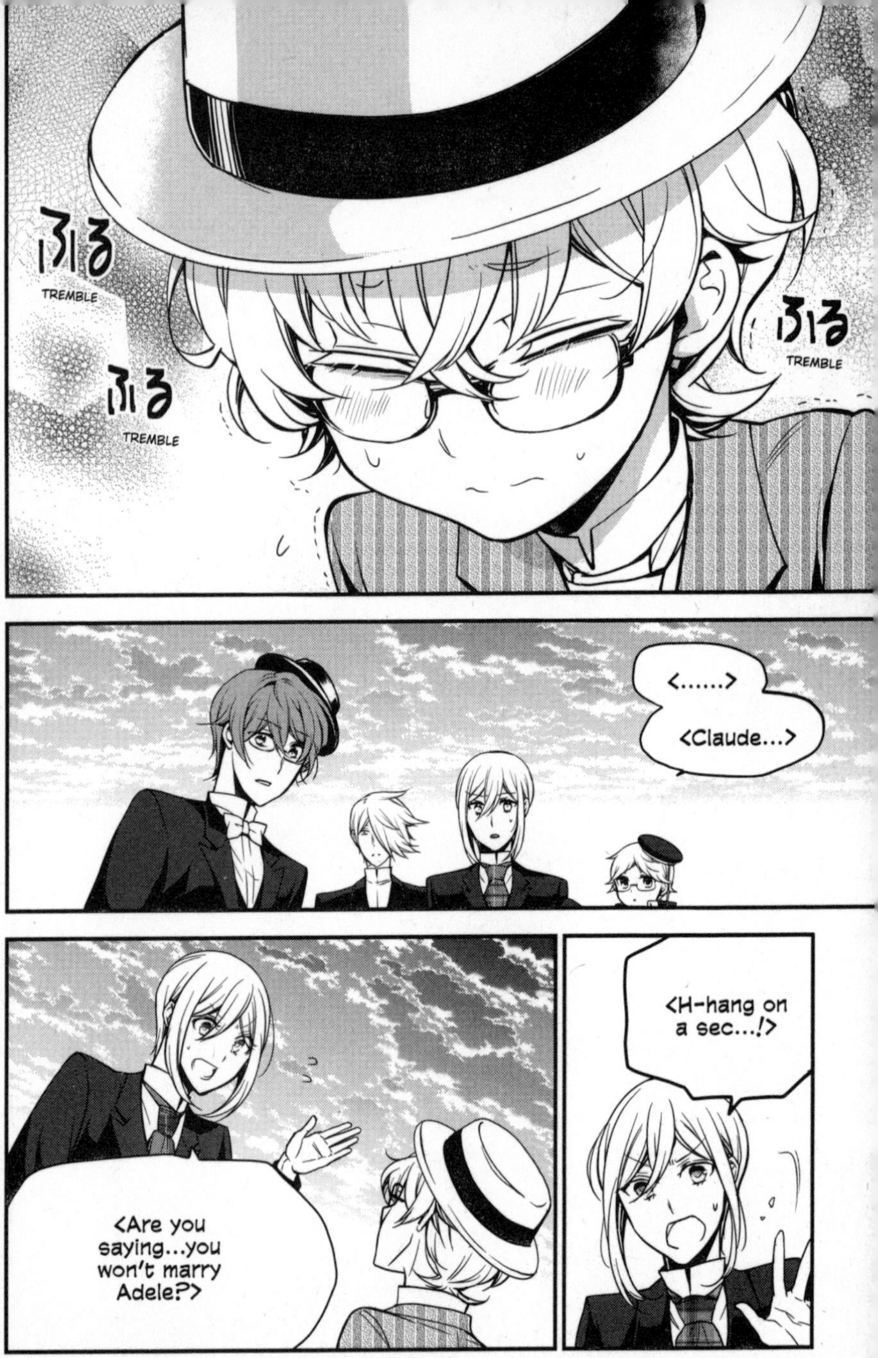
ふる
TREMBLE
ふる
TREMBLE
ふる
TREMBLE
<......>
<Claude...>
<H-hang on a sec...!>
<Are you saying...you won't marry Adele?>

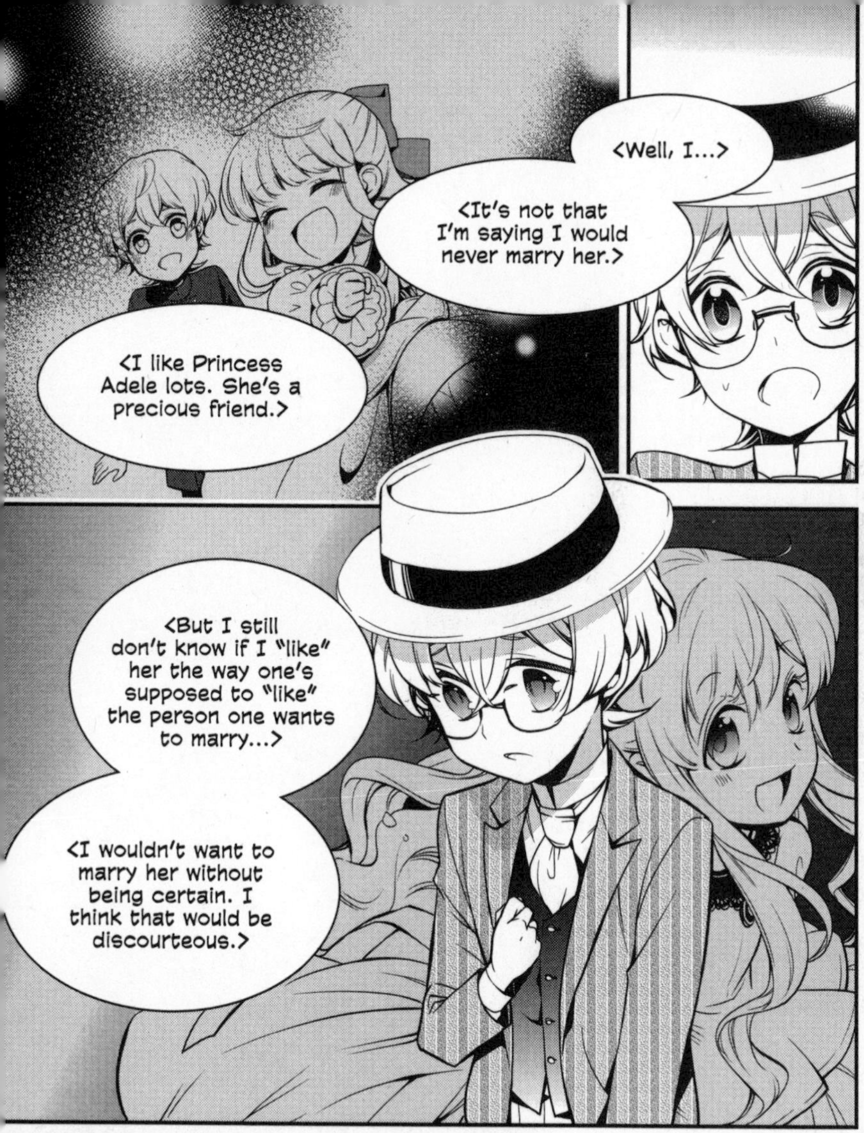
<Well, I...>
<It's not that I'm saying I would never marry her.>
<I like Princess Adele lots. She's a precious friend.>
<But I still don't know if I "like" her the way one's supposed to "like" the person one wants to marry...>
<I wouldn't want to marry her without being certain. I think that would be discourteous.>

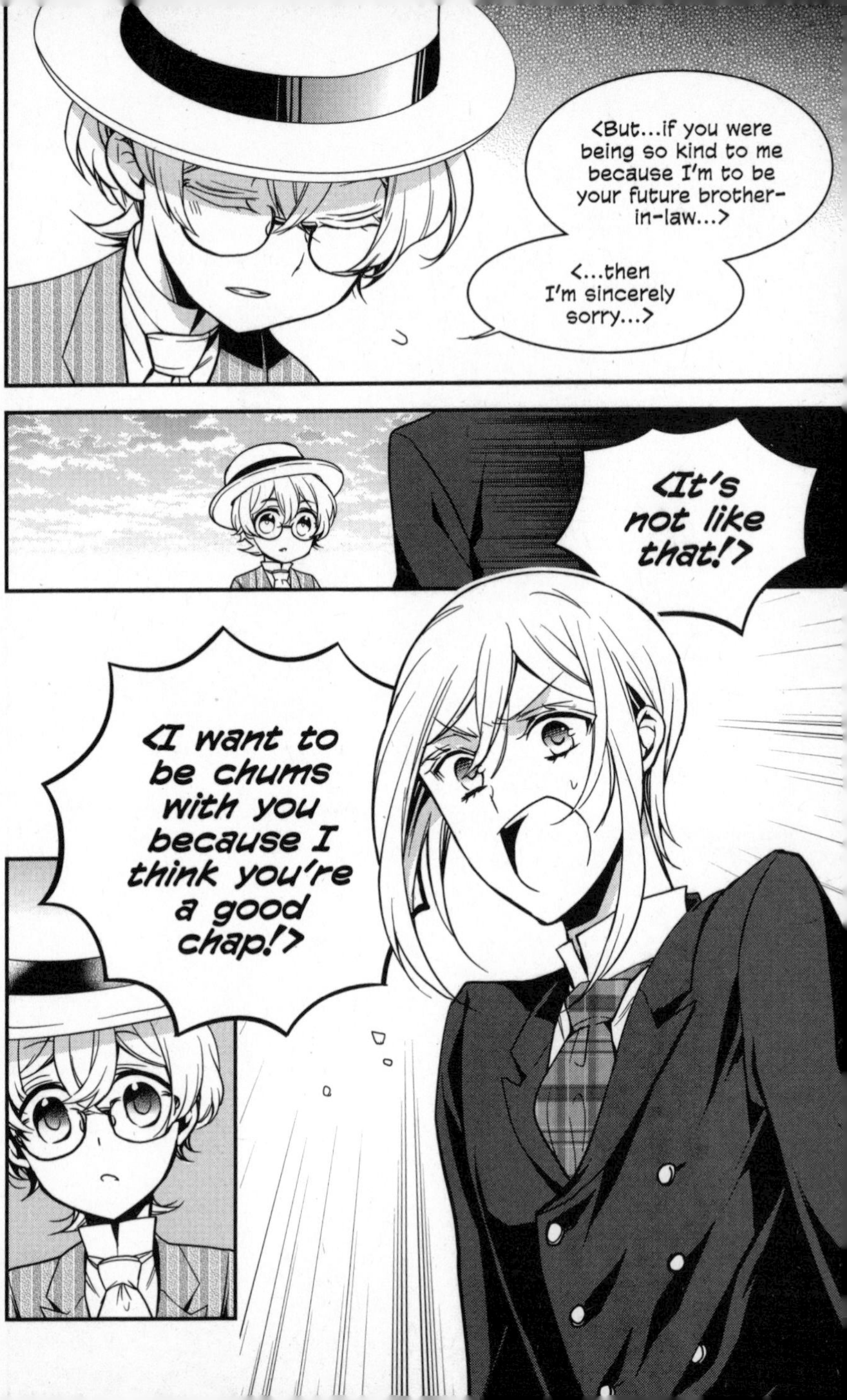
<But...if you were being so kind to me because I'm to be your future brother-in-law...>
<...then I'm sincerely sorry...>
<It's not like that!>
<I want to be chums with you because I think you're a good chap!>

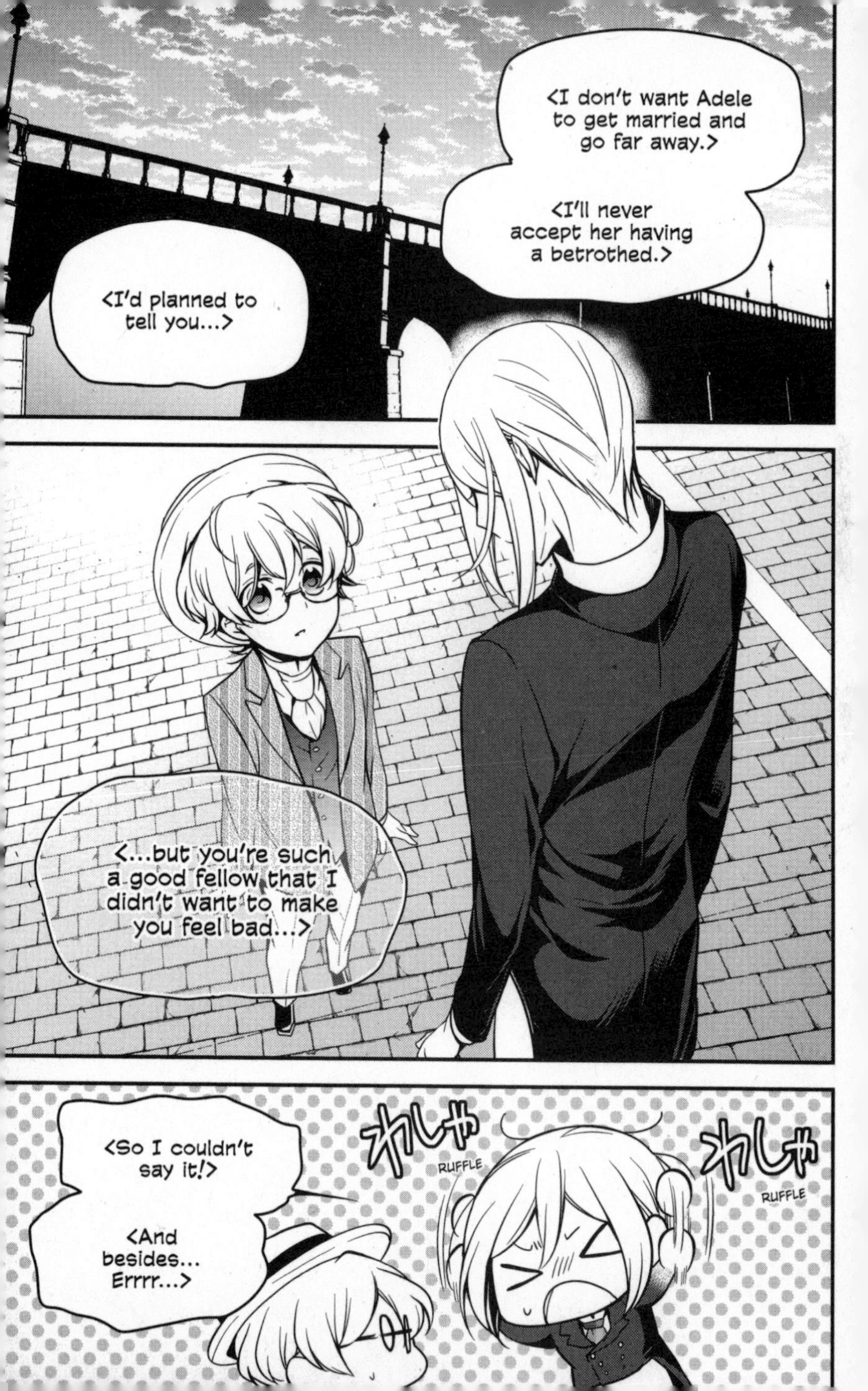
<I don't want Adele to get married and go far away.>
<I'll never accept her having a betrothed.>
<I'd planned to tell you...>
<...but you're such a good fellow that I didn't want to make you feel bad...>
わしゃ
RUFFLE
わしゃ
RUFFLE
<So I couldn't say it!>
<And besides... Errrr...>

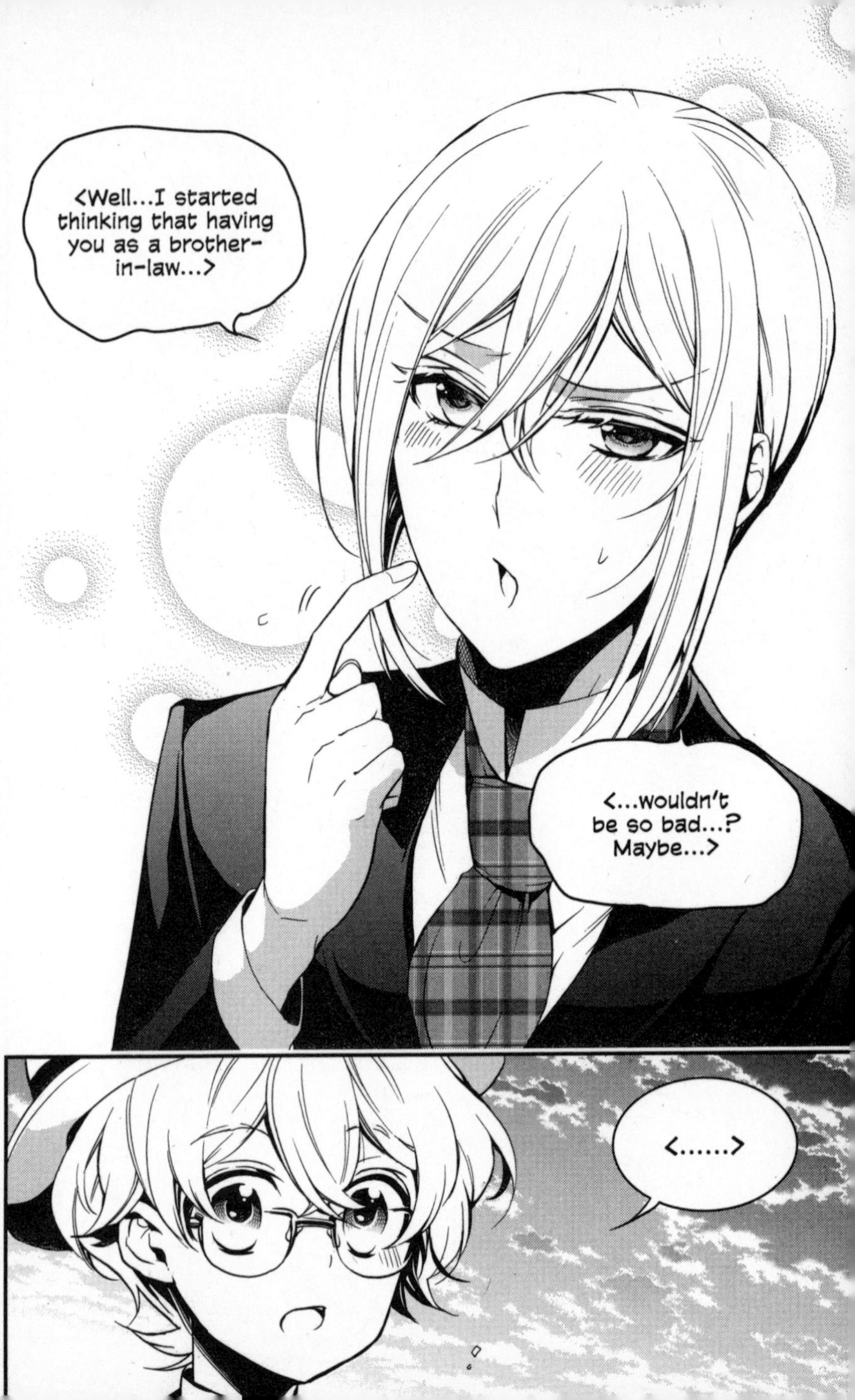
<Well...I started thinking that having you as a brother-in-law...>
<...wouldn't be so bad...? Maybe...>
<......>

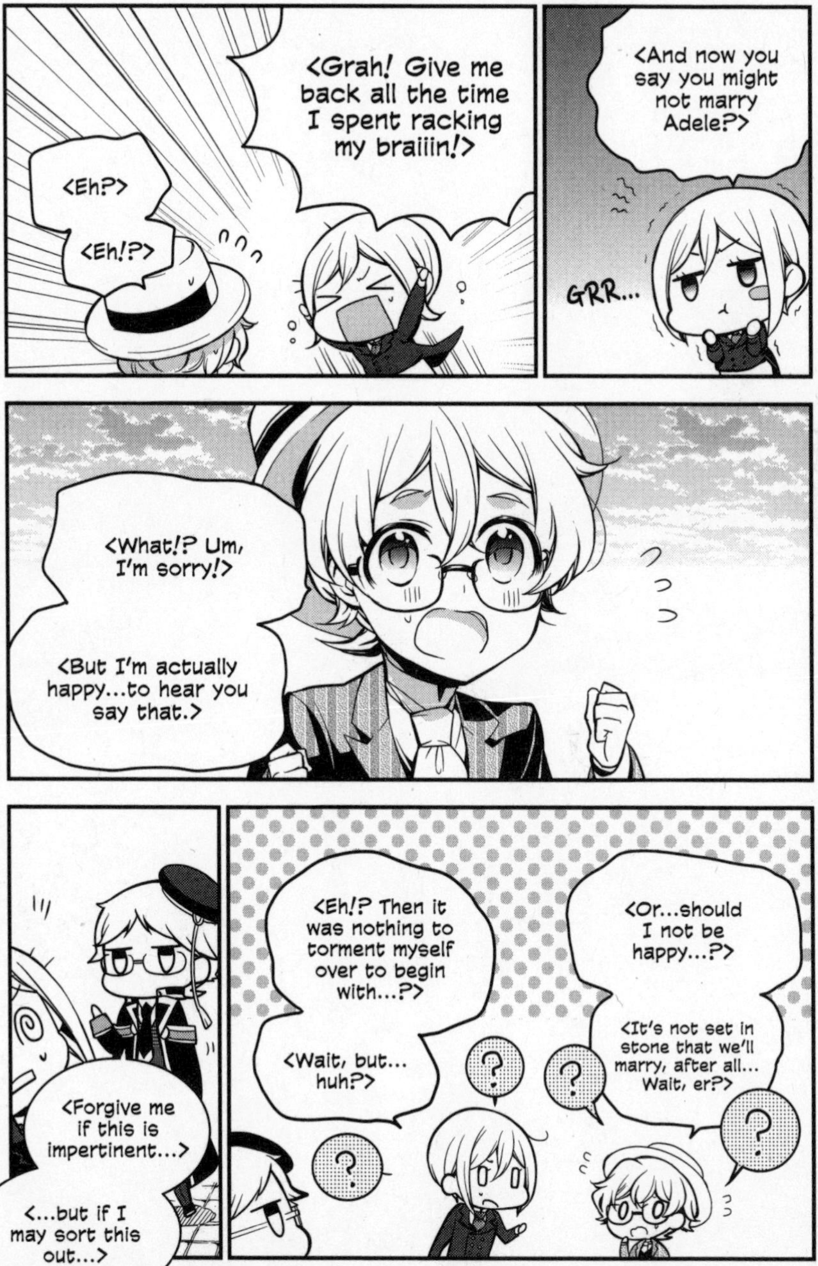
<And now you say you might not marry Adele?>
GRR...
<Grah! Give me back all the time I spent racking my braiiin!>
<Eh?>
<Eh!?>
<What!? Um, I'm sorry!>
<But I'm actually happy...to hear you say that.>
<Or...should I not be happy...?>
<It's not set in stone that we'll marry, after all... Wait, er?>
<Eh!? Then it was nothing to torment myself over to begin with...?>
<Wait, but... huh?>
<Forgive me if this is impertinent...>
<...but if I may sort this out...>

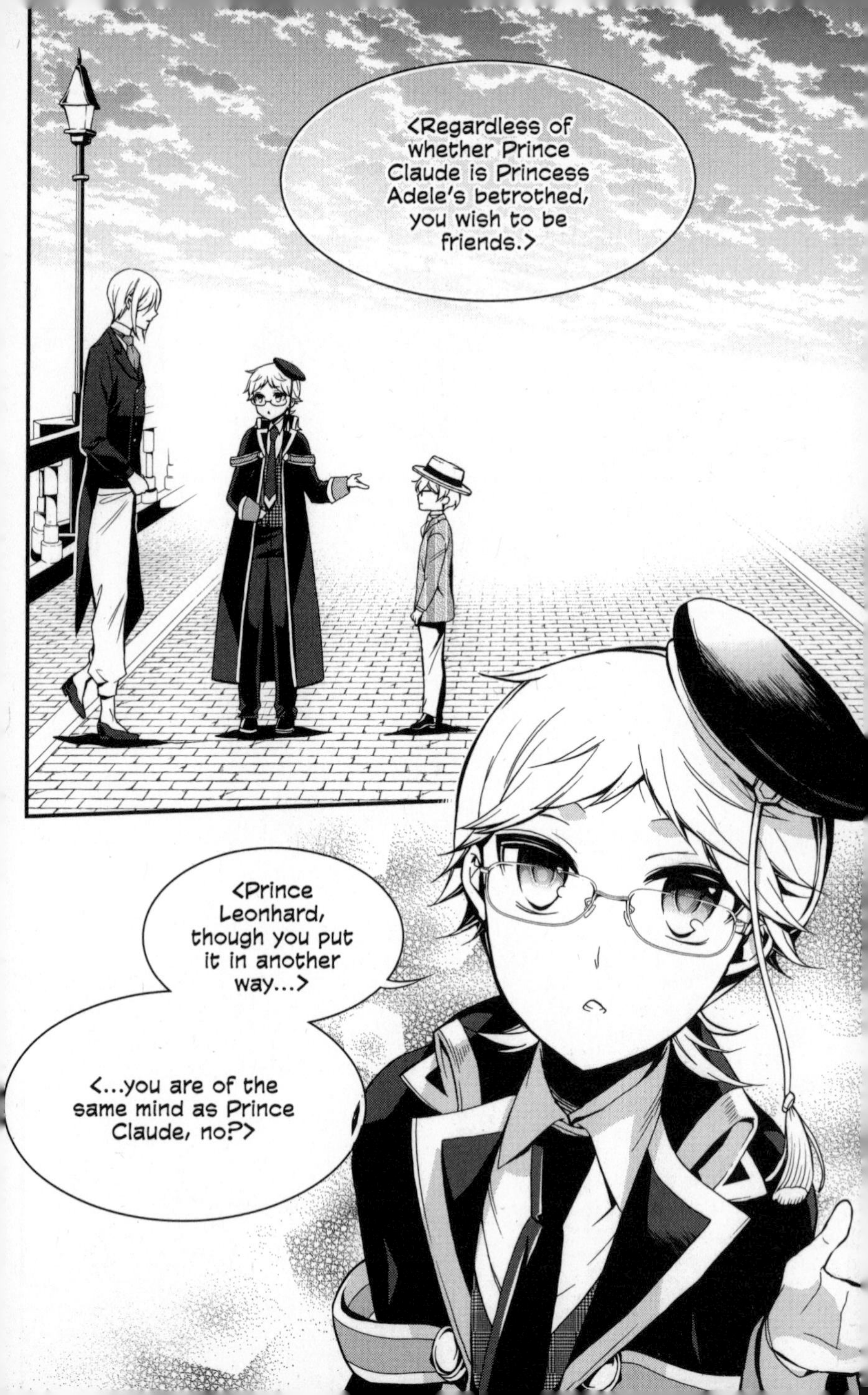
<Regardless of whether Prince Claude is Princess Adele's betrothed, you wish to be friends.>
<Prince Leonhard, though you put it in another way...>
<...you are of the same mind as Prince Claude, no?>

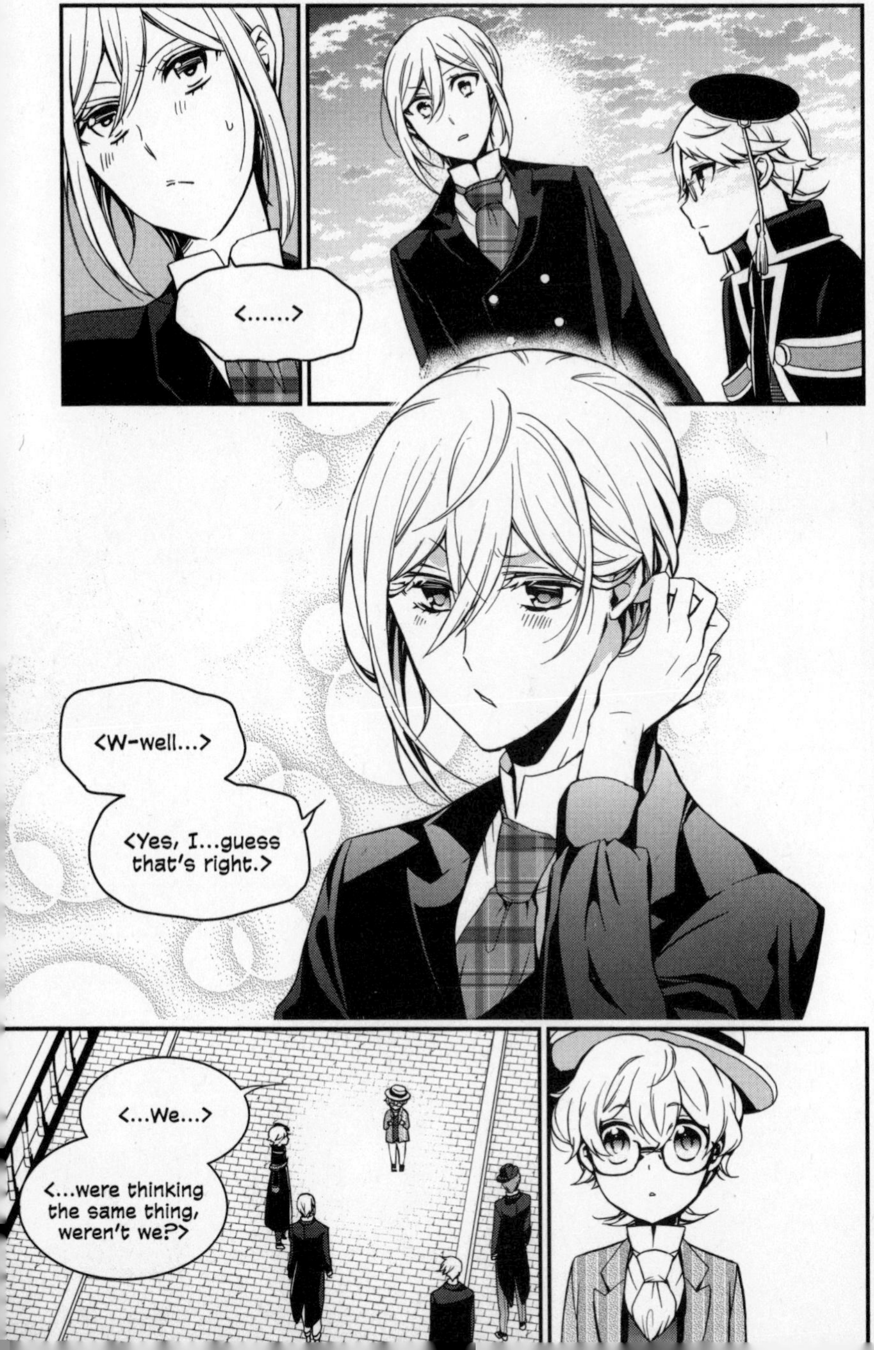
<......>
<W-well...>
<Yes, I...guess that's right.>
<...We...>
<...were thinking the same thing, weren't we?>

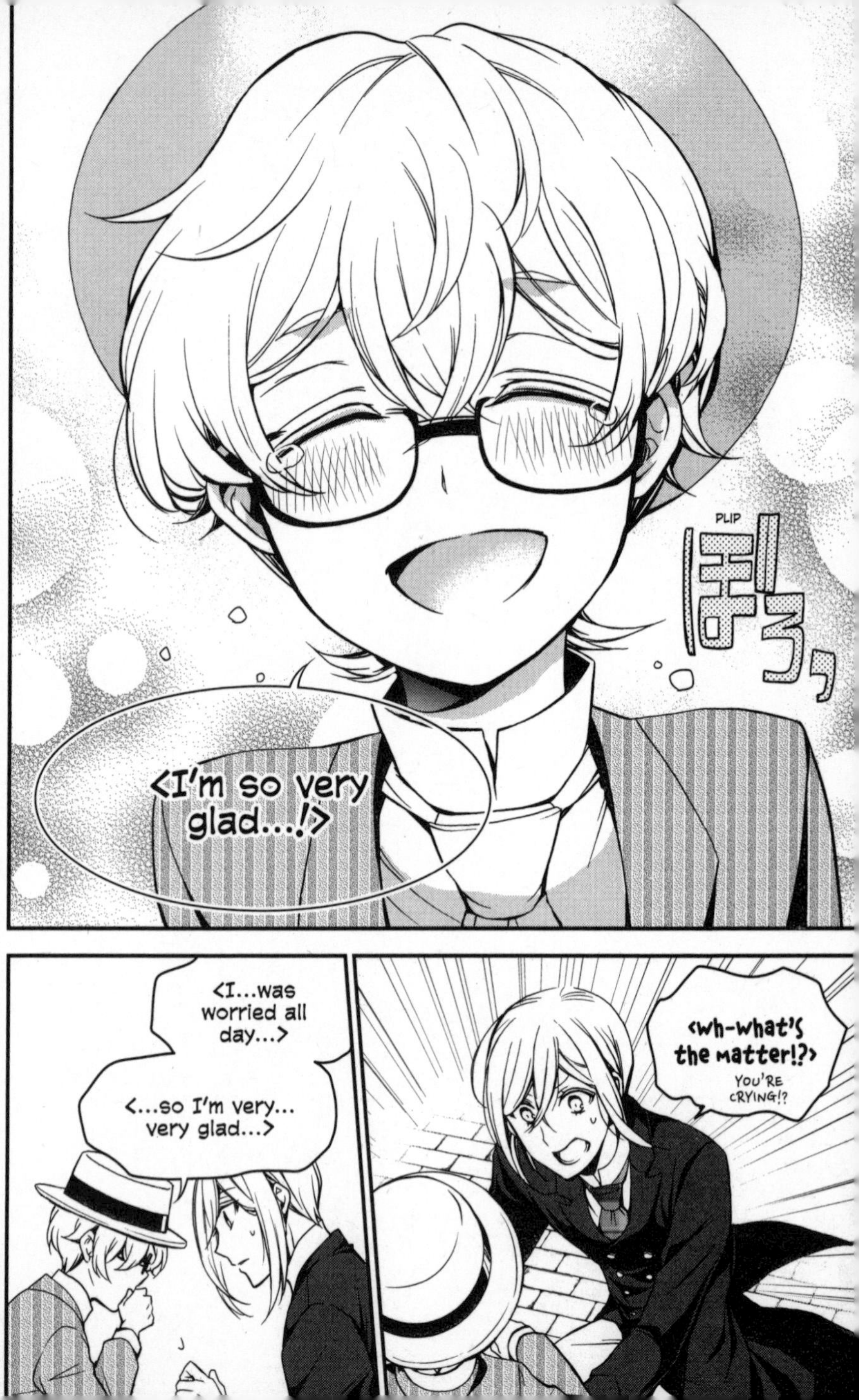
PLIP
<I'm so very glad...!>
‹wh-what's the matter!?›
YOU'RE CRYING!?
<I...was worried all day...>
<...so I'm very... very glad...>

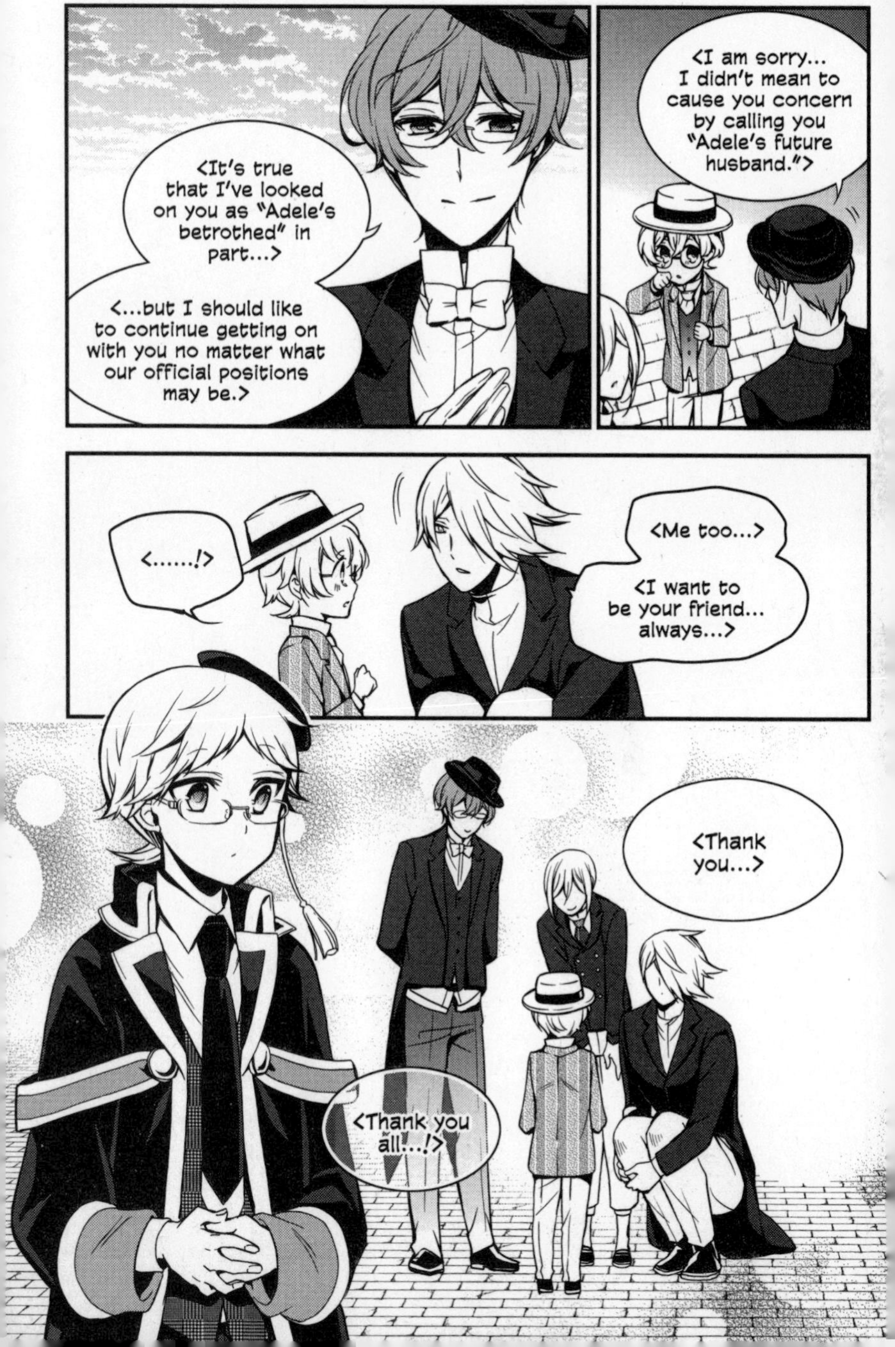

<I am sorry... I didn't mean to cause you concern by calling you "Adele's future husband.">
<It's true that I've looked on you as "Adele's betrothed" in part...>
<...but I should like to continue getting on with you no matter what our official positions may be.>
<Me too...>
<I want to be your friend... always...>
<......!>
<Thank you...>
<Thank you all...!>

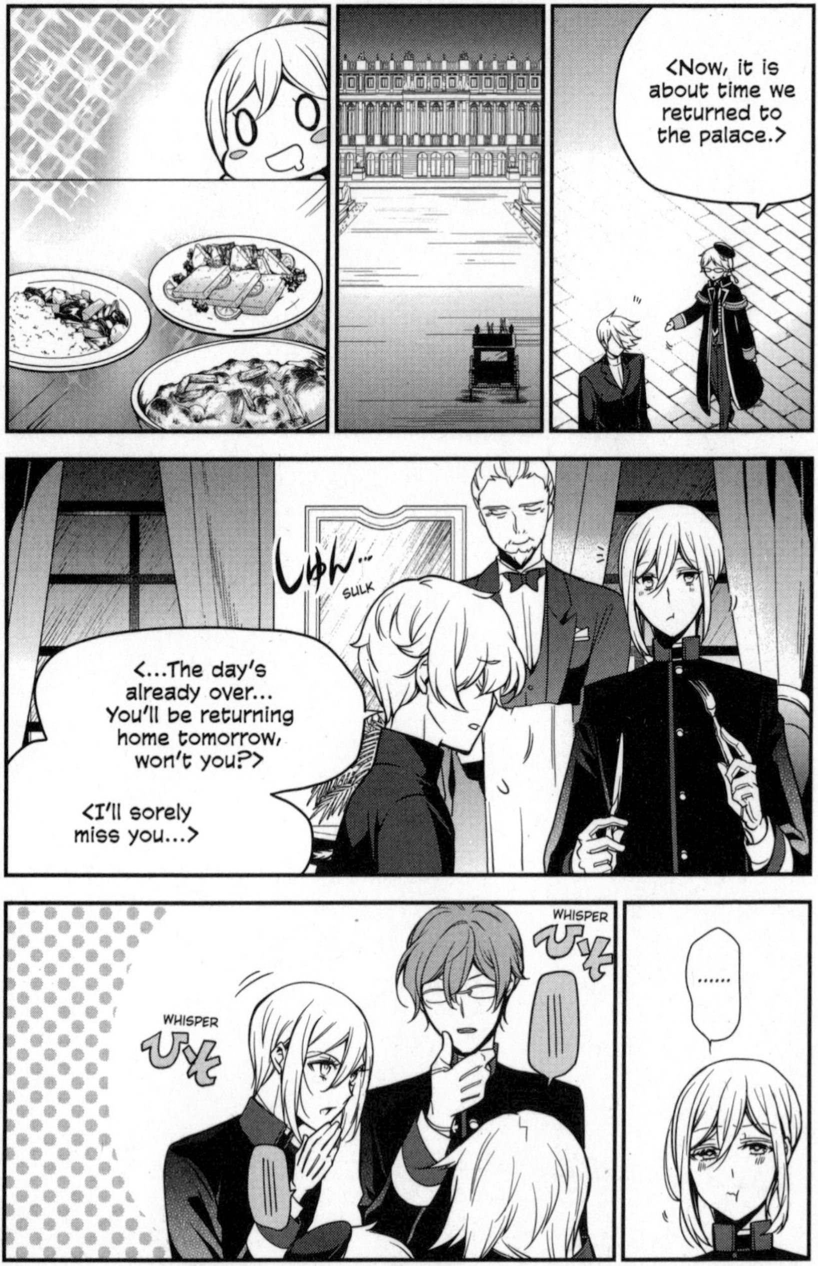
<Now, it is about time we returned to the palace.>
しゅん…
SULK
<...The day's already over... You'll be returning home tomorrow, won't you?>
<I'll sorely miss you...>
......
WHISPER
ひそ
WHISPER
ひそ

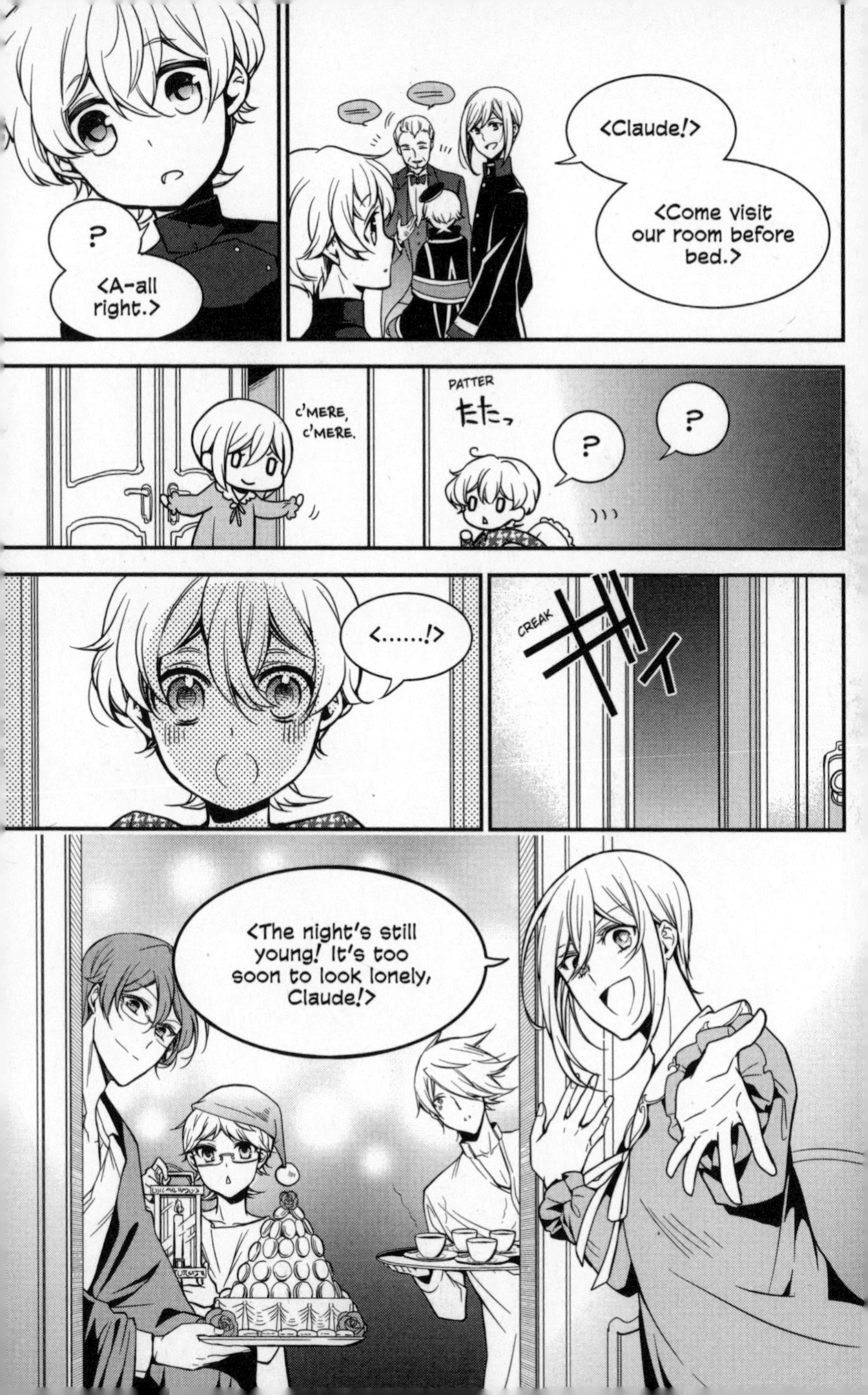
<Claude!>
<Come visit our room before bed.>
?
<A-all right.>
PATTER
たたっ
?
?
C'MERE, C'MERE.
CREAK
ギィ
<......!>
<The night's still young! It's too soon to look lonely, Claude!>

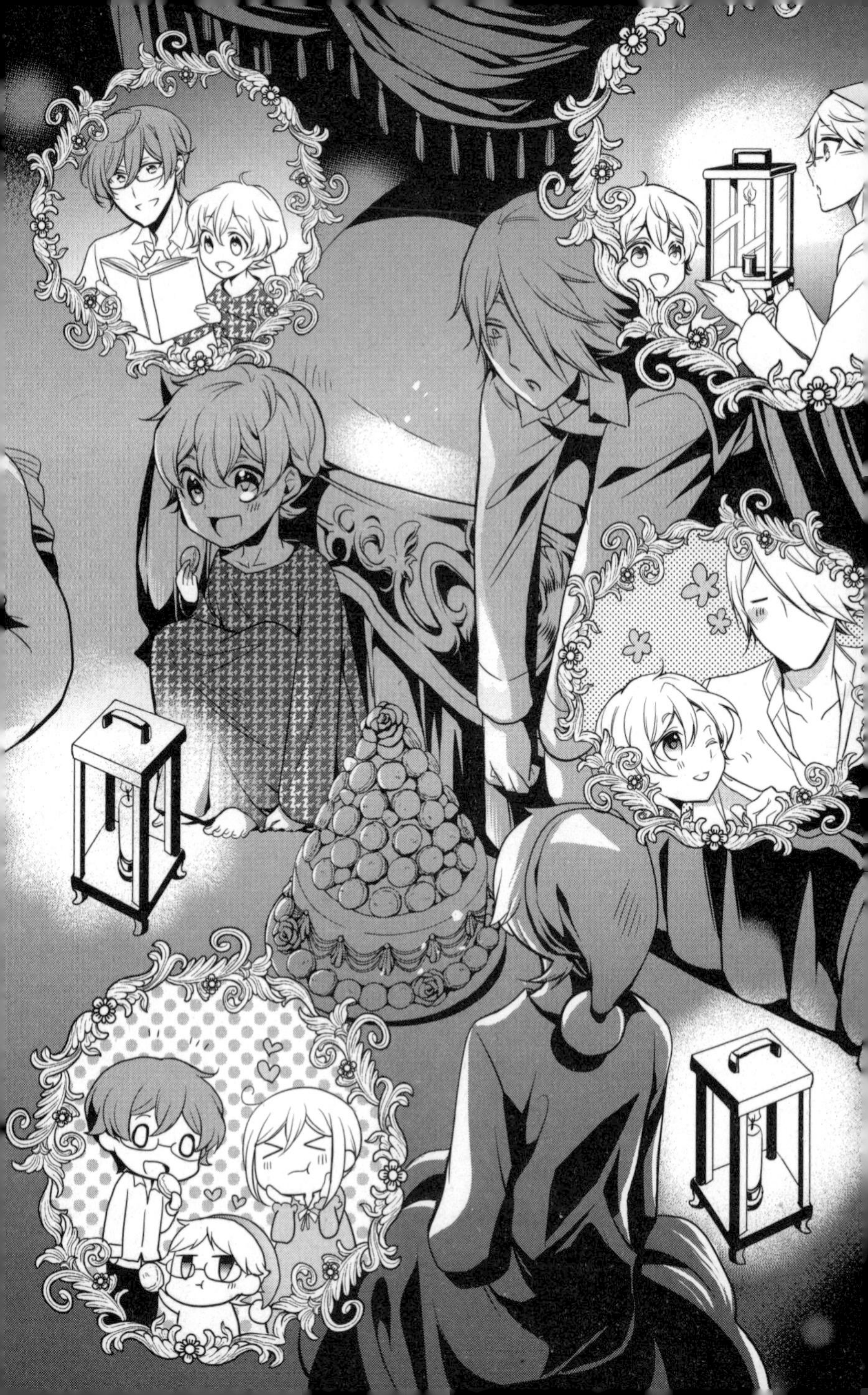

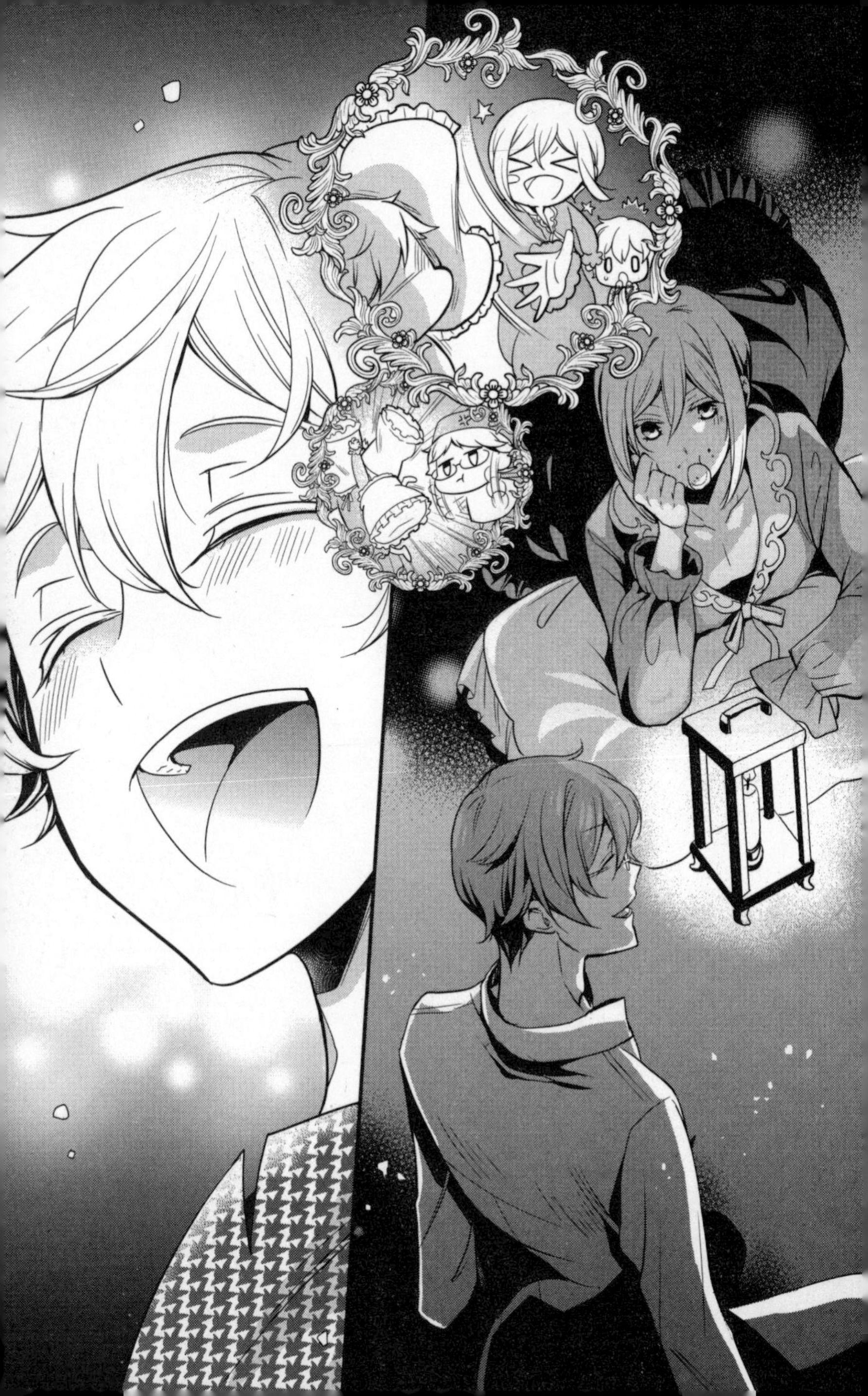

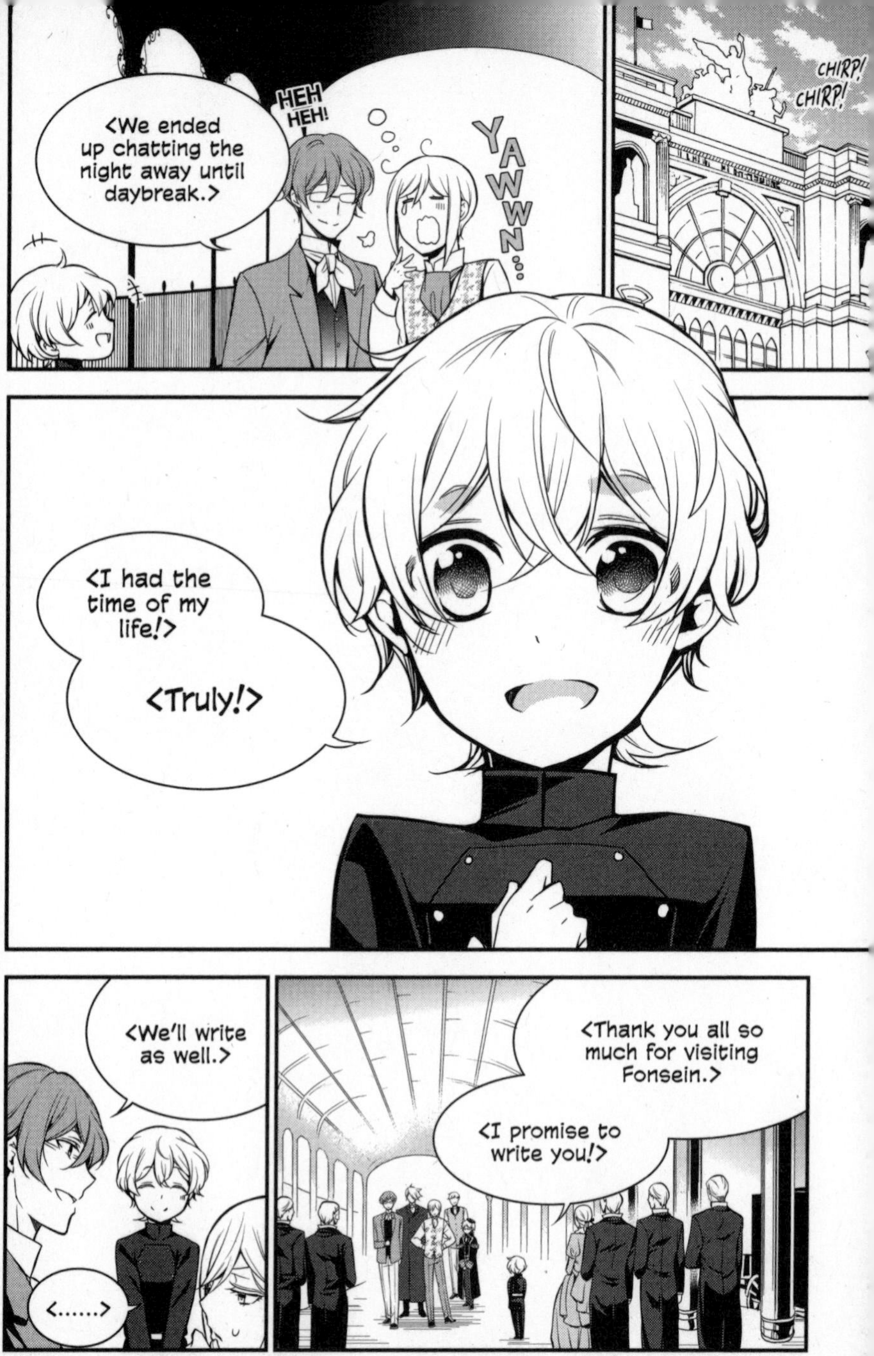
CHIRP! CHIRP!
YAWWN...
HEH HEH!
<We ended up chatting the night away until daybreak.>
<I had the time of my life!>
<Truly!>
<Thank you all so much for visiting Fonsein.>
<I promise to write you!>
<We'll write as well.>
<......>

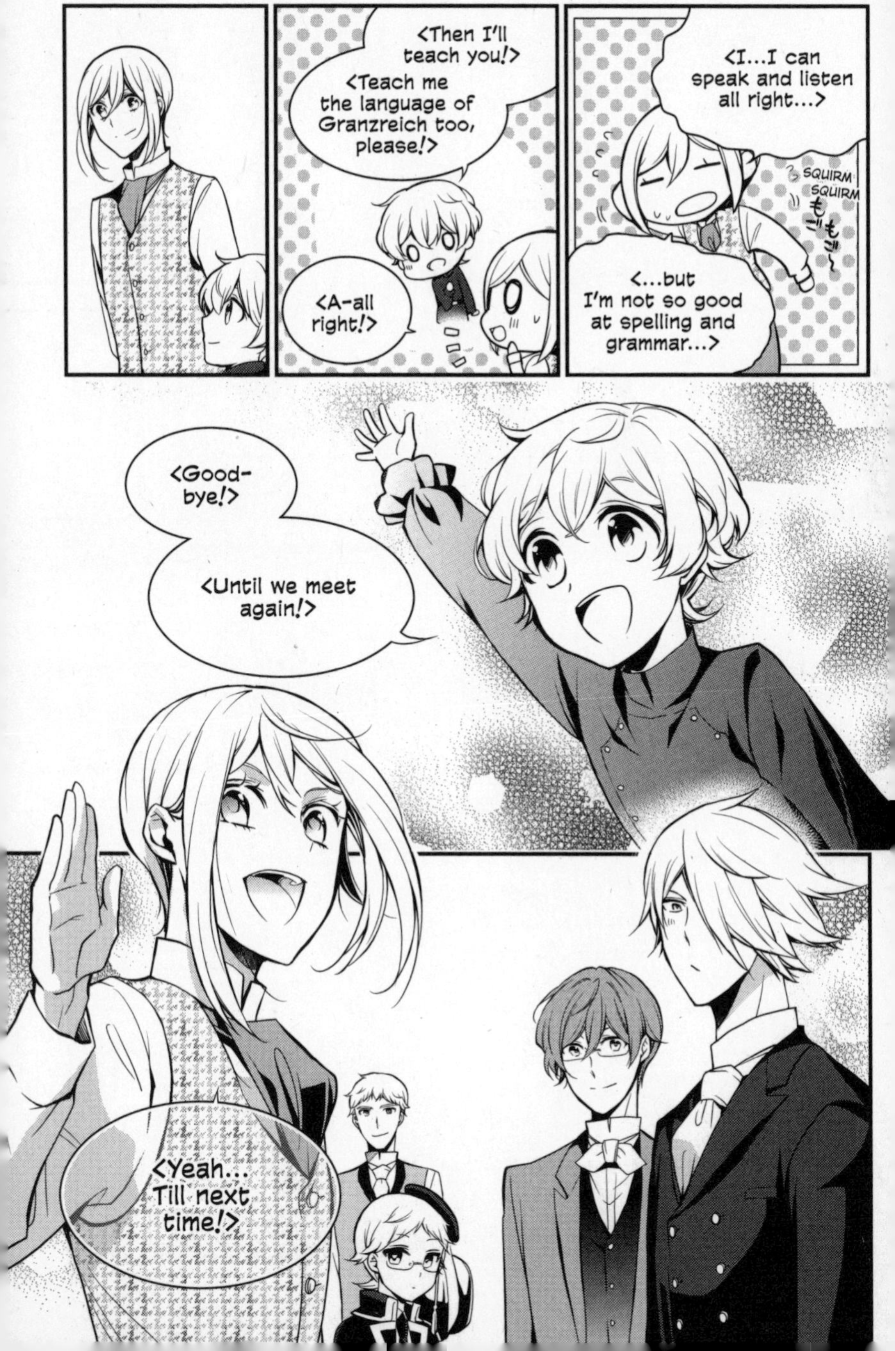
<I...I can speak and listen all right...>
SQUIRM SQUIRM
もごもご~
<...but I'm not so good at spelling and grammar...>
<Then I'll teach you!>
<Teach me the language of Granzreich too, please!>
<A-all right!>
<Good-bye!>
<Until we meet again!>
<Yeah... Till next time!>

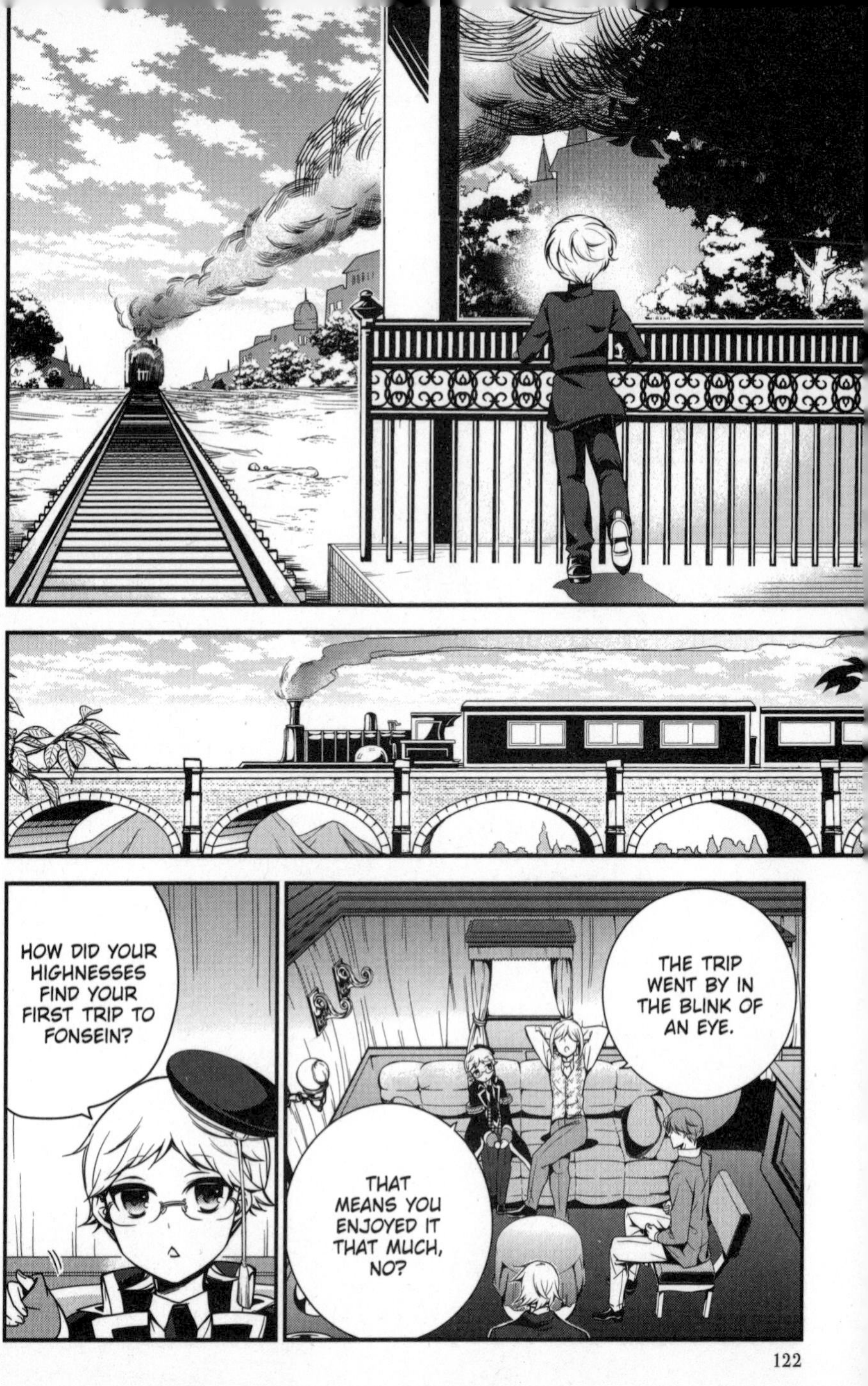
THE TRIP WENT BY IN THE BLINK OF AN EYE.
THAT MEANS YOU ENJOYED IT THAT MUCH, NO?
HOW DID YOUR HIGHNESSES FIND YOUR FIRST TRIP TO FONSEIN?

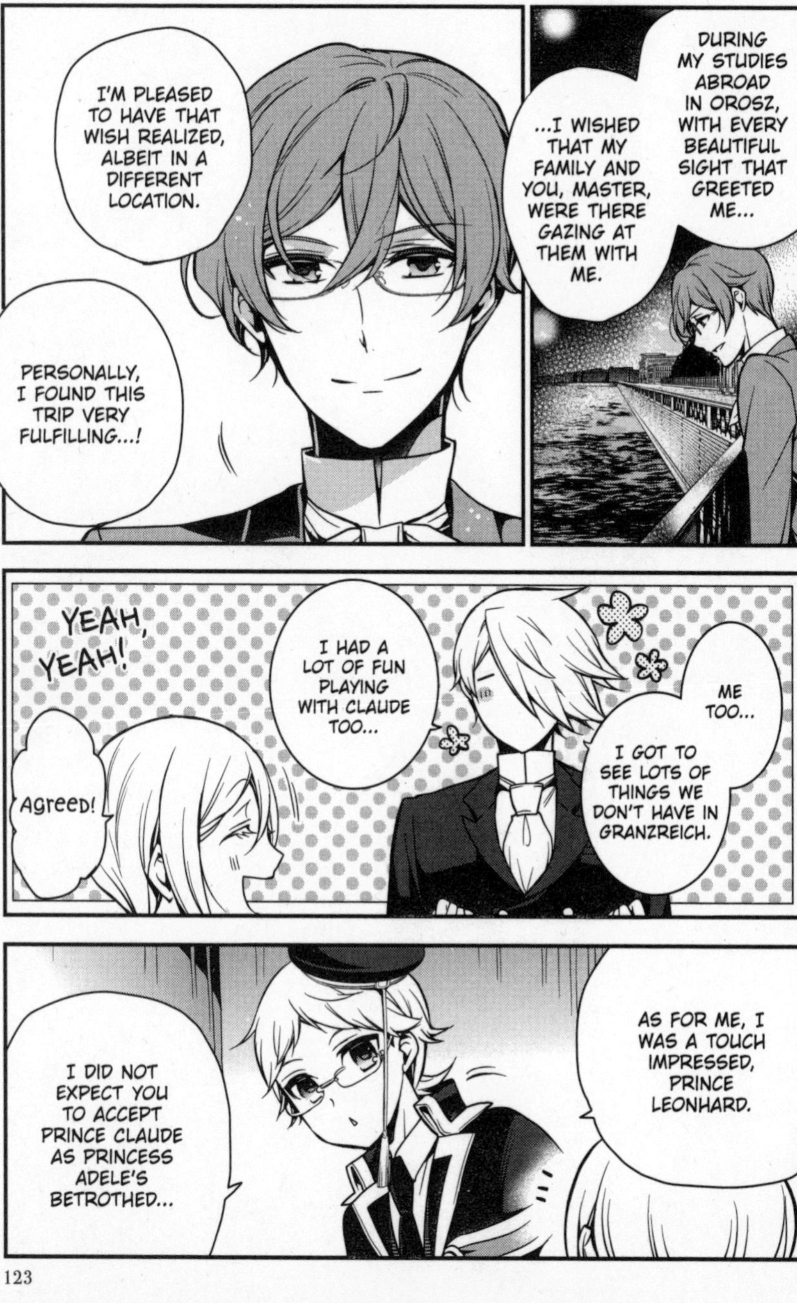
DURING MY STUDIES ABROAD IN OROSZ, WITH EVERY BEAUTIFUL SIGHT THAT GREETED ME...
...I WISHED THAT MY FAMILY AND YOU, MASTER, WERE THERE GAZING AT THEM WITH ME.
I'M PLEASED TO HAVE THAT WISH REALIZED, ALBEIT IN A DIFFERENT LOCATION.
PERSONALLY, I FOUND THIS TRIP VERY FULFILLING...!
ME TOO...
I GOT TO SEE LOTS OF THINGS WE DON'T HAVE IN GRANZREICH.
I HAD A LOT OF FUN PLAYING WITH CLAUDE TOO...
YEAH, YEAH!
Agreed!
AS FOR ME, I WAS A TOUCH IMPRESSED, PRINCE LEONHARD.
I DID NOT EXPECT YOU TO ACCEPT PRINCE CLAUDE AS PRINCESS ADELE'S BETROTHED...

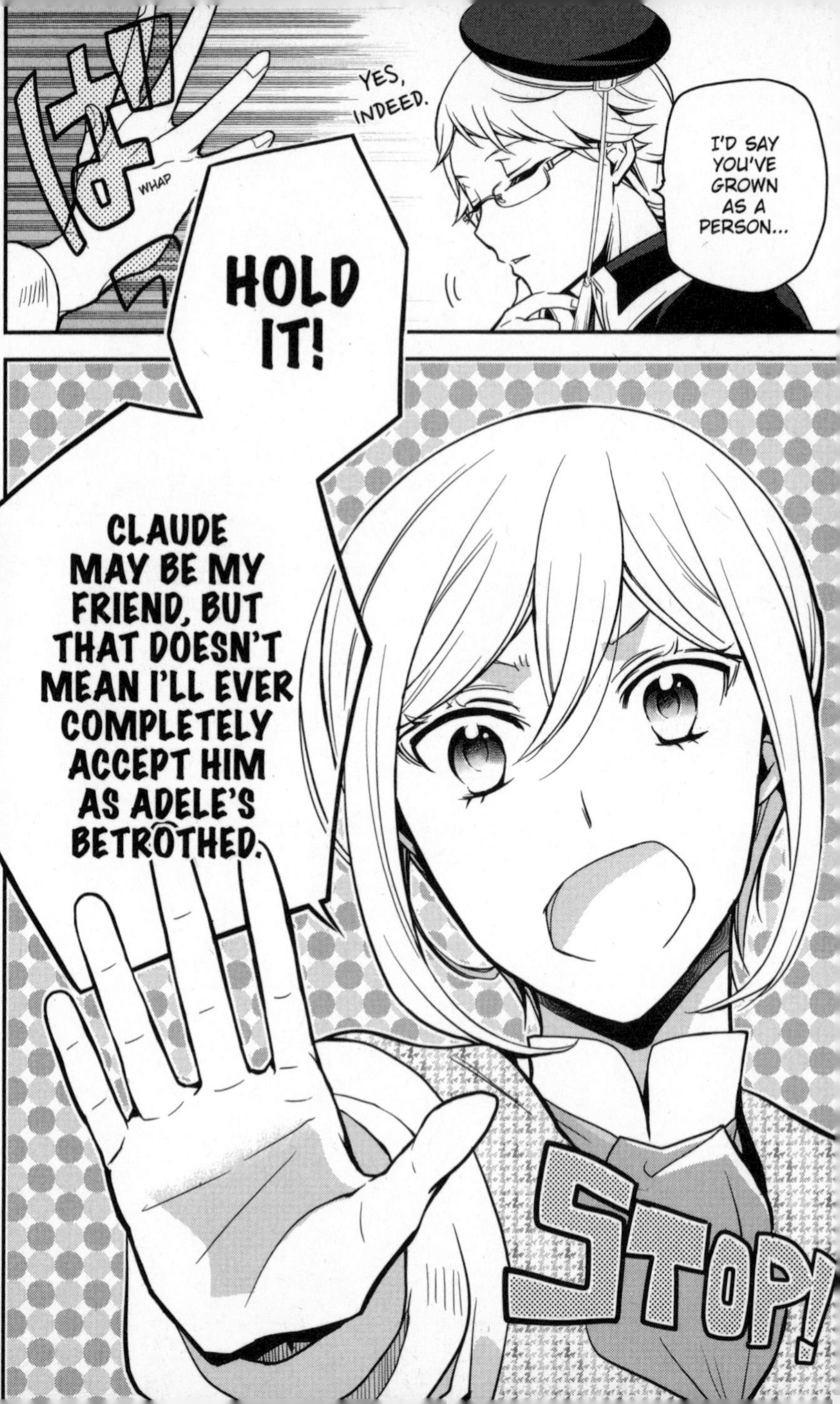
I'D SAY YOU'VE GROWN AS A PERSON...
YES, INDEED.
WHAP
HOLD IT!
CLAUDE MAY BE MY FRIEND, BUT THAT DOESN'T MEAN I'LL EVER COMPLETELY ACCEPT HIM AS ADELE'S BETROTHED.
STOP!

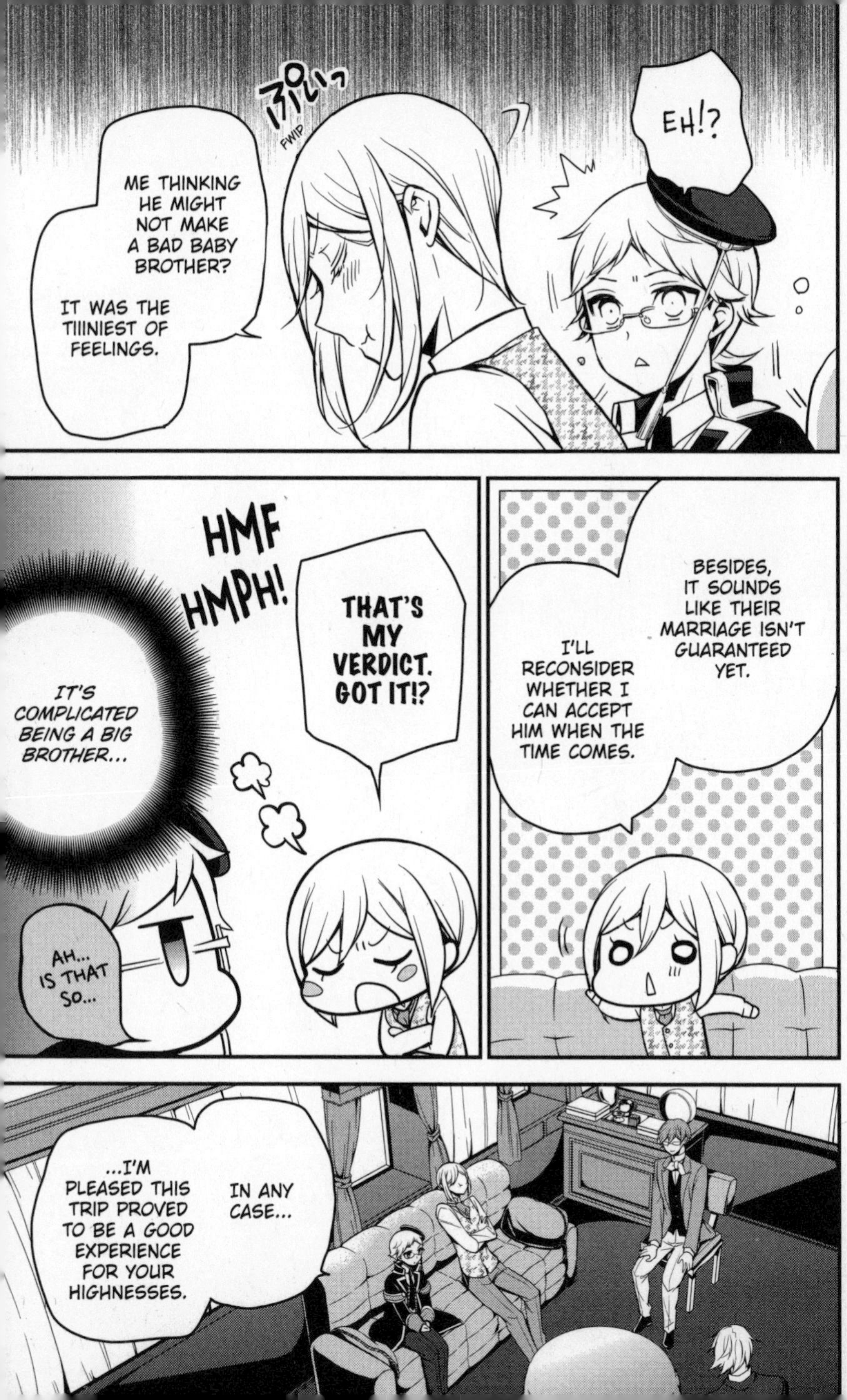
EH!?
ぷいっ
FWIP
ME THINKING HE MIGHT NOT MAKE A BAD BABY BROTHER?
IT WAS THE TIIINIEST OF FEELINGS.
BESIDES, IT SOUNDS LIKE THEIR MARRIAGE ISN'T GUARANTEED YET.
I'LL RECONSIDER WHETHER I CAN ACCEPT HIM WHEN THE TIME COMES.
HMF HMPH!
THAT'S MY VERDICT. GOT IT!?
IT'S COMPLICATED BEING A BIG BROTHER...
AH... IS THAT SO...
IN ANY CASE...
...I'M PLEASED THIS TRIP PROVED TO BE A GOOD EXPERIENCE FOR YOUR HIGHNESSES.

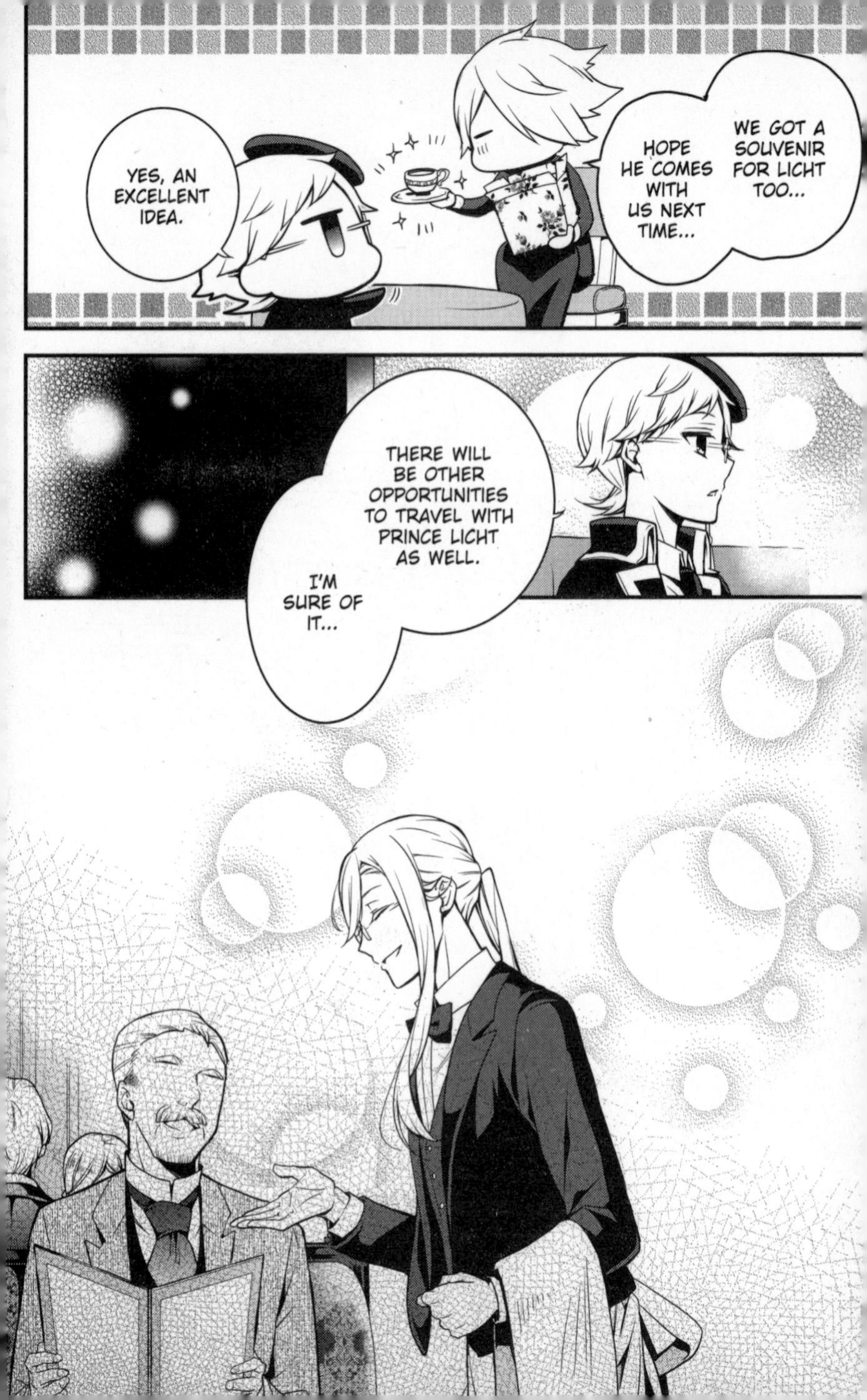
WE GOT A SOUVENIR FOR LICHT TOO...
HOPE HE COMES WITH US NEXT TIME...
YES, AN EXCELLENT IDEA.
THERE WILL BE OTHER OPPORTUNITIES TO TRAVEL WITH PRINCE LICHT AS WELL.
I'M SURE OF IT...

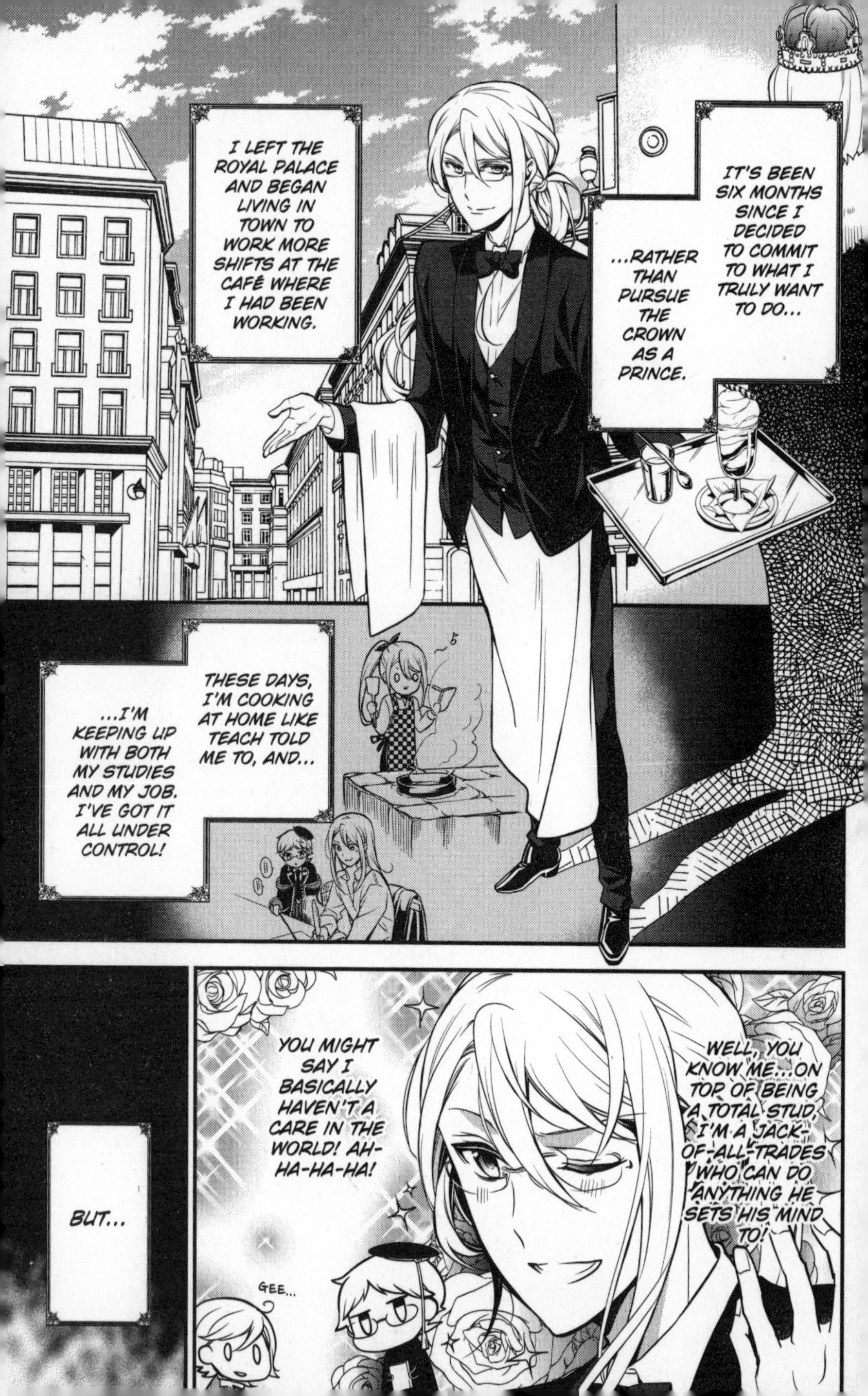
IT'S BEEN SIX MONTHS SINCE I DECIDED TO COMMIT TO WHAT I TRULY WANT TO DO...
...RATHER THAN PURSUE THE CROWN AS A PRINCE.
I LEFT THE ROYAL PALACE AND BEGAN LIVING IN TOWN TO WORK MORE SHIFTS AT THE CAFÉ WHERE I HAD BEEN WORKING.
THESE DAYS, I'M COOKING AT HOME LIKE TEACH TOLD ME TO, AND...
...I'M KEEPING UP WITH BOTH MY STUDIES AND MY JOB. I'VE GOT IT ALL UNDER CONTROL!
WELL, YOU KNOW ME...ON TOP OF BEING A TOTAL STUD, I'M A JACK-OF-ALL-TRADES WHO CAN DO ANYTHING HE SETS HIS MIND TO!
YOU MIGHT SAY I BASICALLY HAVEN'T A CARE IN THE WORLD! AH-HA-HA-HA!
GEE...
BUT...

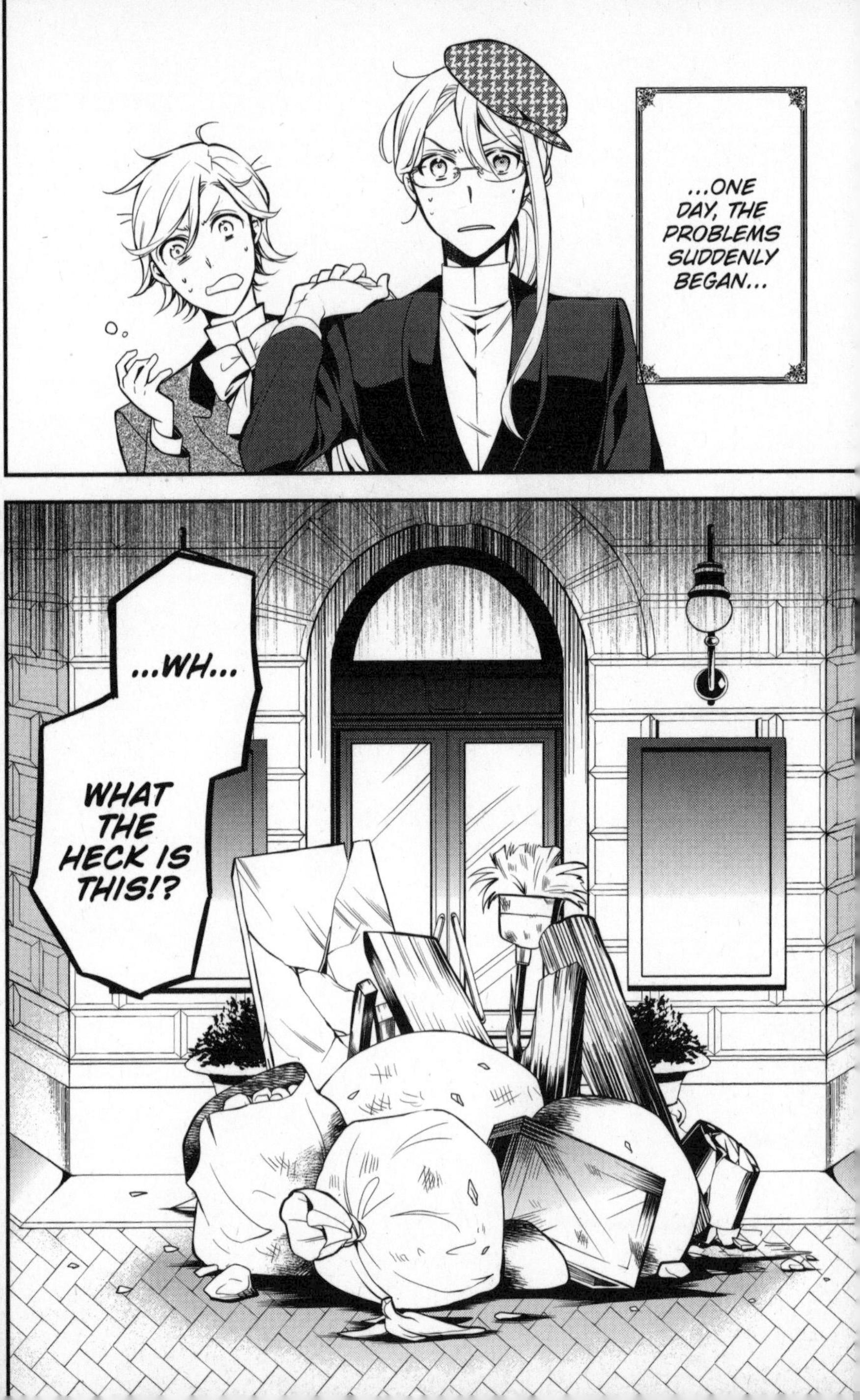
...ONE DAY, THE PROBLEMS SUDDENLY BEGAN...
...WH...
WHAT THE HECK IS THIS!?

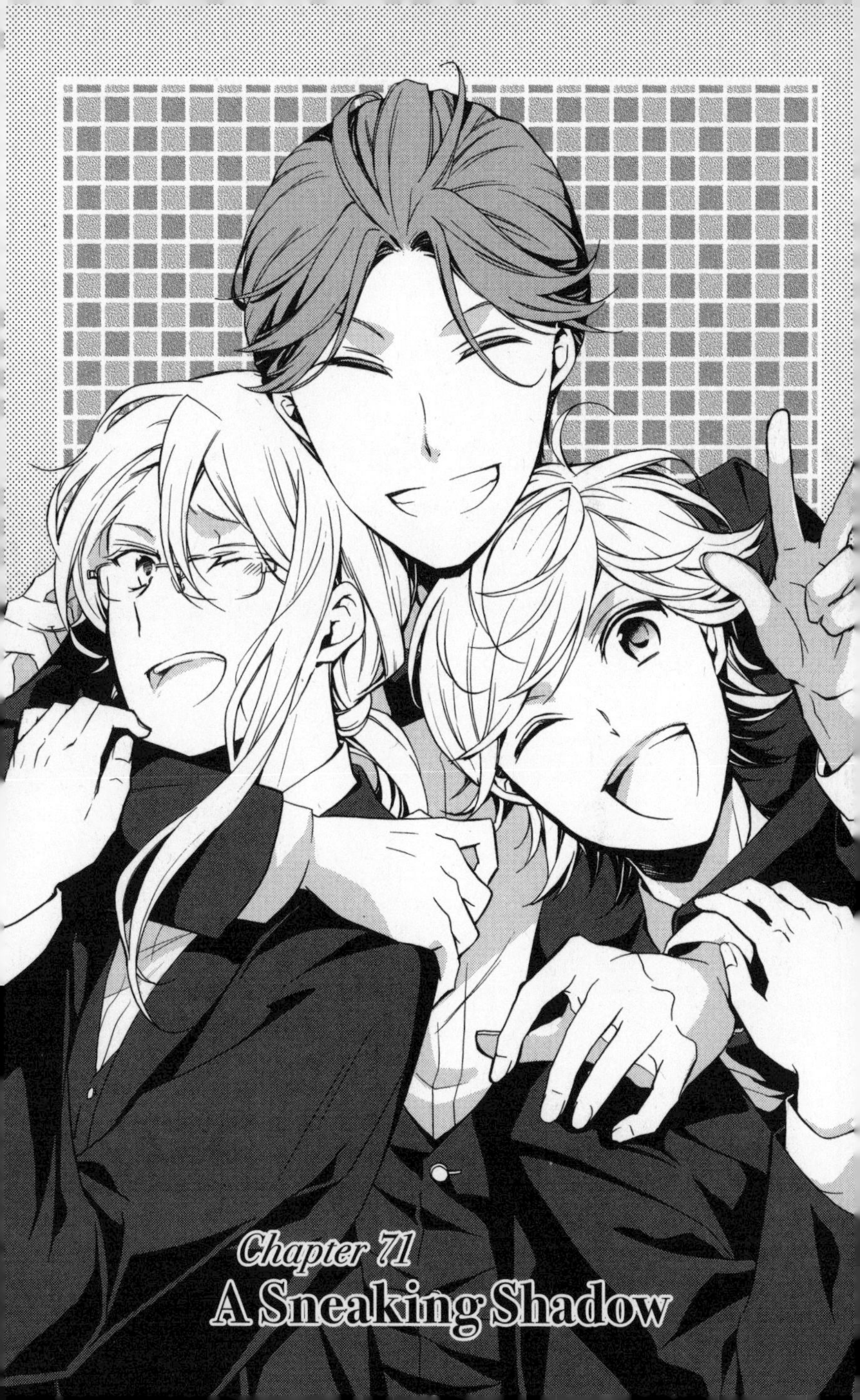
Chapter 71
A Sneaking Shadow

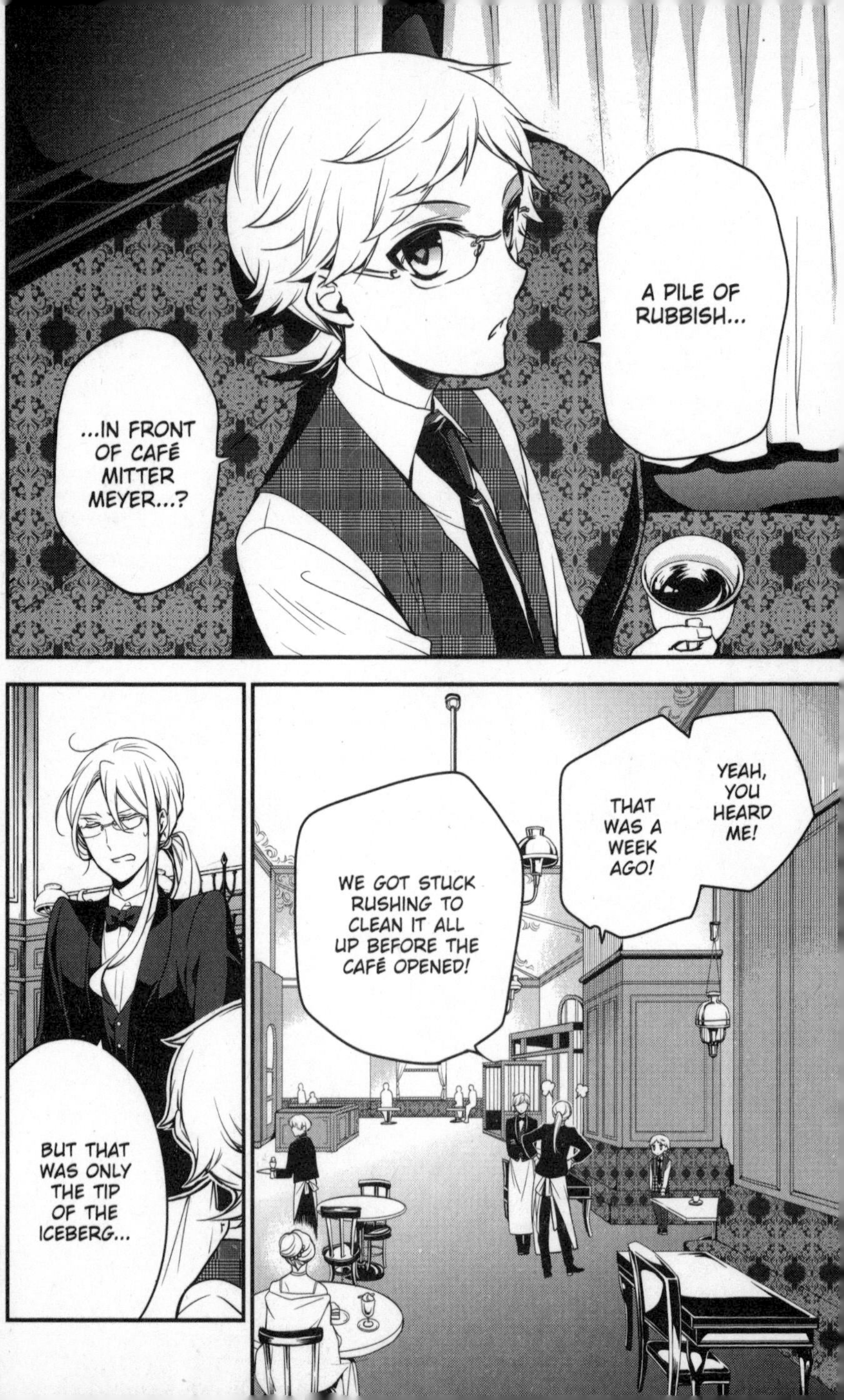
A PILE OF RUBBISH...
...IN FRONT OF CAFÉ MITTER MEYER...?
YEAH, YOU HEARD ME!
THAT WAS A WEEK AGO!
WE GOT STUCK RUSHING TO CLEAN IT ALL UP BEFORE THE CAFÉ OPENED!
BUT THAT WAS ONLY THE TIP OF THE ICEBERG...

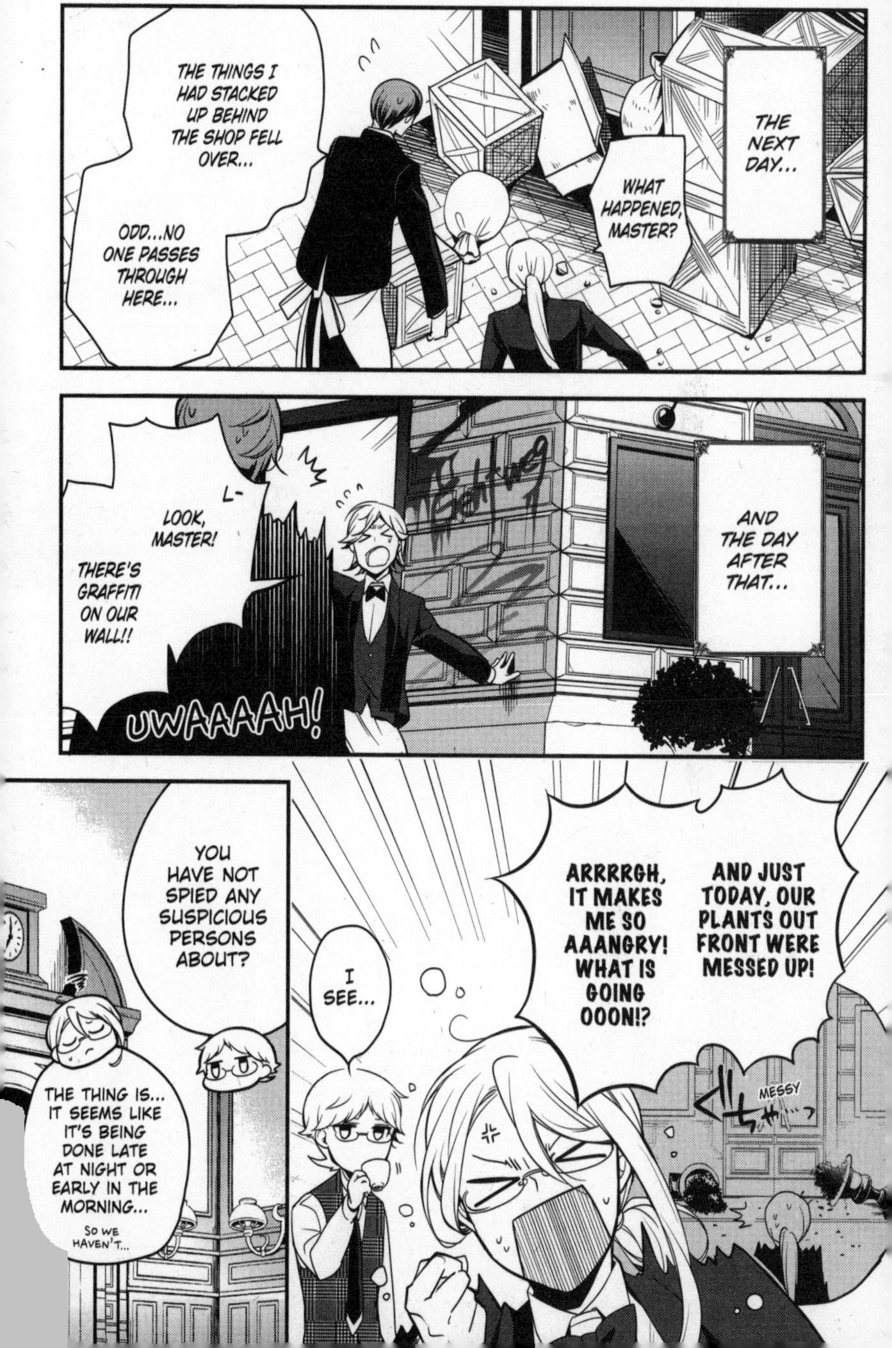
THE NEXT DAY...
WHAT HAPPENED, MASTER?
THE THINGS I HAD STACKED UP BEHIND THE SHOP FELL OVER...
ODD...NO ONE PASSES THROUGH HERE...
AND THE DAY AFTER THAT...
L-
LOOK, MASTER! THERE'S GRAFFITI ON OUR WALL!!
UWAAAAH!
AND JUST TODAY, OUR PLANTS OUT FRONT WERE MESSED UP!
ARRRRGH, IT MAKES ME SO AAANGRY! WHAT IS GOING OOON!?
MESSY
I SEE...
YOU HAVE NOT SPIED ANY SUSPICIOUS PERSONS ABOUT?
THE THING IS... IT SEEMS LIKE IT'S BEING DONE LATE AT NIGHT OR EARLY IN THE MORNING...
SO WE HAVEN'T...

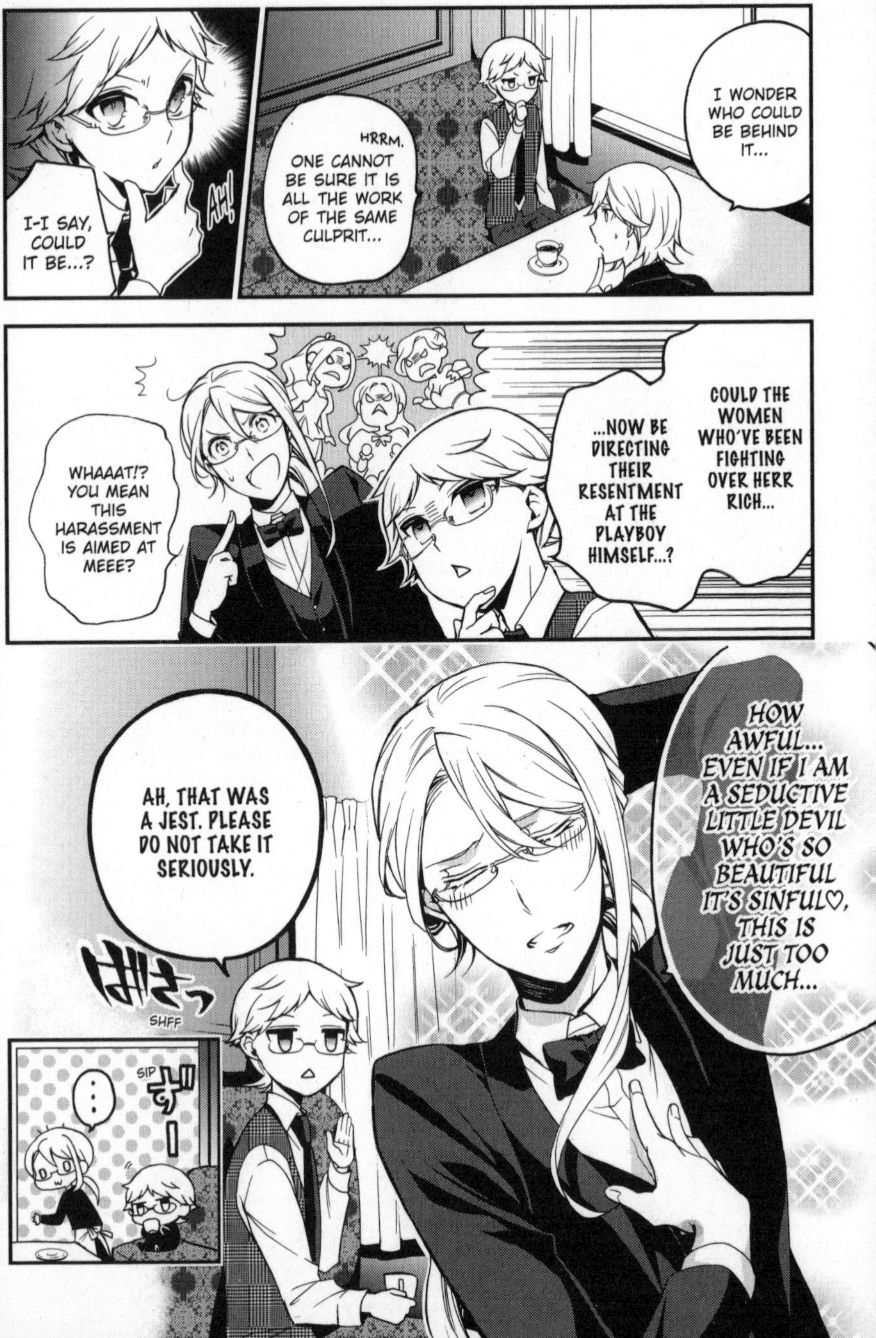
I WONDER WHO COULD BE BEHIND IT...
HRRM. ONE CANNOT BE SURE IT IS ALL THE WORK OF THE SAME CULPRIT...
AH!
I-I SAY, COULD IT BE...?
COULD THE WOMEN WHO'VE BEEN FIGHTING OVER HERR RICH...
...NOW BE DIRECTING THEIR RESENTMENT AT THE PLAYBOY HIMSELF...?
WHAAAT!? YOU MEAN THIS HARASSMENT IS AIMED AT MEEE?
HOW AWFUL... EVEN IF I AM A SEDUCTIVE LITTLE DEVIL WHO'S SO BEAUTIFUL IT'S SINFUL♡, THIS IS JUST TOO MUCH...
AH, THAT WAS A JEST. PLEASE DO NOT TAKE IT SERIOUSLY.
SHFF
...
SIP

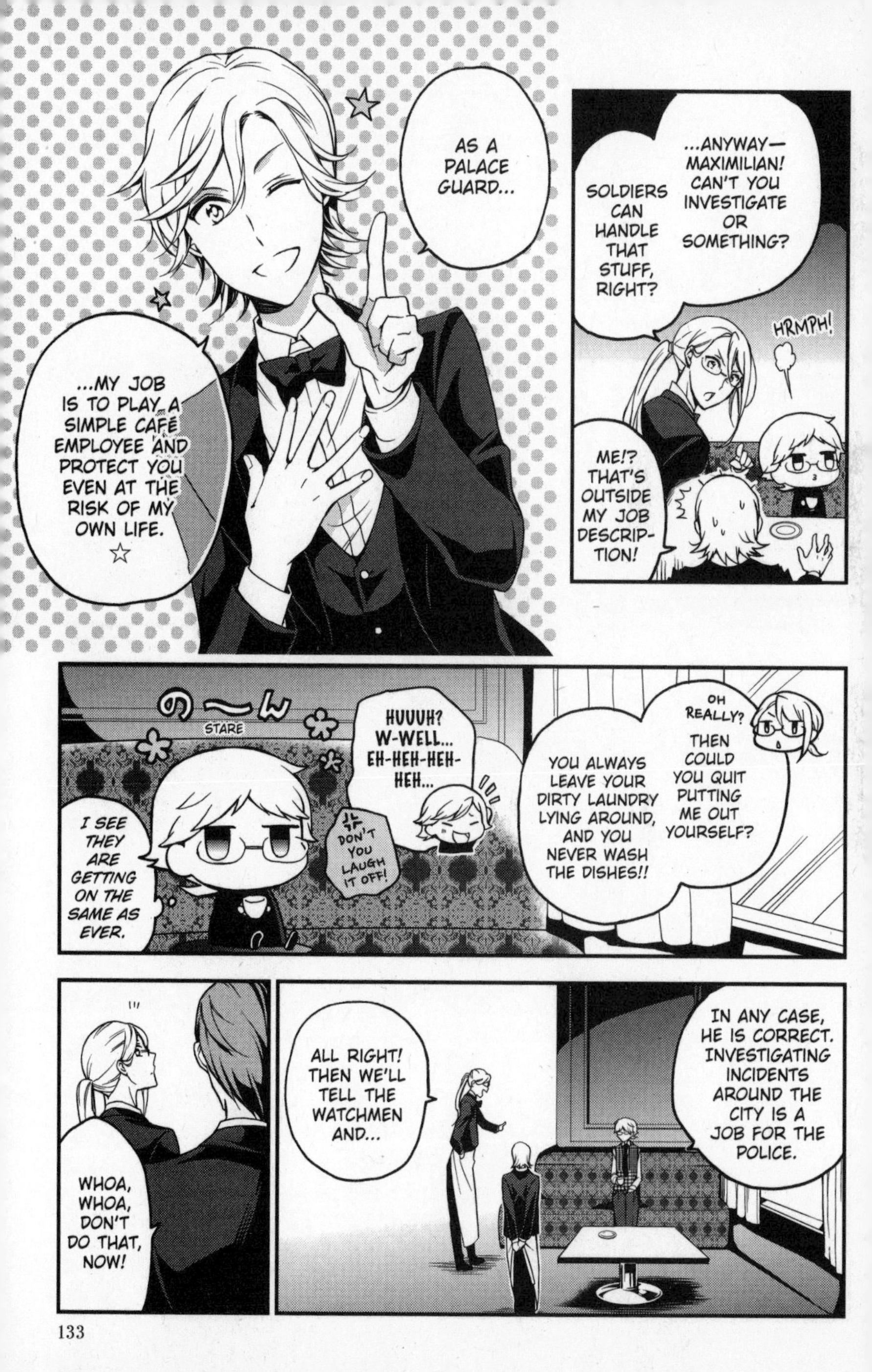
...ANYWAY— MAXIMILIAN! CAN'T YOU INVESTIGATE OR SOMETHING?
SOLDIERS CAN HANDLE THAT STUFF, RIGHT?
HRMPH!
ME!? THAT'S OUTSIDE MY JOB DESCRIPTION!
AS A PALACE GUARD...
...MY JOB IS TO PLAY A SIMPLE CAFÉ EMPLOYEE AND PROTECT YOU EVEN AT THE RISK OF MY OWN LIFE. ☆
OH REALLY?
THEN COULD YOU QUIT PUTTING ME OUT YOURSELF?
YOU ALWAYS LEAVE YOUR DIRTY LAUNDRY LYING AROUND, AND YOU NEVER WASH THE DISHES!!
HUUUH? W-WELL... EH-HEH-HEH-HEH...
DON'T YOU LAUGH IT OFF!
のーん
STARE
I SEE THEY ARE GETTING ON THE SAME AS EVER.
IN ANY CASE, HE IS CORRECT. INVESTIGATING INCIDENTS AROUND THE CITY IS A JOB FOR THE POLICE.
ALL RIGHT! THEN WE'LL TELL THE WATCHMEN AND...
WHOA, WHOA, DON'T DO THAT, NOW!

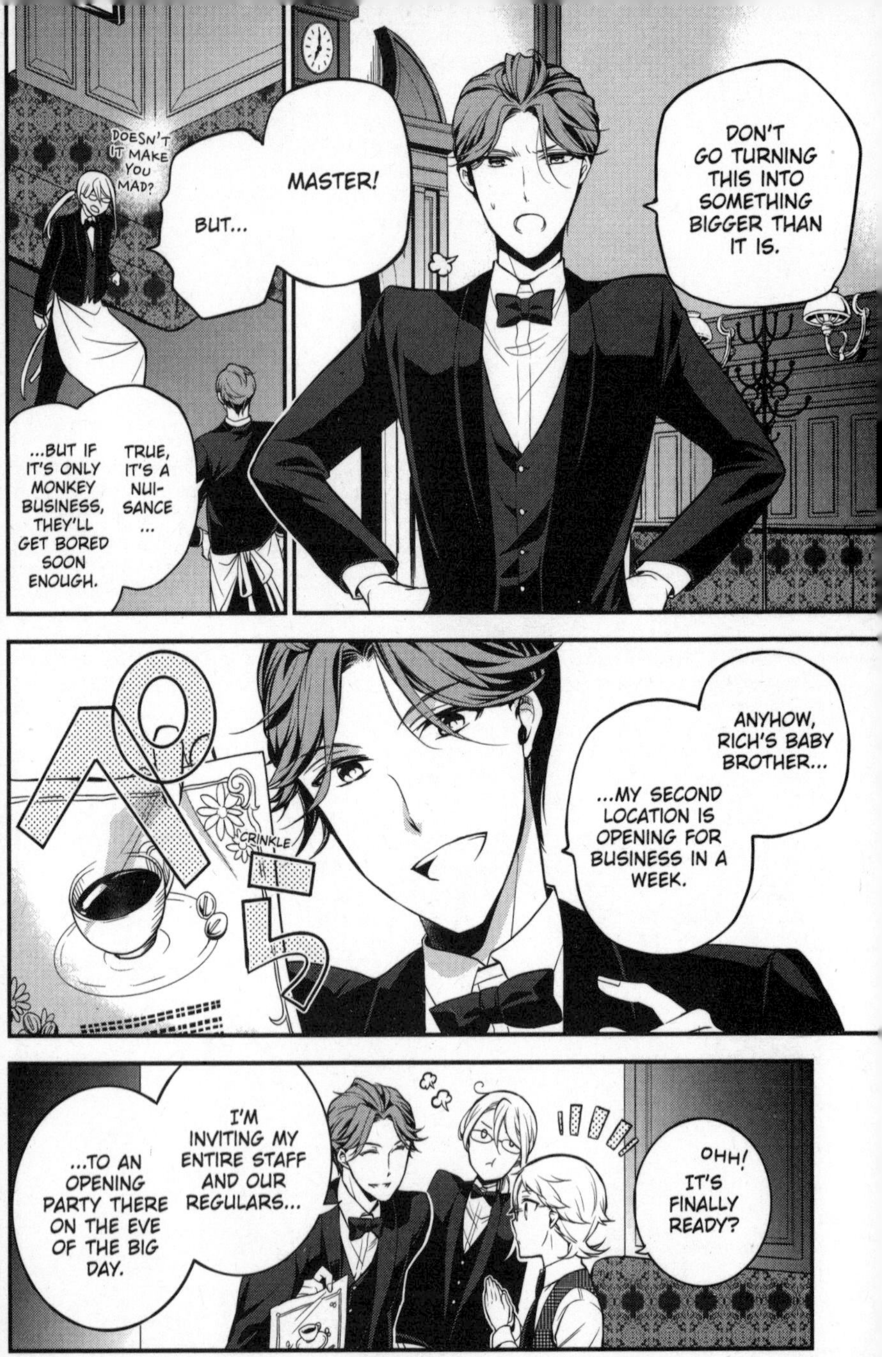
DON'T GO TURNING THIS INTO SOMETHING BIGGER THAN IT IS.
MASTER!
BUT...
DOESN'T IT MAKE YOU MAD?
TRUE, IT'S A NUI-SANCE ...
...BUT IF IT'S ONLY MONKEY BUSINESS, THEY'LL GET BORED SOON ENOUGH.
ANYHOW, RICH'S BABY BROTHER...
...MY SECOND LOCATION IS OPENING FOR BUSINESS IN A WEEK.
CRINKLE
OHH! IT'S FINALLY READY?
I'M INVITING MY ENTIRE STAFF AND OUR REGULARS...
...TO AN OPENING PARTY THERE ON THE EVE OF THE BIG DAY.

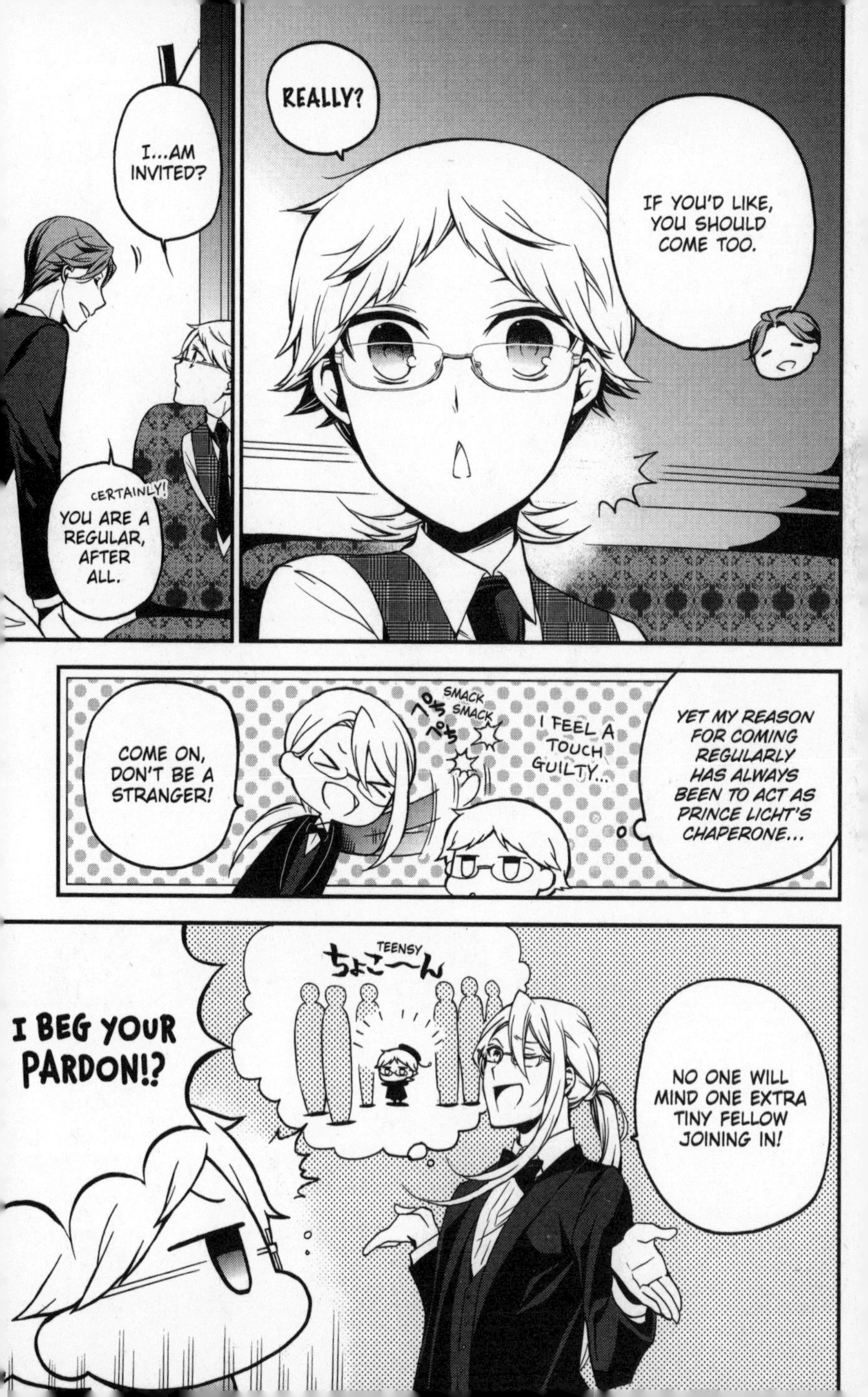
IF YOU'D LIKE, YOU SHOULD COME TOO.
REALLY?
I...AM INVITED?
CERTAINLY!
YOU ARE A REGULAR, AFTER ALL.
YET MY REASON FOR COMING REGULARLY HAS ALWAYS BEEN TO ACT AS PRINCE LICHT'S CHAPERONE...
I FEEL A TOUCH GUILTY...
ぺちぺち
SMACK SMACK
COME ON, DON'T BE A STRANGER!
NO ONE WILL MIND ONE EXTRA TINY FELLOW JOINING IN!
ちょこ〜ん
TEENSY
I BEG YOUR PARDON!?

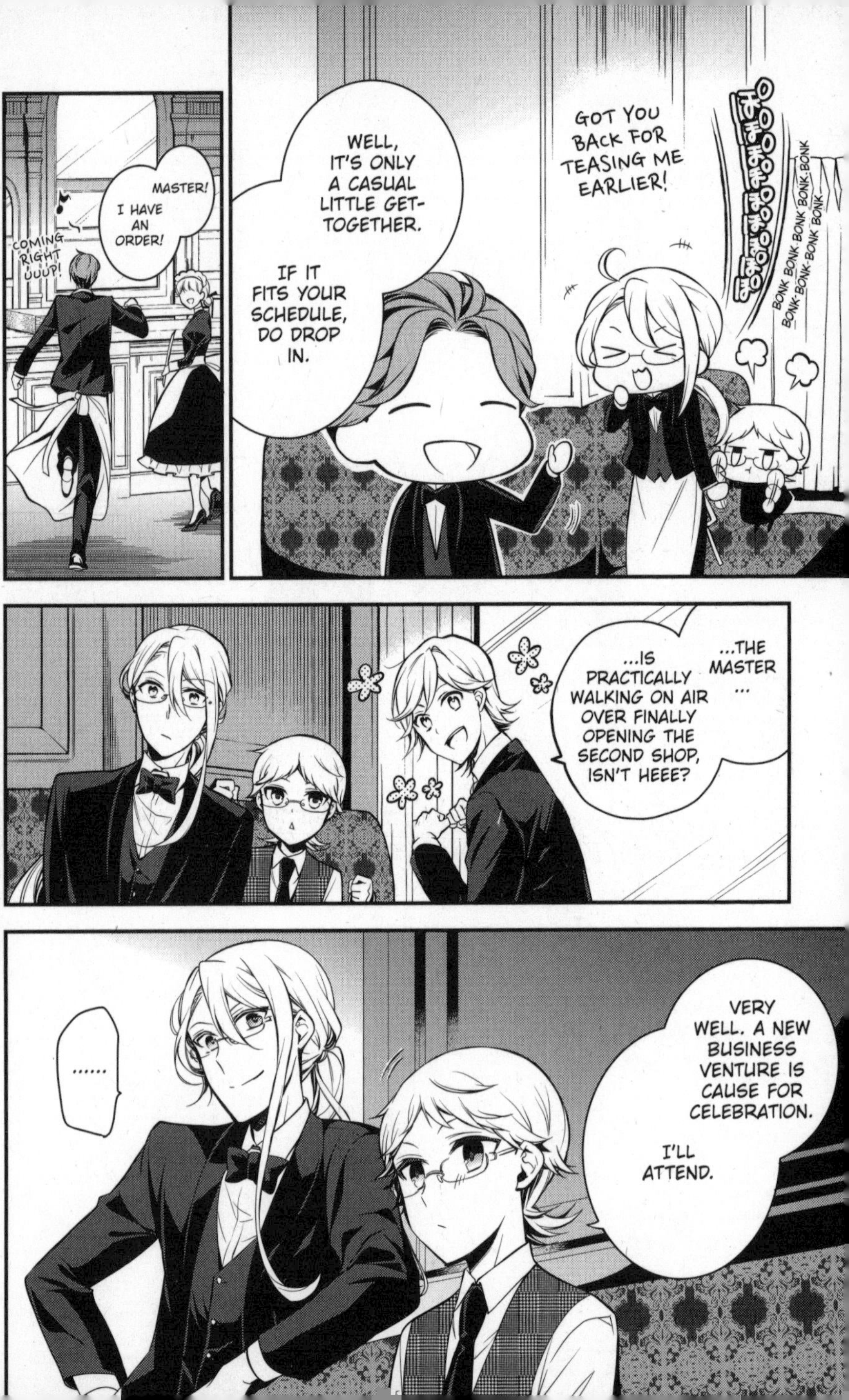
BONK BONK BONK-BONK BONK-BONK-BONK-BONK
GOT YOU BACK FOR TEASING ME EARLIER!
WELL, IT'S ONLY A CASUAL LITTLE GET-TOGETHER.
IF IT FITS YOUR SCHEDULE, DO DROP IN.
MASTER! I HAVE AN ORDER!
COMING RIGHT UUUP!
...THE MASTER ...
...IS PRACTICALLY WALKING ON AIR OVER FINALLY OPENING THE SECOND SHOP, ISN'T HEEE?
VERY WELL. A NEW BUSINESS VENTURE IS CAUSE FOR CELEBRATION.
I'LL ATTEND.
......

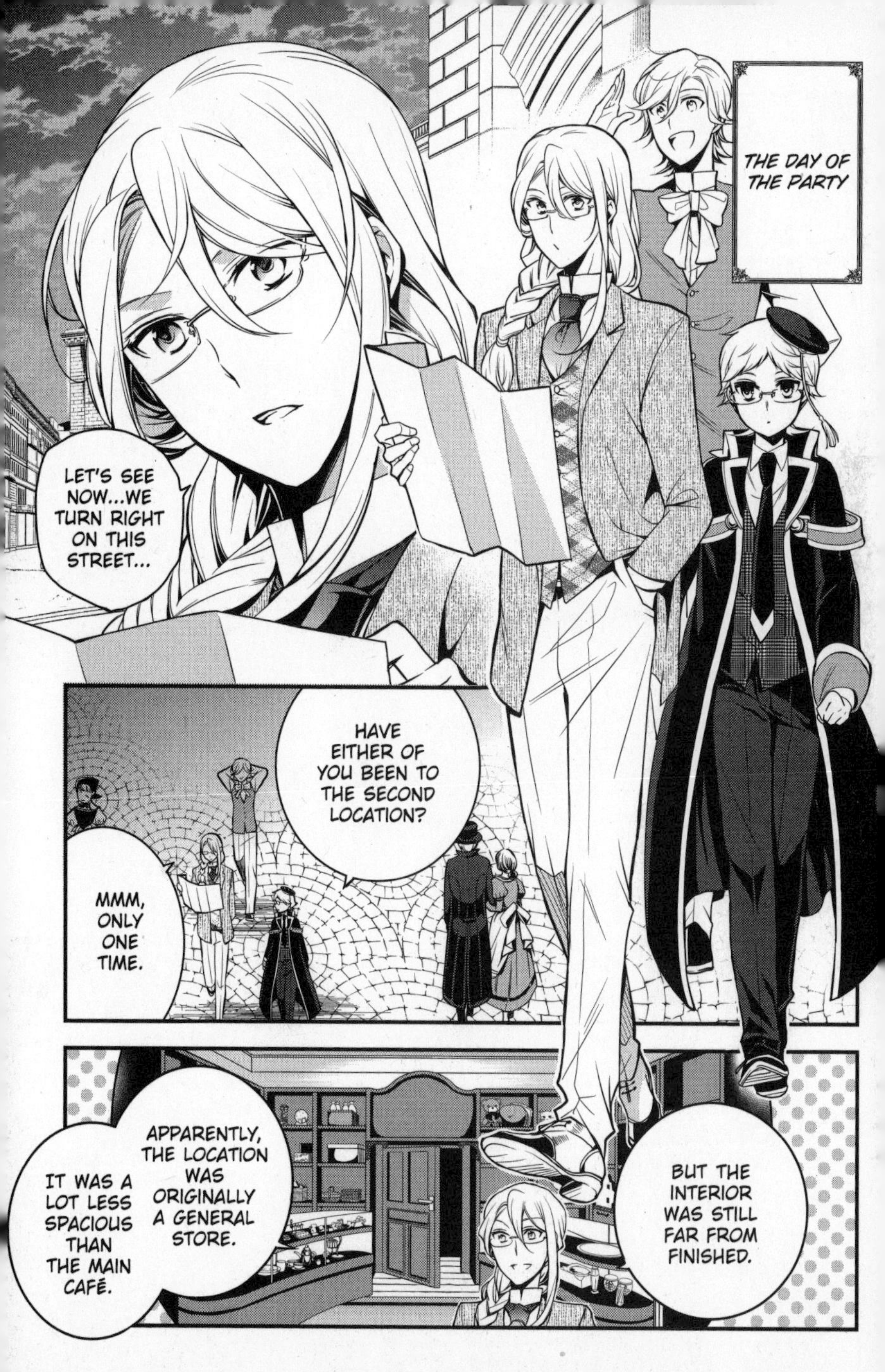
THE DAY OF THE PARTY
LET'S SEE NOW...WE TURN RIGHT ON THIS STREET...
HAVE EITHER OF YOU BEEN TO THE SECOND LOCATION?
MMM, ONLY ONE TIME.
BUT THE INTERIOR WAS STILL FAR FROM FINISHED.
APPARENTLY, THE LOCATION WAS ORIGINALLY A GENERAL STORE.
IT WAS A LOT LESS SPACIOUS THAN THE MAIN CAFÉ.

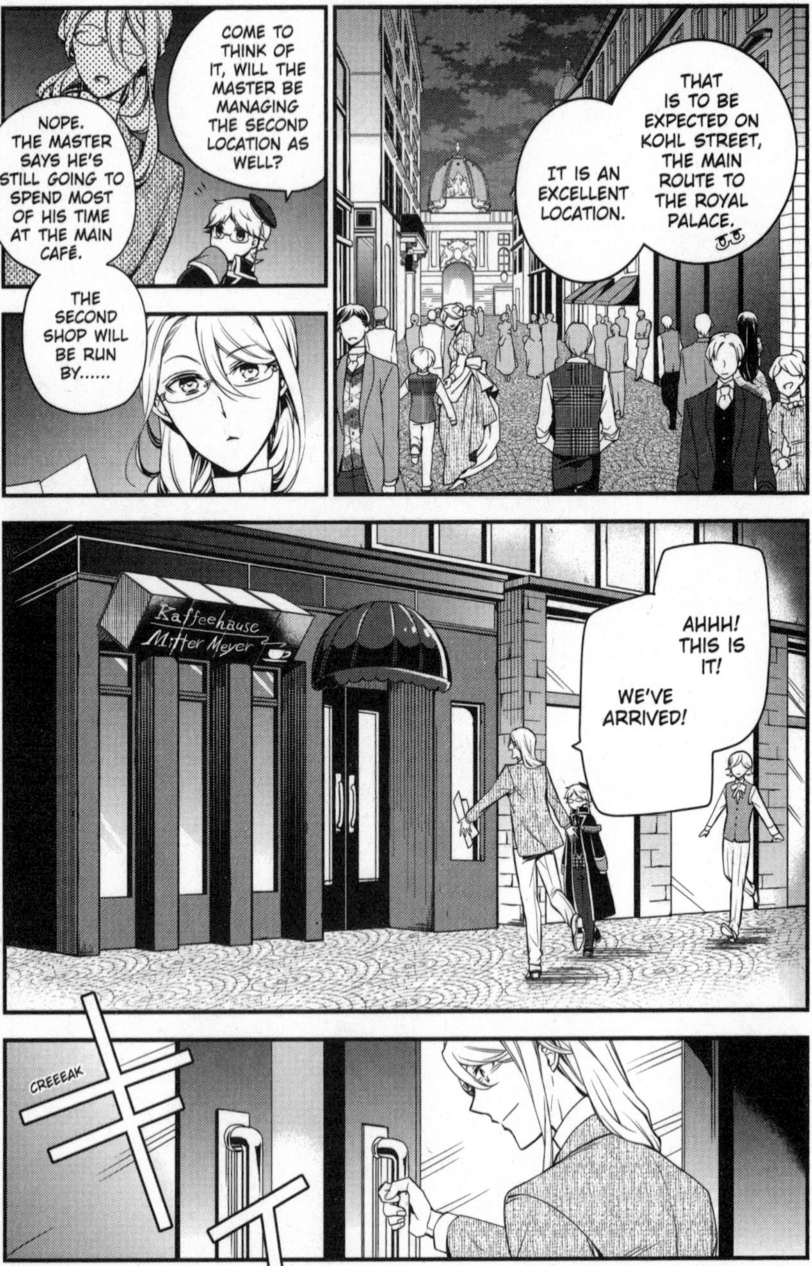
THAT IS TO BE EXPECTED ON KOHL STREET, THE MAIN ROUTE TO THE ROYAL PALACE.
IT IS AN EXCELLENT LOCATION.
COME TO THINK OF IT, WILL THE MASTER BE MANAGING THE SECOND LOCATION AS WELL?
NOPE. THE MASTER SAYS HE'S STILL GOING TO SPEND MOST OF HIS TIME AT THE MAIN CAFÉ.
THE SECOND SHOP WILL BE RUN BY......
AHHH! THIS IS IT!
WE'VE ARRIVED!
Kaffeehause Mitter Meyer
CREEEAK

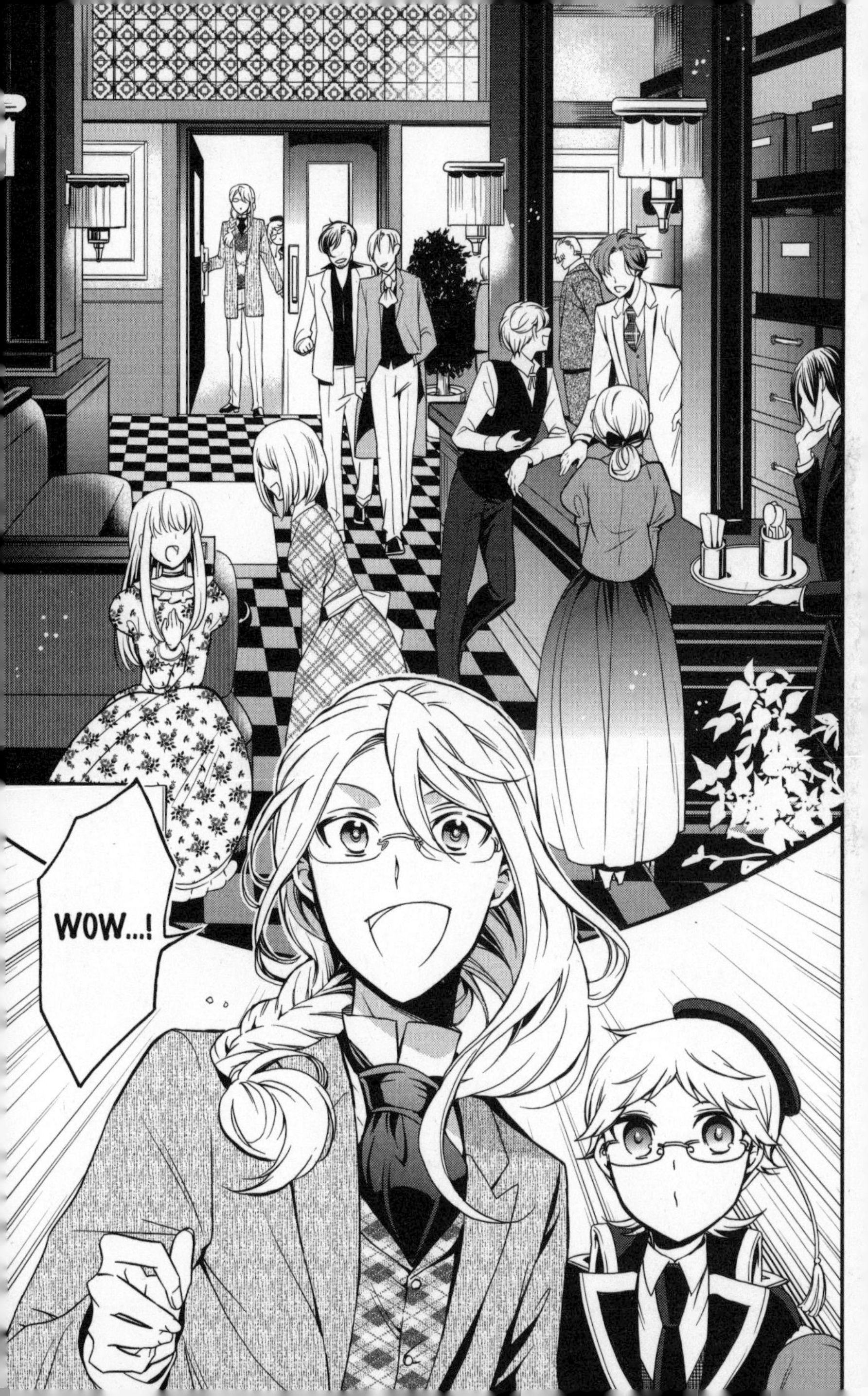
WOW...!

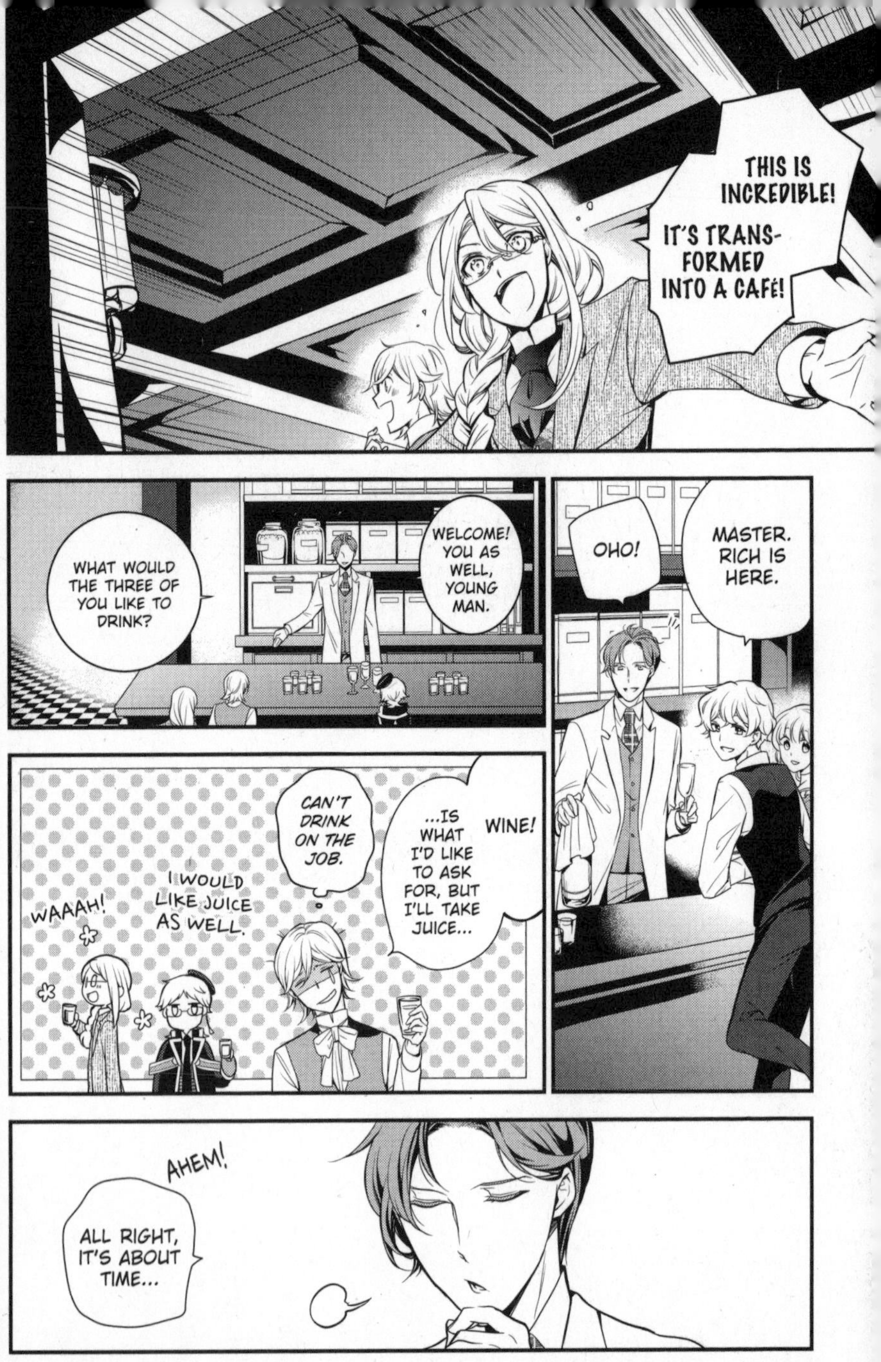
THIS IS INCREDIBLE!
IT'S TRANS-FORMED INTO A CAFÉ!
MASTER. RICH IS HERE.
OHO!
WELCOME! YOU AS WELL, YOUNG MAN.
WHAT WOULD THE THREE OF YOU LIKE TO DRINK?
WINE!
...IS WHAT I'D LIKE TO ASK FOR, BUT I'LL TAKE JUICE...
CAN'T DRINK ON THE JOB.
I WOULD LIKE JUICE AS WELL.
WAAAH!
AHEM!
ALL RIGHT, IT'S ABOUT TIME...

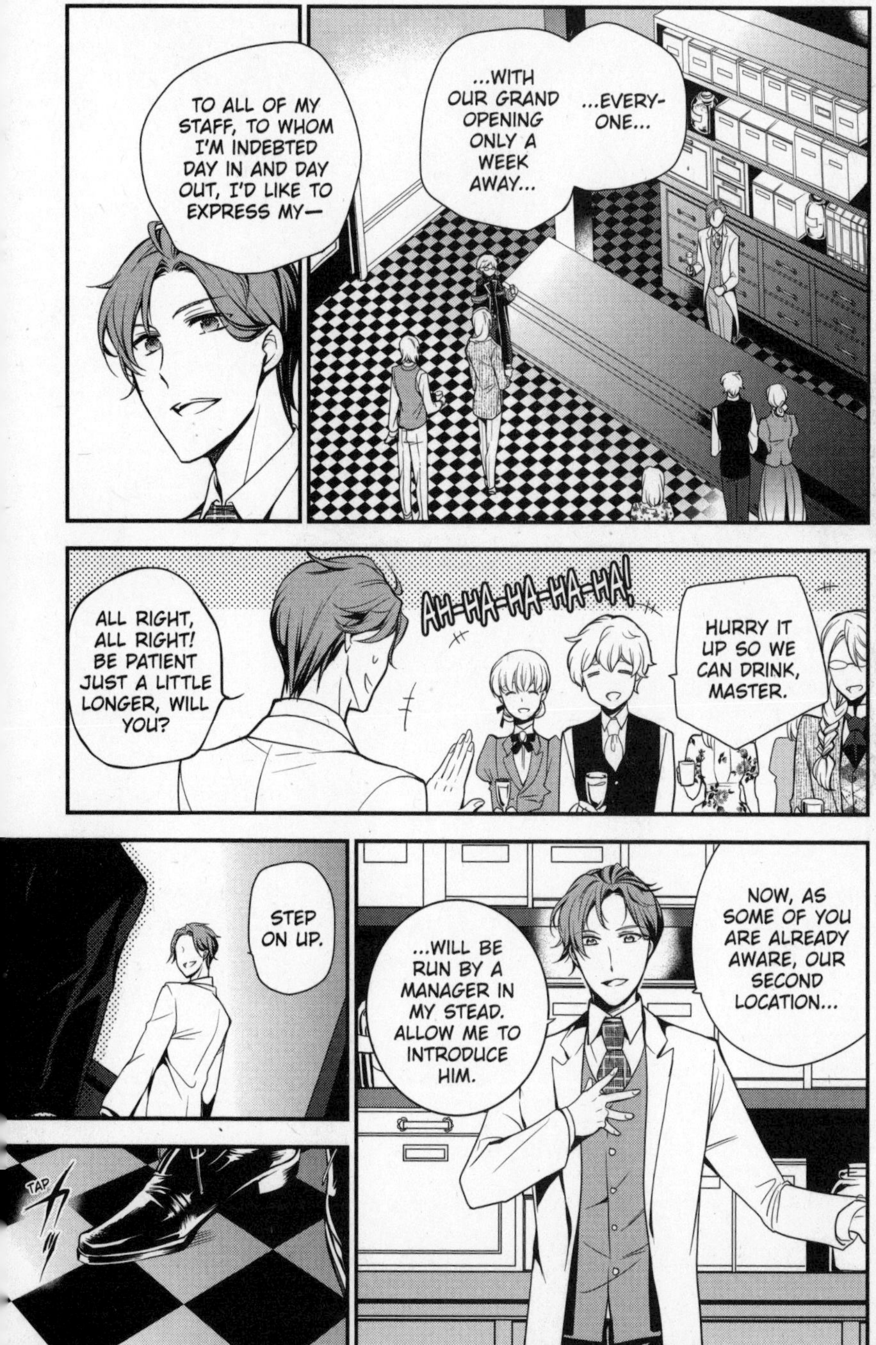
...EVERY-ONE...
...WITH OUR GRAND OPENING ONLY A WEEK AWAY...
TO ALL OF MY STAFF, TO WHOM I'M INDEBTED DAY IN AND DAY OUT, I'D LIKE TO EXPRESS MY—
HURRY IT UP SO WE CAN DRINK, MASTER.
AH-HA-HA-HA-HA!
ALL RIGHT, ALL RIGHT! BE PATIENT JUST A LITTLE LONGER, WILL YOU?
NOW, AS SOME OF YOU ARE ALREADY AWARE, OUR SECOND LOCATION...
...WILL BE RUN BY A MANAGER IN MY STEAD. ALLOW ME TO INTRODUCE HIM.
STEP ON UP.
TAP

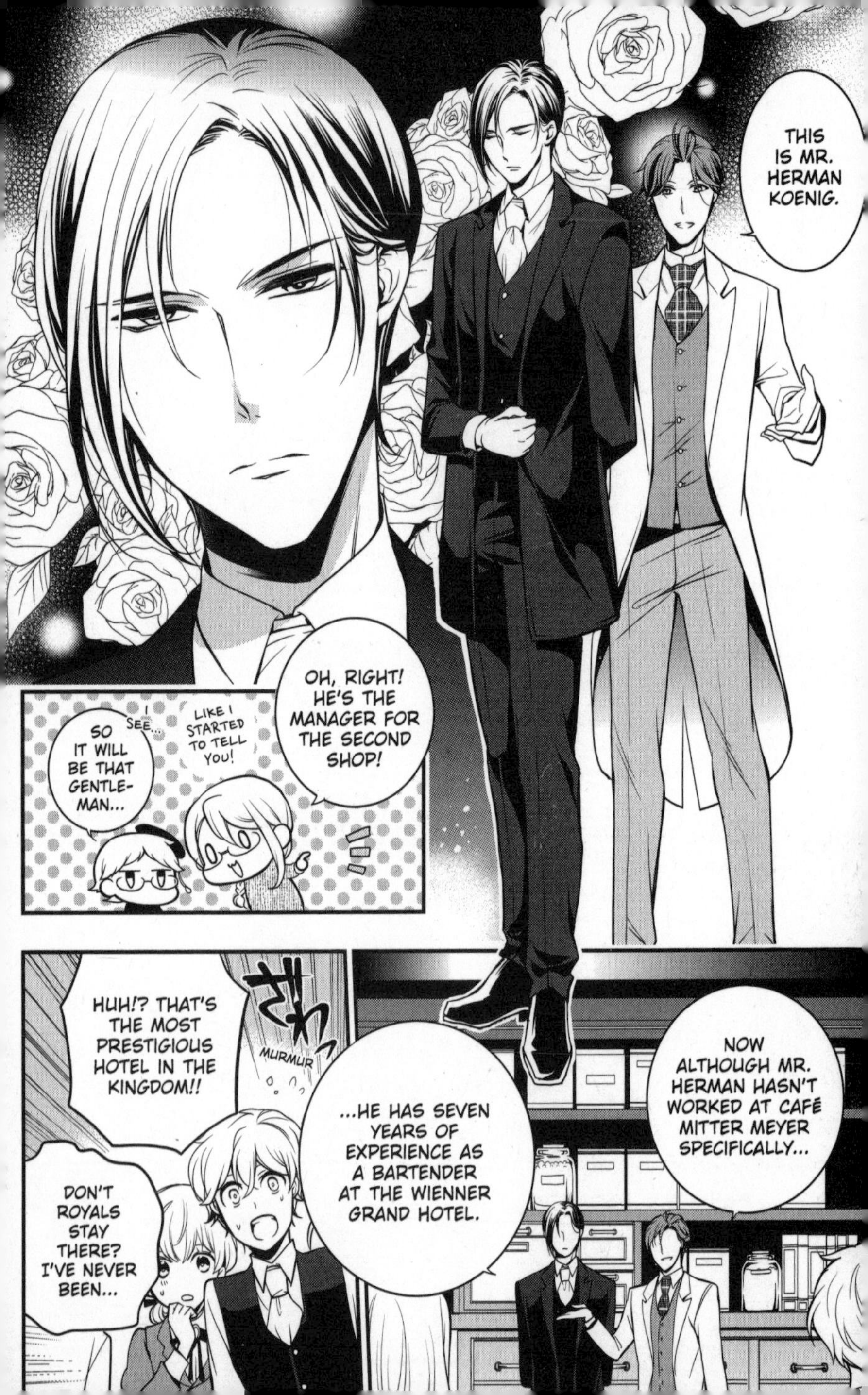
THIS IS MR. HERMAN KOENIG.
OH, RIGHT! HE'S THE MANAGER FOR THE SECOND SHOP!
LIKE I STARTED TO TELL YOU!
I SEE...
SO IT WILL BE THAT GENTLEMAN...
NOW ALTHOUGH MR. HERMAN HASN'T WORKED AT CAFÉ MITTER MEYER SPECIFICALLY...
...HE HAS SEVEN YEARS OF EXPERIENCE AS A BARTENDER AT THE WIENNER GRAND HOTEL.
ざわ
MURMUR
HUH!? THAT'S THE MOST PRESTIGIOUS HOTEL IN THE KINGDOM!!
DON'T ROYALS STAY THERE? I'VE NEVER BEEN...

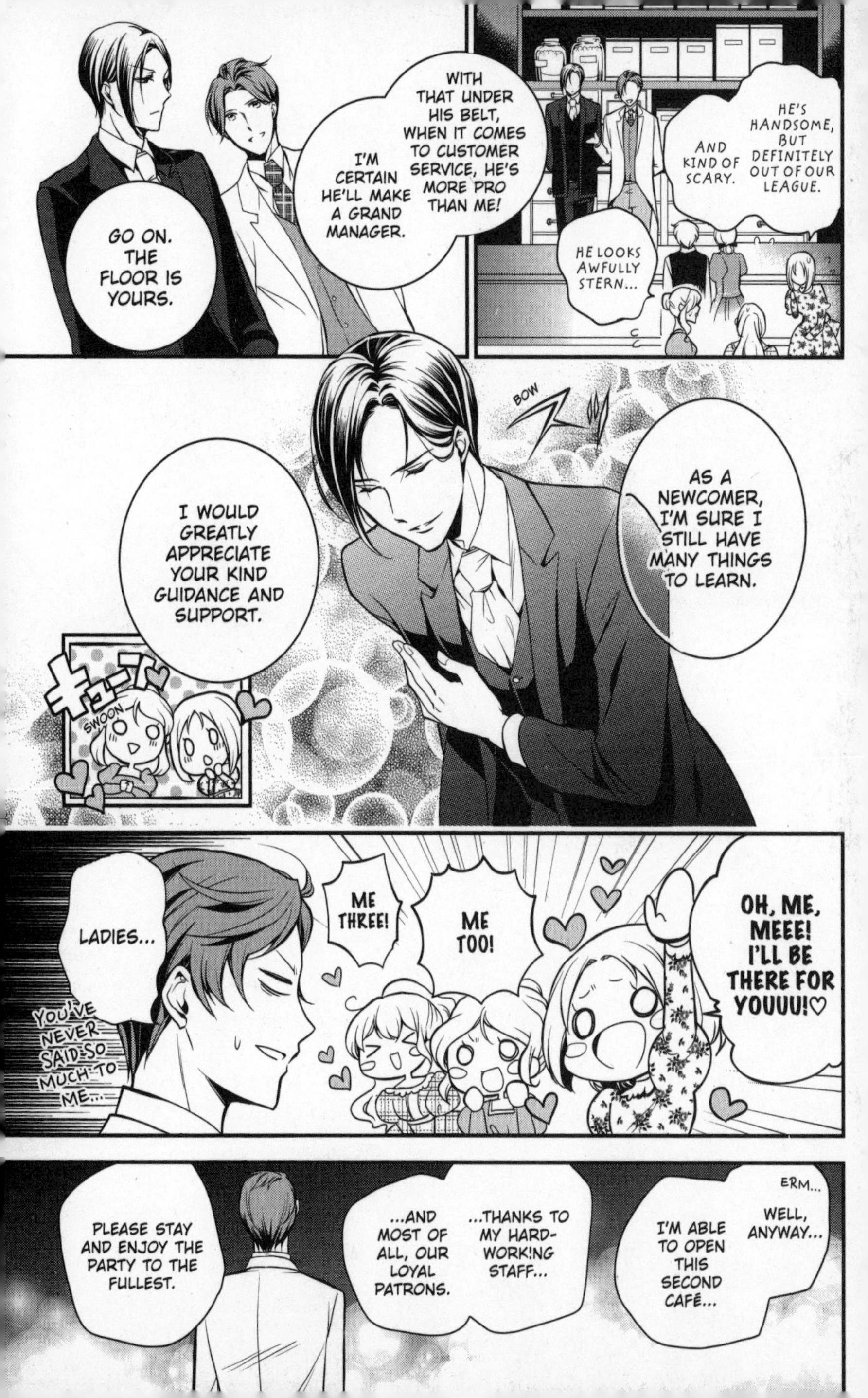
HE'S HANDSOME, BUT DEFINITELY OUT OF OUR LEAGUE.
AND KIND OF SCARY.
HE LOOKS AWFULLY STERN...
WITH THAT UNDER HIS BELT, WHEN IT COMES TO CUSTOMER SERVICE, HE'S MORE PRO THAN ME!
I'M CERTAIN HE'LL MAKE A GRAND MANAGER.
GO ON. THE FLOOR IS YOURS.
BOW
AS A NEWCOMER, I'M SURE I STILL HAVE MANY THINGS TO LEARN.
I WOULD GREATLY APPRECIATE YOUR KIND GUIDANCE AND SUPPORT.
キューン♡
SWOON
OH, ME, MEEE! I'LL BE THERE FOR YOUUU!♡
ME TOO!
ME THREE!
LADIES...
YOU'VE NEVER SAID SO MUCH TO ME...
ERM...
WELL, ANYWAY...
I'M ABLE TO OPEN THIS SECOND CAFÉ...
...THANKS TO MY HARD-WORKING STAFF...
...AND MOST OF ALL, OUR LOYAL PATRONS.
PLEASE STAY AND ENJOY THE PARTY TO THE FULLEST.

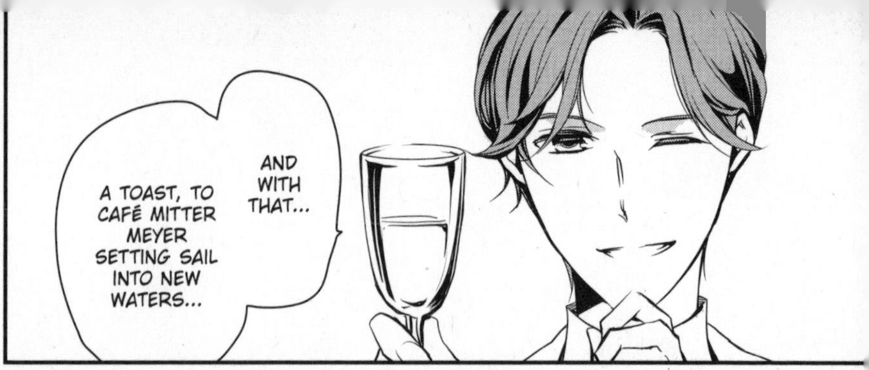
AND WITH THAT...
A TOAST, TO CAFÉ MITTER MEYER SETTING SAIL INTO NEW WATERS...

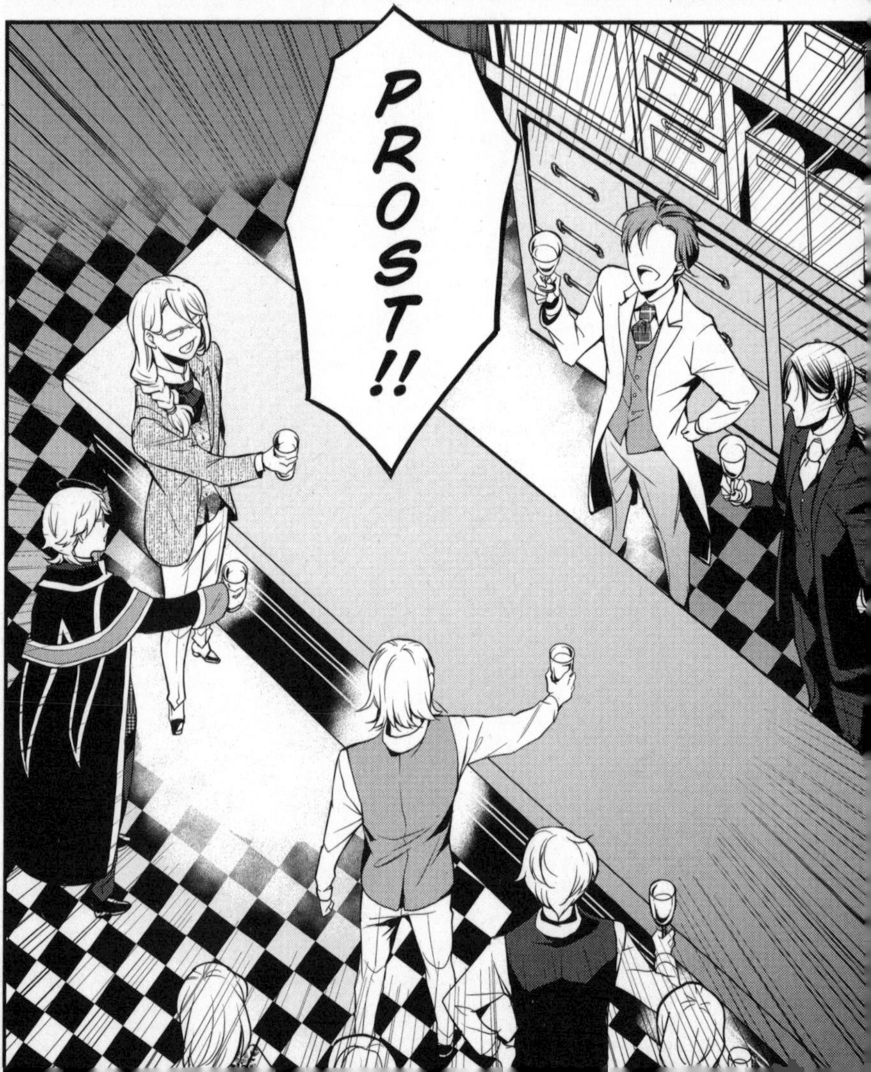
PROST!!

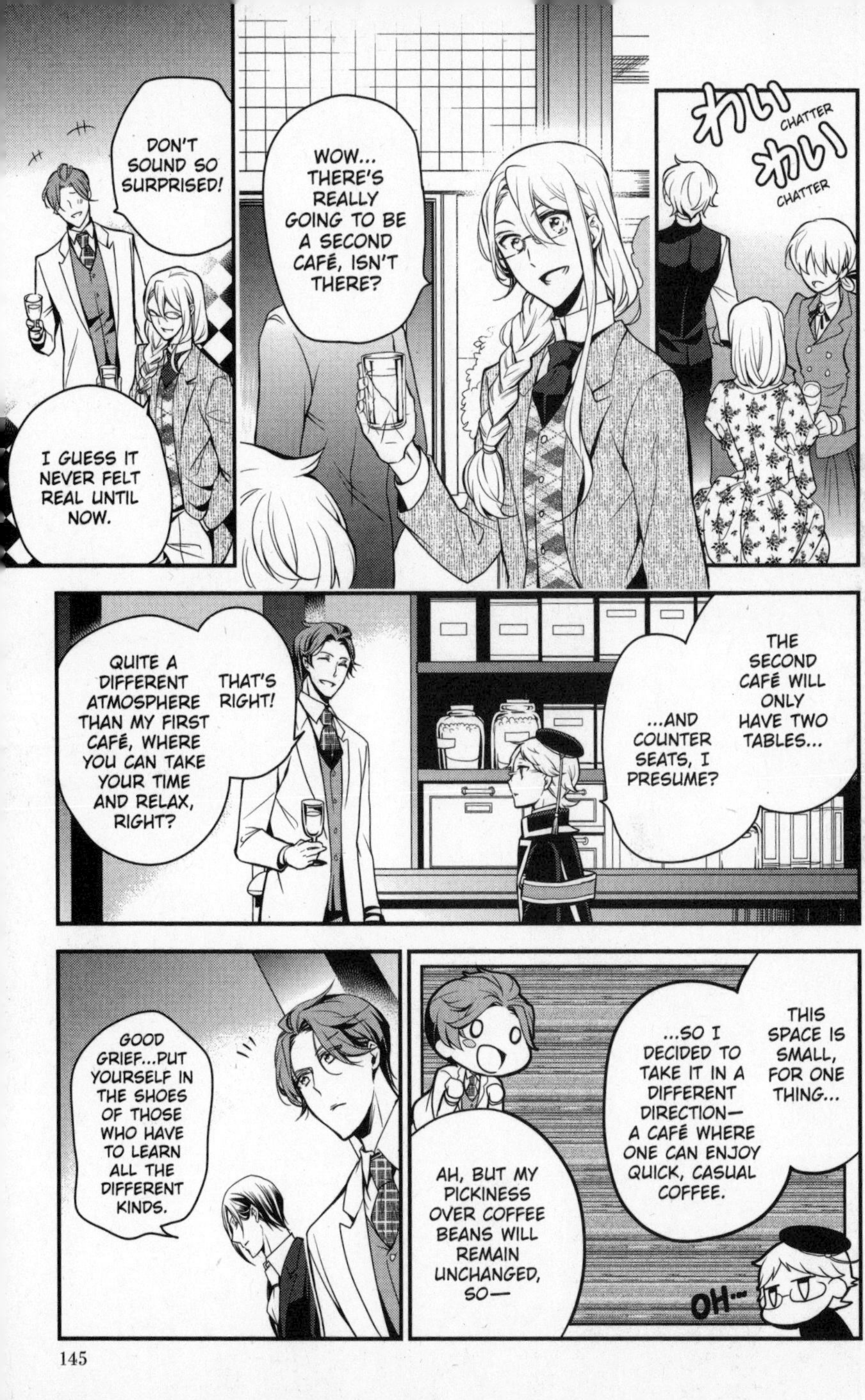
わいわい
CHATTER CHATTER
WOW... THERE'S REALLY GOING TO BE A SECOND CAFÉ, ISN'T THERE?
DON'T SOUND SO SURPRISED!
I GUESS IT NEVER FELT REAL UNTIL NOW.
THE SECOND CAFÉ WILL ONLY HAVE TWO TABLES...
...AND COUNTER SEATS, I PRESUME?
THAT'S RIGHT!
QUITE A DIFFERENT ATMOSPHERE THAN MY FIRST CAFÉ, WHERE YOU CAN TAKE YOUR TIME AND RELAX, RIGHT?
THIS SPACE IS SMALL, FOR ONE THING...
...SO I DECIDED TO TAKE IT IN A DIFFERENT DIRECTION—A CAFÉ WHERE ONE CAN ENJOY QUICK, CASUAL COFFEE.
AH, BUT MY PICKINESS OVER COFFEE BEANS WILL REMAIN UNCHANGED, SO—
OH...
GOOD GRIEF...PUT YOURSELF IN THE SHOES OF THOSE WHO HAVE TO LEARN ALL THE DIFFERENT KINDS.

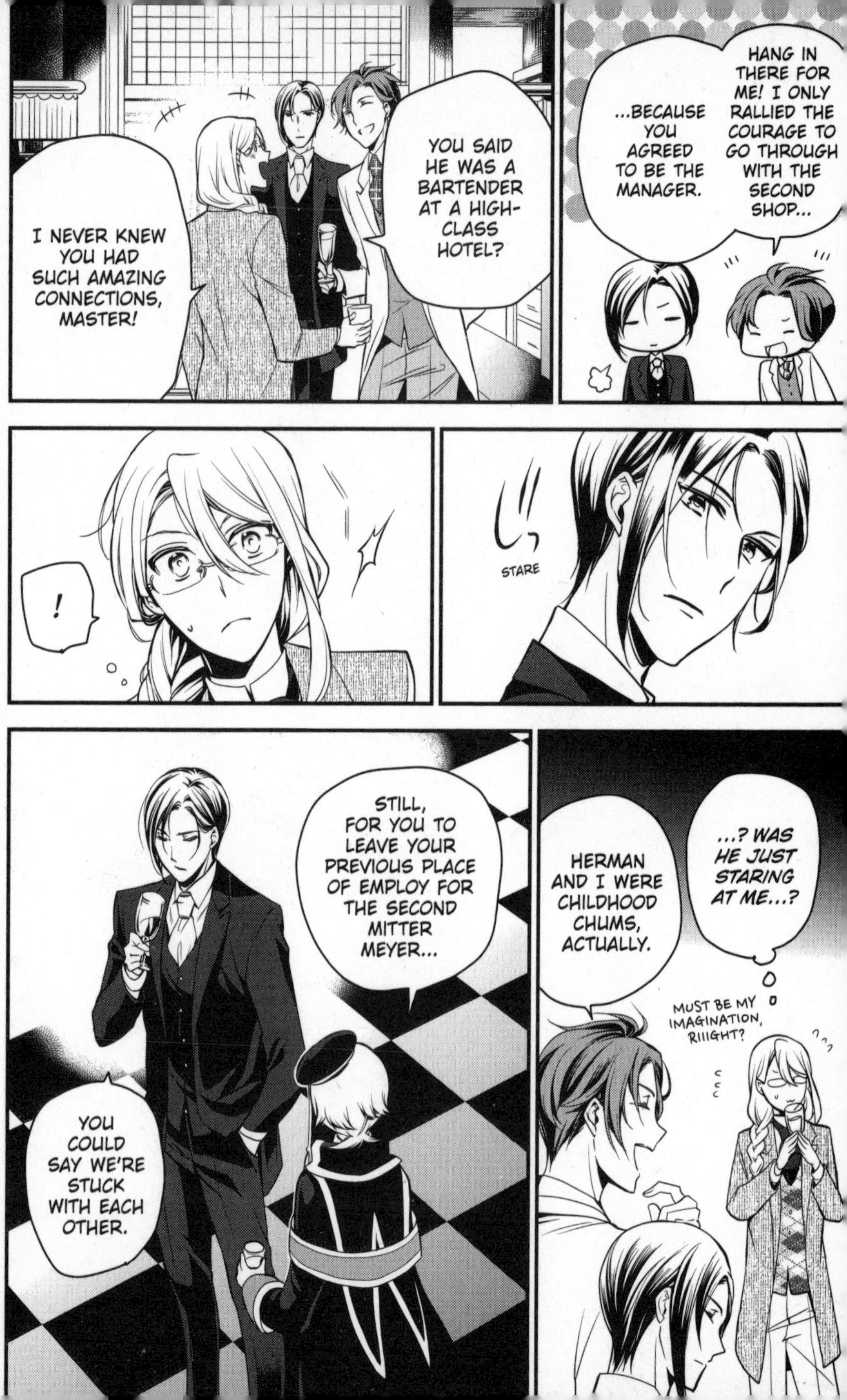
HANG IN THERE FOR ME! I ONLY RALLIED THE COURAGE TO GO THROUGH WITH THE SECOND SHOP...
...BECAUSE YOU AGREED TO BE THE MANAGER.
YOU SAID HE WAS A BARTENDER AT A HIGH-CLASS HOTEL?
I NEVER KNEW YOU HAD SUCH AMAZING CONNECTIONS, MASTER!
STARE
!
...? WAS HE JUST STARING AT ME...?
HERMAN AND I WERE CHILDHOOD CHUMS, ACTUALLY.
MUST BE MY IMAGINATION, RIIIGHT?
STILL, FOR YOU TO LEAVE YOUR PREVIOUS PLACE OF EMPLOY FOR THE SECOND MITTER MEYER...
YOU COULD SAY WE'RE STUCK WITH EACH OTHER.

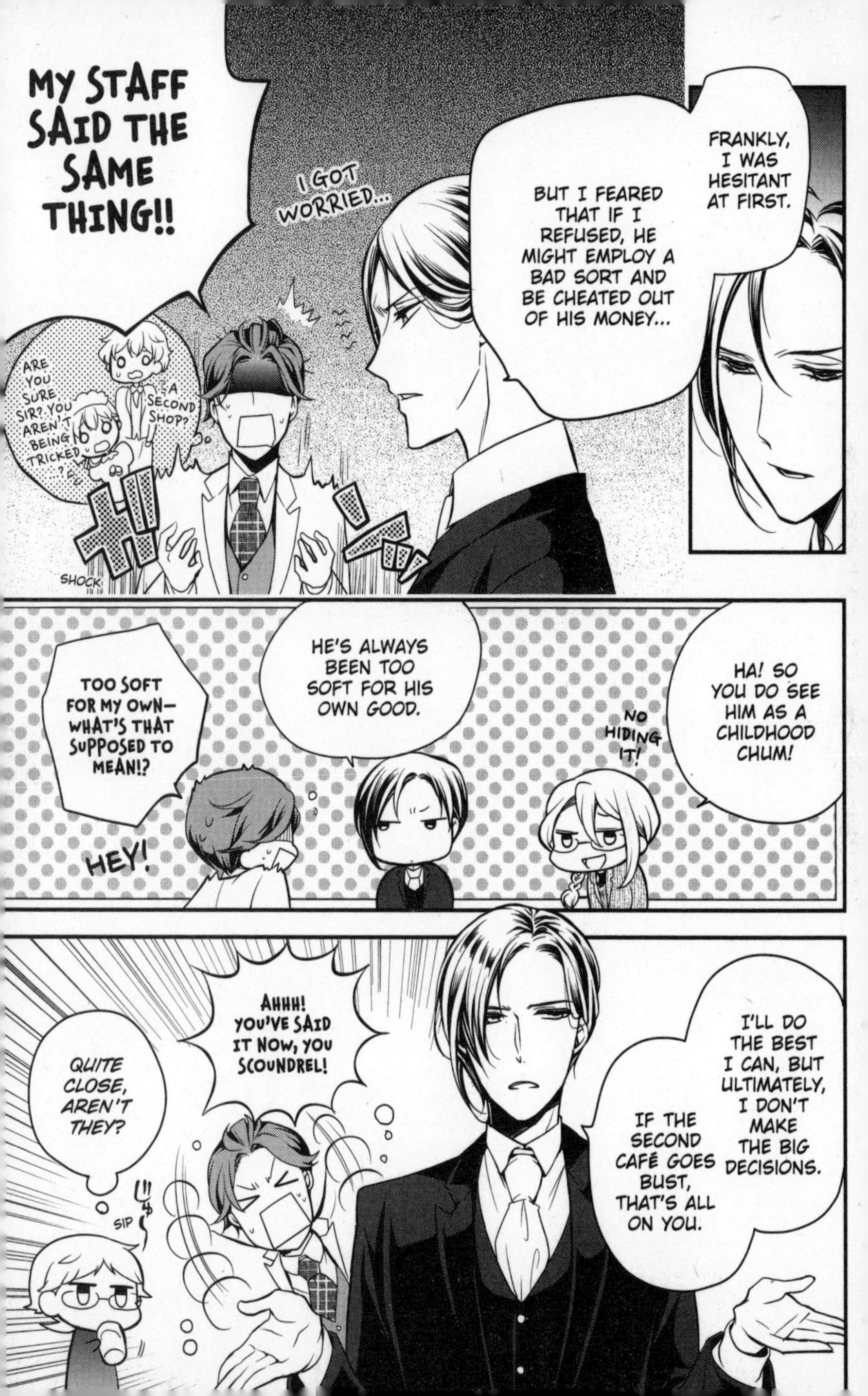
FRANKLY, I WAS HESITANT AT FIRST.
BUT I FEARED THAT IF I REFUSED, HE MIGHT EMPLOY A BAD SORT AND BE CHEATED OUT OF HIS MONEY...
I GOT WORRIED...
MY STAFF SAID THE SAME THING!!
A SECOND SHOP?
ARE YOU SURE SIR? YOU AREN'T BEING TRICKED...?
SHOCK
HA! SO YOU DO SEE HIM AS A CHILDHOOD CHUM!
NO HIDING IT!
HE'S ALWAYS BEEN TOO SOFT FOR HIS OWN GOOD.
TOO SOFT FOR MY OWN— WHAT'S THAT SUPPOSED TO MEAN!?
HEY!
I'LL DO THE BEST I CAN, BUT ULTIMATELY, I DON'T MAKE THE BIG DECISIONS.
IF THE SECOND CAFÉ GOES BUST, THAT'S ALL ON YOU.
AHHH! YOU'VE SAID IT NOW, YOU SCOUNDREL!
QUITE CLOSE, AREN'T THEY?
SIP

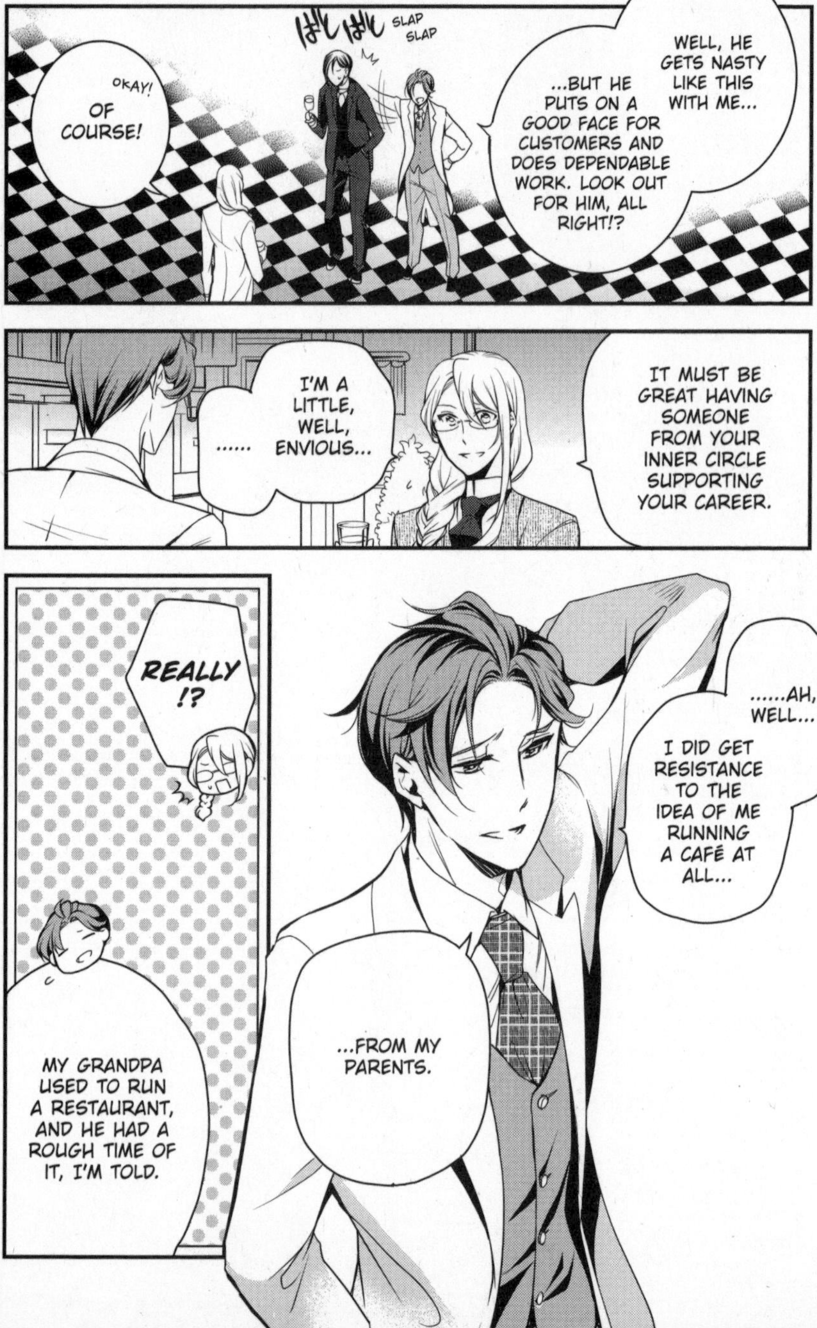
WELL, HE GETS NASTY LIKE THIS WITH ME...
...BUT HE PUTS ON A GOOD FACE FOR CUSTOMERS AND DOES DEPENDABLE WORK. LOOK OUT FOR HIM, ALL RIGHT!?
ぱしぱし SLAP SLAP
OKAY! OF COURSE!
IT MUST BE GREAT HAVING SOMEONE FROM YOUR INNER CIRCLE SUPPORTING YOUR CAREER.
I'M A LITTLE, WELL, ENVIOUS...
......
......AH, WELL...
I DID GET RESISTANCE TO THE IDEA OF ME RUNNING A CAFÉ AT ALL...
...FROM MY PARENTS.
REALLY!?
MY GRANDPA USED TO RUN A RESTAURANT, AND HE HAD A ROUGH TIME OF IT, I'M TOLD.

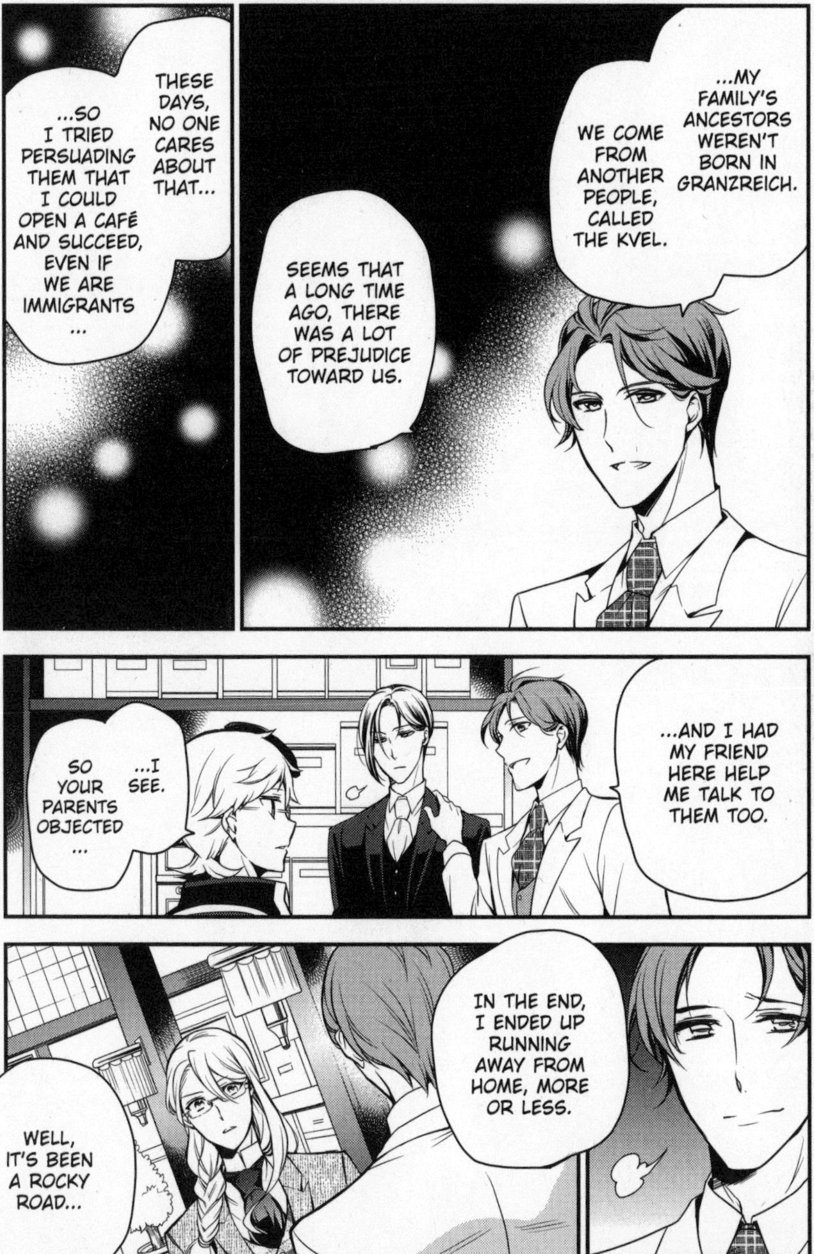
...MY FAMILY'S ANCESTORS WEREN'T BORN IN GRANZREICH.
WE COME FROM ANOTHER PEOPLE, CALLED THE KVEL.
SEEMS THAT A LONG TIME AGO, THERE WAS A LOT OF PREJUDICE TOWARD US.
THESE DAYS, NO ONE CARES ABOUT THAT...
...SO I TRIED PERSUADING THEM THAT I COULD OPEN A CAFÉ AND SUCCEED, EVEN IF WE ARE IMMIGRANTS...
...AND I HAD MY FRIEND HERE HELP ME TALK TO THEM TOO.
...I SEE.
SO YOUR PARENTS OBJECTED...
IN THE END, I ENDED UP RUNNING AWAY FROM HOME, MORE OR LESS.
WELL, IT'S BEEN A ROCKY ROAD...

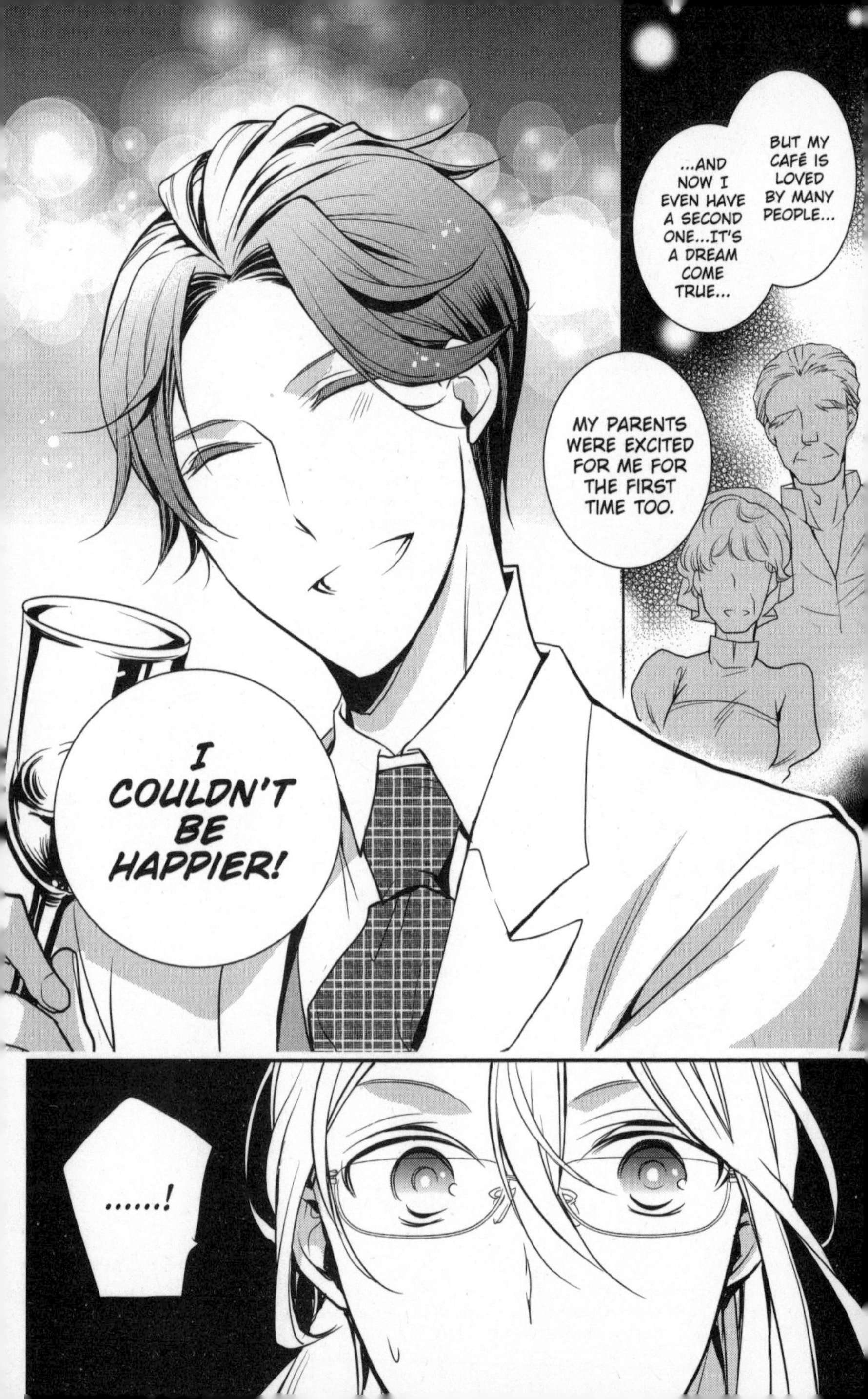
BUT MY CAFÉ IS LOVED BY MANY PEOPLE...
...AND NOW I EVEN HAVE A SECOND ONE...IT'S A DREAM COME TRUE...
MY PARENTS WERE EXCITED FOR ME FOR THE FIRST TIME TOO.
I COULDN'T BE HAPPIER!
......!

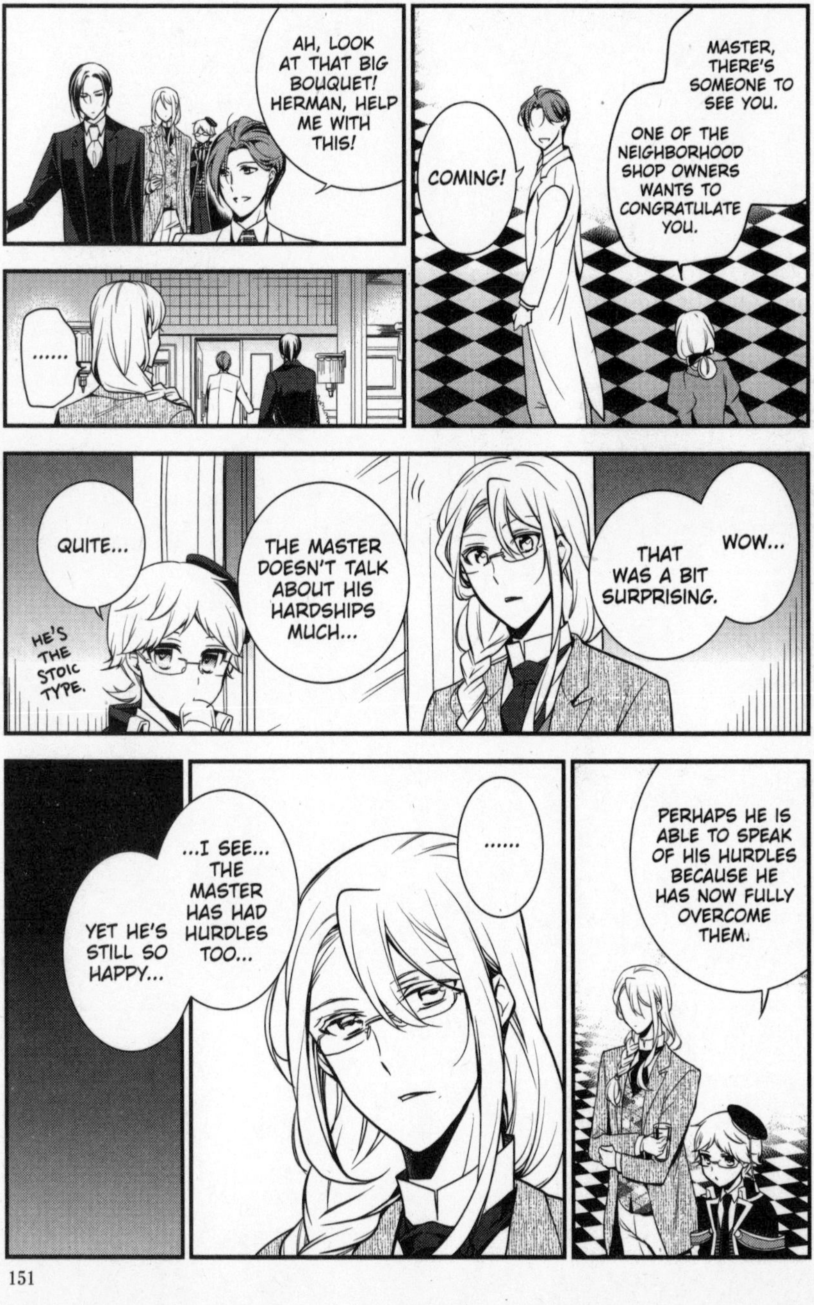
MASTER, THERE'S SOMEONE TO SEE YOU.
ONE OF THE NEIGHBORHOOD SHOP OWNERS WANTS TO CONGRATULATE YOU.
COMING!
AH, LOOK AT THAT BIG BOUQUET! HERMAN, HELP ME WITH THIS!
......
WOW...
THAT WAS A BIT SURPRISING.
THE MASTER DOESN'T TALK ABOUT HIS HARDSHIPS MUCH...
QUITE...
HE'S THE STOIC TYPE.
PERHAPS HE IS ABLE TO SPEAK OF HIS HURDLES BECAUSE HE HAS NOW FULLY OVERCOME THEM.
......
...I SEE... THE MASTER HAS HAD HURDLES TOO...
YET HE'S STILL SO HAPPY...

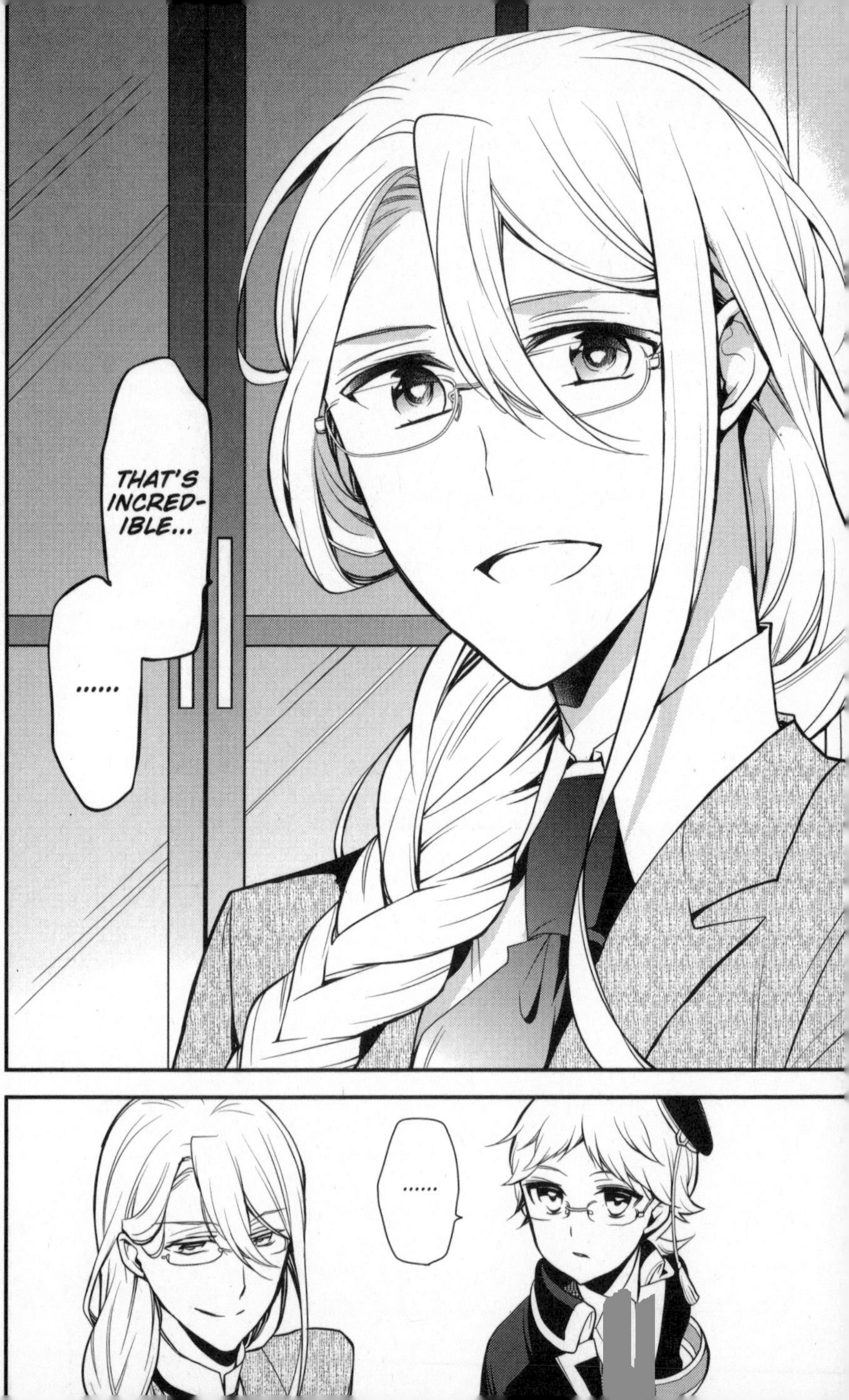
THAT'S INCRED-IBLE...
......
......

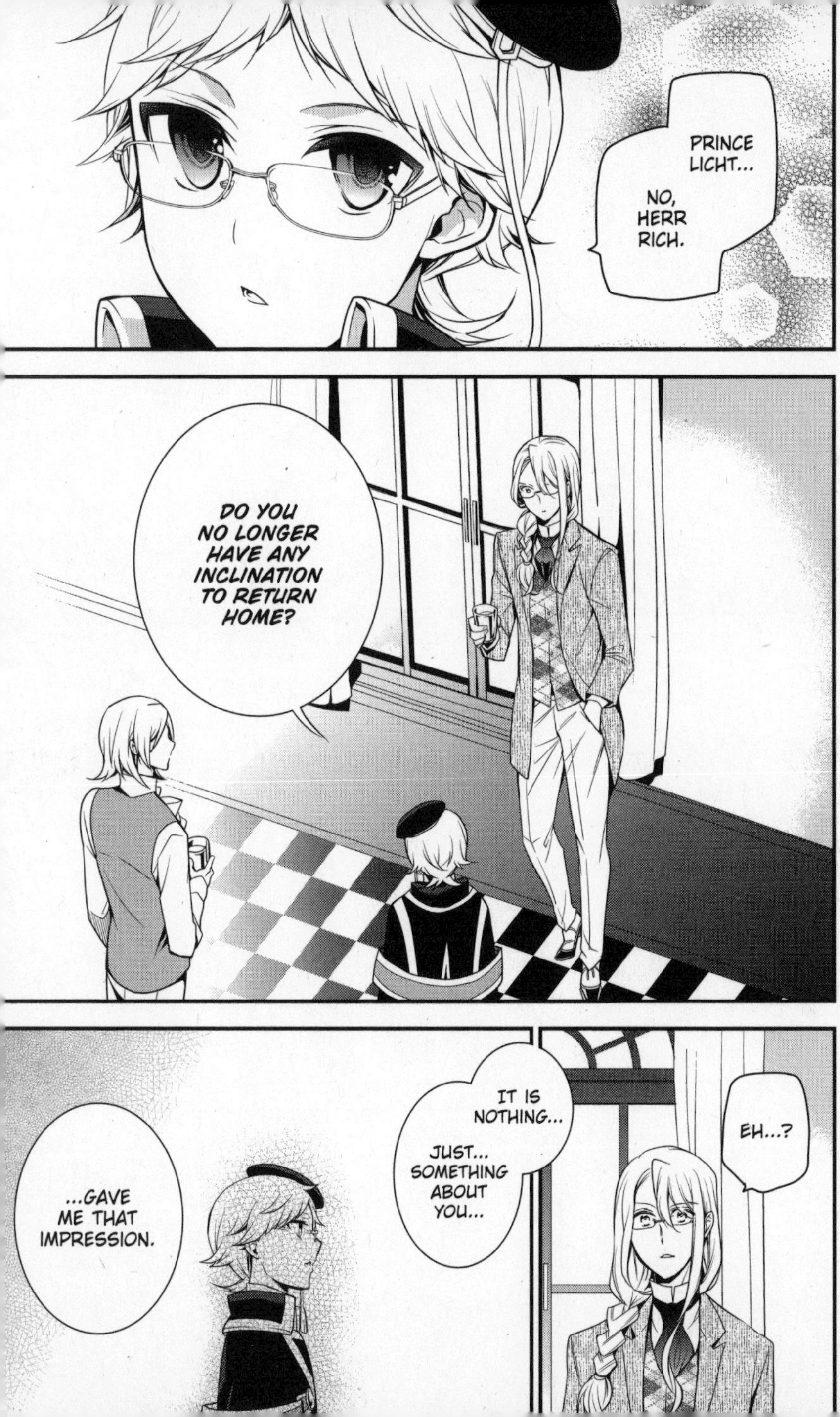
PRINCE LICHT...
NO, HERR RICH.
DO YOU NO LONGER HAVE ANY INCLINATION TO RETURN HOME?
EH...?
IT IS NOTHING...
JUST... SOMETHING ABOUT YOU...
...GAVE ME THAT IMPRESSION.

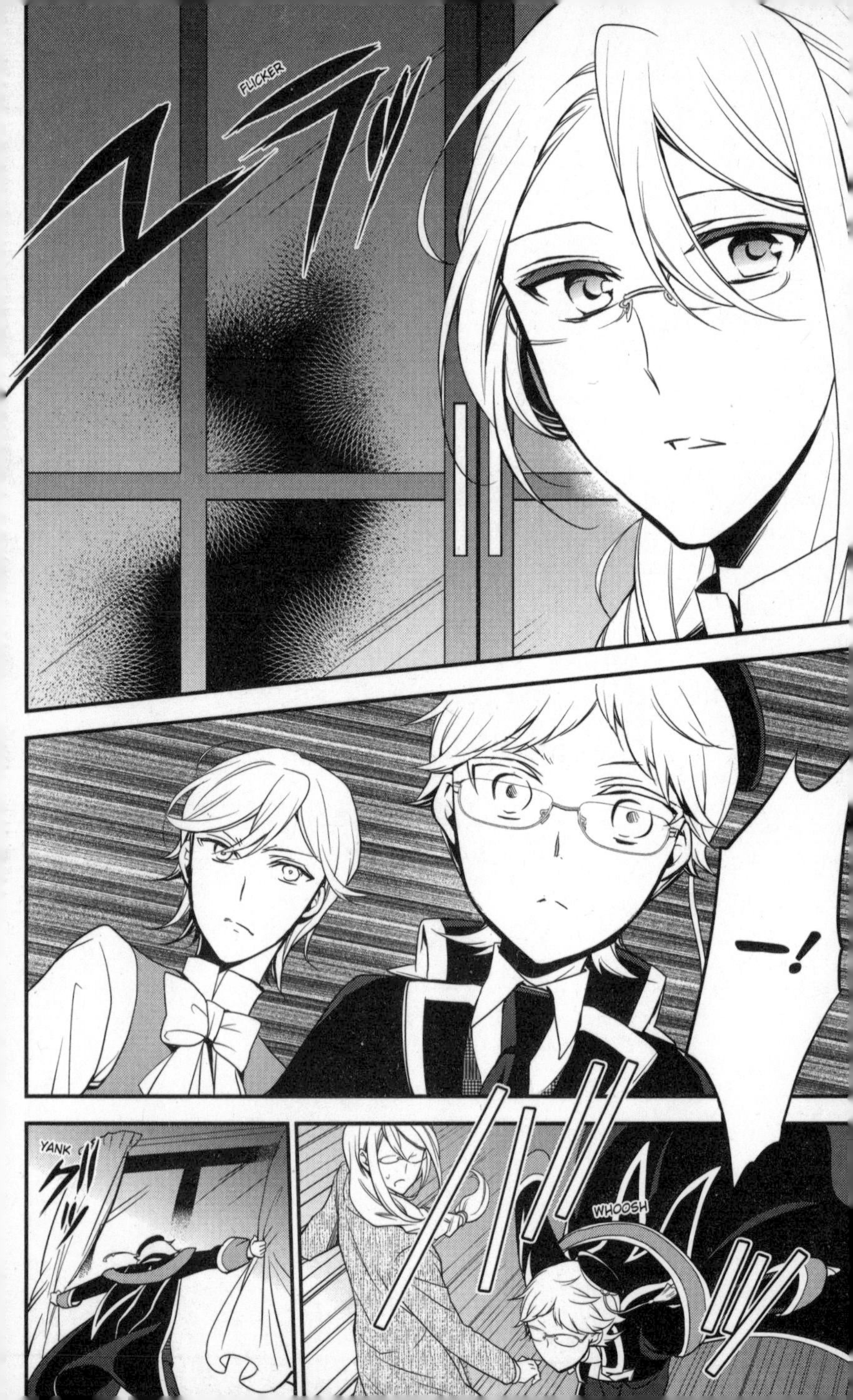
FLICKER
—!
WHOOSH
YANK

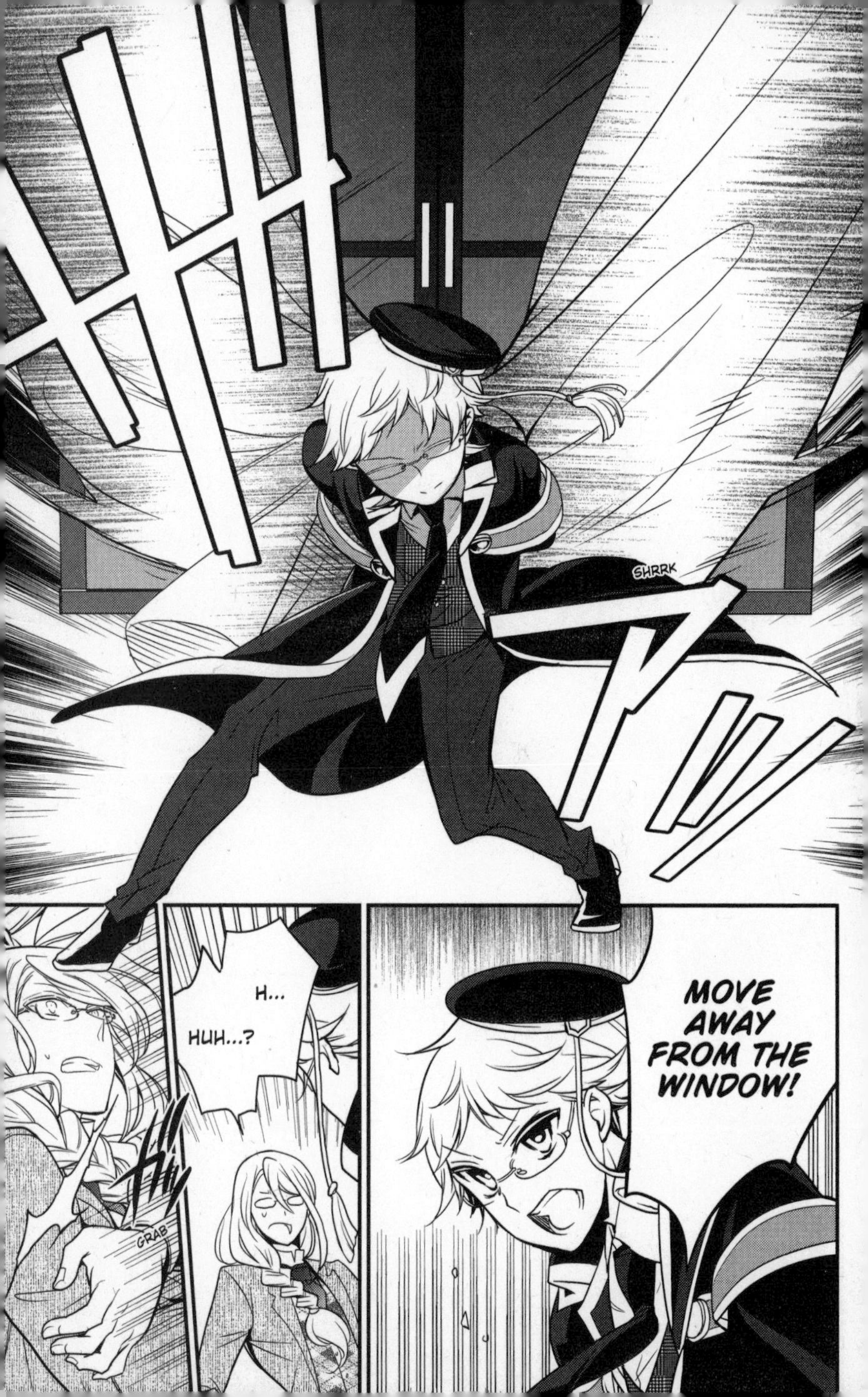
SHRRK
MOVE AWAY FROM THE WINDOW!
H...
HUH...?
GRAB

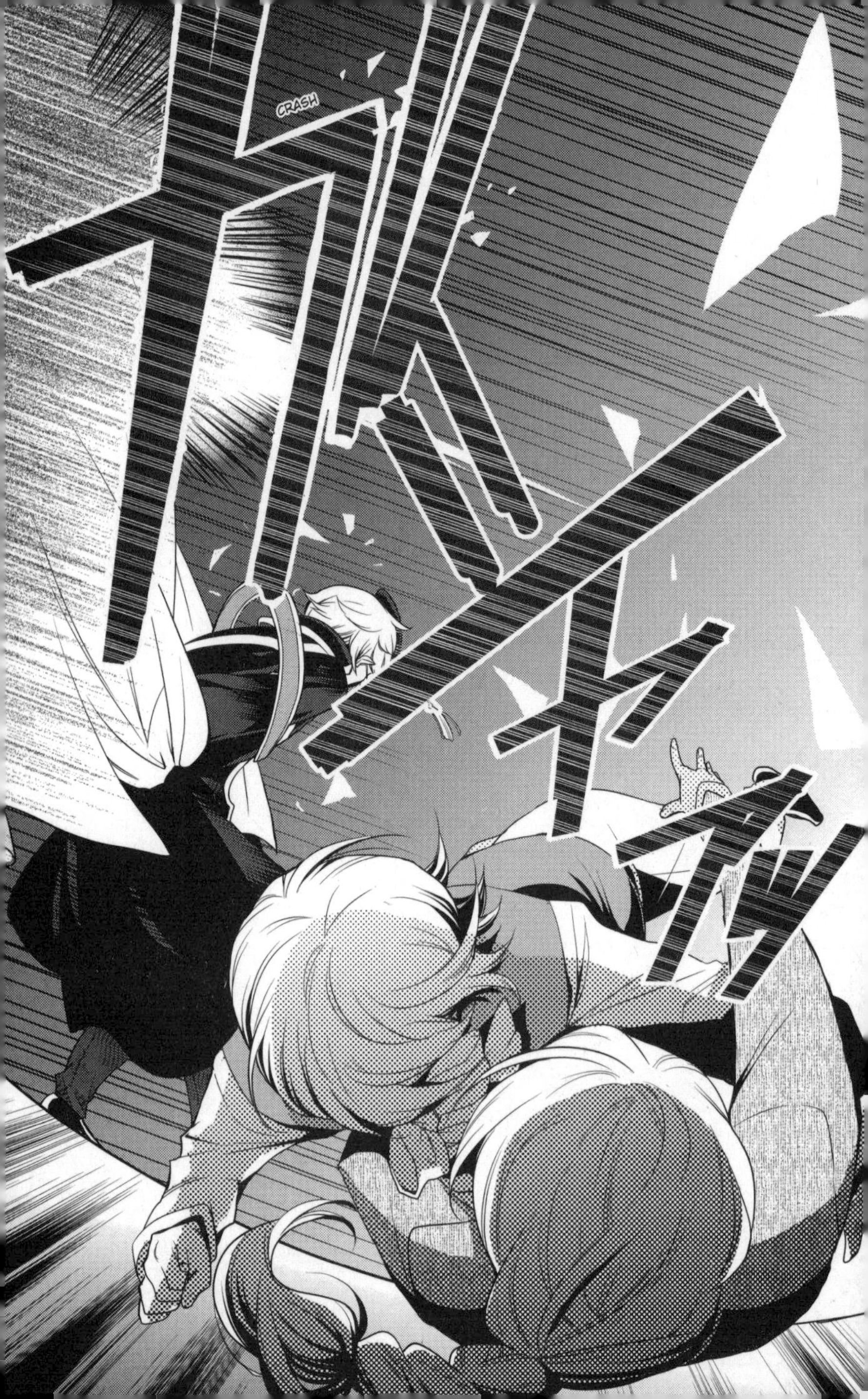
CRASH

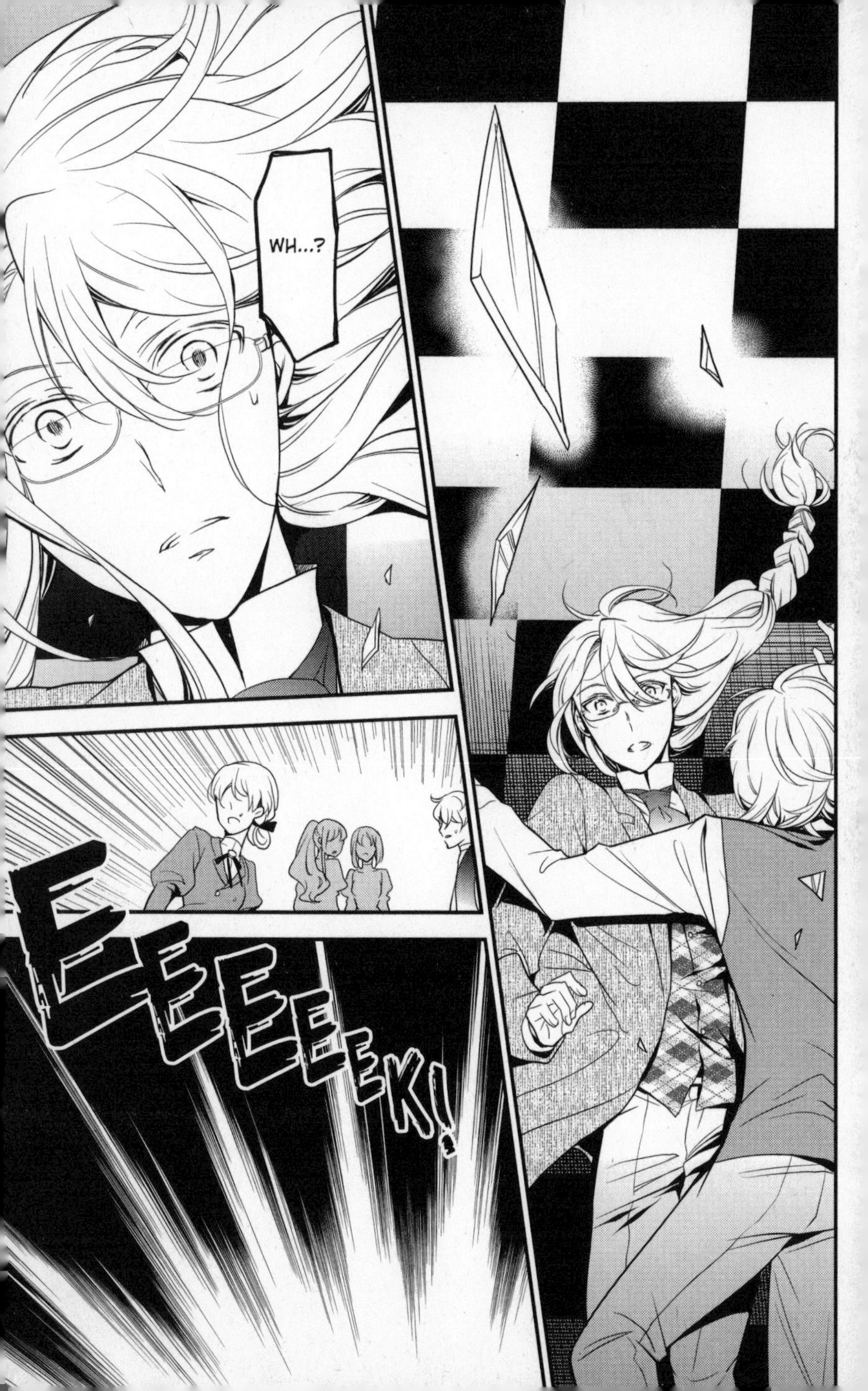
WH...?
EEEEEEK!

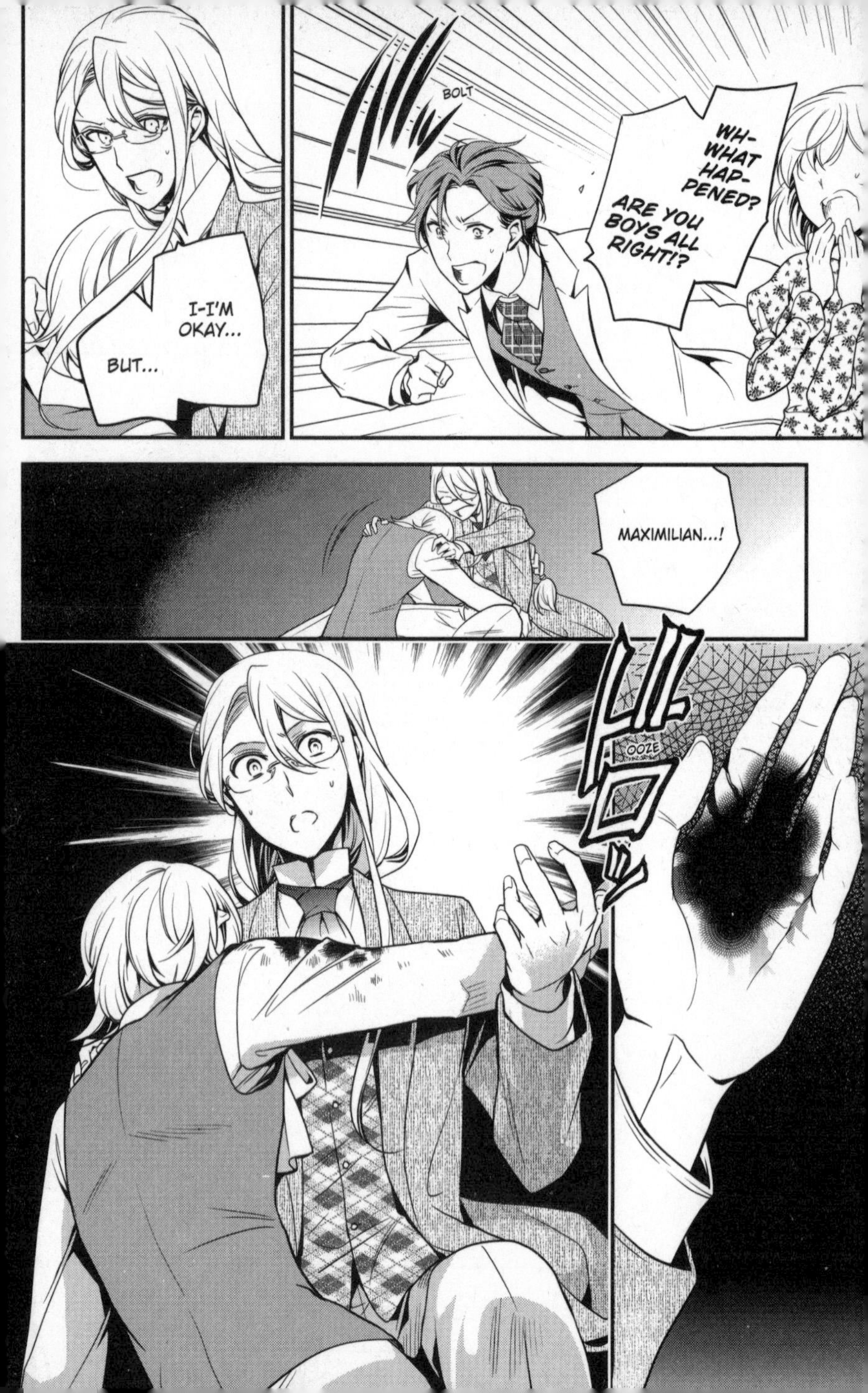
WH- WHAT HAP- PENED? ARE YOU BOYS ALL RIGHT!?
BOLT
I-I'M OKAY...
BUT...
MAXIMILIAN...!
OOZE

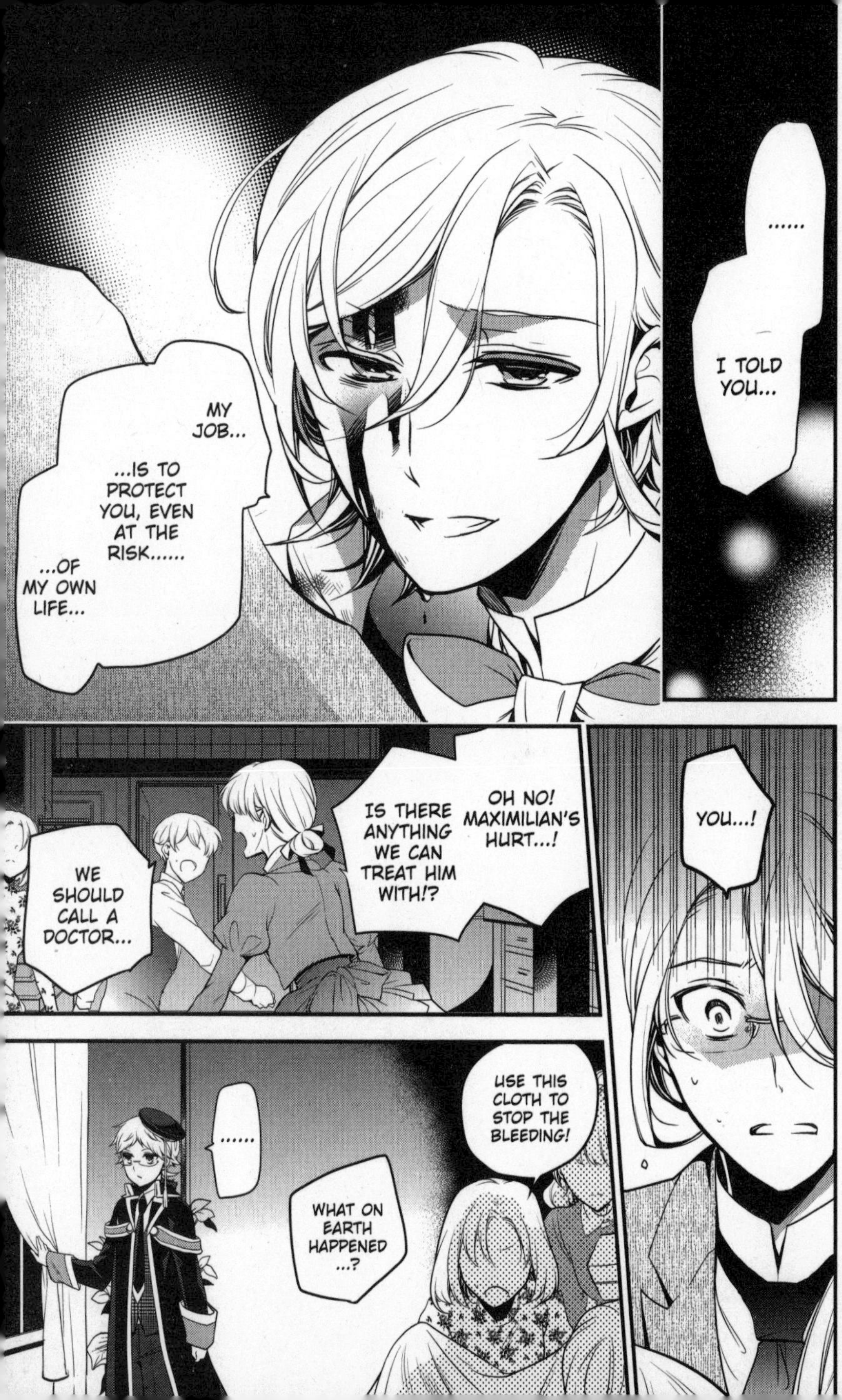
......
I TOLD YOU...
MY JOB...
...IS TO PROTECT YOU, EVEN AT THE RISK......
...OF MY OWN LIFE...
YOU...!
OH NO! MAXIMILIAN'S HURT...!
IS THERE ANYTHING WE CAN TREAT HIM WITH!?
WE SHOULD CALL A DOCTOR...
USE THIS CLOTH TO STOP THE BLEEDING!
......
WHAT ON EARTH HAPPENED ...?

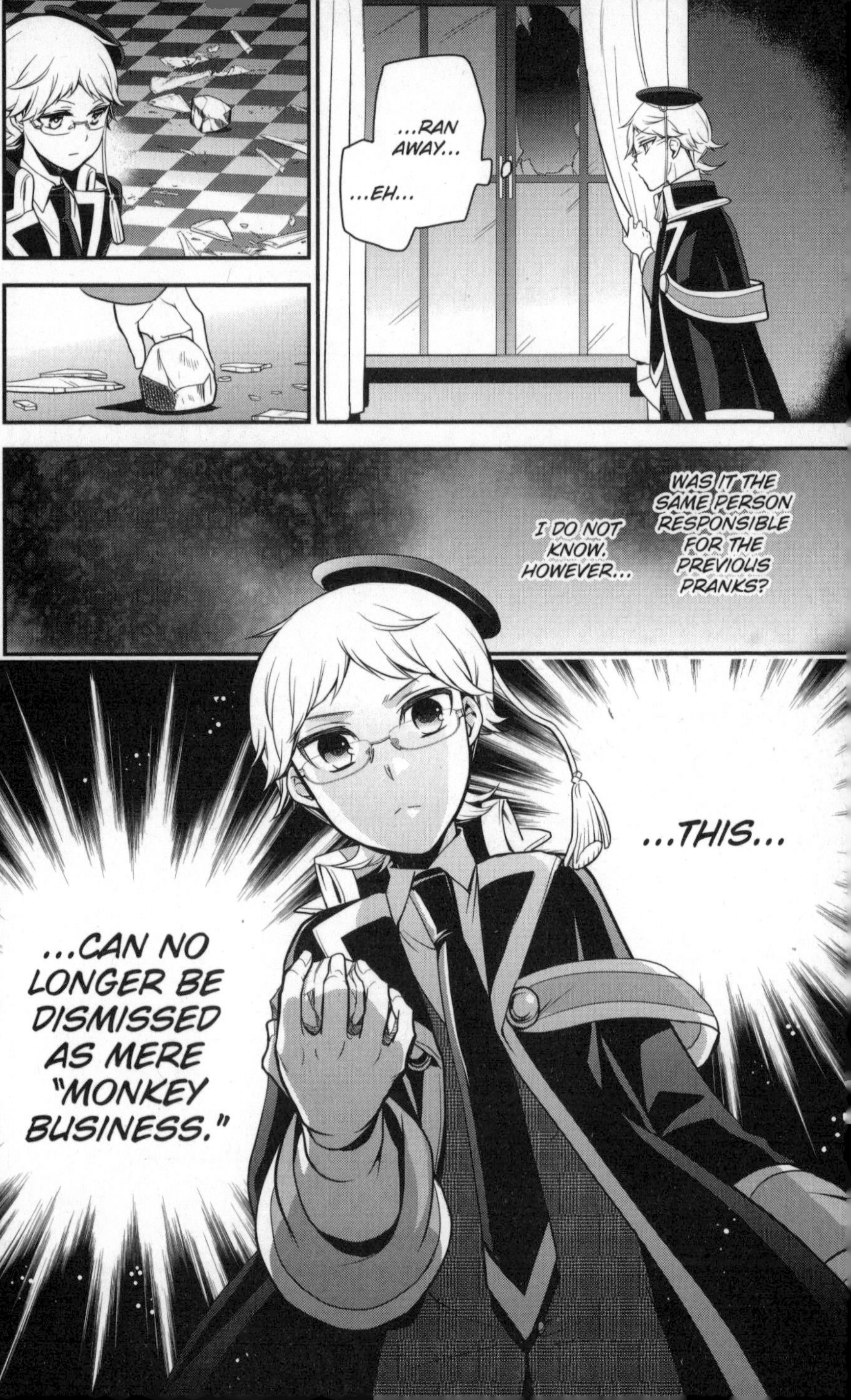
...RAN AWAY...
...EH...
WAS IT THE SAME PERSON RESPONSIBLE FOR THE PREVIOUS PRANKS?
I DO NOT KNOW. HOWEVER...
...THIS...
...CAN NO LONGER BE DISMISSED AS MERE "MONKEY BUSINESS."

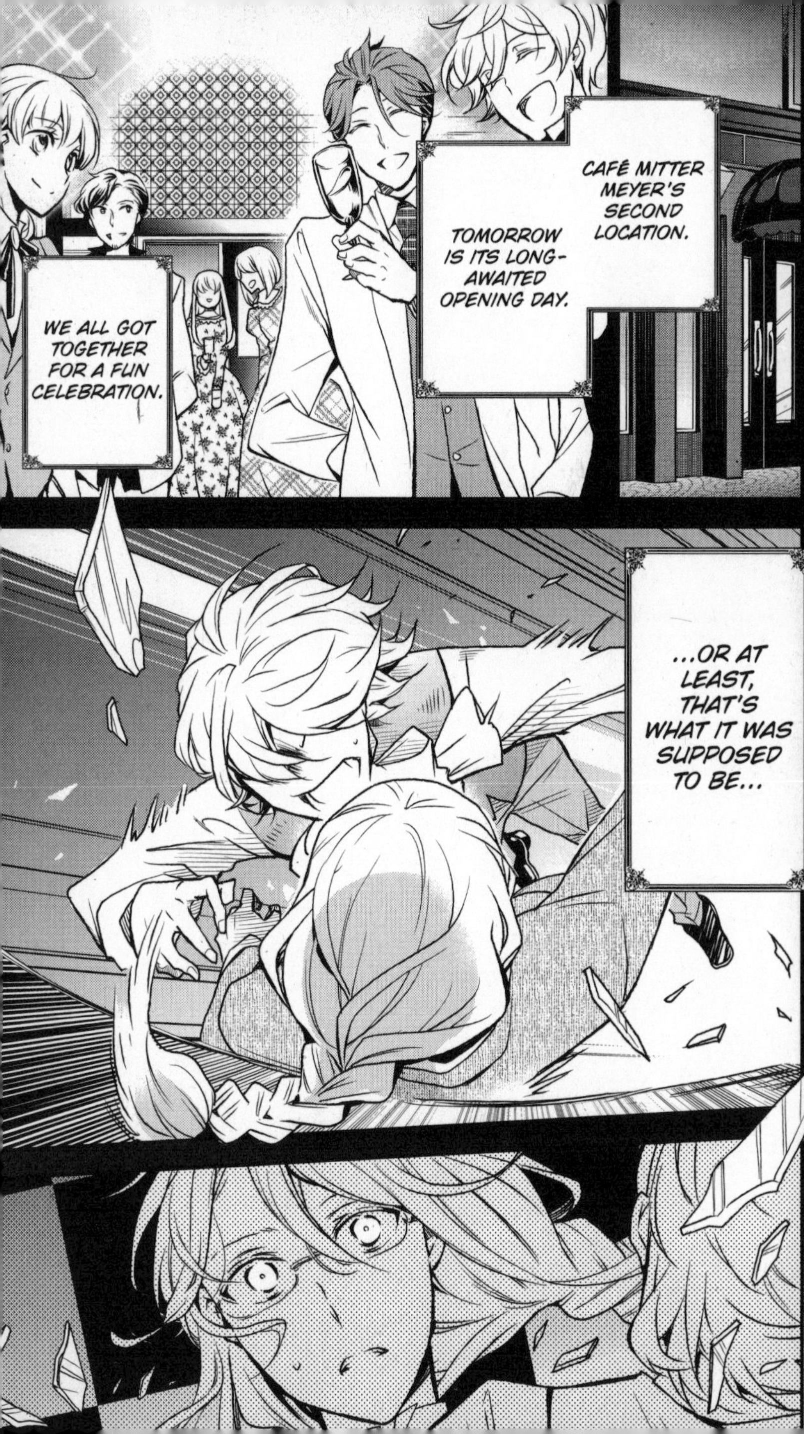
CAFÉ MITTER MEYER'S SECOND LOCATION.
TOMORROW IS ITS LONG-AWAITED OPENING DAY.
WE ALL GOT TOGETHER FOR A FUN CELEBRATION.
...OR AT LEAST, THAT'S WHAT IT WAS SUPPOSED TO BE...

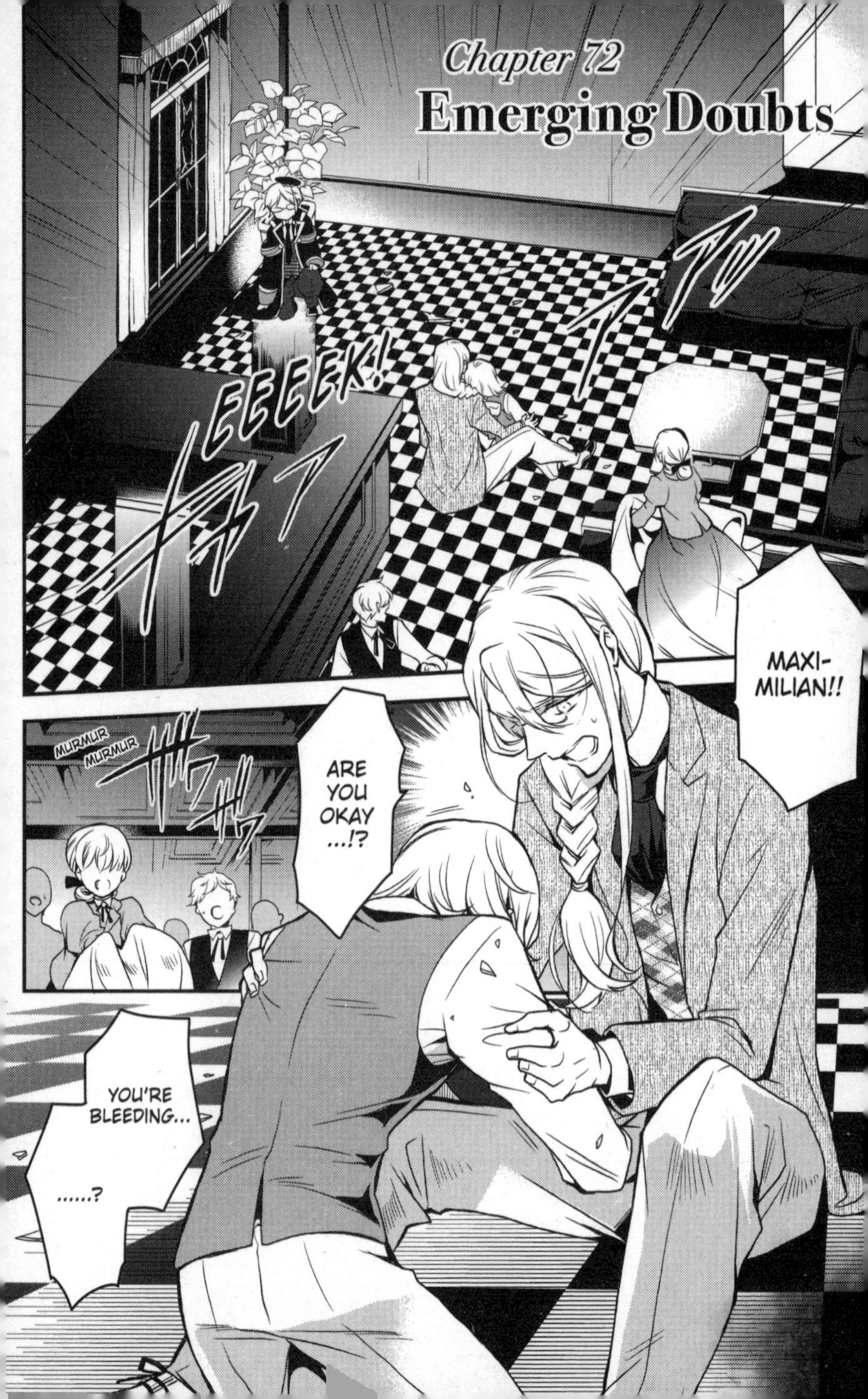
Chapter 72
Emerging Doubts
EEEEEK!!
MAXI-MILIAN!!
ARE YOU OKAY ...!?
MURMUR MURMUR
YOU'RE BLEEDING...
......?

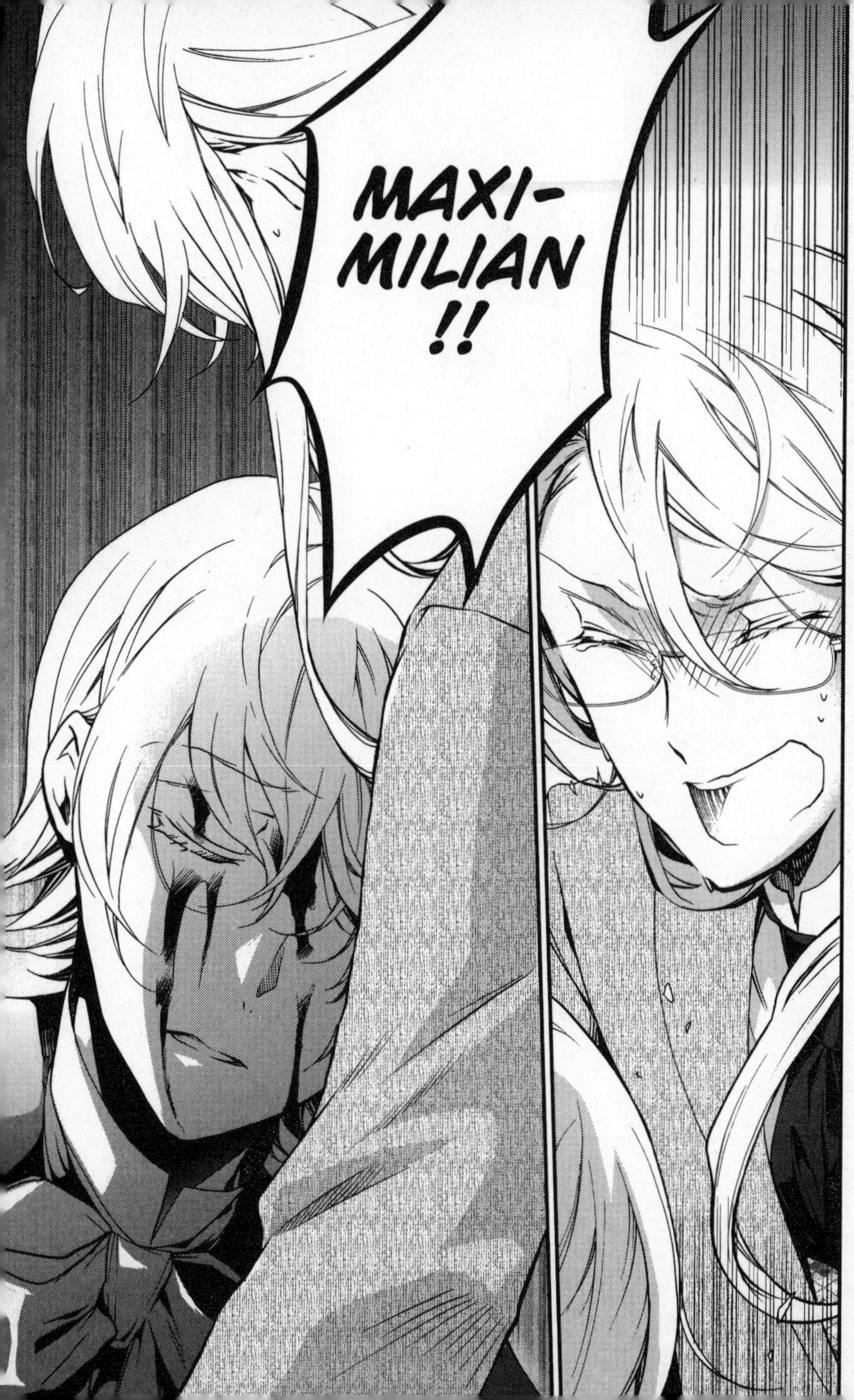
MAXI-
MILIAN
!!

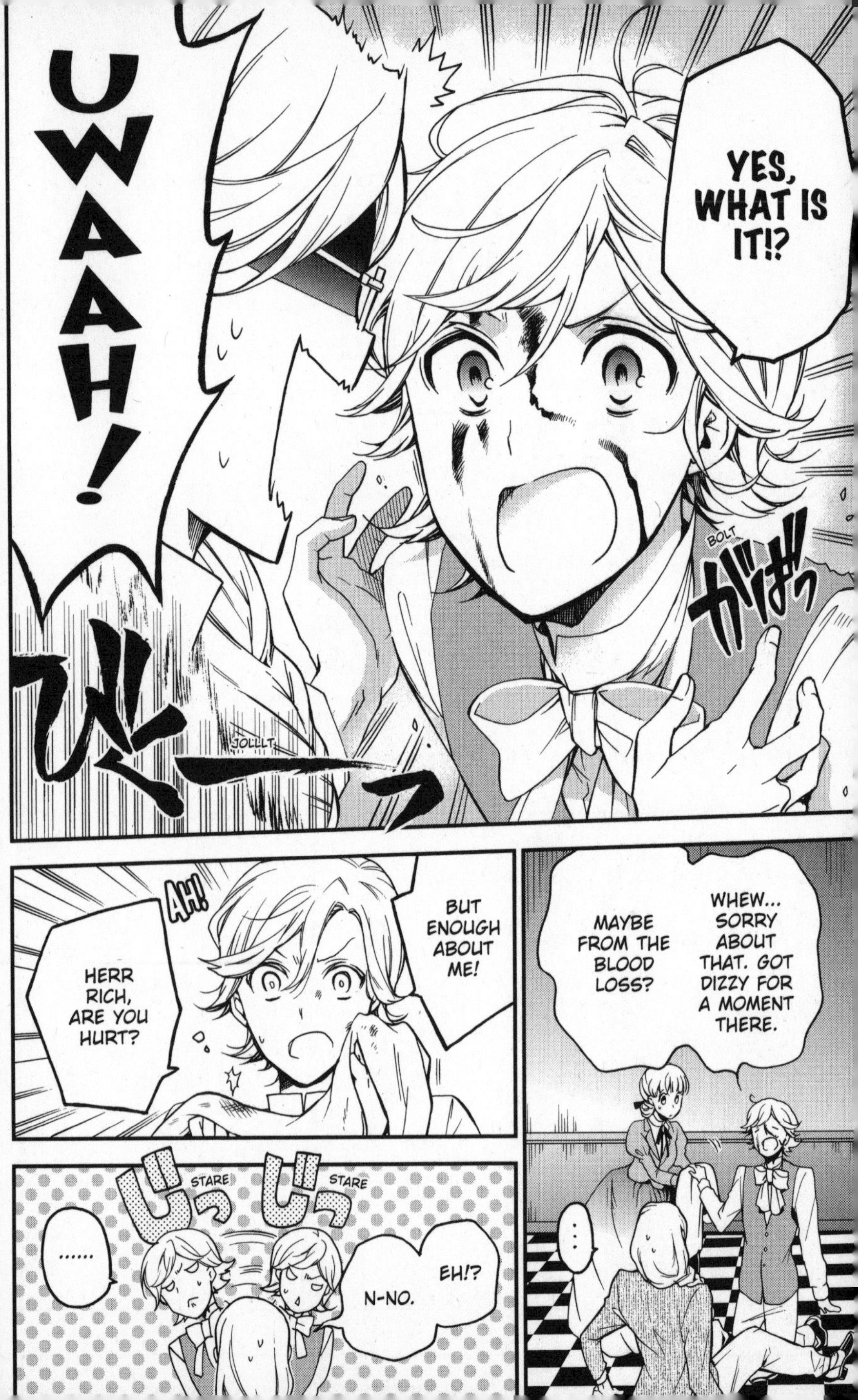
YES, WHAT IS IT!?
UWAH!
BOLT
JOLLLT
WHEW... SORRY ABOUT THAT. GOT DIZZY FOR A MOMENT THERE.
MAYBE FROM THE BLOOD LOSS?
...
BUT ENOUGH ABOUT ME!
AH!
HERR RICH, ARE YOU HURT?
STARE
STARE
EH!?
N-NO.
......

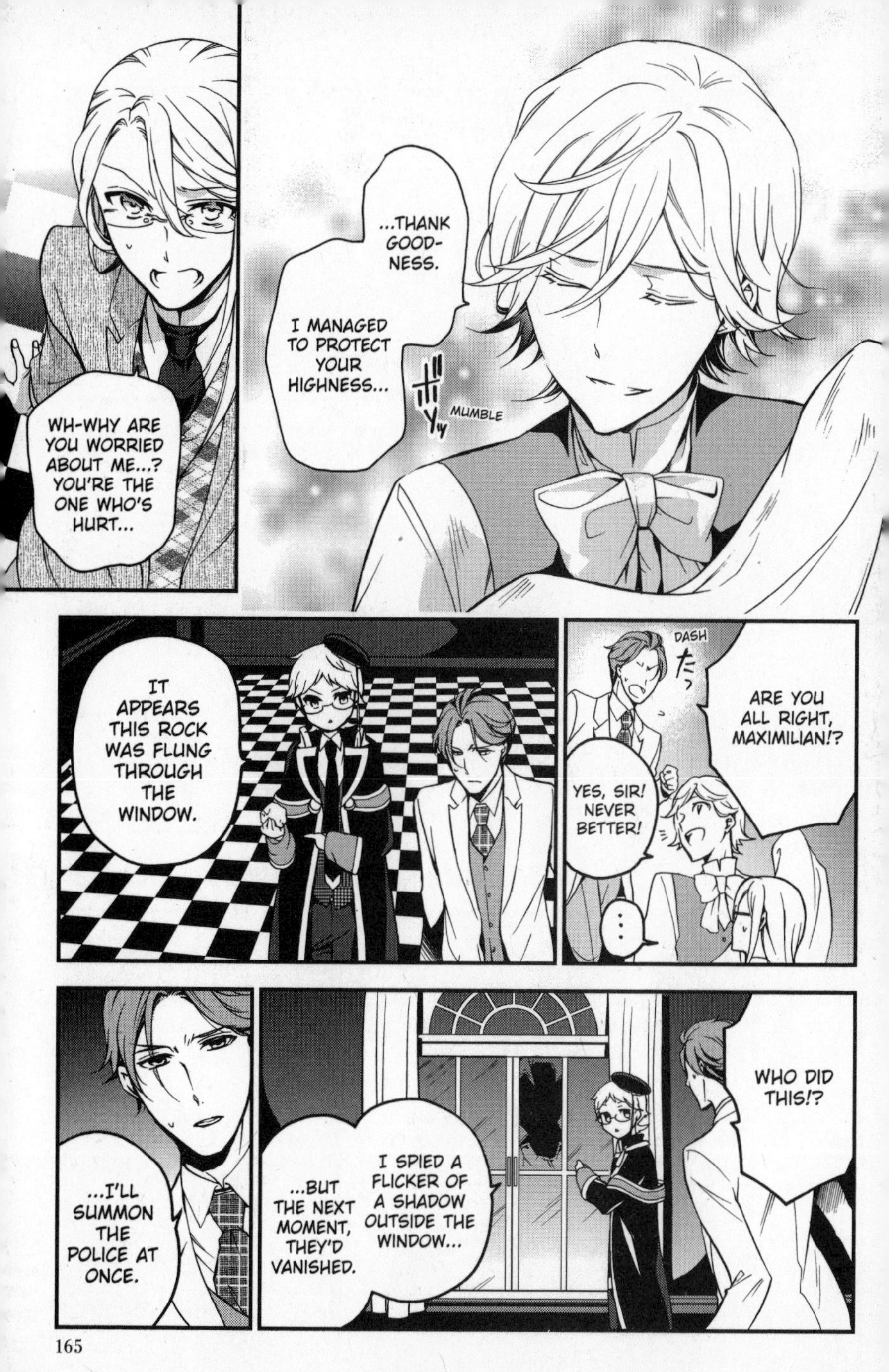
...THANK GOODNESS.
I MANAGED TO PROTECT YOUR HIGHNESS...
MUMBLE
WH-WHY ARE YOU WORRIED ABOUT ME...? YOU'RE THE ONE WHO'S HURT...
DASH
ARE YOU ALL RIGHT, MAXIMILIAN!?
YES, SIR! NEVER BETTER!
...
IT APPEARS THIS ROCK WAS FLUNG THROUGH THE WINDOW.
WHO DID THIS!?
I SPIED A FLICKER OF A SHADOW OUTSIDE THE WINDOW...
...BUT THE NEXT MOMENT, THEY'D VANISHED.
...I'LL SUMMON THE POLICE AT ONCE.

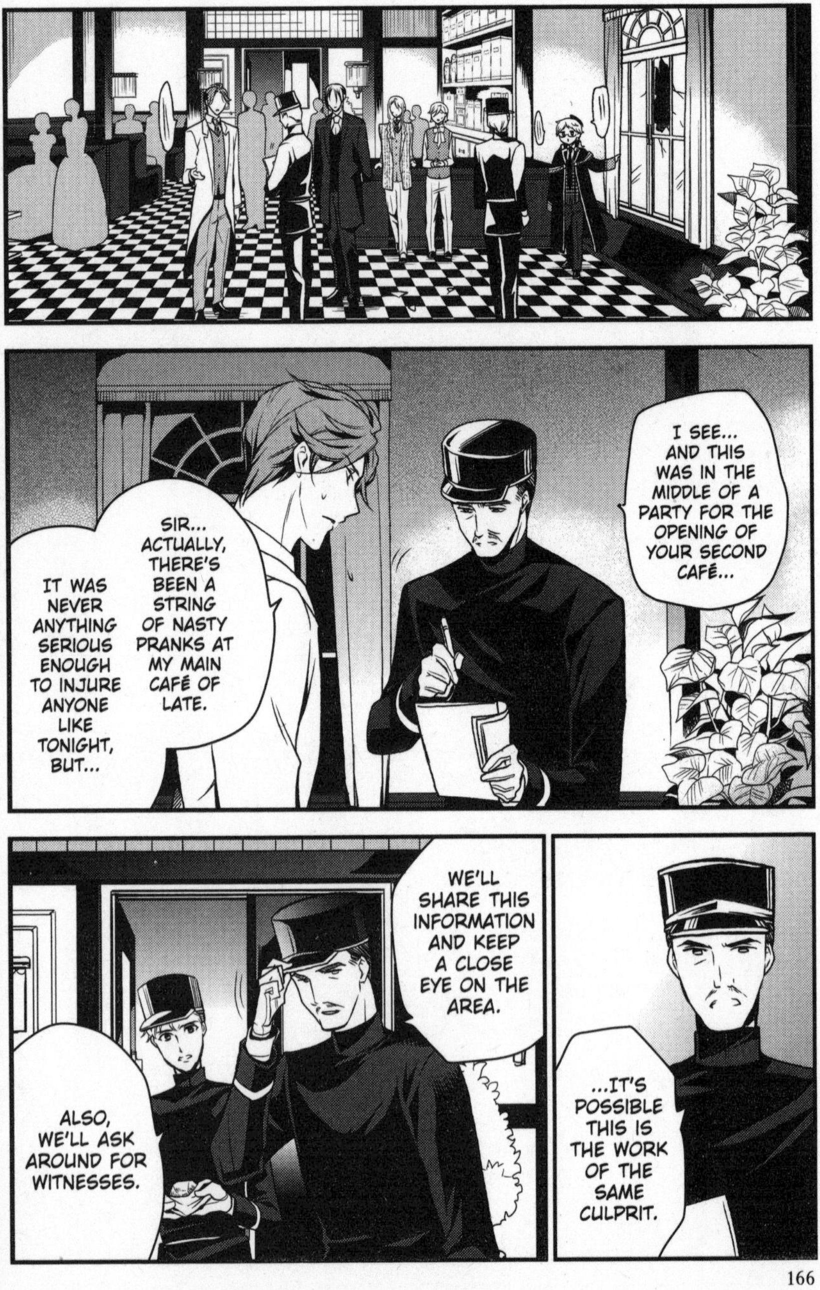
I SEE... AND THIS WAS IN THE MIDDLE OF A PARTY FOR THE OPENING OF YOUR SECOND CAFÉ...
SIR... ACTUALLY, THERE'S BEEN A STRING OF NASTY PRANKS AT MY MAIN CAFÉ OF LATE.
IT WAS NEVER ANYTHING SERIOUS ENOUGH TO INJURE ANYONE LIKE TONIGHT, BUT...
...IT'S POSSIBLE THIS IS THE WORK OF THE SAME CULPRIT.
WE'LL SHARE THIS INFORMATION AND KEEP A CLOSE EYE ON THE AREA.
ALSO, WE'LL ASK AROUND FOR WITNESSES.

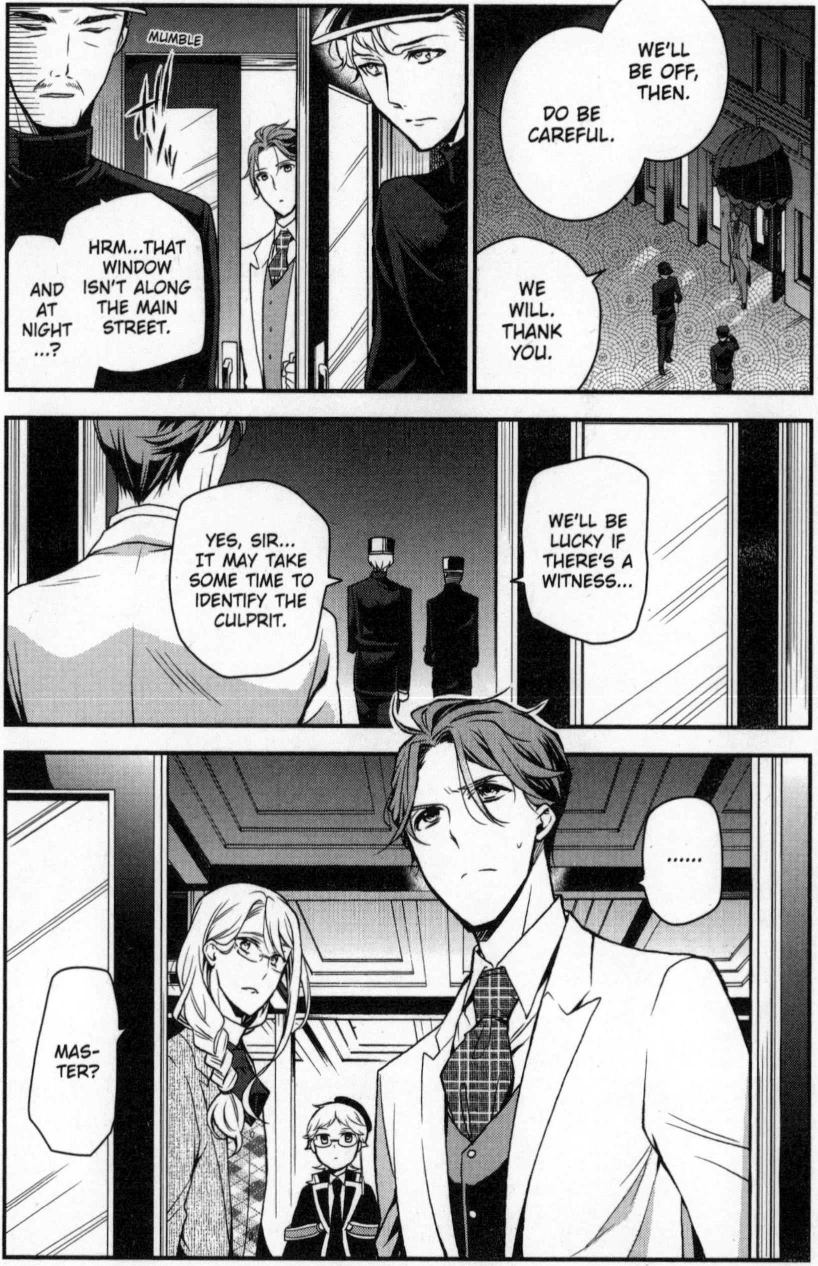
WE'LL BE OFF, THEN.
DO BE CAREFUL.
WE WILL. THANK YOU.
MUMBLE
HRM...THAT WINDOW ISN'T ALONG THE MAIN STREET.
AND AT NIGHT ...?
WE'LL BE LUCKY IF THERE'S A WITNESS...
YES, SIR... IT MAY TAKE SOME TIME TO IDENTIFY THE CULPRIT.
......
MAS-TER?

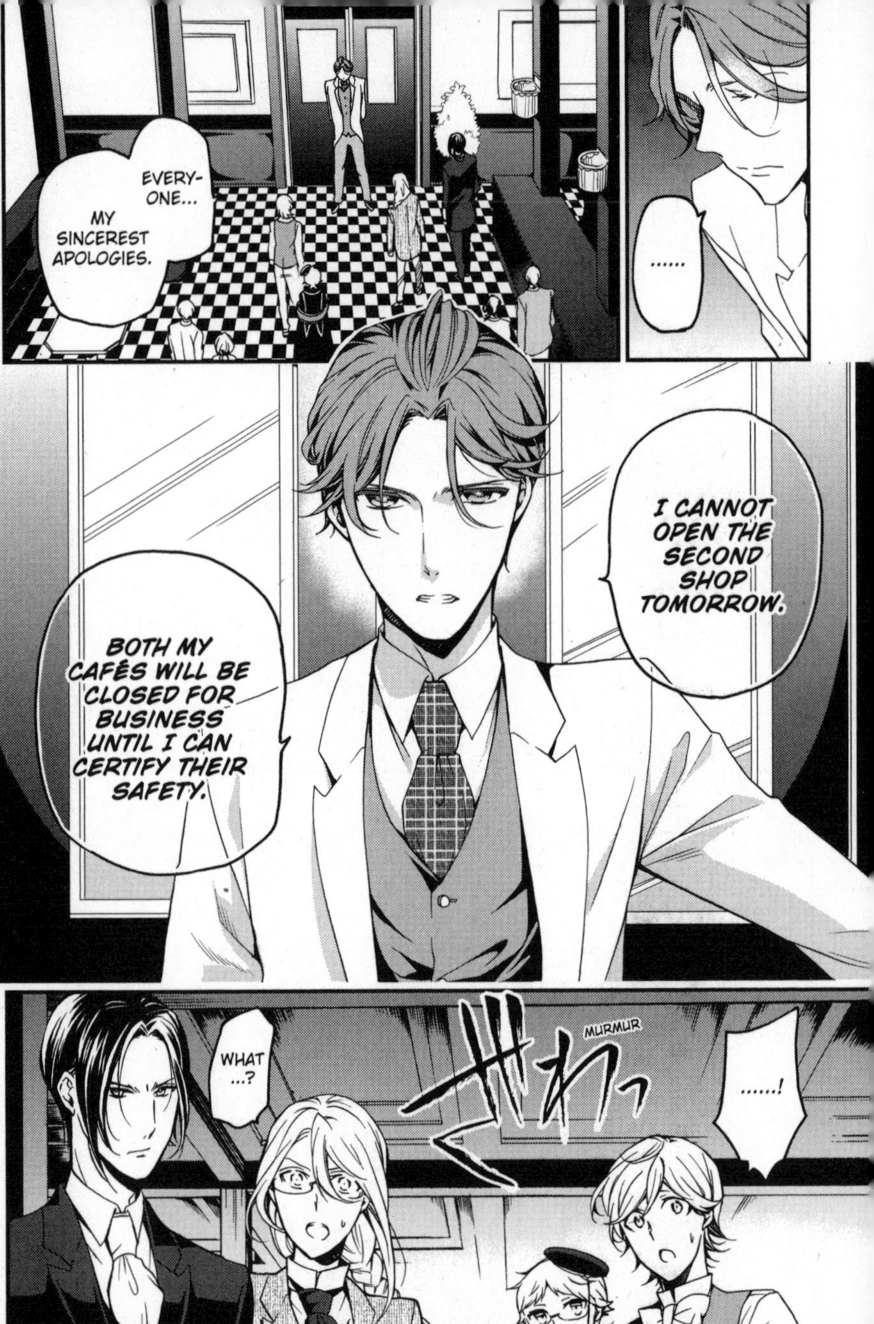

......
EVERY-ONE...
MY SINCEREST APOLOGIES.
I CANNOT OPEN THE SECOND SHOP TOMORROW.
BOTH MY CAFÉS WILL BE CLOSED FOR BUSINESS UNTIL I CAN CERTIFY THEIR SAFETY.
......!
MURMUR
WHAT ...?

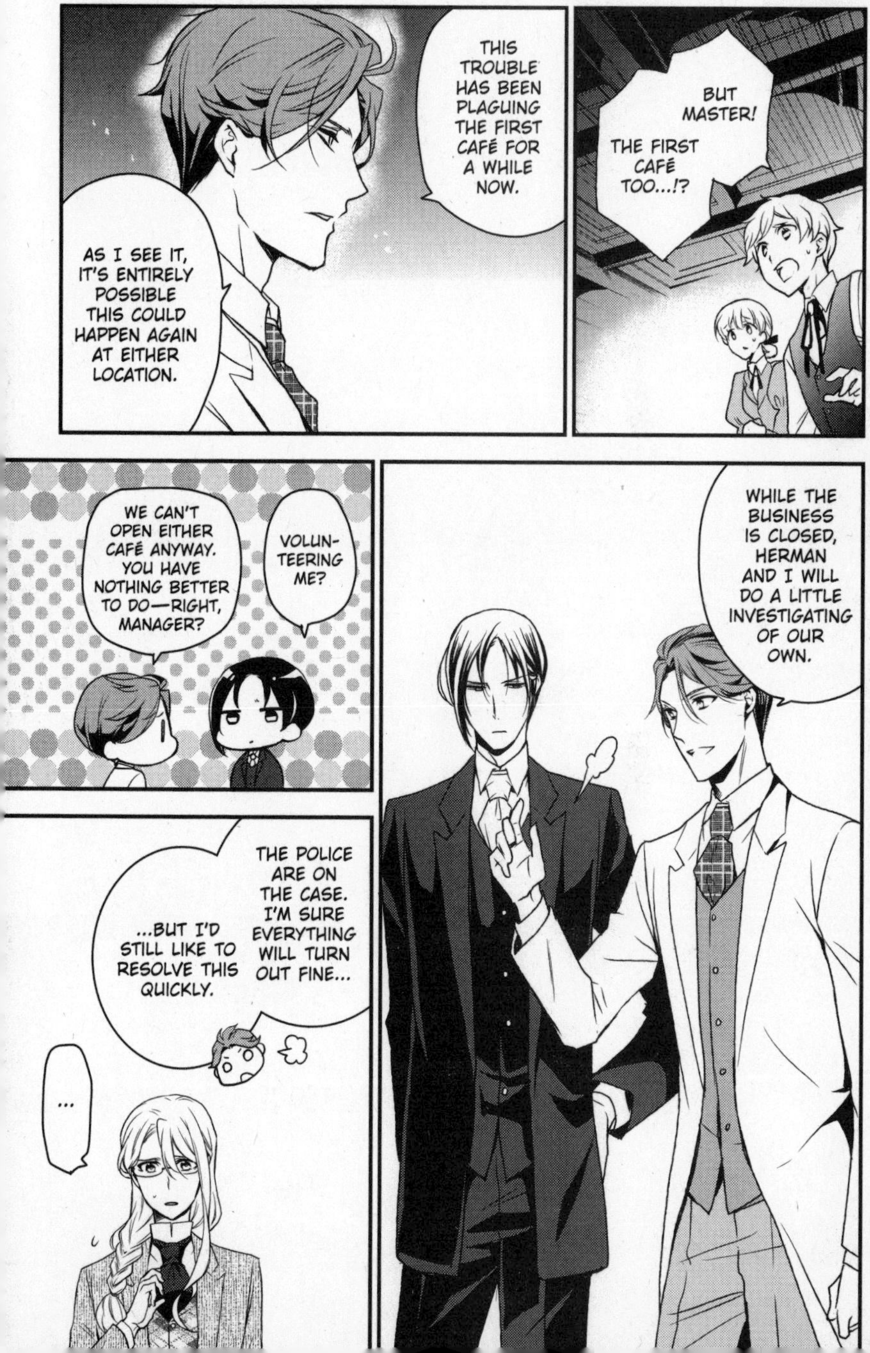
BUT MASTER!
THE FIRST CAFÉ TOO...!?
THIS TROUBLE HAS BEEN PLAGUING THE FIRST CAFÉ FOR A WHILE NOW.
AS I SEE IT, IT'S ENTIRELY POSSIBLE THIS COULD HAPPEN AGAIN AT EITHER LOCATION.
WHILE THE BUSINESS IS CLOSED, HERMAN AND I WILL DO A LITTLE INVESTIGATING OF OUR OWN.
VOLUN-TEERING ME?
WE CAN'T OPEN EITHER CAFÉ ANYWAY. YOU HAVE NOTHING BETTER TO DO—RIGHT, MANAGER?
THE POLICE ARE ON THE CASE. I'M SURE EVERYTHING WILL TURN OUT FINE...
...BUT I'D STILL LIKE TO RESOLVE THIS QUICKLY.
...

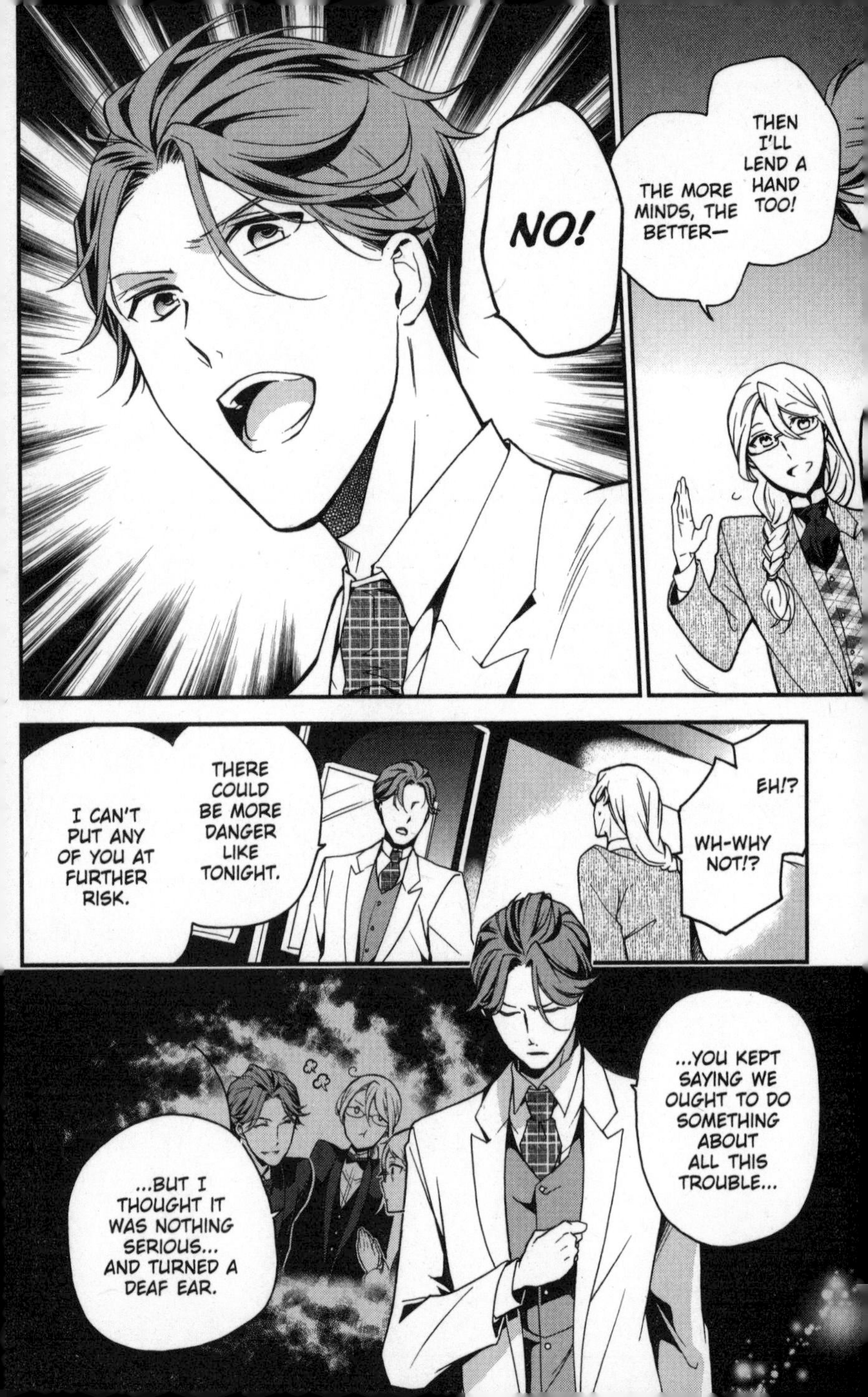
THEN I'LL LEND A HAND TOO!
THE MORE MINDS, THE BETTER—
NO!
EH!?
WH-WHY NOT!?
THERE COULD BE MORE DANGER LIKE TONIGHT.
I CAN'T PUT ANY OF YOU AT FURTHER RISK.
...YOU KEPT SAYING WE OUGHT TO DO SOMETHING ABOUT ALL THIS TROUBLE...
...BUT I THOUGHT IT WAS NOTHING SERIOUS... AND TURNED A DEAF EAR.

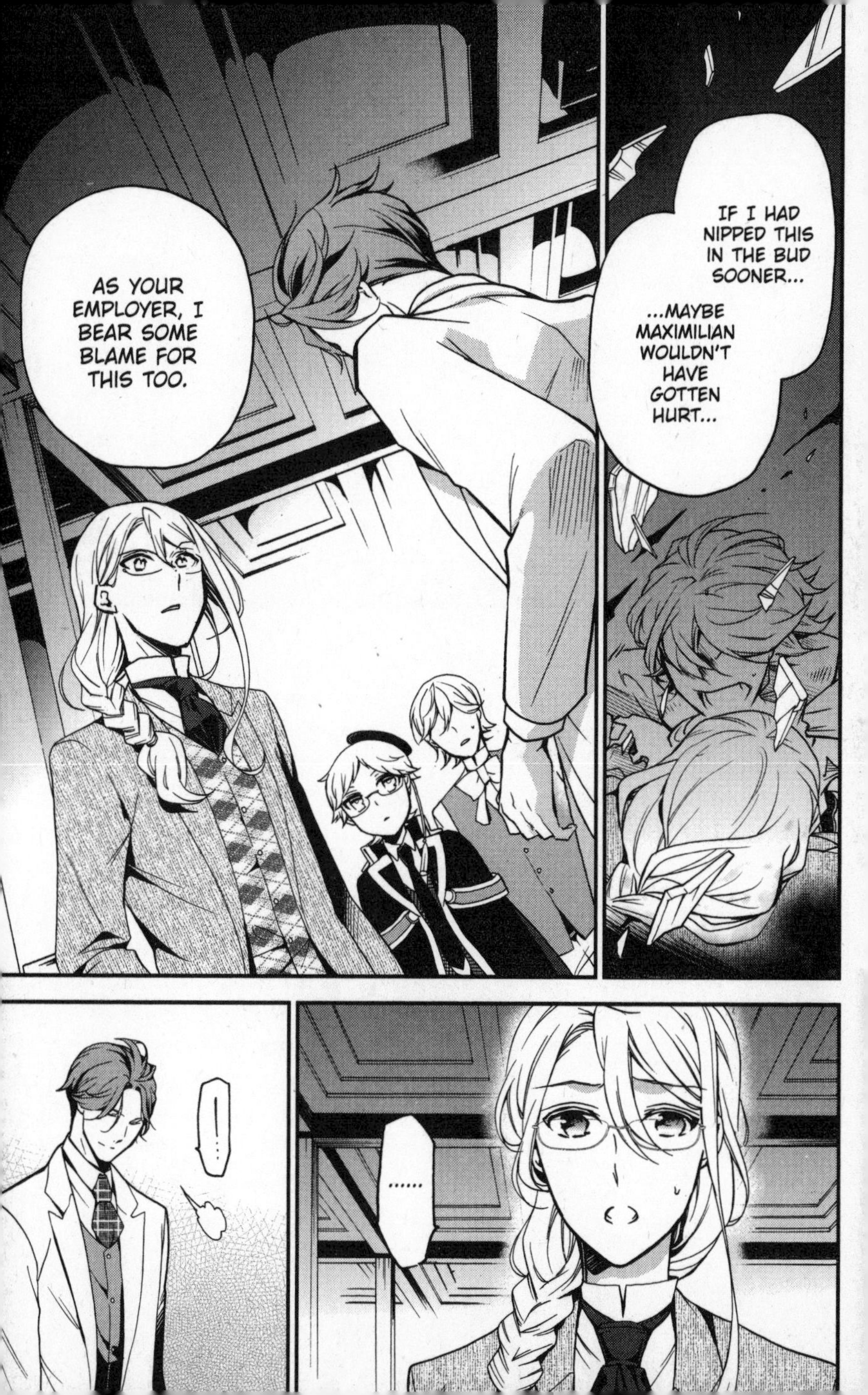
IF I HAD NIPPED THIS IN THE BUD SOONER...
...MAYBE MAXIMILIAN WOULDN'T HAVE GOTTEN HURT...
AS YOUR EMPLOYER, I BEAR SOME BLAME FOR THIS TOO.
......
!...

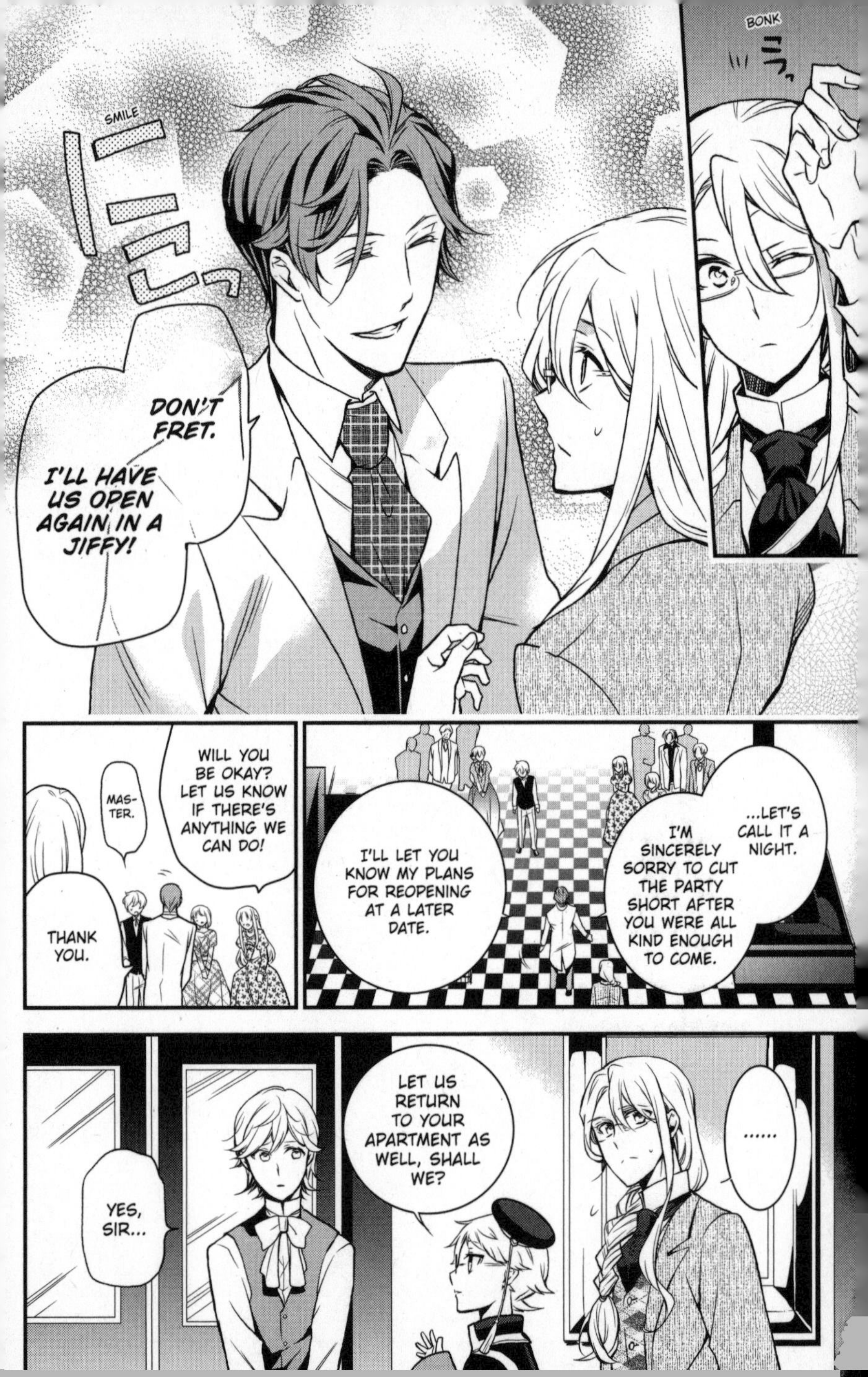
BONK
SMILE
DON'T FRET.
I'LL HAVE US OPEN AGAIN IN A JIFFY!
...LET'S CALL IT A NIGHT.
I'M SINCERELY SORRY TO CUT THE PARTY SHORT AFTER YOU WERE ALL KIND ENOUGH TO COME.
I'LL LET YOU KNOW MY PLANS FOR REOPENING AT A LATER DATE.
WILL YOU BE OKAY? LET US KNOW IF THERE'S ANYTHING WE CAN DO!
MASTER.
THANK YOU.
......
LET US RETURN TO YOUR APARTMENT AS WELL, SHALL WE?
YES, SIR...

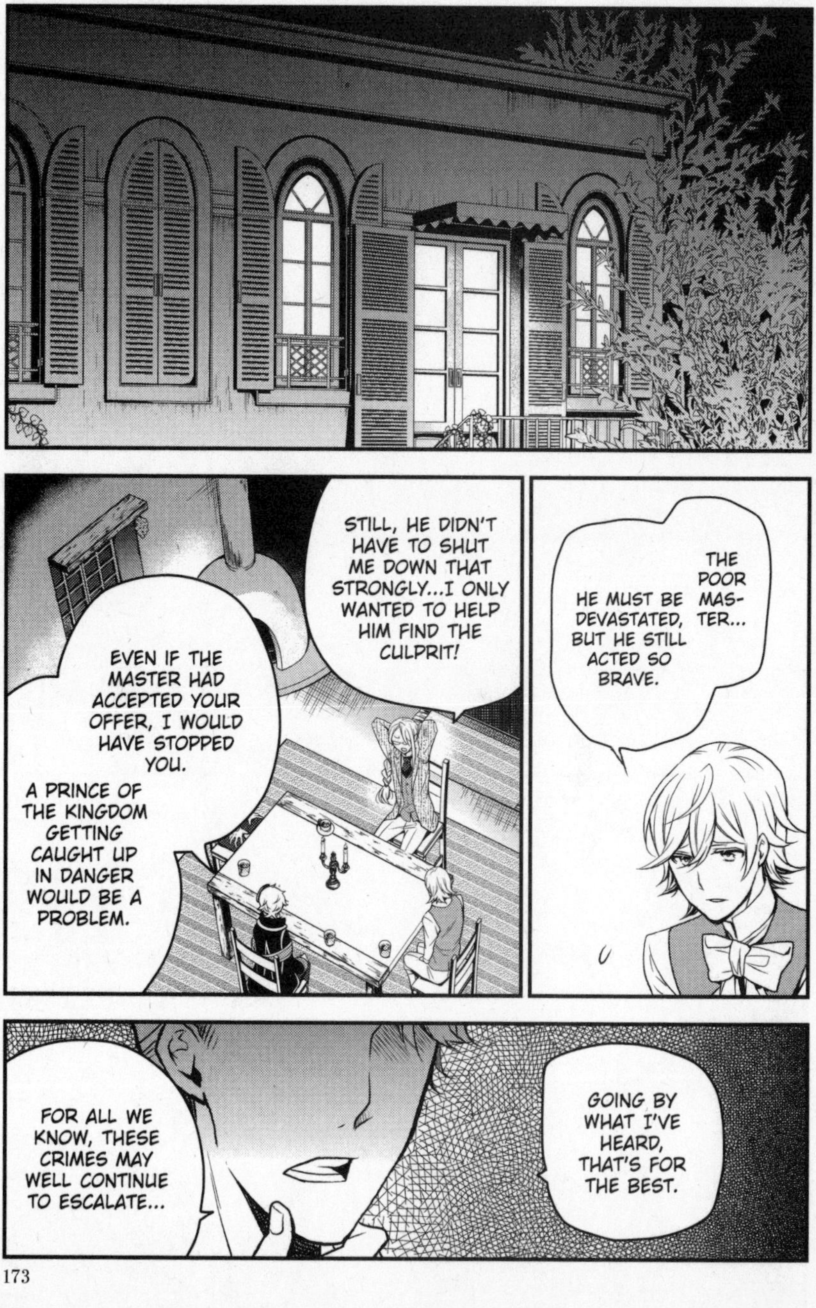
THE POOR MASTER...
HE MUST BE DEVASTATED, BUT HE STILL ACTED SO BRAVE.
STILL, HE DIDN'T HAVE TO SHUT ME DOWN THAT STRONGLY...I ONLY WANTED TO HELP HIM FIND THE CULPRIT!
EVEN IF THE MASTER HAD ACCEPTED YOUR OFFER, I WOULD HAVE STOPPED YOU.
A PRINCE OF THE KINGDOM GETTING CAUGHT UP IN DANGER WOULD BE A PROBLEM.
GOING BY WHAT I'VE HEARD, THAT'S FOR THE BEST.
FOR ALL WE KNOW, THESE CRIMES MAY WELL CONTINUE TO ESCALATE...

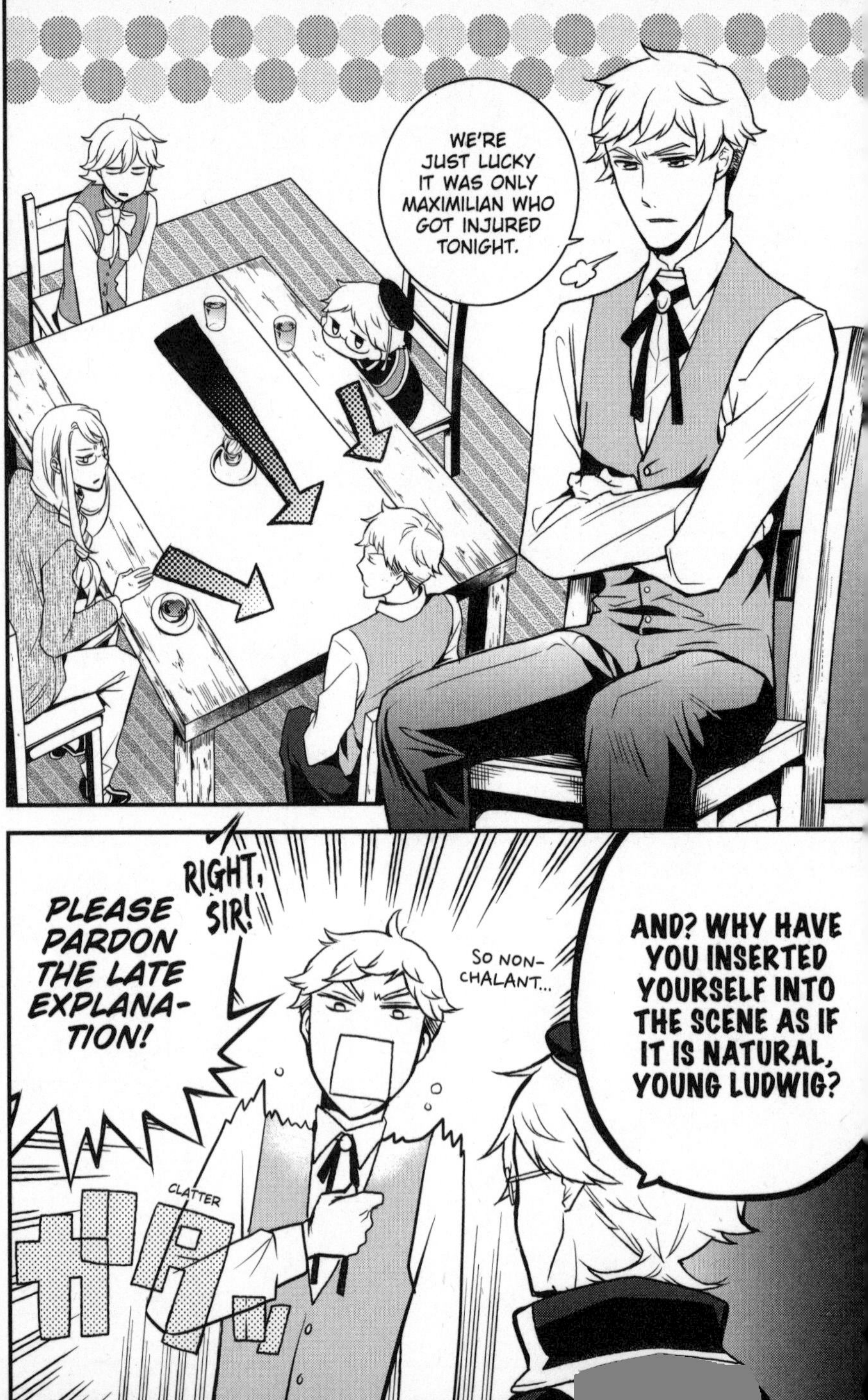
WE'RE JUST LUCKY IT WAS ONLY MAXIMILIAN WHO GOT INJURED TONIGHT.
AND? WHY HAVE YOU INSERTED YOURSELF INTO THE SCENE AS IF IT IS NATURAL, YOUNG LUDWIG?
SO NON-CHALANT...
RIGHT, SIR!
PLEASE PARDON THE LATE EXPLANA-TION!
CLATTER

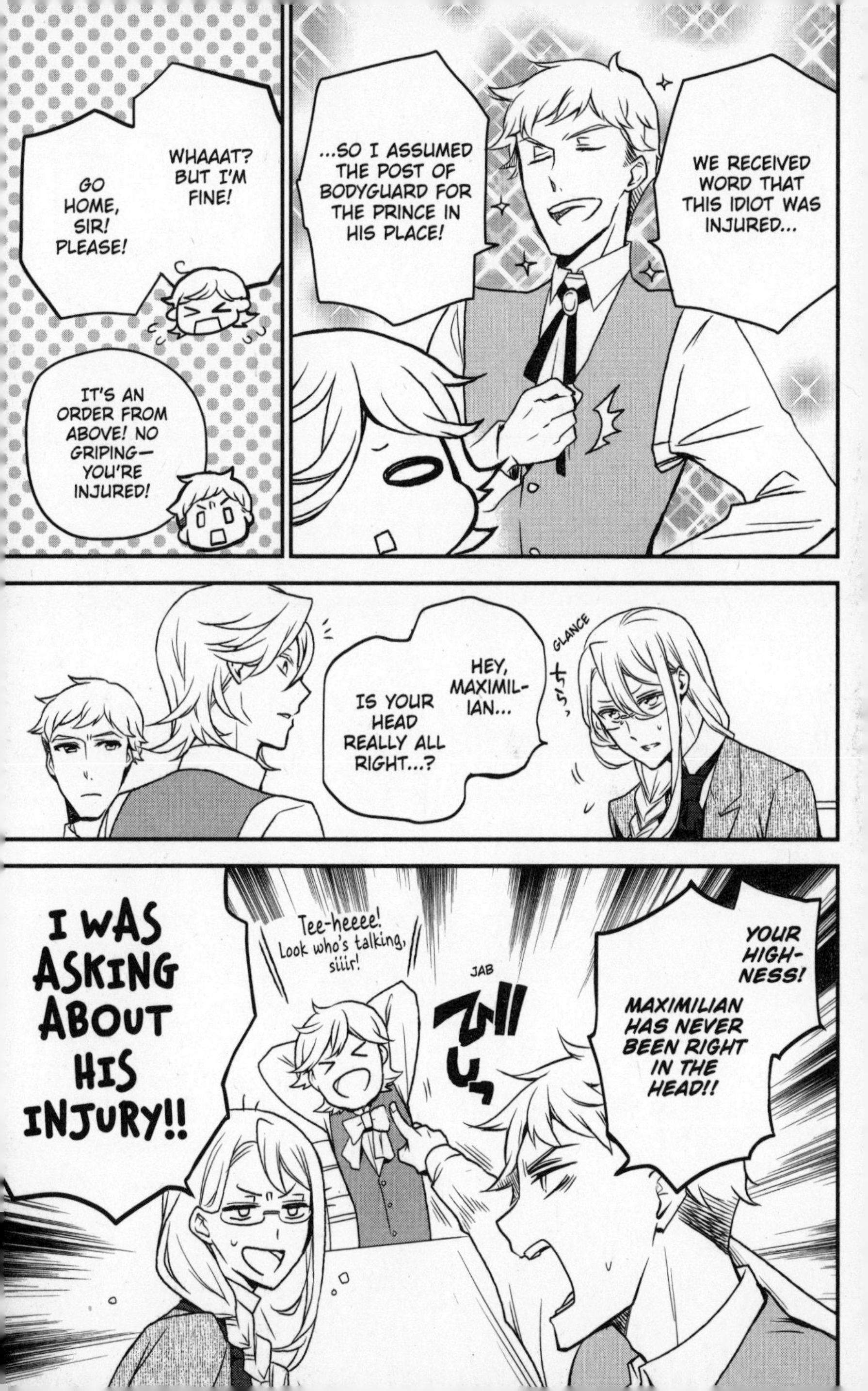
WE RECEIVED WORD THAT THIS IDIOT WAS INJURED...
...SO I ASSUMED THE POST OF BODYGUARD FOR THE PRINCE IN HIS PLACE!
WHAAAT? BUT I'M FINE!
GO HOME, SIR! PLEASE!
IT'S AN ORDER FROM ABOVE! NO GRIPING—YOU'RE INJURED!
GLANCE
HEY, MAXIMILIAN...
IS YOUR HEAD REALLY ALL RIGHT...?
YOUR HIGHNESS!
MAXIMILIAN HAS NEVER BEEN RIGHT IN THE HEAD!!
JAB
Tee-heeee! Look who's talking, siiir!
I WAS ASKING ABOUT HIS INJURY!!

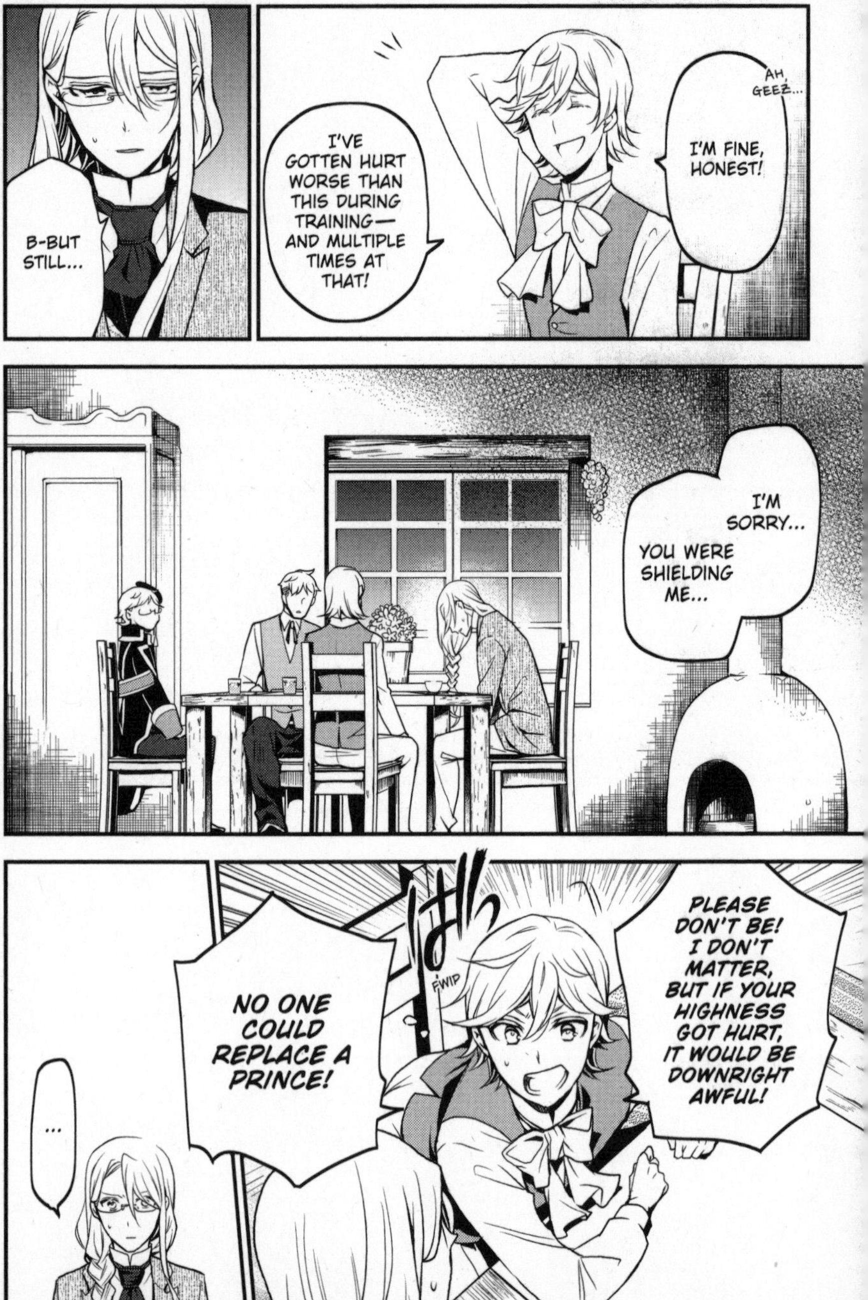
AH, GEEZ...
I'M FINE, HONEST!
I'VE GOTTEN HURT WORSE THAN THIS DURING TRAINING—AND MULTIPLE TIMES AT THAT!
B-BUT STILL...
I'M SORRY...
YOU WERE SHIELDING ME...
FWIP
PLEASE DON'T BE! I DON'T MATTER, BUT IF YOUR HIGHNESS GOT HURT, IT WOULD BE DOWNRIGHT AWFUL!
NO ONE COULD REPLACE A PRINCE!
...

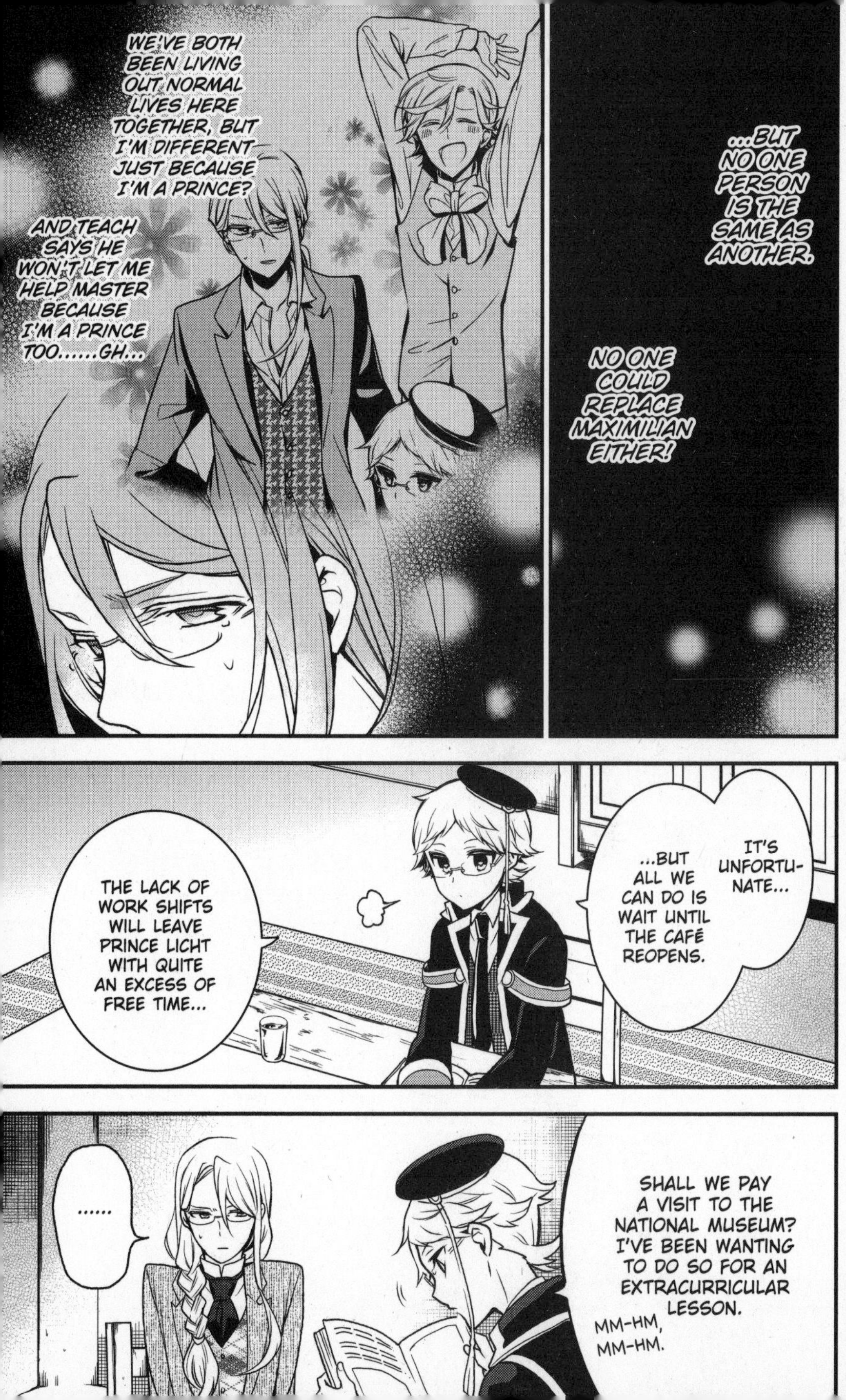
...BUT NO ONE PERSON IS THE SAME AS ANOTHER.
NO ONE COULD REPLACE MAXIMILIAN EITHER!
WE'VE BOTH BEEN LIVING OUT NORMAL LIVES HERE TOGETHER, BUT I'M DIFFERENT JUST BECAUSE I'M A PRINCE?
AND TEACH SAYS HE WON'T LET ME HELP MASTER BECAUSE I'M A PRINCE TOO......GH...
IT'S UNFORTUNATE...
...BUT ALL WE CAN DO IS WAIT UNTIL THE CAFÉ REOPENS.
THE LACK OF WORK SHIFTS WILL LEAVE PRINCE LICHT WITH QUITE AN EXCESS OF FREE TIME...
SHALL WE PAY A VISIT TO THE NATIONAL MUSEUM? I'VE BEEN WANTING TO DO SO FOR AN EXTRACURRICULAR LESSON.
MM-HM, MM-HM.
......

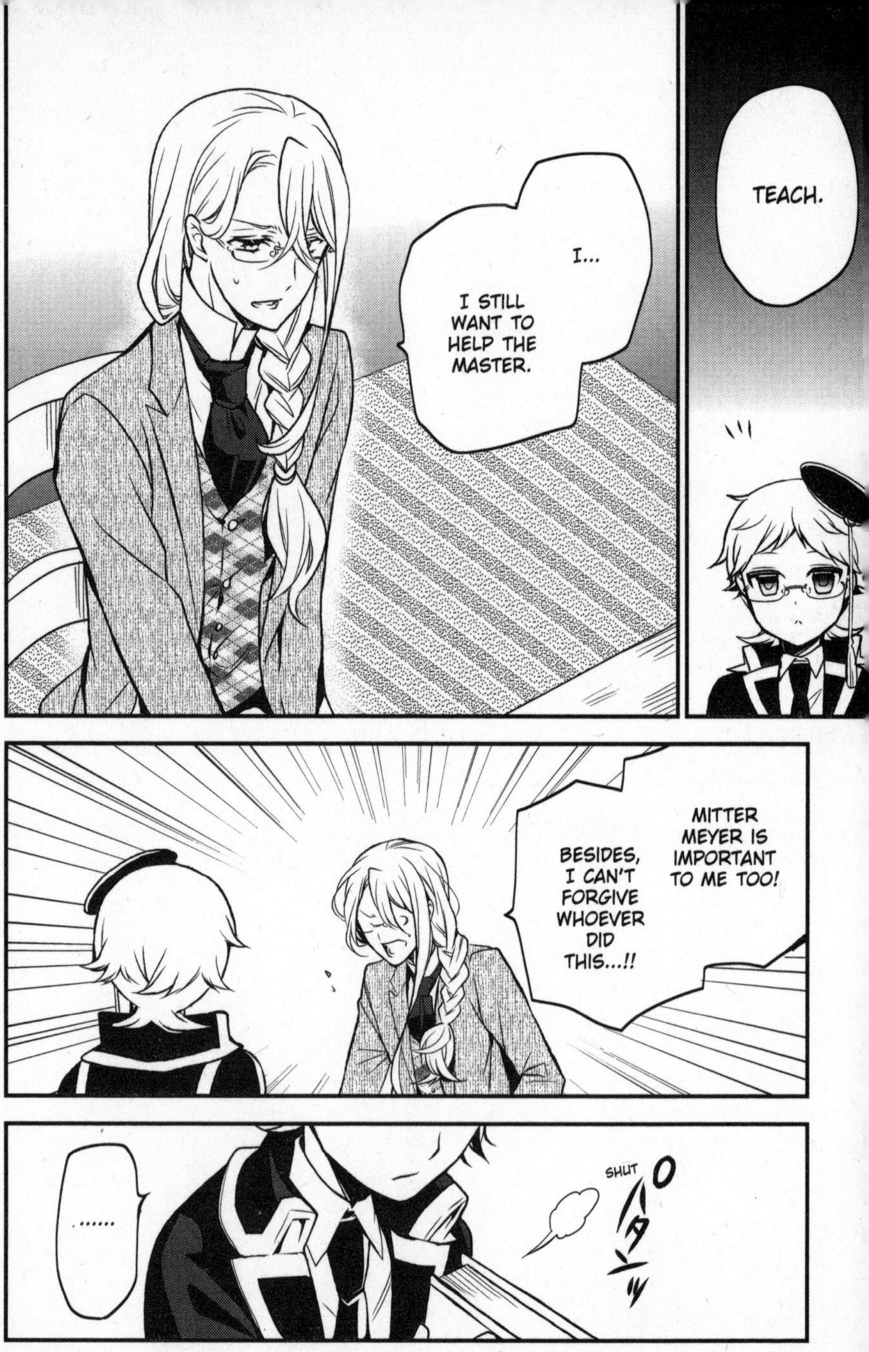
TEACH.
I...
I STILL WANT TO HELP THE MASTER.
MITTER MEYER IS IMPORTANT TO ME TOO!
BESIDES, I CAN'T FORGIVE WHOEVER DID THIS...!!
パタンッ
SHUT
....

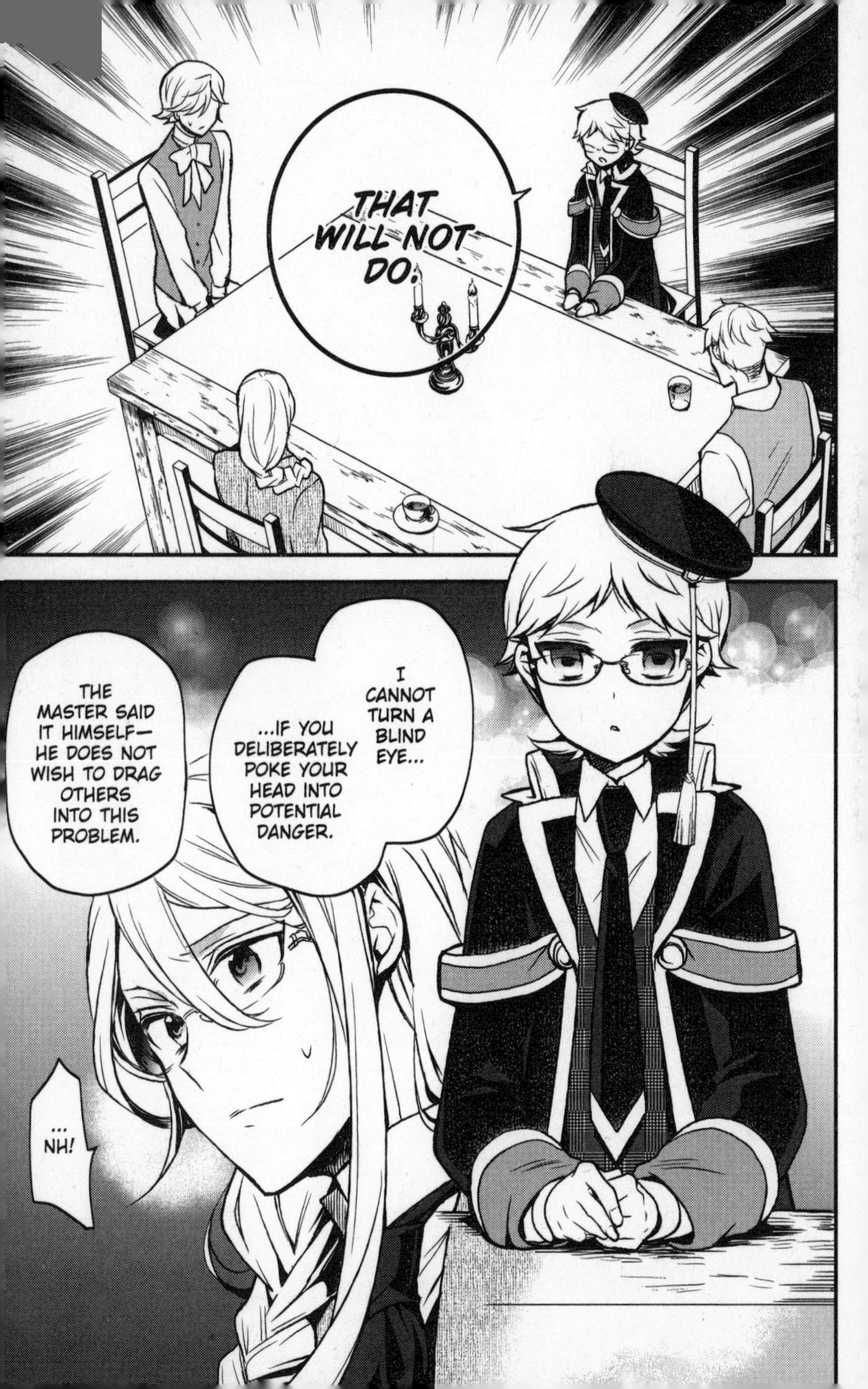
THAT WILL NOT DO.
I CANNOT TURN A BLIND EYE...
...IF YOU DELIBERATELY POKE YOUR HEAD INTO POTENTIAL DANGER.
THE MASTER SAID IT HIMSELF—HE DOES NOT WISH TO DRAG OTHERS INTO THIS PROBLEM.
...NH!

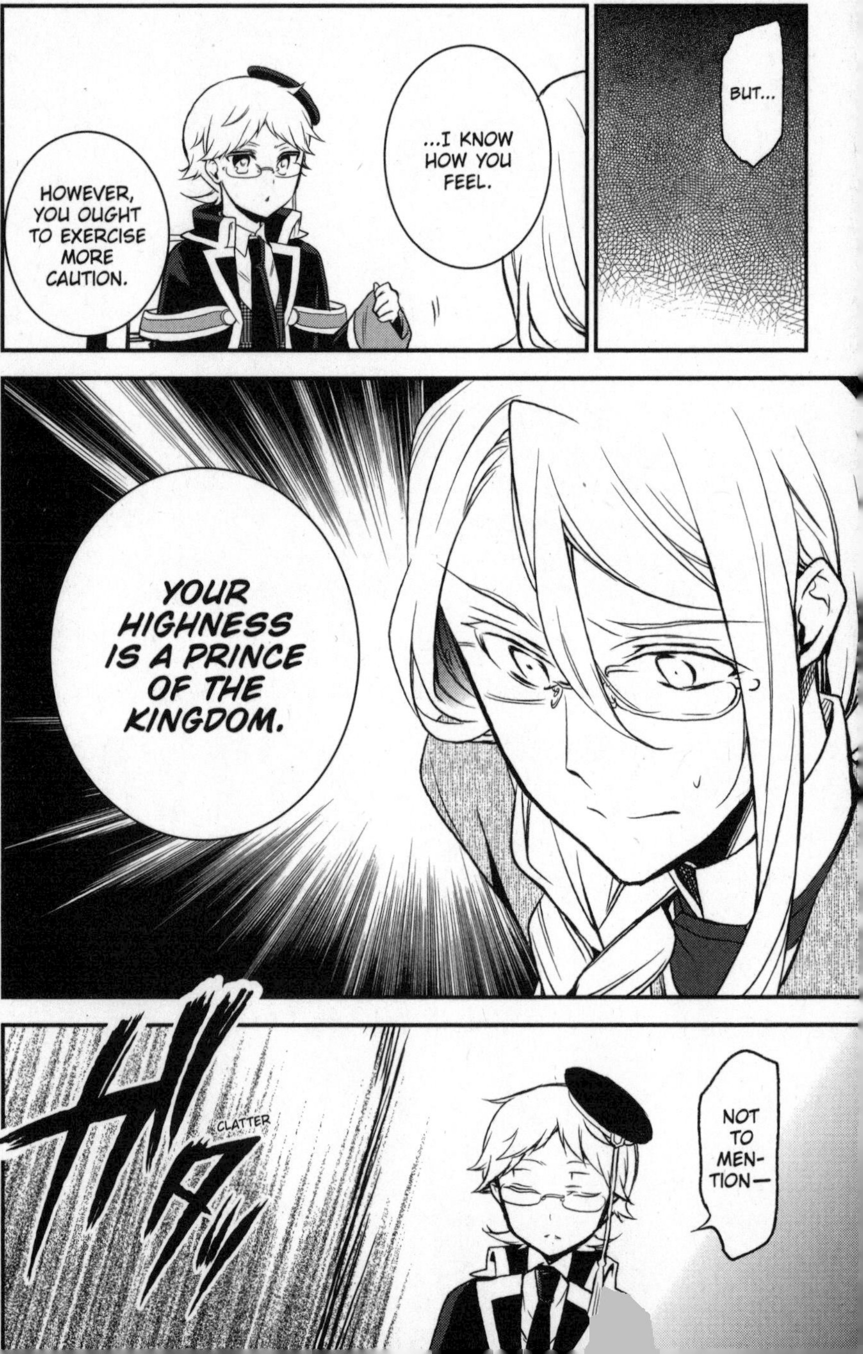
BUT...
...I KNOW HOW YOU FEEL.
HOWEVER, YOU OUGHT TO EXERCISE MORE CAUTION.
YOUR HIGHNESS IS A PRINCE OF THE KINGDOM.
NOT TO MEN-TION—
CLATTER

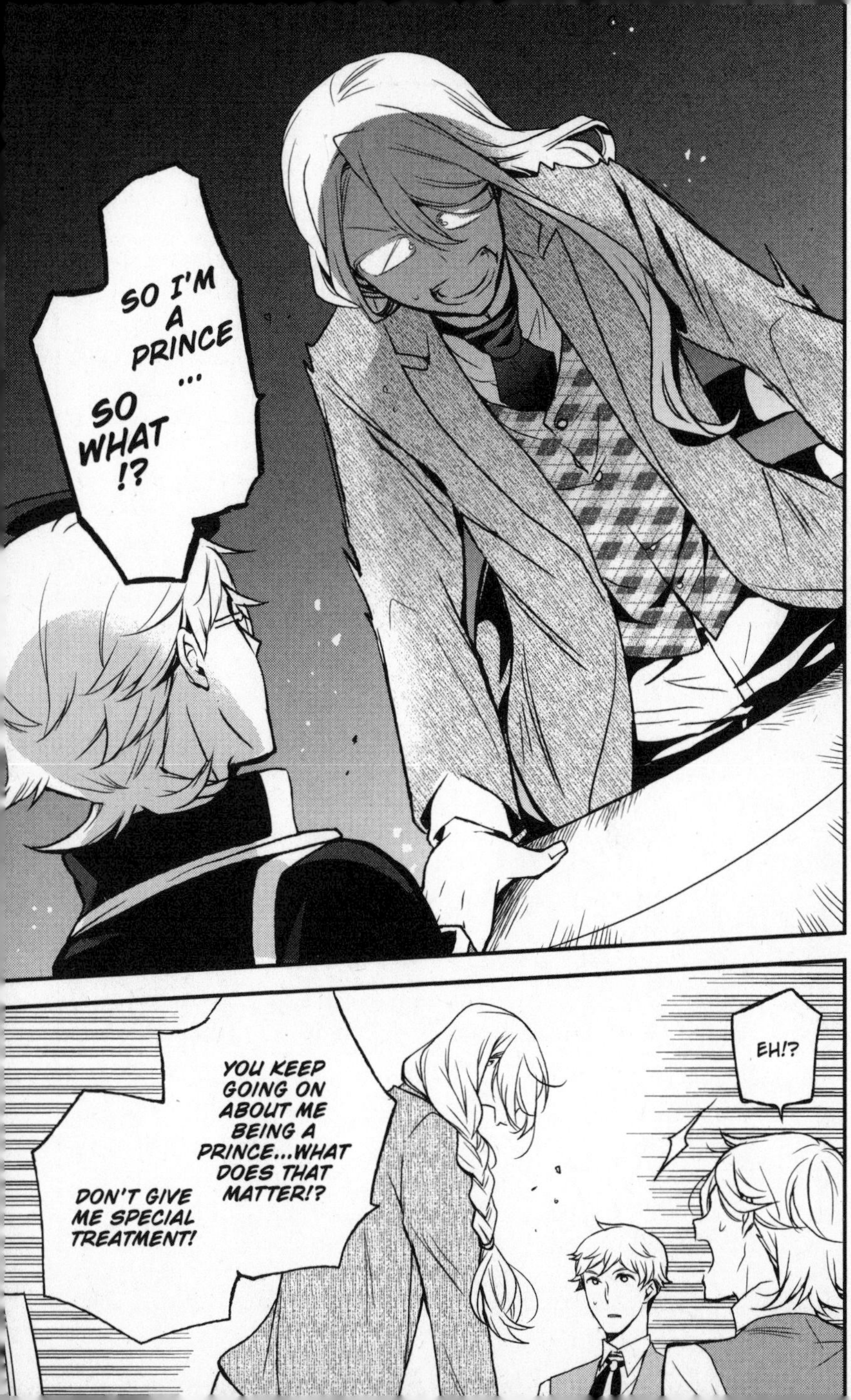
SO I'M A PRINCE... SO WHAT!?
EH!?
YOU KEEP GOING ON ABOUT ME BEING A PRINCE...WHAT DOES THAT MATTER!?
DON'T GIVE ME SPECIAL TREATMENT!

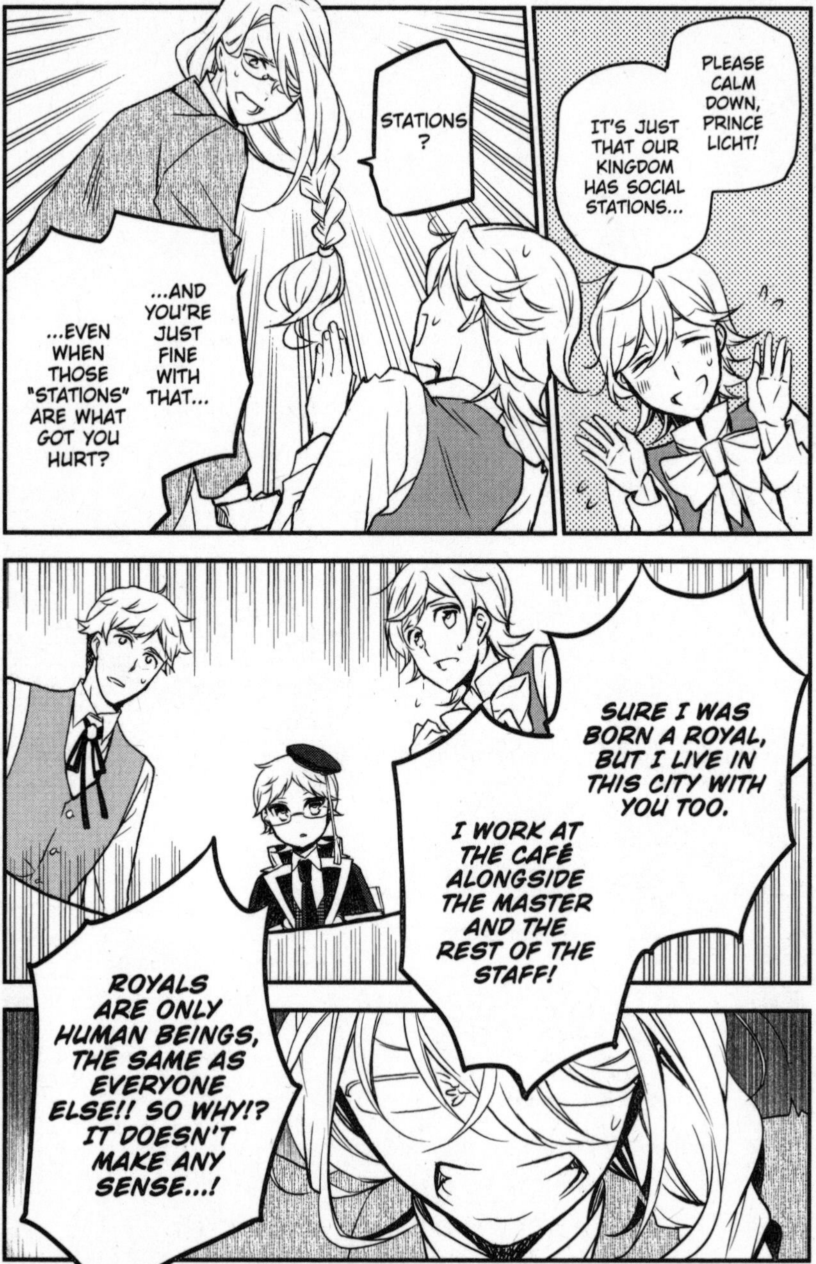
PLEASE CALM DOWN, PRINCE LICHT!
IT'S JUST THAT OUR KINGDOM HAS SOCIAL STATIONS...
STATIONS?
...AND YOU'RE JUST FINE WITH THAT...
...EVEN WHEN THOSE "STATIONS" ARE WHAT GOT YOU HURT?
SURE I WAS BORN A ROYAL, BUT I LIVE IN THIS CITY WITH YOU TOO.
I WORK AT THE CAFÉ ALONGSIDE THE MASTER AND THE REST OF THE STAFF!
ROYALS ARE ONLY HUMAN BEINGS, THE SAME AS EVERYONE ELSE!! SO WHY!? IT DOESN'T MAKE ANY SENSE...!

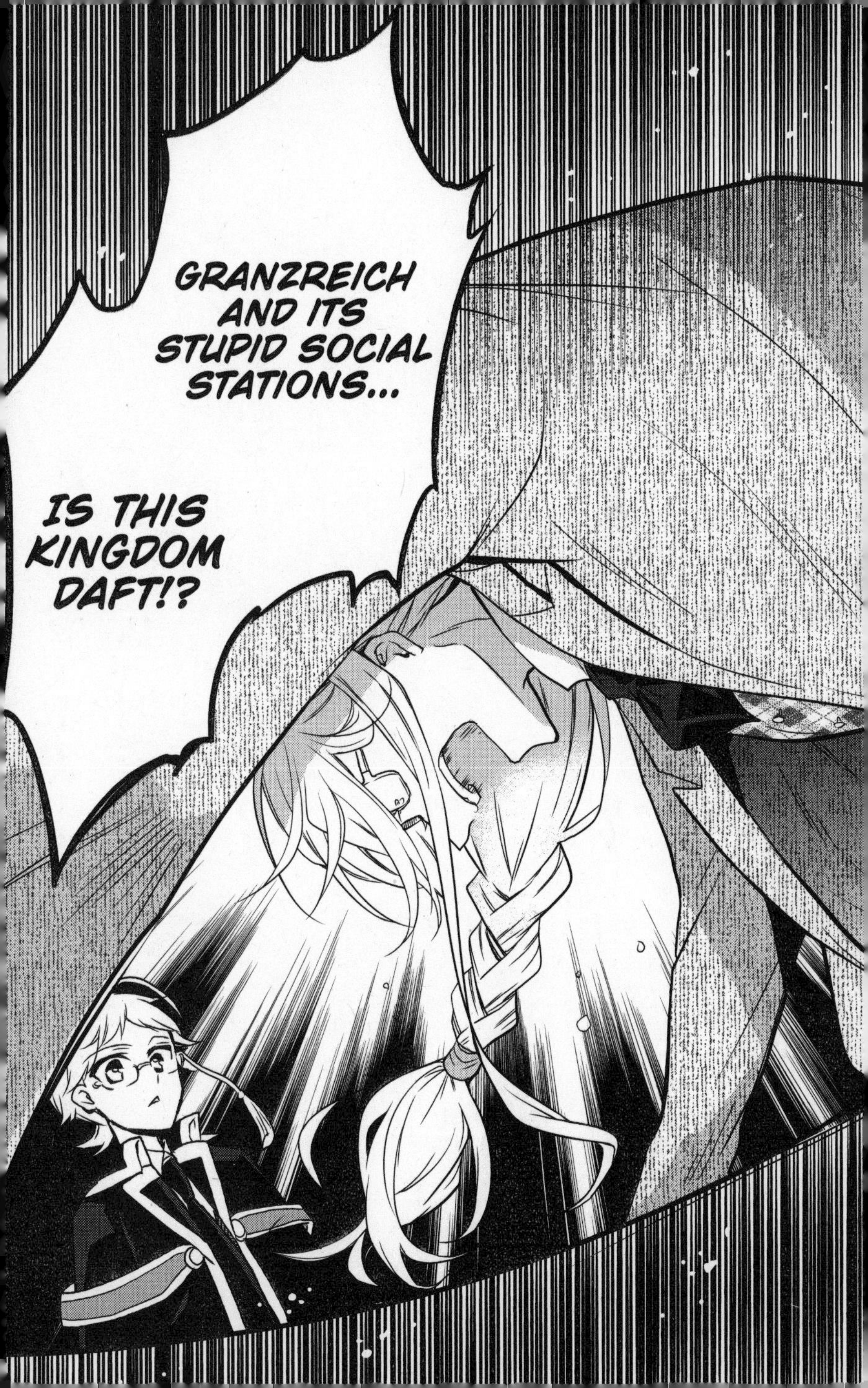
GRANZREICH AND ITS STUPID SOCIAL STATIONS...
IS THIS KINGDOM DAFT!?

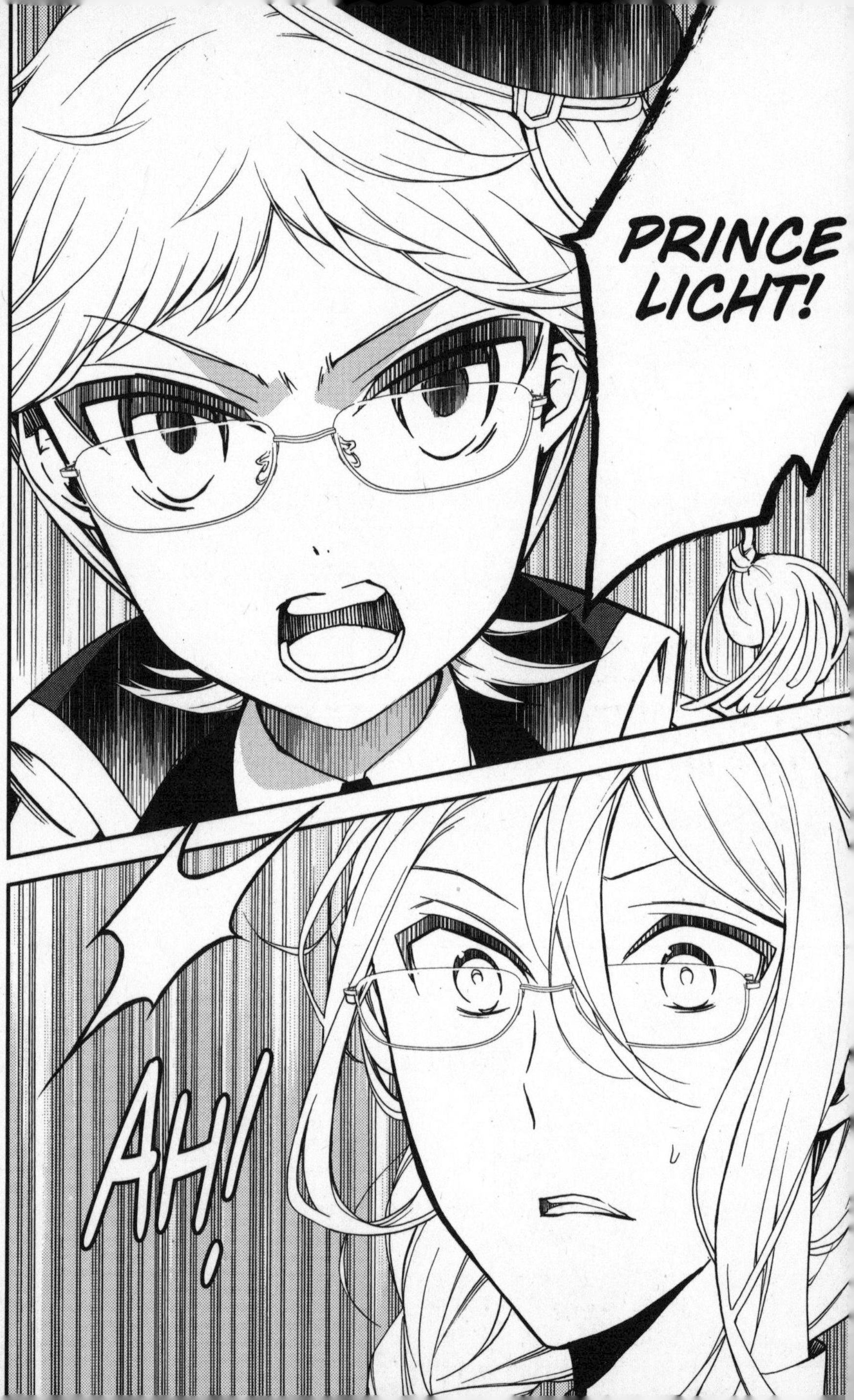
PRINCE LICHT!
AH!

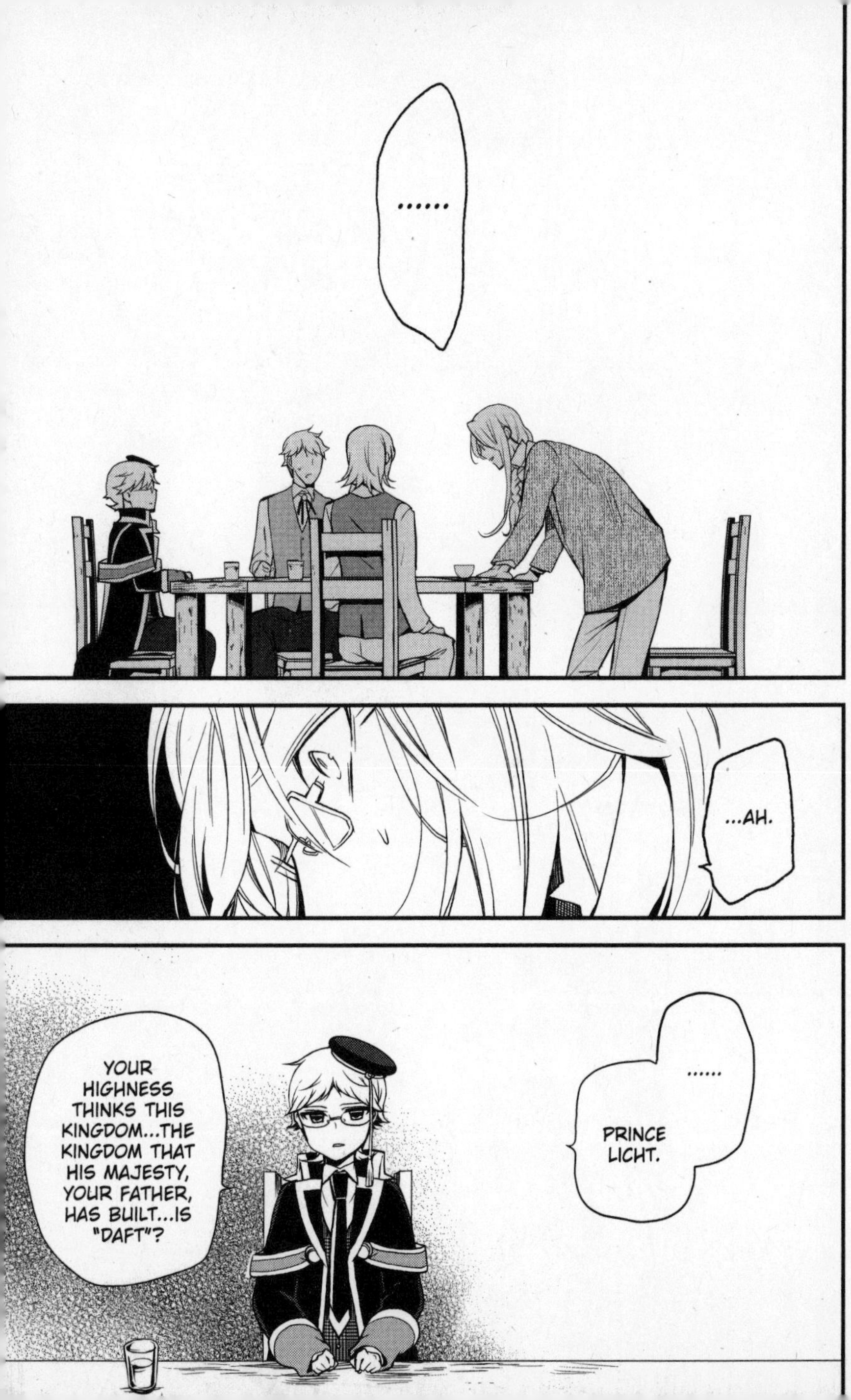
......
...AH.
......
PRINCE LICHT.
YOUR HIGHNESS THINKS THIS KINGDOM...THE KINGDOM THAT HIS MAJESTY, YOUR FATHER, HAS BUILT...IS "DAFT"?

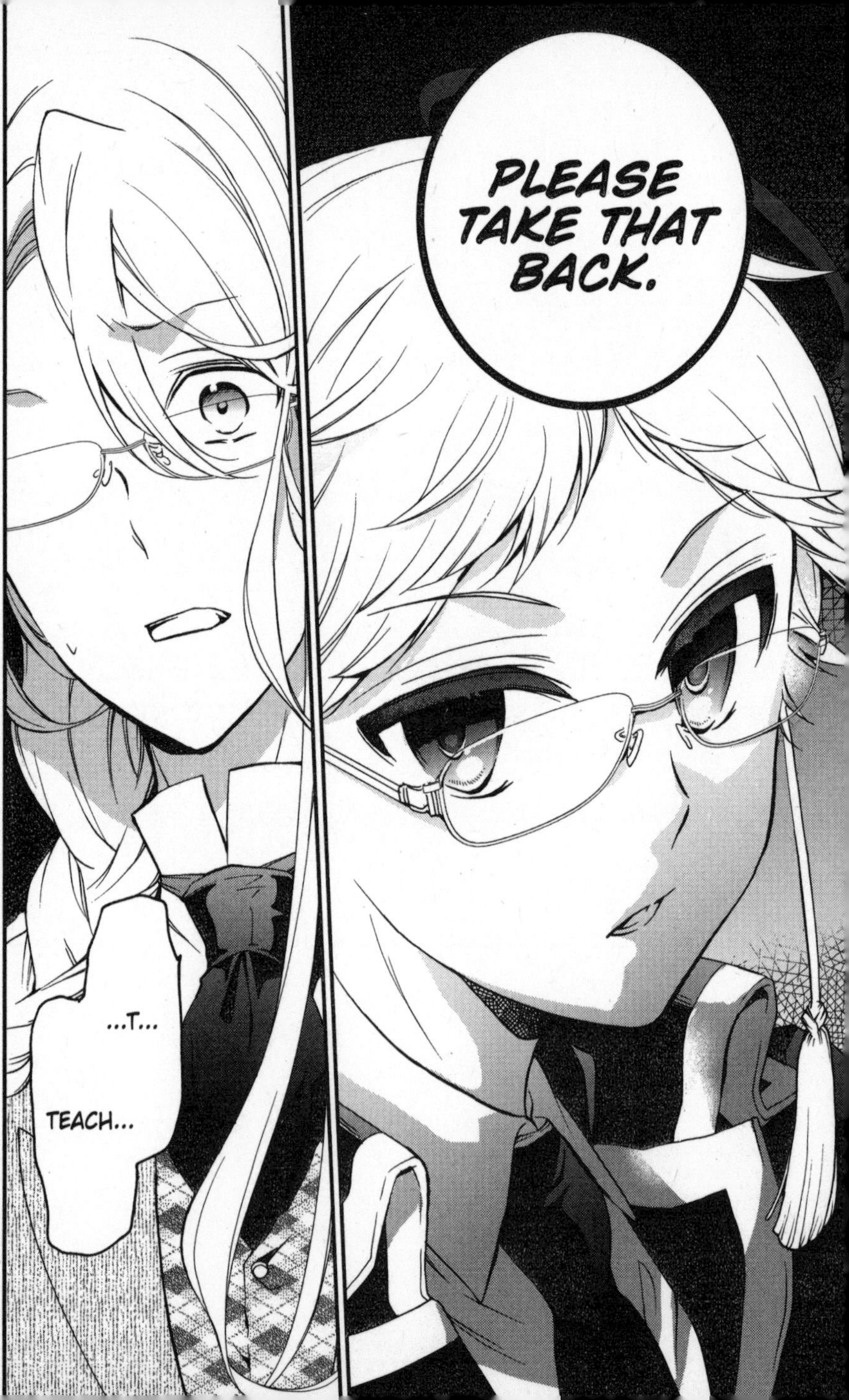
PLEASE TAKE THAT BACK.
...T...
TEACH...

CHAPTER 66 EXTRA

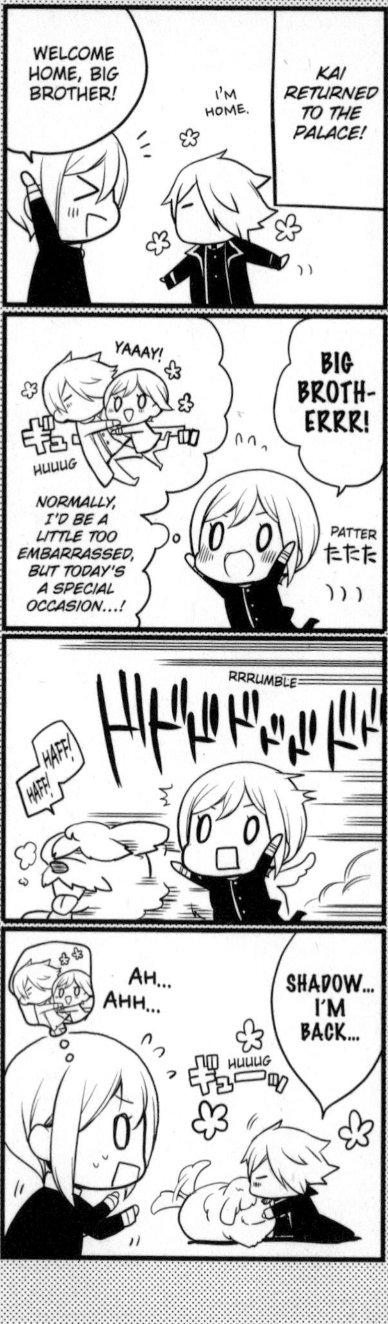

KAI RETURNED TO THE PALACE!
I'M HOME.
WELCOME HOME, BIG BROTHER!
BIG BROTH-ERRR!
YAAAY!
ギュー
HUUUG
NORMALLY, I'D BE A LITTLE TOO EMBARRASSED, BUT TODAY'S A SPECIAL OCCASION...!
PATTER
たたた
RRRUMBLE
HAFF! HAFF!
SHADOW... I'M BACK...
HUUUG
ギューッ
AH... AHH...

CHAPTER 69 EXTRA

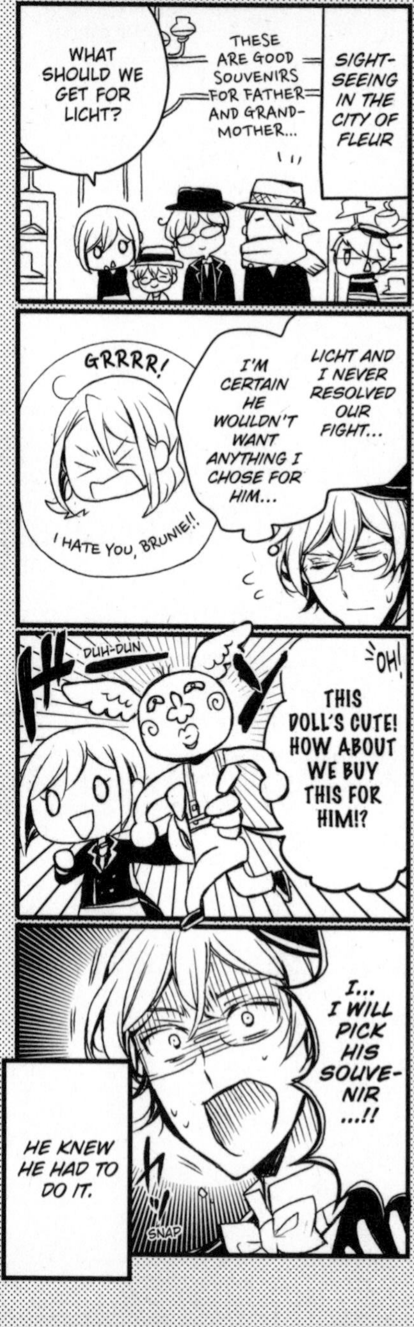

SIGHT-SEEING IN THE CITY OF FLEUR
THESE ARE GOOD SOUVENIRS FOR FATHER AND GRAND-MOTHER...
WHAT SHOULD WE GET FOR LICHT?
LICHT AND I NEVER RESOLVED OUR FIGHT...
I'M CERTAIN HE WOULDN'T WANT ANYTHING I CHOSE FOR HIM...
GRRRR!
I HATE YOU, BRUNIE!!
OH!
THIS DOLL'S CUTE! HOW ABOUT WE BUY THIS FOR HIM!?
DUH-DUN
I... I WILL PICK HIS SOUVENIR...!!
HE KNEW HE HAD TO DO IT.
SNAP

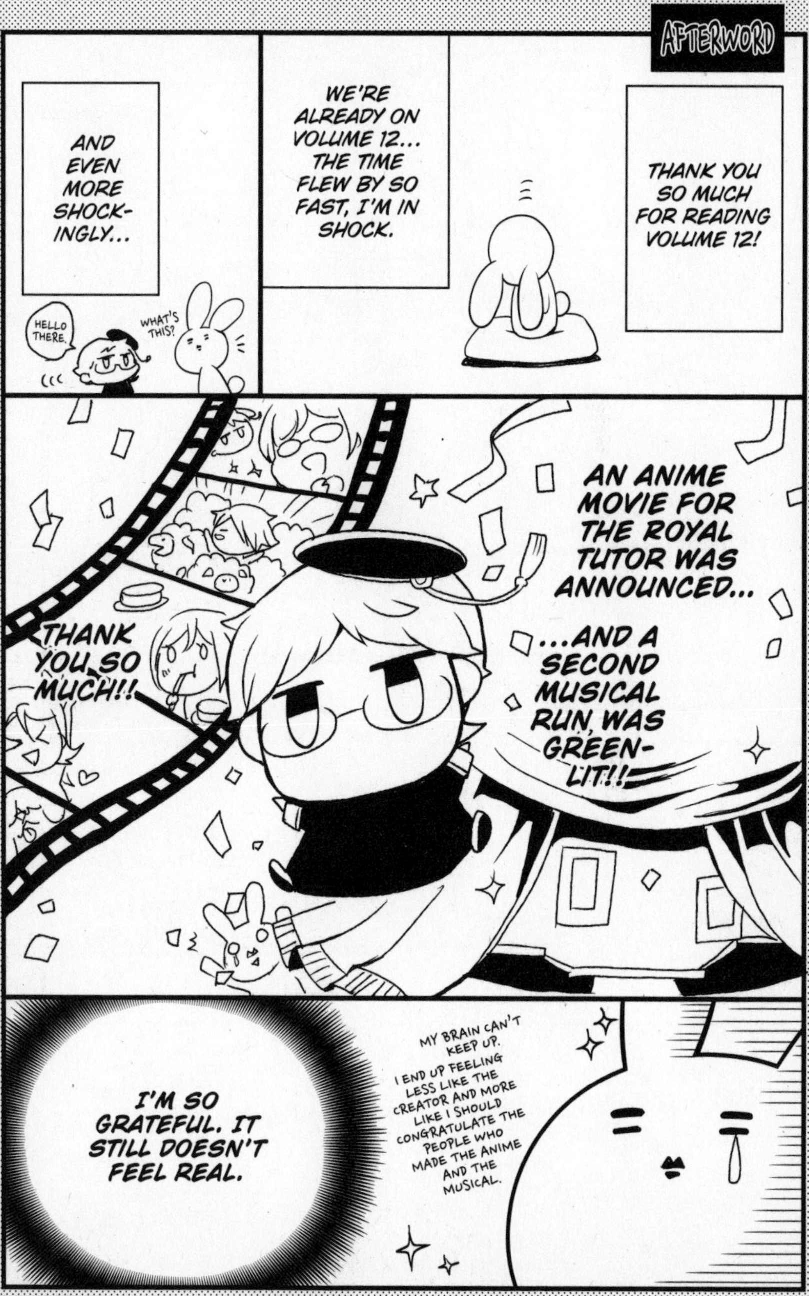
AFTERWORD
THANK YOU SO MUCH FOR READING VOLUME 12!
WE'RE ALREADY ON VOLUME 12... THE TIME FLEW BY SO FAST, I'M IN SHOCK.
AND EVEN MORE SHOCKINGLY...
WHAT'S THIS?
HELLO THERE.
AN ANIME MOVIE FOR THE ROYAL TUTOR WAS ANNOUNCED...
...AND A SECOND MUSICAL RUN, WAS GREENLIT!!
THANK YOU SO MUCH!!
MY BRAIN CAN'T KEEP UP. I END UP FEELING LESS LIKE THE CREATOR AND MORE LIKE I SHOULD CONGRATULATE THE PEOPLE WHO MADE THE ANIME AND THE MUSICAL.
I'M SO GRATEFUL. IT STILL DOESN'T FEEL REAL.

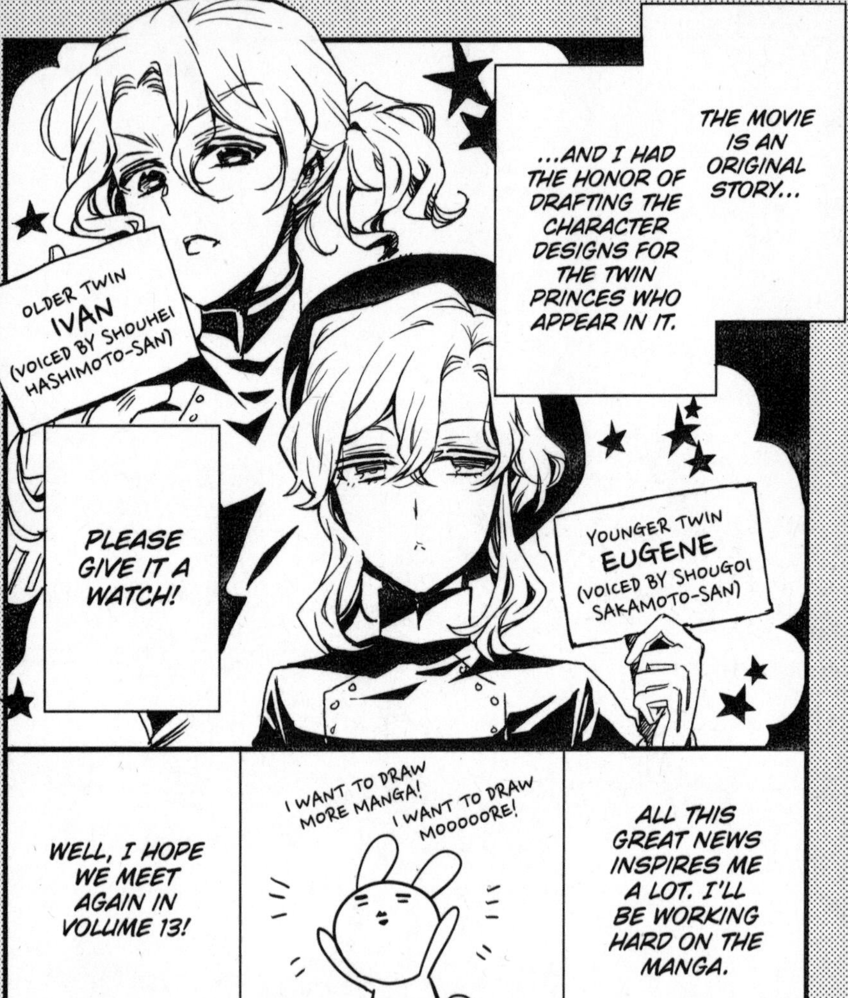
THE MOVIE IS AN ORIGINAL STORY...
...AND I HAD THE HONOR OF DRAFTING THE CHARACTER DESIGNS FOR THE TWIN PRINCES WHO APPEAR IN IT.
OLDER TWIN IVAN (VOICED BY SHOUHEI HASHIMOTO-SAN)
YOUNGER TWIN EUGENE (VOICED BY SHOUGOI SAKAMOTO-SAN)
PLEASE GIVE IT A WATCH!
ALL THIS GREAT NEWS INSPIRES ME A LOT. I'LL BE WORKING HARD ON THE MANGA.
I WANT TO DRAW MORE MANGA!
I WANT TO DRAW MOOOOORE!
WELL, I HOPE WE MEET AGAIN IN VOLUME 13!

SPECIAL THANKS

TSUCHIYA-SAN

MY EDITOR, AKIYAMA-SAN

THE ROYAL TUTOR: THE MOVIE PRODUCTION COMMITTEE

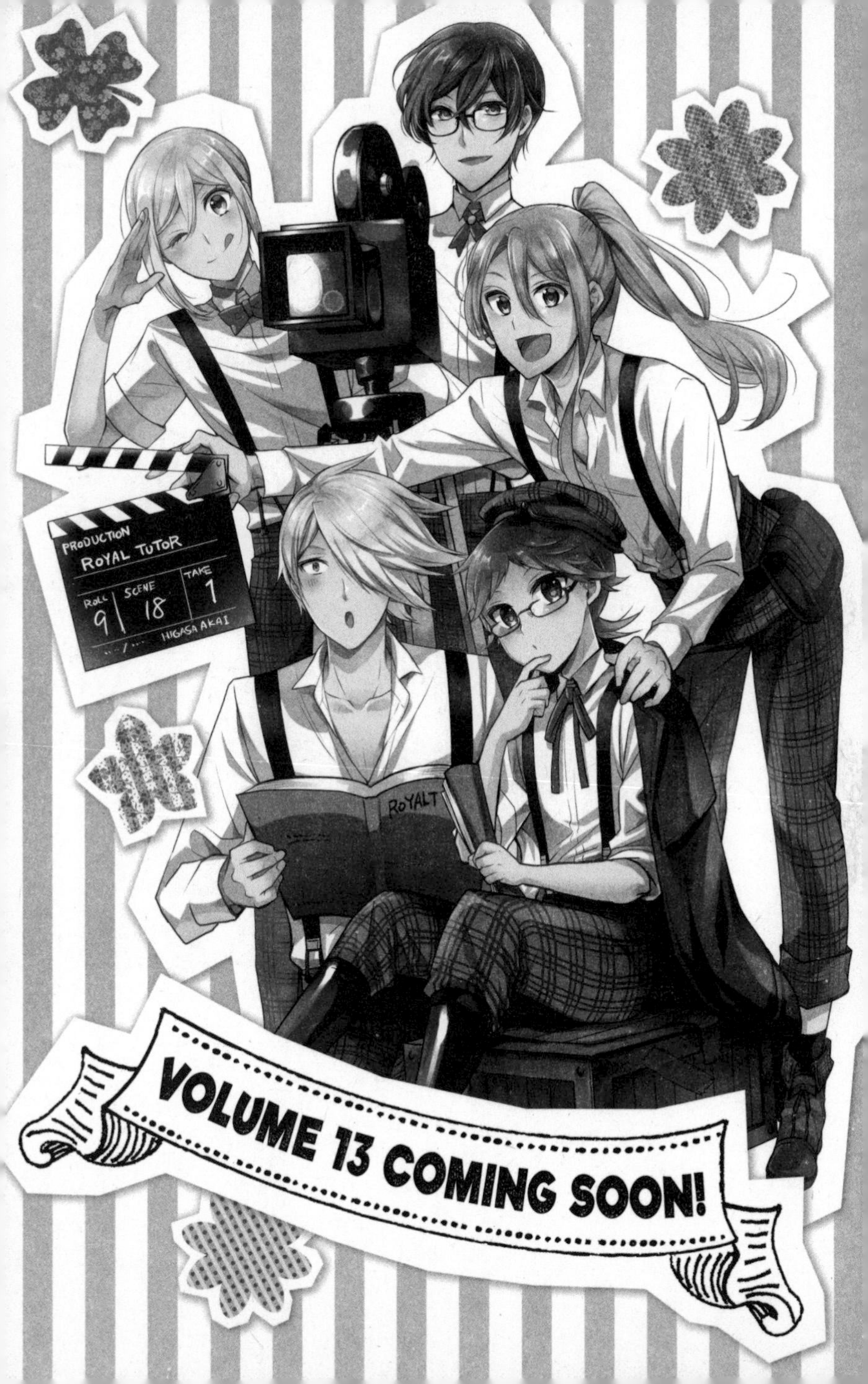
PRODUCTION
ROYAL TUTOR
ROLL 9
SCENE 18
TAKE 1
HIGASA AKAI
ROYALT
VOLUME 13 COMING SOON!

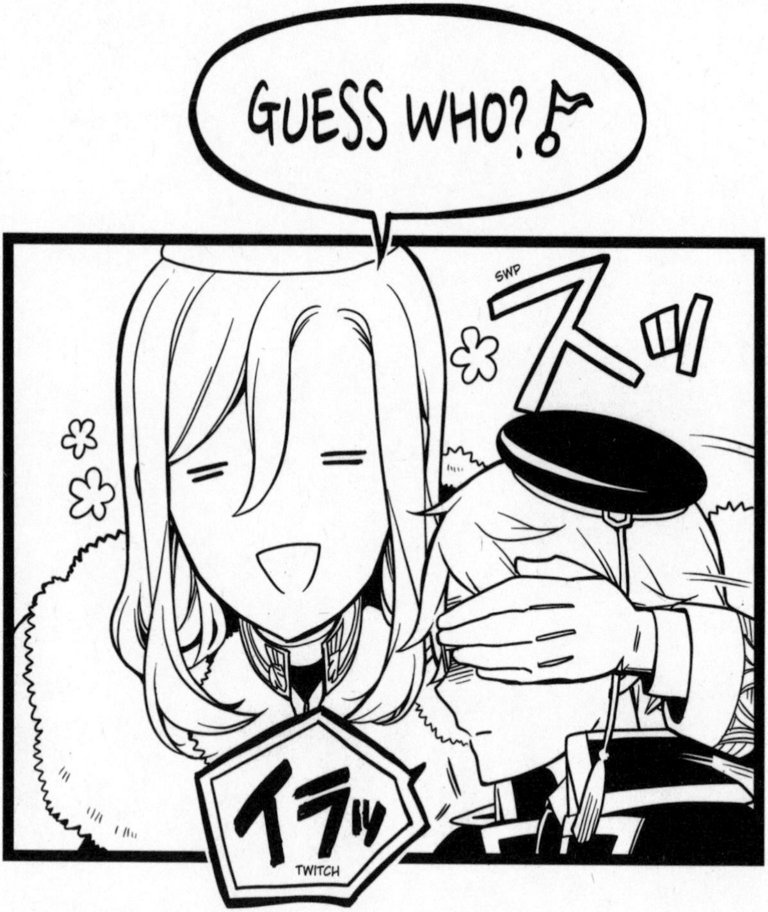
GUESS WHO?♪
SWP
スッ
イラッ
TWITCH

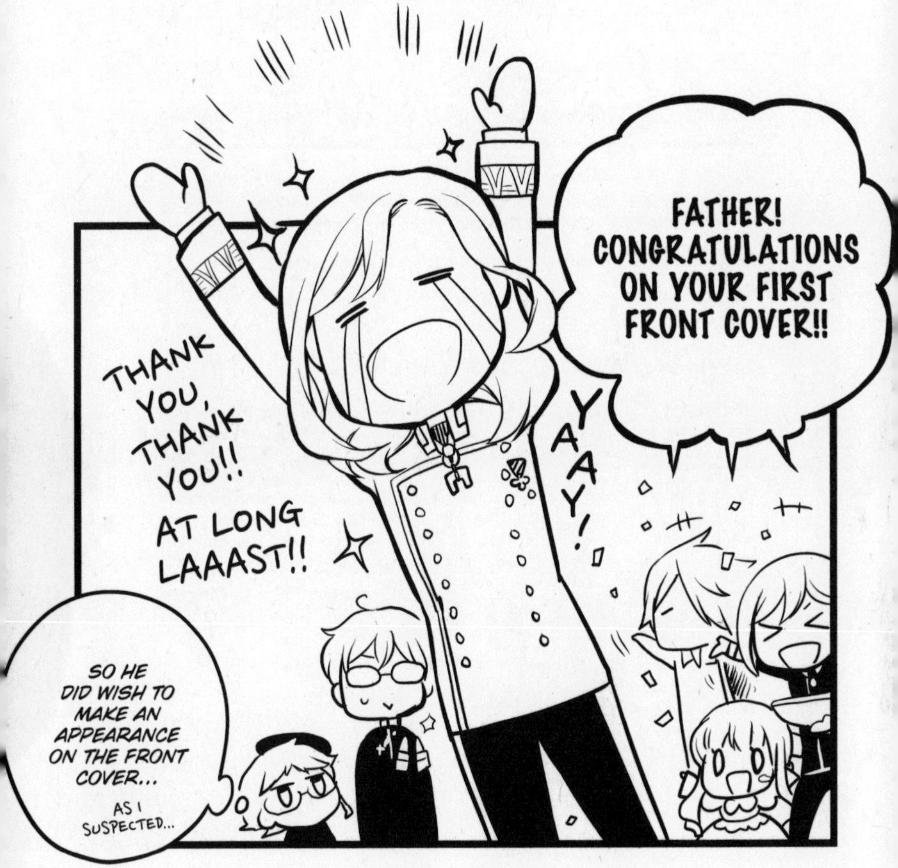
FATHER! CONGRATULATIONS ON YOUR FIRST FRONT COVER!!
YAAAY!
THANK YOU, THANK YOU!!
AT LONG LAAAST!!
SO HE DID WISH TO MAKE AN APPEARANCE ON THE FRONT COVER...
AS I SUSPECTED...

The Royal Tutor ⑫

Higasa Akai

Translation: Amanda Haley • Lettering: Abigail Blackman

THE ROYAL TUTOR Vol. 12 © 2019 Higasa Akai / SQUARE ENIX CO., LTD. First published in Japan in 2019 by SQUARE ENIX CO., LTD. English translation rights arranged with SQUARE ENIX CO., LTD. and Yen Press, LLC through Tuttle-Mori Agency, Inc., Tokyo.

English translation © 2019 by SQUARE ENIX CO., LTD.

Yen Press
150 West 30th Street, 19th Floor
New York, NY 10001

Visit us at yenpress.com
facebook.com/yenpress
twitter.com/yenpress
yenpress.tumblr.com
instagram.com/yenpress

First Yen Press Edition: August 2019
The chapters in this volume were originally published as ebooks by Yen Press.

Yen Press is an imprint of Yen Press, LLC.
The Yen Press name and logo are trademarks of Yen Press, LLC.

The publisher is not responsible for websites (or their content) that are not owned by the publisher.

Library of Congress Control Number: 2017938422

ISBNs: 978-1-9753-8511-8 (paperback)
       978-1-9753-8512-5 (ebook)

10 9 8 7 6 5 4 3 2 1

WOR

Printed in the United States of America